# Intellectual Disabilities

# and

# Personality Disorder

## An integrated

Zillah Webb

# Intellectual Disabilities and Personality Disorder: An integrated approach

© Zillah Webb

The author has asserted her rights in accordance with the Copyright, Designs and Patents Act (1988) to be identified as the author of this work.

Published by:
Pavilion Publishing and Media Ltd
Rayford House, School Road,
Hove, BN3 5HX
Tel: 01273 434943
Fax: 01273 227308
Email: info@pavpub.com
Web: www.pavpub.com

Published 2014. Reprinted 2016.

A catalogue record for this book is available from the British Library.

Print ISBN: 978-1-909810-35-8
EPDF: 978-1-909810-69-3
EPub: 978-1-909810-70-9
MOBI: 978-1-909810-71-6

*Pavilion is the leading training and development provider and publisher in the health, social care and allied fields, providing a range of innovative training solutions underpinned by sound research and professional values. We aim to put our customers first, through excellent customer service and value.*

**Author:** Zillah Webb
**Production editor:** Catherine Ansell-Jones, Pavilion Publishing and Media Ltd
**Cover design:** Phil Morash, Pavilion Publishing and Media Ltd
**Page layout and typesetting:** Phil Morash, Pavilion Publishing and Media Ltd
**Printing:** Print on Demand Worldwide

# Contents

# About the author

Prior to training as a clinical psychologist, Zillah worked in a number of different hospitals for people with intellectual disabilities or mental health problems, including as a volunteer support worker, psychiatric nursing assistant and assistant psychologist.

Zillah completed her BSc in Psychology in 1981 at the University of Birmingham and in 1984 she gained her MSc in Clinical Psychology at the University of Surrey. She then undertook two years training in family therapy resulting in a Certificate in Family Therapy from Birkbeck College and the Institute of Family Therapy. In 2004 she gained her doctorate in clinical psychology from Canterbury Christ Church University College. The specialist focus of her doctorate was autistic spectrum disorders.

In 1989 Zillah became a chartered clinical psychologist with the British Psychological Society and from June 2011 she has been a registered clinical psychologist with the Health and Care Professions Council.

Since qualifying, Zillah has worked in a range of roles in the NHS in services for children (CAMHS and paediatrics) and individuals with intellectual disabilities including community and inpatient settings. She has also worked in the voluntary sector in a specialist service for individuals on the autistic spectrum. Her current role is in a specialist inpatient service for individuals with intellectual disabilities and mental health problems.

Zillah is joint author of *Working with Adults with Asperger Syndrome: A practical toolkit* (2009).

# Acknowledgements

I would like to thank the many staff from Surrey and Borders Partnership Foundation NHS Trust who have helped me develop the ideas in this book, including Patrick Howarth who is the epitome of compassionate distance. Particular thanks must go to the staff team at April Cottage who continue to inspire me with their determination to help everyone admitted to their unit, however severe or intractable their problems may seem.

Thanks are also due to Karen Dodd, Valerie Barden and Anna Sellen for dipping into and commenting on the final draft of the book. I must also thank Valerie Barden, Carol Hagland and Rowena Rossiter for their encouragement, wisdom and stimulating discussions over tea and cakes in some of the loveliest settings in Sussex.

Finally, thanks are due to Philip Hunt who has patiently read and commented on each chapter many times in an effort to promote consistency, coherence and logic of both the content and structure of the book. Without his efforts this book would have been finished much earlier but certainly would never have made sense to anyone but me.

# Preface

This book is the result of my efforts to help staff teams support individuals with intellectual disabilities with (often undiagnosed) personality disorders. Staff would seek my help, looking for ways to manage a constantly changing array of challenging behaviours and emotional turmoil. Although I tried my best, I was often left feeling that I had failed both the staff team and the individual.

To resolve this I set out to understand more about personality disorder and how it might be influenced by the individual who also has intellectual disabilities. I looked at a range of research literature and books. More importantly I listened to individuals and staff. I shamelessly picked the brains of staff attending training sessions, of my colleagues and of trainees and assistants I have had the privilege of working with. As I learnt, I put my learning into practice. Almost without realising it, I moved from feeling overwhelmed, to a position of confident curiosity. By working collaboratively with staff and individuals I found I was able to help them resolve what seemed like insurmountable problems.

The following chapters aim to pull together what I have learnt. Rather than considering individual personality disorders, every chapter addresses a number of related difficulties or symptoms. This avoids the repetition that would otherwise occur given the overlap between different personality disorders. It also highlights the importance of individual assessment and a person-centred approach. It means that the book can be used even where there is no clarity around diagnosis, which is often the case when working with this group. It also fits better with the varied presentation of personality disorder in people with intellectual disabilities. The chapters look at how these problems arise and how they may be addressed. Each chapter is designed to be able to be read independently, allowing the reader to focus on the issues that are most relevant to the individuals they support. However, to avoid repetition, readers are directed to useful techniques or explanations in other chapters.

The book is intended to be used by a range of professionals. Hence I have included some more basic information on psychological processes. I have also found that re-visiting these basics is an important part of working with this client group as so often they can induce a feeling of being separate, special, different and beyond what applies to other people. Recognising basic human processes that apply to everyone can be a useful starting point for challenging this thinking and opening possibilities for change.

To make the book more readable I have avoided having too many references in the text. Only those directly quoted are referenced. Each chapter finishes with a further reading section. This includes the key texts that have I have drawn on in the chapter and sources that will give more detailed information on specific topics.

Finally, I must mention my discomfort with the term 'personality disorder'. I have used it here only because there is, as yet, no widely understood and accepted alternative. I look forward to a time when there is a more accurate and less derogatory name for this constellation of difficulties.

Intellectual Disabilities and Personality Disorder: An integrated approach
© Pavilion Publishing and Media Ltd and its licensors 2014.

# Chapter 1: Personality disorder and individuals with intellectual disabilities

This chapter explores what is meant by the terms 'personality' and 'personality disorder'. It examines the possible causes of personality disorder and the impact of having a personality disorder for the individual and society. It also looks at what an intellectual disability is and why individuals with intellectual disabilities may be vulnerable to developing personality disorders. It explores the impact of intellectual disabilities on the presentation and diagnosis of personality disorder. It looks at the challenges presented by individuals with intellectual disabilities and personality disorder and identifies approaches to intervention with these individuals.

## Key topics

- Personality
- Personality disorders
- Problems associated with having a personality disorder
- Causes
- Intellectual disabilities
- Personality disorder in individuals with intellectual disabilities
- Diagnosis of personality disorder in individuals with intellectual disabilities
- Intervention

# Personality

Personality may be understood as the lasting characteristics that influence a person's thoughts, feelings and behaviour. It shapes a person's view of themselves (their identity), other people and the world in general. It influences how they engage in relationships. Personality also underpins how people respond to situations (both emotionally and behaviourally) and how they cope with problems. Personality comprises an integrated system of traits and attributes that characterise the person.

Everyone's personality is unique. However, everyone's personality characteristics or 'traits' can be seen as falling somewhere on a range. For example, people differ in how sociable they are, from the most extravert and outgoing to the most introvert and reclusive. Box 1.1 shows the 'big five', the overarching personality traits consistently identified in research.

---

## Box 1.1: The big five personality traits

The diagram below shows the 'big five' personality traits. The label on the arrow is the term often used to describe the personality trait. The labels at the ends of the arrow describe the extremes of that trait. If points are marked to show where individuals fall on each dimension they can be joined to create a profile. While there may be similarities, everyone will have a unique profile.

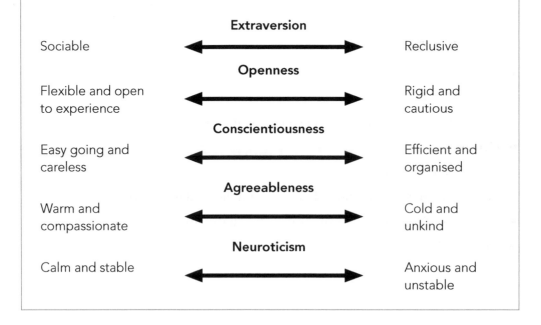

---

While personality is a major influence, it is not the only cause of how people behave. For example, people may be influenced by factors such as changes in their mood or the characteristics of the situation they find themselves in.

Personality develops from childhood as a result of a person's biology, relationships and experiences. There appears to be a genetic component to personality as differences in temperament are evident from birth. Babies have been shown to differ in characteristics such as activity, sociability and emotional reactivity. Other personality traits become apparent during childhood but these are flexible and change as the person develops. A more consistent pattern of traits emerges in late teens or early adulthood. In adulthood, personality is much less flexible but it can and often does change as people mature and undergo different life experiences.

A healthy personality is central to successful functioning. It helps people to:

- have a stable sense of themselves (identity)
- have coherent internal experiences (perceptions, emotions and thoughts)
- have a stable sense of other people
- form successful relationships
- function independently
- function in groups
- function in wider society.

Consequently, an unhealthy personality will impact on all aspects of a person's functioning. The current term for difficulties arising from an unhealthy personality is 'personality disorder'.

# Personality disorders

## Definition

There is much debate about the term 'personality disorder', how it should be defined and whether it should be used at all. In many ways it is a clumsy and unhelpful label. As research progresses it is to be hoped that a more helpful and less stigmatising name will be found for this constellation of difficulties. However, for the time-being this is the only widely understood term for these difficulties.

Hence it is used here as shorthand for the problems that individuals experience, without necessarily accepting the 'medicalisation' of those difficulties implied by the term 'disorder'.

Personality disorder is the current term used when an adult has enduring personal characteristics (personality traits) that significantly impair their well-being and social functioning. Their approach to life will cause suffering to themselves, those close to them or to the wider community. In recognition of the greater flexibility of personality traits in childhood, personality disorder is not diagnosed in people younger than 18 years. One widely used definition of personality disorder is given in Box 1.2.

---

### Box 1.2: Definition of personality disorder

Personality disorder is *'an enduring pattern of inner experience and behaviour that deviates markedly from the expectations of the individual's culture, is pervasive and inflexible, has an onset in adolescence or early adulthood, is stable over time, and leads to distress or impairment'*.

American Psychiatric Association (2013) *DSM-IV*. Arlington. VA: APA.

---

A number of different types of personality disorders have been suggested, depending on the most noticeable characteristics. Some examples are given in Box 1.3. Where different diagnostic systems give different names for similar patterns of symptoms, both names have been included.

Box 1.3 shows one approach to grouping personality disorders according to the most prominent characteristics. Personality disorders may also be grouped on the basis of whether the main characteristics are related to behavioural 'acting out' or are more internalised and characterised by anxiety and over-thinking.

However, the diagnosis of specific types of personality disorder is unreliable; different assessors and different assessment tools can lead to the same individual being given different diagnoses. There is even disagreement between the two main diagnostic systems used by doctors; the *Diagnostic and Statistical Manual of Mental Disorders 5* (DSM-V) and the *International Classification of Diseases 10* (ICD-10). These systems give different names and slightly different diagnostic criteria for some of the most common personality disorders.

| Box 1.3: Types of personality disorder and their characteristics | |
| --- | --- |
| Type/cluster of personality disorder | Main characteristics/pervasive patterns of behaviour |
| **A. Odd/eccentric** | |
| Paranoid | Distrust and suspicion of others |
| Schizoid | Lack of social connection (few friends, does not seek social contact) and limited emotional expression (coldness, detached or flat emotions) |
| Schizotypal | Social discomfort, cognitive distortions and behavioural eccentricities |
| **B. Dramatic/erratic** | |
| Antisocial/dissocial | Ignore and break the rights of others |
| Borderline/emotionally unstable | Impulsive behaviour, unstable relationships and feelings |
| Histrionic | Excessive emotion and need for attention |
| Narcissistic | Pattern of grandiosity, need for admiration and lack of empathy |
| **C. Anxious/fearful** | |
| Avoidant/anxious | Social inhibition, feel inadequate, oversensitive to criticism |
| Obsessive-compulsive | Need for order, perfection and control |
| Dependent | Excessive need to be taken care of, submissive, unassertive and clinging behaviour, fear of separation/being alone, difficulties with decision making and taking responsibility, difficulties with initiating project |
| **Other** | |
| Personality disorder – mixed/trait specified | Where individual does not fit one category |

The term 'personality disorder' implies that there is a clear distinction between a healthy personality and an unhealthy personality and also between different types of personality disorder. In reality, the picture is much more complex and confusing. Some individuals may have only a few problematic characteristics and would not meet the diagnostic criteria for personality disorder despite these characteristics causing them extensive problems. Other individuals may have multiple problematic characteristics and could be diagnosed with several personality disorders. (The DSM-5 gives a proposed research model for personality disorder based on a dimensional model in recognition of the potential advantages of such an approach.)

Rather than thinking only of diagnostic categories, it can be helpful to think of individuals as falling on a spectrum of personality functioning. This is shown in Figure 1.4.

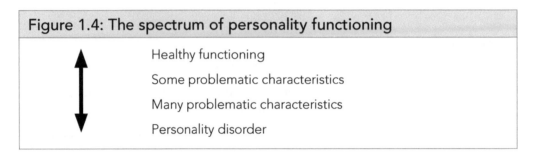

**Figure 1.4: The spectrum of personality functioning**

Healthy functioning

Some problematic characteristics

Many problematic characteristics

Personality disorder

In a similar way, the problematic characteristics can be seen as falling towards the extreme end of the range on certain personality traits. For example, an individual with antisocial personality disorder, who disregards the needs of others, would be expected to fall at the far end of the 'agreeableness' trait (cold and unkind).

## Occurrence

Research suggests that about 10% of the general adult population has a personality disorder, with borderline personality disorder being by far the most frequent (about six per cent) (Alwin *et al*, 2006). Personality disorders occur in similar numbers in men and women. However, specific types of personality disorder may have different gender ratios, for example, borderline personality disorder is more commonly diagnosed in women, while antisocial personality disorder is more commonly diagnosed in men. There are some differences in rates of diagnosis between different ethnic groups. However it is not clear if these are real differences or just reflect differences in diagnostic practices (for example, the influence of gender or other stereotypes).

Individuals with cluster B or 'acting out' personality disorders, such as borderline and antisocial personality disorder, are most frequently seen by health services.

## Outcome

It used to be thought that the outcome for individuals with personality disorder was inevitably poor; individuals do not respond to short-term treatment and there is a high suicide rate (almost 10%). However, more recently research has shown more positive outcomes for individuals with a cluster B personality disorder; many individuals 'mature out' of the diagnosis by their mid-thirties. Many individuals respond well to longer term, specialist treatment approaches. After regular treatment for at least 15 months about half of individuals improve sufficiently to no longer meet the diagnostic criteria for personality disorder.

Research has identified a number of factors that are associated with more positive outcomes for individuals with cluster B personality disorders (Kreisman & Straus, 2004). These are given in Table 1.5.

| Table 1.5: Factors associated with outcome in cluster B personality disorder | |
|---|---|
| Favourable outcome | Unfavourable outcome |
| Short-term | |
| Early and rapid progress in treatment<br>Supportive relationships<br>Friendliness and likeability | Chronic symptoms<br>Severe symptoms<br>Co-morbidity<br>Greater impulsivity<br>Impaired relationship with parents<br>Disability<br>Poor physical health eg. diabetes, arthritis, obesity |
| Long-term | |
| Higher intelligence<br>Physical attractiveness<br>Artistic talent<br>Self-discipline<br>Involvement in 12-step treatment programme if have addiction (eg. Alcoholics Anonymous) | Chronic hostility and irritability<br>History of antisocial behaviour<br>History of severe parental abuse<br>Severe jealousy<br>Poverty<br>Addiction but not in 12-step |

# Problems associated with having a personality disorder

Individuals with personality disorder are more likely to experience a range of problems including: problems with self-image and self-esteem, high levels of emotional distress or anxiety, difficulties with impulsive behaviours and substance misuse, and distorted thinking patterns. Individuals often appear to be entangled in a complex web of unhelpful and abusive relationships. They are also more likely to experience adverse life events, including difficulties with accommodation and employment.

Individuals with personality disorder may engage in a range of high risk or antisocial behaviours. A diagnosis of a cluster B personality disorder is linked to future aggression and re-offending in those who have committed crimes.

Individuals with borderline personality disorder often experience crises which rapidly escalate and may include self-harm or suicidal behaviour. They frequently use services such as A&E departments and often have contact with many different services. However, individuals often have negative experiences with services. They may receive poor care as the result of misunderstanding or prejudice and may be excluded from accessing some services. Many individuals with personality disorder find it very difficult to engage with services; they may repeatedly ask for help only to fail to attend appointments or fail to follow the advice given.

Individuals can provoke strong emotional reactions in those trying to help and support them. Staff members may feel deskilled, manipulated, powerless or angry. Members within a team may have very different images of the person and there may be conflict or 'splitting' within and between teams.

# Causes

The causes of personality disorder are not fully understood and there are many different theories. One helpful way of understanding personality disorder is the biosocial developmental model developed to help understand borderline personality disorder. This approach suggests that for biologically vulnerable individuals certain psychological, social and environmental experiences can combine to shape their emotions, thoughts and behaviours, leading to the patterns of responding that are called personality disorder. Some of these factors and the way they influence development are explored next.

Intellectual Disabilities and Personality Disorder: An integrated approach
© Pavilion Publishing and Media Ltd and its licensors 2014.

# Biological vulnerability

Some individuals appear to be biologically vulnerable to developing personality disorder. Genetics may play a role in this. A study of twins suggested that an inheritability factor for borderline personality disorder is 0.69 (Torgersen *et al*, 2000). There may be inherited traits, such as impulsivity, that contribute to developing a personality disorder. Individuals who develop personality disorder may also have some differences in the way parts of their brains are structured or function, or the levels of key chemicals (neurotransmitters) in areas of their brains. These differences may make it more difficult to control emotions and behaviour.

# Parenting

**Note:** The terms 'parent' and 'parenting' will be used throughout to include all those who care for children, including biological, step, foster and adopted parents and paid carers.

Individuals with personality disorders are likely to have grown up in families where both parents found bringing up a child very difficult. The parents may have had problems with addiction or mental health problems that led them to be emotionally unavailable and neglectful of their children. In these circumstances family life may be unstable and uncaring. Parents may have been so absorbed in their own difficulties that they could not see things from the child's perspective or recognise the child's needs.

Some children may also have experienced the care system. Sadly, paid carers may also not provide good enough parenting. 'Looked after' children may experience multiple relocations and placement failures. These experiences will impair an individual's ability to form attachments and manage their emotions.

# Abuse

A high proportion of individuals with personality disorder have experienced physical, sexual and/or emotional abuse. Children who are neglected or abused often learn to think only of themselves. They need to be selfish and ruthless to protect themselves and get as much as they can in situations where there is not enough to go round. Children who are exposed to harsh or neglectful parenting will absorb negative views of themselves and the world. They will also learn a narrow range of unhelpful ways of interacting with others. For example, individuals may adopt the role of either victim or bully depending on who they are interacting with and be unaware that there are other ways of behaving in these situations. However, many individuals survive abuse with healthy personalities. It is thought that how other people respond to the abuse is important. Personality disorder may develop when no one is able to recognise the child's pain and support them in coming to terms with the abuse.

## Attachments

Experiences of neglect, rejection, inconsistency and confusion make it difficult for a child to form healthy bonds or attachments to their parents. These early bonds with parents form the pattern for all future relationships. Individuals with personality disorder often form attachments that are described as 'insecure' or 'disorganised'. These styles are explored more fully in Chapter 4. Their early experiences meant that they did not gain confidence from their parents but rather were anxious and unsure about them. Where abuse or neglect was more extreme, the child would be very confused; they would both fear and need their parents. After such experiences it is very hard for an individual to trust others not to hurt or abandon them. Consequently, relationships become a source of anxiety and it is hard to draw comfort from others.

Attachment problems can also arise where there is a mismatch between the personality of the child and the parent. This mismatch can make it difficult for the parent to relate to the child and understand their needs. These misunderstandings then distress and upset the child, making it harder for the parent to relate to them. Such mismatches can also occur when a baby has additional needs. Where there are serious health problems, sensory problems, difficulties feeding or the baby cries a lot and cannot be comforted, parents may struggle to meet the child's needs. Some parents may struggle to accept and love such a child. These difficulties may also result in insecure attachments.

## Understanding mental states (mentalising)

Consistent and caring parents help children to understand their own and others' actions. Parents explain the child's emotions to them and signal that it is OK to feel that way. They also explain why others might have behaved in certain ways. For example, *'John hit you because he was tired of waiting for a go on the swing, you are upset because it was your turn'*. This develops into the ability to understand actions by working out what is going on in their own and other people's minds. This process is called 'mentalising', 'social cognition' or more informally, 'mind-reading'. It is thought that the early experiences of individuals with personality disorder interfere with learning how to understand their own and others' thoughts, feelings and behaviour. Without the ability to mentalise, a person's own behaviour and emotions and those of others will often be experienced as confusing, unpredictable and frightening. Lacking this ability may make it very hard for an individual to consider others' needs; they may even be totally oblivious of the pain they cause others.

## Managing emotions

Parents also teach children how to manage their emotions and to calm themselves when distressed. Initially the parent does this for the baby but, as the child grows, parents gradually teach the child to manage alone. When parents are unable to do this, the child can find emotions overwhelming and unmanageable and may develop extreme responses such as self-harm to block them out.

## Reinforcement of unhelpful behaviour patterns

In families where parents are overwhelmed by their own needs and the pressures of daily life, children's needs are often overlooked. Children who behave appropriately are often ignored. However, it is difficult to ignore extreme behaviours such as screaming or running away. Hence children learn that only extreme behaviours are effective in getting their needs met and these will increasingly be their first response.

In summary, personality disorders may develop in biologically vulnerable individuals when their early family environment is unable to meet their needs. This leads to the pervasive social, cognitive, emotional and behavioural problems that contribute to the diagnosis of personality disorder.

## Intellectual disabilities

The term 'intellectual disabilities' is used here synonymously with the British term 'learning disabilities' to represent the presence of:

- a significantly reduced ability to understand new or complex information, to learn new skills (impaired intelligence), with;
- a reduced ability to cope independently (impaired social functioning);
- which started before adulthood, with a lasting effect on development.

Estimates of the prevalence of intellectual disabilities vary. It is suggested that between two and three per cent of the population may have intellectual disabilities (Emerson & Hatton, 2008). The great majority of these individuals (more than 75%) will have mild intellectual disabilities (Emerson & Hatton 2008). Intellectual disabilities may be caused by a number of factors, including genetic and chromosomal disorders, but for many the cause is not known. Intellectual disabilities are not a mental health problem and most individuals with intellectual disabilities have good mental health. However, a significant minority (10–40%) also experience mental health problems (Emerson & Hatton, 2008; Deb *et al*, 2001). It is also possible for an individual with intellectual disabilities to have a personality disorder.

## Personality and intellectual disabilities

It might be assumed that individuals with intellectual disabilities would have personalities that show the same 'big five' traits that have been identified in the general population. However, there is some research that suggests the experience of growing up with intellectual disabilities has a profound effect on the development of personality. It has been suggested that repeated experiences of failure may shape the approach of individuals with intellectual disabilities to new challenges; making them avoid new tasks, expect failure and look to others for cues as to how to solve problems. These experiences might make individuals with intellectual disabilities less open to new experiences and more anxious. The impact of these experiences is such that some researchers have suggested that the personality of individuals with intellectual disabilities may be characterised by seven personality traits (see Box 1.6).

Intellectual Disabilities and Personality Disorder: An integrated approach
© Pavilion Publishing and Media Ltd and its licensors 2014.

> ## Box 1.6: Seven personality dimensions identified in children with intellectual disabilities
>
> 1. Positive reaction tendency – a heightened motivation to interact with and be dependent upon a supportive adult
> 2. Negative reaction tendency – initial wariness shown with interacting with strange adults
> 3. Expectancy of success – degree to which the individual expects to succeed or fail when presented with a new task
> 4. Outer directedness – tendency to look to others for solutions to difficult or ambiguous tasks
> 5. Efficacy motivation – the pleasure derived from tackling and solving difficult problems
> 6. Obedience
> 7. Curiosity/creativity
>
> Zigler *et al* (2002)

At first glance the seven traits bear little resemblance to the 'big five'. They also do not include factors related to mood or emotion. These differences may reflect genuine differences in the personality structure of individuals with intellectual disabilities.

However, they may also be influenced by characteristics of the research approach that developed them. These traits were identified in children, using observation of behaviour on different tasks or ratings by teachers. There was no attempt to talk to the participants to explore their inner worlds. The researchers were looking for traits that distinguished individuals with intellectual disabilities from their more able peers and hence did not explore areas of similarity.

The language used to describe the traits may also reflect the unconscious bias of the researchers about the position of children with intellectual disabilities in society. This may make the traits appear more different from the 'big five' than is perhaps the case. For example, 'obedience' might reflect the dimension of conscientiousness, 'positive reaction tendency' might relate to extraversion and 'curiosity/creativity' to openness. It is to be hoped that these issues will be clarified by future research.

# Personality disorder in individuals with intellectual disabilities

Some individuals with intellectual disabilities show the enduring patterns of inner experience and behaviour that constitute personality disorder. However many people with intellectual disabilities who show problem behaviours will not have personality disorders. Therefore it is important that the possibility that an individual has personality disorder is considered when assessing problematic behaviours. An individual with intellectual disabilities may also have a personality disorder if they show a range of severe, persistent problems with managing their own behaviour and relating to other people.

Some of the types of problems likely to be encountered in individuals with personality disorder and intellectual disabilities are given in Box 1.7.

---

### Box 1.7: Problems experienced by individuals with intellectual disabilities and personality disorder

- Unhealthy self-image and low self-esteem
- Emotional distress eg. intense, changeable emotions
- Interpersonal difficulties eg. difficulty making and keeping friendships, conflict with other individuals
- Difficulties with self-control and impulsivity including substance misuse and offending behaviour
- Distorted thinking eg. black and white thinking
- Problems with physical health eg. poor treatment compliance
- Co-morbid mental health problems eg. depression, anxiety
- Challenging behaviours eg. verbal and physical aggression
- Suicidal behaviour and self-harm including self-injury and self-poisoning
- Frequent crises eg. placement breakdown and multiple admissions to hospital
- Difficulties engaging with services eg. missed appointments
- Creating tensions and disagreements within and between teams
- Complex family and relationship networks, including people who may exploit or abuse the individual and may come into conflict with the services supporting them

---

The types of problems encountered are very similar to those found in more able individuals with personality disorder. However, the presence of intellectual disabilities adds another layer of complexity to the presentation of difficulties and the approach to intervention. Each of these problem areas are explored in more depth in subsequent chapters.

Individuals with intellectual disabilities and personality disorder often require significant, long-term support and intervention from health and social services. However, if the personality disorder is not recognised or if staff do not understand the needs of individuals with personality disorder, individuals are unlikely to get the specialist help that they need.

## Prevalence

The prevalence of personality disorders in individuals with intellectual disabilities is still unclear, mainly as the result of a number of issues that make diagnosis difficult and inconsistent. A review of published research found rates ranging from 1–91% (Alexander & Cooray, 2003). This was attributed to inconsistencies in the approaches taken by different researchers and also to the many difficulties of research in this area. Overall, the research suggests that the patterns of thoughts, feelings and behaviour that characterise personality disorder are common in individuals with intellectual disabilities, particularly those in forensic services (up to 50%) (Lindsay, 2007) but that frequently the condition has not been diagnosed (Khan *et al*, 1997). The most frequently identified personality disorders in this population are antisocial personality disorder and borderline personality disorder. However, this may be because the 'acting out' that characterises these personality disorders means that they are more likely to be referred to services.

There is some evidence that individuals with intellectual disabilities and personality disorder make frequent use of health services. One study found that 59% of individuals with intellectual disabilities identified as having personality disorder had had at least one hospital admission in the previous five years and had needed intensive behavioural support (Khan *et al*, 1997). One case study reported an individual who had over 100 admissions as a result of self-harm (Wink *et al*, 2010).

## Outcome

Looking at the factors associated with favourable and unfavourable outcomes in personality disorder in the general population suggests that individuals with intellectual disabilities and personality disorder are likely to have a poor prognosis. Individuals with intellectual disabilities are more likely to have additional physical health problems and disabilities, to be poor and socially isolated. Individuals with intellectual disabilities are often more dependent on their families and have greater difficulties 'escaping' enmeshed, over-protective, exploitative or abusive families. The difficulties recognising personality disorder in people with intellectual disabilities and lack of information on how to help them once it has been diagnosed also mean they are unlikely to get timely and appropriate treatment.

There is some evidence that individuals with intellectual disabilities and personality disorder may benefit less from standard inpatient treatment than individuals with intellectual disabilities and other mental health problems. However, case studies suggest that, once a personality disorder has been diagnosed and appropriate support and treatment is given, outcome can improve significantly. For example, individuals may be on less and fewer medications, they may have fewer admissions to hospital and may have better relationships with family members and the staff who support them. However, progress was dependent on them being in a consistent, supportive residential setting; those lacking such support did not improve. Medication also appears to play a significant role by helping individuals to engage with those offering social and psychological support.

## Causes

The underlying causes of personality disorder are likely to be the same for individuals with intellectual disabilities as for the general population. It is likely that some individuals with intellectual disabilities have the biological vulnerabilities that appear to underlie personality disorder and it would be expected that growing up in damaging family environments would have similar consequences for them as for more able individuals with these vulnerabilities. In addition, there are a number of factors that might make this group more vulnerable to developing personality disorders. Some of these are given in Box 1.8.

## Box 1.8: Factors that make individuals with intellectual disabilities vulnerable to developing personality disorders

- Problems at birth and in early childhood eg. being hospitalised, difficulties feeding, being slow and unresponsive making them more difficult to parent successfully.

- Experience of abuse by parents and others (individuals with learning disabilities are more likely to be abused).

- Grief reaction of parents to having a child with learning disabilities can interfere with successful attachment/bonding between parent and child

- Vulnerability to extreme over-protection by parents (eg. being treated like a young child through adolescence and into adulthood). This reduces opportunities to learn a range of skills, resulting in reduced social skills and increased dependence in personal and social situations.

- Growing up in an institution. Some older individuals were placed in hospitals from as young as two years of age. Many institutions had policies of regularly moving staff to try to avoid bonds forming between nurses and the children they cared for. Institutions created a distorted environment and are associated with aggression, physical and sexual abuse. They may foster patterns of dependent or oppositional behaviour.

- Cognitive impairment may increase vulnerability to the effects of poor parenting. It may reduce the ability to think about and process experiences and to learn new ways of responding.

- Narrower social networks reducing the likelihood of forming protective relationships.

- Repeated experiences of failure, rejection, discrimination and stigmatisation impact on a person's sense of self.

Figure 1.9 tries to draw together the factors that may lead to the development of the patterns of thoughts, emotions and behaviour that characterise personality disorder in individuals with intellectual disabilities and which may lead to personality disorder being diagnosed

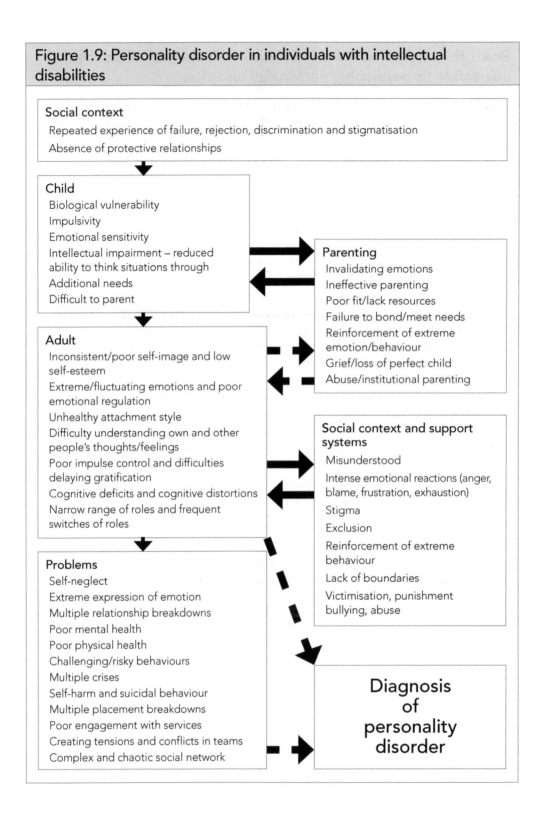

Figure 1.9: Personality disorder in individuals with intellectual disabilities

**Social context**
Repeated experience of failure, rejection, discrimination and stigmatisation
Absence of protective relationships

**Child**
Biological vulnerability
Impulsivity
Emotional sensitivity
Intellectual impairment – reduced ability to think situations through
Additional needs
Difficult to parent

**Parenting**
Invalidating emotions
Ineffective parenting
Poor fit/lack resources
Failure to bond/meet needs
Reinforcement of extreme emotion/behaviour
Grief/loss of perfect child
Abuse/institutional parenting

**Adult**
Inconsistent/poor self-image and low self-esteem
Extreme/fluctuating emotions and poor emotional regulation
Unhealthy attachment style
Difficulty understanding own and other people's thoughts/feelings
Poor impulse control and difficulties delaying gratification
Cognitive deficits and cognitive distortions
Narrow range of roles and frequent switches of roles

**Social context and support systems**
Misunderstood
Intense emotional reactions (anger, blame, frustration, exhaustion)
Stigma
Exclusion
Reinforcement of extreme behaviour
Lack of boundaries
Victimisation, punishment bullying, abuse

**Problems**
Self-neglect
Extreme expression of emotion
Multiple relationship breakdowns
Poor mental health
Poor physical health
Challenging/risky behaviours
Multiple crises
Self-harm and suicidal behaviour
Multiple placement breakdowns
Poor engagement with services
Creating tensions and conflicts in teams
Complex and chaotic social network

**Diagnosis of personality disorder**

# Diagnosis of personality disorder in individuals with intellectual disabilities

Identifying personality disorder is not easy even without the complication of the individual having intellectual disabilities. The characteristics that make up personality disorder are not in themselves abnormal; it is their frequency, severity and intensity that make them problematic. Many symptoms may also come and go depending on the situation the individual is in. Consequently, a diagnosis of personality disorder is made by looking at patterns of behaviour over time and in different situations.

Diagnosis becomes even more difficult when the individual has intellectual disabilities. Some of the issues that complicate diagnosis in this group are given in Box 1.10.

## Approaches to diagnosis of personality disorder in individuals with intellectual disabilities

As a result of these difficulties a number of authors have explored how the diagnosis of personality disorder in individuals with intellectual disabilities can be made more reliable and valid. In keeping with the confusion that often surrounds personality disorder, these approaches differ significantly and give different recommendations. These approaches include:

- adaptation of the International Classification of Diseases (ICD-10) to give the Classification of Diseases – Learning Disabilities (CD-LD)

- adaptation of Diagnostic and Statistical Manual (DSM-IV) to give the Diagnostic Manual – Intellectual Disabilities (DM-ID)

- a step-by-step approach using specific assessment tools or clinical judgement to rate individuals against the standard ICD-10 or DSM-IV diagnostic criteria.

Currently there is little research on these approaches and hence it is not clear which approaches are most helpful in practice. The latest DSM version (DSM-5, 2013) is too new for its use with individuals with intellectual disabilities to have been explored.

Each approach has its strengths and weaknesses. As they are not necessarily mutually exclusive it is possible to follow one approach and enrich it with features of the others. The approach suggested in this book is based on CD-LD. This was chosen because of its strong focus on distinguishing intellectual disabilities and personality disorder in general, rather than focusing on the diagnosis of specific personality disorders. The former is more compatible with a person-centred approach that focuses on each individual's unique combination of 'symptoms' rather than fitting them into categories that, in reality, are overlapping and of limited help in treatment planning.

---

### Box 1.10: Issues that complicate diagnosis of personality disorder in individuals with intellectual disabilities

- Individuals with intellectual disabilities mature later than the general population hence it can be difficult to distinguish 'lasting characteristics' from traits that may resolve with maturity.

- It is difficult to determine whether a particular characteristic or behaviour is due to the intellectual disabilities or personality disorder as both are related to development. For example, aggression and impulsivity may be found in each condition.

- There is overlap between the diagnosis of personality disorder and behavioural disorders (challenging behaviour) in adults with intellectual disabilities.

- There is overlap between the characteristics of some personality disorders and disorders on the autistic spectrum eg. schizoid and obsessive compulsive personality disorders.

- There are difficulties using the standard personality disorder diagnostic criteria in individuals with intellectual disabilities as some characteristics that may indicate personality disorder in the general population may arise from having intellectual disabilities. For example, being immature, dependent, suggestible and impulsive.

- Individuals with intellectual disability have often led more restrictive lives, which may have limited their opportunities, influenced the development of certain personality traits and reduced access to important areas of social functioning, including restricted opportunities for:
  - intimate/sexual relationships
  - decision making
  - employment/vocational experiences.

- Individual's sense of self may have been shaped by repeated experiences of failure and by negative self-evaluation in relation to non-disabled peers.

- Individuals with intellectual disabilities may have grown up/live in institutions. This abnormal environment creates a culture and learning experiences that foster behaviour patterns that appear maladaptive outside of the environment that produced them.

Continued...

---

- Some diagnostic criteria for personality disorder are linked to the individual's thoughts, perceptions and emotions eg. feelings of emptiness and confused identity. The more severe an individual's intellectual disability, the more difficult it is to accurately access these inner experiences as a result of:
  - difficulties with expressive and receptive communication
  - difficulties understanding abstract/complex ideas.
- Diagnosis requires historical information. Individuals with intellectual disabilities may have difficulty recalling or communicating this information and may struggle with concepts of time. There may not be a reliable informant who can provide this information on their behalf.
- There are no reliable and valid assessment tools for assessing personality disorder for use with individuals with intellectual disabilities.
- There is reluctance to label individuals with intellectual disabilities with an additional, potentially stigmatising condition.

## Assessment

While different authors prefer different assessment tools, there is some consensus on steps that can be taken to make diagnosis as reliable as possible. These include raising the age at which personality disorder can be diagnosed from 18 to 21 to allow for maturation and using information from more than one source rather than simply interviewing the individual. Many authors suggest combining interviews, questionnaires, informant information and direct observation. They suggest that a diagnosis of personality disorder should only be given when these sources give a consistent picture of pervasive difficulties.

## Reviewing a diagnosis

DM-ID recommends that caution should be exercised where there is evidence to suggest that the 'symptoms' of personality disorder may have arisen as the result of adaptation to an abnormal environment (for example, institutionalisation), abnormal learning experiences or lack of learning. In such situations they suggest that the diagnosis of personality disorder should be given on a provisional basis. The diagnosis should be reviewed annually to determine if living in a healthier environment and being exposed to social learning, treatment and contingency management have changed the individual's behaviours and attitudes to the extent that they no longer meet the diagnostic criteria.

Given that it is now recognised that individuals without intellectual disabilities may 'mature' out of personality disorder, the approach of regularly reviewing a diagnosis of personality disorder would appear sensible even if individuals have not experienced such abnormal environments.

# CD-LD

Developed by the Royal College of Psychiatrists, CD-LD addresses a number of the concerns about the diagnosis of personality disorder in individuals with intellectual disabilities. This approach is attractive in that the focus is on whether or not the individual has a personality disorder first and only once this has been established does it look at specific clusters of symptoms. The CD-LD diagnostic criteria are summarised in Box 1.11.

---

## Box 1.11: Diagnosis of personality disorder in individuals with intellectual disabilities

To be given a diagnosis of personality disorder an individual with intellectual disability must:

1. Be over 21 years of age

2. Not have severe or profound intellectual disabilities

3. Have specific characteristics that cannot be explained by the intellectual disability, a pervasive developmental disability (eg. autism) or other physical or mental health problems

4. Meet the following general criteria for personality disorder:
   a. Traits deviate markedly from what is culturally expected and involve several areas of functioning eg. emotions, arousal, impulsivity, outlook and thinking, style of interaction
   b. Traits developed in adolescence and show a continuous development from the time they were identified
   c. Traits are chronic, pervasive and maladaptive across a broad range of personal and social situations
   d. Traits cause considerable distress for the individual and others
   e. Traits cause significant problems with social or occupational functioning

If they satisfy the above then it is appropriate to consider whether they meet the criteria for a subtype of personality disorder:

- Odd/eccentric group:
  - paranoid

- Dramatic/erratic group:
  - dissocial (antisocial)
  - emotionally unstable – impulsive type
  - emotionally unstable – borderline type (borderline)
  - histrionic

Adapted from Royal College of Psychiatrists (2001)

---

# Subcategories of personality disorder

The Royal College of Psychiatrists recommends that certain subcategories of personality disorder **should not** be diagnosed in individuals with intellectual disabilities. They are:

- schizoid (lacking social connection and emotional expression)
- dependent (excessive need to be cared for)
- anxious/avoidant (social inhibition, feelings of inadequacy).

The Royal College of Psychiatrists suggests that these subcategories are inappropriate for use with individuals with intellectual disabilities for a number of reasons. Some diagnostic features of these subgroups overlap with core features of intellectual disabilities and disorders on the autistic spectrum. Other characteristics are likely to arise directly from the experience of growing up with intellectual disabilities; for example, being dependent, being sensitive to criticism, being fearful of new situations. Use of these subcategories risks applying the diagnosis of personality disorder to the majority of individuals with intellectual disabilities or disorder on the autistic spectrum and consequently would be meaningless and stigmatising.

However DM-ID takes a different approach suggesting that all categories of personality disorder may be diagnosed in individuals with intellectual disabilities provided they are interpreted thoughtfully and take into account the cultural expectations and experiences of individuals with intellectual disabilities and some minor adjustment to the criteria.

There is some research evidence that suggests the concept of dependent personality disorder can be meaningful in individuals with intellectual disabilities. It appears that thoughtful assessment can distinguish appropriate dependence from maladaptive, pervasive over-dependence. There is also some evidence that all personality disorders except schizotypal (difficulties with close relationships and eccentric behaviour) can be reliably diagnosed in people with intellectual disabilities.

However, there is also a lot of evidence that suggests that the sub-categories of personality disorder are not discrete and individuals may meet the criteria for more than one disorder. There is some evidence that difficult personality traits in individuals with intellectual disabilities might be more accurately described as falling into two groups: 'acting out' or 'externalising' and 'internalising' (anxious/ruminating).

The subcategories of personality disorders used with individuals with intellectual disabilities are likely to change as more research evidence becomes available.

Boxes 1.12–15 give more detail of the characteristics of the personality disorders the CD-LD considers identifiable in individuals with intellectual disabilities. The characteristics listed have been collated from both CD-LD and DM-ID to give as full a picture as possible. Each diagnostic system sets different criteria in terms of the number and type of characteristics required for a diagnosis. Hence any individual with a diagnosis would not show all the characteristics listed.

---

### Box 1.12: Paranoid personality disorder

A pervasive distrust of others and misinterpretation of their motives including:

- excessive sensitivity to setbacks and rebuffs not apparent to others and quick to counterattack
- persistently bearing grudges, inability to 'forgive and forget'
- suspicious of others
- misunderstanding actions of others as hostile, contemptuous, exploitative or deceptive
- reluctant to confide in others for fear that it will be used to harm them
- disproportionate sense of personal rights
- think only of themselves and how situations impact on them, talk about themselves and assume things overheard must be about them
- preoccupation with conspiratorial explanations of events
- recurrent unjustified suspicions about faithfulness of partners, loyalty or trustworthiness of friends or associates.

---

Intellectual Disabilities and Personality Disorder: An integrated approach
© Pavilion Publishing and Media Ltd and its licensors 2014.

## Box 1.13: Antisocial (dissocial) personality disorder

A pervasive disregard for and violation of the rights of others and disregard for personal responsibilities including:

- ability to make but not sustain relationships
- lack of concern for the feelings of others
- lack of concern about risks to others
- highly irresponsible behaviour with:
    - disregard for social norms, rules
    - failure to sustain work behaviour
    - failure to meet obligations
- disregard of laws to the extent of behaving in ways that would give grounds for arrest
- impulsivity or failure to plan ahead
- very low tolerance for frustration
- very low threshold for aggressive and violent behaviour
- not experiencing guilt or learning from negative experiences
- not taking responsibility for actions; blaming others or rationalising what they have done rather than showing remorse
- deceitfulness and lying to take others in.

## Box 1.14: Emotionally unstable personality disorder and borderline personality disorder

Emotionally unstable personality disorder – impulsive type

A pervasive pattern of impulsivity and unpredictability including:

- argumentative, especially when impulsive acts are criticised or thwarted
- frequently acts without thinking about the consequences
- impulsive acts that are potentially self-damaging in more than one area of functioning (spending, sexual behaviour, substance abuse, driving, binge eating)
- frequent and uncontrolled outbursts of anger or violence
- difficulty maintaining any action that does not offer immediate reward
- frequent sudden and unpredictable changes in mood
- instability of attention as a result of marked reactivity of mood.

Emotionally unstable personality disorder – borderline type (borderline)

A pervasive pattern of instability in personal relationships, self-image and emotions with marked impulsivity including:

As for impulsive type, and:

- disturbances in and uncertainty about self-image, aims and personal preferences
- tendency to become involved in intense and unstable relationships often leading to emotional crises
- unstable and intense relationships characterised by alternating idealisation and devaluation
- excessive/frantic efforts to avoid abandonment (real or imagined)
- recurrent threats or acts of self-harm
- chronic feelings of emptiness
- transient stress-related symptoms such as paranoid thinking or dissociation.

Intellectual Disabilities and Personality Disorder: An integrated approach
© Pavilion Publishing and Media Ltd and its licensors 2014.

> ## Box 1.15: Histrionic personality disorder
>
> A pervasive pattern of excessive emotionality and attention-seeking including:
> - self-dramatisation or exaggerated expression of emotion
> - superficial/shallow and rapidly changing emotions
> - continually seeking excitement or need to be the centre of attention
> - inappropriate seductiveness in appearance or behaviour
> - over concern with physical attractiveness
> - style of speech that is excessively impressionistic and lacking in detail (must be considered in the light of communication difficulties characteristic of intellectual disabilities).
>
> The following are diagnostic characteristics of histrionic personality disorder in the general population but should not be applied to individuals with intellectual disability because of the high frequency with which they occur as a direct consequence of having intellectual disabilities:
> - suggestibility (easily influenced by others)
> - considers relationships to be more important than they are.

The personality disorder subtypes most frequently encountered in services for individuals with intellectual disabilities are antisocial and borderline personality disorder. Individuals with intellectual disabilities and antisocial personality disorder are more likely to be encountered in forensic settings such as secure units. Borderline personality disorder is also often seen in individuals in these services. Individuals with borderline and histrionic personality disorders are frequently found amongst the individuals receiving support from specialist intellectual disabilities services. These individuals may be in supported living and residential care services and inpatient mental health wards (both general and specialist intellectual disabilities services). Most frequently, individuals with intellectual disabilities and personality disorder will meet the CD-LD general diagnostic criteria but have one or two characteristics from several of the subtypes.

## Individual diagnoses

Formal diagnosis of personality disorder can only be made by a health professional, drawing on a range of information including direct observation and interviews with the individual and people who know the individual well. If it is thought that an individual may have a personality disorder, it may be helpful, with the individual's consent, to seek assessment by a health professional (usually a psychiatrist) through a local mental health or intellectual disabilities team.

Whatever service the professional works in, it is important that they have a good understanding of both personality disorder and intellectual disabilities.

It will help the health professional making the assessment to have an accurate picture of the individual's current behaviour and also as much information about their past as possible. Assessment can be a stressful process for the individual and it may help if a trusted person can help them prepare for the assessment.

Sometimes the picture can remain unclear even after professional assessment. To meet the diagnostic criteria an individual must show a certain number of characteristics. Where they do not have difficulties in all the areas required, a diagnosis cannot be made. However this does not make the difficulties they experience disappear. Part of the problem with diagnosis is that it imposes an artificial cut-off on a continuum; one side is considered 'normal' and the other 'abnormal'. Where an individual cannot be given a diagnosis it can sometimes be productive to think about the unhelpful traits or patterns of responding that the individual shows. Once these are identified it is possible to develop specialised support and intervention plans even though the individual does not have a 'diagnosis' of personality disorder. The formulation approach to challenging behaviour explored in Chapter 10 can be very helpful for such individuals.

## Stigma, discrimination and perceptions

A diagnosis of personality disorder in addition to intellectual disabilities may sometimes make it much harder for the individual to access the support and empathetic care that they often desperately need. This is because of the ways individuals with personality disorder are sometimes viewed.

In the past it was thought that anyone with a personality disorder, regardless of their ability level, was 'untreatable' and being labelled as having a personality disorder often meant people were excluded from services and treatment.

There is now a much better understanding of personality disorder, its causes and how to help people overcome it. Specific treatment approaches have been developed or adapted to address the needs of individuals with personality disorder. It is now recognised that personality can be influenced by positive, nurturing, emotionally containing and insightful experiences during adulthood. While change is not easy, some people can move on from personality disorder by slowly learning from life and their experiences. Despite these positive developments individuals with personality disorder still frequently encounter negative attitudes, misunderstanding and discrimination in health services.

*Challenging Behaviour: A unified approach* (RCPsych, 2006) recommends that assessments of challenging behaviour in people with intellectual disabilities should consider 'enduring abnormalities of personality' but cautions:

*'The term personality disorder however should be used with care; it can be used pejoratively in people whose behaviours are intractable, are considered socially unacceptable, or invoke strong emotional responses in others.'*

The label 'personality disorder' can also be experienced by the individual as an attack on their identity. By saying that their personality is disordered, the diagnosis implies that their very being is wrong, ill or unacceptable. 'Personality disorder' is an unfortunate name for enduring unhelpful patterns of thinking, feeling and responding. It is these patterns of responding that need to change rather than the individual's core personality.

Despite these issues, an additional diagnosis of personality disorder can be very helpful in understanding why an individual with intellectual disabilities experiences certain problems. It can be particularly helpful in explaining why some superficially able individuals with mild intellectual disabilities struggle with so many aspects of everyday life. It also helps in identifying unmet needs, and developing care plans.

## Intervention

There are now a number of well-established approaches to helping individuals with personality disorders, particularly borderline personality disorder, although further research is needed to identify the relative effectiveness of different programmes and components of approaches. National guidance has been produced for the treatment and management of borderline personality disorder. However, this guidance highlights that very little is known about how to treat individuals who have both personality disorder and intellectual disabilities. In the absence of specific evidence, it suggests that mental health and intellectual disabilities teams should work together in addressing the needs of individuals with mild intellectual disabilities and borderline personality disorder. It suggests that individuals with moderate or severe intellectual disabilities who show behaviours and symptoms that suggest borderline personality disorder should be assessed and treated by specialist intellectual disabilities services. However, it does not give any advice on how approaches could be adapted for this group or how intervention should be integrated with meeting the needs arising from their intellectual disabilities.

There is growing evidence from case studies that the needs of individuals with intellectual disabilities and personality disorder can be met through an individualised, multidisciplinary/multi-modal approach that considers medication, psychological and behavioural interventions. These studies have also highlighted the importance of a consistent, containing environment with a stable and skilled staff group. They also identify that individuals with intellectual disabilities and personality disorder are at risk of 'over medication' if their difficulties are not correctly diagnosed and the required support is not given.

This book develops the idea that interventions for individuals with intellectual disabilities and personality disorder need to be tailored to the individual, drawing on approaches used with both populations. This person-centred, integrative approach should take into account the individual's unique personal history, their current situation, the extent and pattern of their cognitive deficits and the nature of the problems they present. Interventions for specific problem areas will be explored in subsequent chapters. However, there are two general points that relate to all aspects of intervention: philosophy of care and intervention priorities. These points are discussed below.

## Philosophy of care

Individuals with intellectual disabilities and personality disorder appear to do poorly in services that offer a great degree of personal freedom and choice and expect high levels of personal independence. Rather, they appear to respond much better to sympathetic but firmly enforced boundaries and benefit from long-term personal support. This may be understood as offering 'authoritative support'. This is an approach that shows high levels of sensitivity to and interest in an individual, holds high expectations of the individual but also has clear boundaries that are enforced by staff. This approach, adapted from the work of Cameron and Maginn (2009) on parenting styles, is explored more fully in later chapters.

When looking at the challenges faced by individuals with intellectual disabilities, it is important to consider the philosophy of the service supporting them and whether there is a mismatch between what the service is delivering and what the individual needs. If such a mismatch exists this needs to be addressed if intervention is to be successful.

## Intervention priorities

Individuals with intellectual disabilities and personality disorder often present with multiple problems and in crisis. It is therefore useful to think about the most helpful sequence for interventions. The priorities for intervention are given in Box 1.16.

---

### Box 1.16: Priorities for interventions

1. Proactive development of contingency plans to anticipate, minimise and safely manage crises.
2. Establishing a working relationship and dealing with immediate problems (such as panic attacks or depression).
3. Creating a long-term support plan to maintain stability.
4. Developing individual's skills in controlling feelings and impulses.
5. Working to explore, process and potentially resolve longstanding psychological issues.

---

It is important to recognise that not all individuals with intellectual disabilities and personality disorder will be able to progress beyond step 3 in Box 1.16; it is likely that a number of individuals will not be able to engage in or benefit from therapy. However, by managing crises, building positive working relationships and giving long-term stability it is possible to greatly increase an individual's quality of life and promote optimal functioning. It is also important to recognise that many individuals are unable to benefit from individual therapy because the first three priorities have not been addressed. It is easy to fall into labelling the individual as 'untreatable' when in fact they might be able to engage with and benefit from therapy if their needs for containment and stability were addressed and the foundations for a working relationship were developed.

# Key learning points

- Personality is the unique combination of enduring personal characteristics that shape an individual's thoughts, feelings and behaviour.

- Personality disorder occurs when individuals with certain biological vulnerabilities have adverse experiences in childhood. It leads to patterns of inner experience and behaviour that have detrimental effects on the individual, their relationships and their ability to function in society.

- Individuals with intellectual disabilities may also develop personality disorders. This is likely to be the result of the same process that leads to personality disorder in more able individuals, although the presentation may be slightly different.

- The process for diagnosing personality disorder needs to be adapted for use with individuals with intellectual disabilities.

- It is recognised that a diagnosis of personality disorder may be associated with stigma and the risk of exclusion from services. However it can be helpful in ensuring that individuals access the specialist support that they need.

- Individuals with intellectual disabilities and personality disorder will need a person-centred, integrated care plan that draws on knowledge of both intellectual disabilities and personality disorder, which explicitly considers service philosophy and is delivered in the correct sequence.

# References

Alexander R & Cooray S (2003) Diagnosis of personality disorders in learning disability. *British Journal of Psychiatry* **44** 28–31.

Alwin N, Blackburn R, Davidson K, Hilton M, Logan C & Shine J (2006) *Understanding Personality Disorder: A report by the British Psychological Society*. Leicester: The British Psychological Society.

American Psychiatric Association (2013) *DSM-IV*. Arlington, VA: APA.

Cameron R & Maginn C (2009) *Achieving Positive Outcomes for Children in Care*. London: Sage.

Deb S, Matthews T, Holt G & Bouras N (2001) *Practice Guidelines for the Assessment and Diagnosis of Mental Health Problems in Adults with Intellectual Disability*. Brighton: Pavilion.

Emerson E & Hatton C (2008) *Estimating Future Need for Adult Social Care Services for People with Learning Disabilities in England. CeDR Report 2008:6*. Centre for Disability Research Lancaster University. Available at: eprints.lancs.ac.uk/21049 (accessed January 2014).

Khan A, Cowan C & Roy A (1997) Personality disorder in people with learning disabilities: a community survey. *Journal of Intellectual Disability Research* **41** (4) 324–330.

Kreisman J & Straus H (2004) *Sometimes I Act Crazy: Living with borderline personality disorder*. New Jersey: Wiley.

Lindsay W (2007) Personality disorder. In N Bouras & G Holt (Eds) *Psychiatric and Behavioural Disorders in Intellectual and Developmental Disabilities*, pp143–153. Cambridge: Cambridge University Press.

Royal College of Psychiatrists (2001) *LD DC-LD: Diagnostic criteria for psychiatric disorders for use with adults with learning disabilities / mental retardation* (occasional paper). London: RCP.

Royal College of Psychiatrists (2006) *Challenging Behaviour: A unified approach*. Available at: http://www.rcpsych.ac.uk/files/pdfversion/cr144.pdf (accessed April 2014).

Torgerson S, Lygren S, Oien P, Skre I, Onstad S, Edvardsen J, Tambs K & Kringlen E (2000) A twin study of personality disorders. *Comprehensive Psychiatry* **41** 416–425.

Wink L, Erikson C, Chamers J & McDougle C (2010) Co-morbid intellectual disability and borderline personality disorder: a case series. *Psychiatry* **73** (3) 277–287.

Zigler E, Bennett-Gates D, Hodapp R & Henrich (2002) Assessing personality traits of individuals with mental retardation. *American Journal on Mental Retardation* **107** (3) 181–193.

# Further reading

Alexander R & Cooray S (2003) Diagnosis of personality disorders in learning disability. *British Journal of Psychiatry* **44** S28–S31.

American Psychiatric Association (1994) *Diagnostic and Statistical Manual of Mental Disorders 4th Edition* (DSM-IV). Washington DC: APA.

American Psychiatric Association (1994) *Diagnostic and Statistical Manual of Mental Disorders 5th Edition* (DSM-5). Washington DC: APA.

Crowell S, Beauchaine T & Linehan M (2009) A biosocial developmental model of borderline personality: elaborating and extending Linehan's theory. *Psychological Bulletin* **135** (3) 495–510.

Deb S, Matthews T, Holt G & Bouras N (2001) *Practice Guidelines for the Assessment and Diagnosis of Mental Health Problems in Adults with Intellectual Disability*. Brighton: Pavilion.

Department of Health (2001) *Valuing People: A new strategy for learning disability for the 21st century*. London: DH.

Dimeff L & Linehan M (2001) Dialectical behaviour therapy in a nutshell. *The California Psychologist* **34** 10–13.

Elliott C & Smith L (2009) *Borderline Personality Disorder for Dummies*. Indianapolis, Indiana: Wiley.

Emerson E & Heslop P (2010) *A Working Definition of Learning Disabilities, Improving Health and Lives Report no 1 Learning Disabilities Observatory*. Available at: www.improvinghealthandlives. uk/uploads/doc/vid_7446_2010-01Working Definition.pdf (accessed April 2014).

Flynn A, Matthews H & Hollins S (2002) Validity of the diagnosis of personality disorder in adults with learning disability and severe behavioural problems. *British Journal of Psychiatry* **180** 543–546.

Green H (2013) Psychiatric diagnosis vs. psychological formulation: A plea for synthesis. *Clinical Psychology Forum* **246** 23–25.

Hollins S & Sineson V (2000) Psychotherapy, learning disabilities and trauma: new perspectives. *British Journal of Psychiatry* **176** 32–36.

Lindsay W, Dana L, Dosen A, Gabriel S & Young S (2007). Personality disorders. In R Fletcher, E Loscen, C Stavrakaki & M First (Eds) *Diagnostic Manual – Intellectual Disability (DM-ID): A clinical guide for diagnosis of mental disorders in persons with intellectual disability*, pp 511-532. USA: NADD.

Mavromatis M (2000) The diagnosis and treatment of borderline personality disorder in persons with developmental disability: three case reports. *Mental Health Aspects of Developmental Disabilities* **3** (3) 89–97.

Naik B, Gangadhara S & Alexander R (2002) Personality disorder in learning disability – the clinical experience. *The British Journal of Developmental Disabilities* **48** 2 95–100.

National Collaboration Centre for Mental Health (2009) *Borderline Personality Disorder. The NICE guideline on treatment and management*. Leicester & London: The British Psychological Society & Royal College of Psychiatrists.

Pridding A & Proctor N (2008) A systematic review of personality disorder amongst people with intellectual disability with implications for the mental health nurse practitioner. *Journal of Clinical Nursing* **17** 2811–2819.

Reid A & Ballinger B (1987) Personality disorder in mental handicap. *Psychological Medicine* **17** 983–987.

Tenneij N, Didden R & Koots H (2011) Predicting change in emotional and behavioural problems during inpatient treatment in clients with mild intellectual disability. *Journal of Applied Research in Intellectual Disabilities* March **24** (2) 142–149.

# Chapter 2: Unhealthy self-image and low self-esteem

This chapter explores what self-image and self-esteem are and how they develop. It looks at how self-image and self-esteem may be influenced by personality disorder and intellectual disabilities. The chapter identifies the problems that poor self-image and low self-esteem may cause individuals and how these problems may be addressed.

## Key topics

- Self-image
- Self-image and self-esteem in individuals with personality disorder
- Self-image and self-esteem in individuals with intellectual disabilities
- Self-image and self-esteem in individuals with intellectual disabilities and personality disorder
- Improving self-image and self-esteem
- Positive support
- Therapeutic activities

## Self-image

Self-image is the mental picture a person has of themselves. Other terms used to describe this sense of self include identity and self-concept. Self-image is a relatively long-term picture; it is how someone sees themselves generally. For example, being in a bad mood would be a passing state but thinking of oneself as grumpy would be part of self-image. However, self-image is never totally fixed; aspects are always adapting and developing in response to life events and the changes brought about by time.

Self-image is complex and encompasses a number of elements; these are given in Box 2.1.

---

### Box 2.1: Elements of self-image

**Person's view of themselves**
- Physical characteristics eg. male/female, fat/slim, tall/short
- Capabilities eg. intelligence, common sense, good driver
- Characteristics eg. loveable, independent
- Roles eg. worker, mother, son
- Group membership eg. working class, Welsh, Liverpool supporter
- Sexuality eg. gay, straight, bisexual
- Political and religious affiliations eg. Christian, Hindu, Conservative, Liberal, Democrat, Republican

**Person's evaluation of themselves (self-esteem)**
- Evaluation of characteristics eg. too fat, too short
- Sense of worth (self-respect)
- Belief in their abilities (self-confidence)

---

A person's self-image may or may not correspond to how other people see them. For example, someone most people consider short might consider themselves to be tall because they are the tallest member of their family. One person may consider themselves fat and another person consider themselves thin despite them both weighing the same on the scales.

People may also value the same characteristic very differently. One person may be happy being overweight, thinking *'big girls have more fun'*. Another may think *'I'll never be invited to a party, I'm too fat.'* This evaluation of personal qualities forms part of 'self-esteem' and is explored more fully in the following sections.

While some aspects of self-image are conscious, others have been absorbed over time and a person may not be fully aware of them. These will form part of their core belief system. Core beliefs are important in shaping how people react emotionally and behaviourally and are explored in greater depth in Chapter 7.

## Developing self-image

Babies have no sense of self. As they develop they become aware of themselves as a separate person and of how others see them. Their self-image develops with experience of the world and interactions with other people. They absorb what others say about them and how others react to them. This process is called 'internalising'.

Small children do not have the capacity to question the judgement of adults and will usually accept what adults say as the truth. Small children will also accept without question an adult's emotional response to them. In a secure and loving family (however that family is constructed), children receive a balance of positive and negative comments. They will also have a strong sense of being loved for themselves regardless of their characteristics or behaviour. This is called 'unconditional positive regard'. These comments and emotional responses form the basis of a healthy self-image including good self-esteem. However, some families are not able to foster a positive sense of self in their children. This may be due to the parents' own experiences as children, to illness, problems with addiction or to circumstances surrounding the birth and early childhood.

Self-image continues to develop throughout life, with experiences and relationships outside the family becoming increasingly influential. Teenage years often see a lot of changes and can be quite turbulent. During this time teenagers may experiment with different personas, making frequent changes to their style of dress, hairstyle, the groups they socialise with, the activities they take part in and their ambitions for the future. However, by early adulthood most people develop a consistent sense of self. This is seen in a stable sense of personal and sexual identity and consistent values, goals and ambitions.

## Self-esteem

Self-esteem is the judgemental part of self-concept. It comprises a person's evaluation of their personal characteristics, their sense of worth (self-respect) and belief in their abilities (self-confidence). Self-esteem underlies a person's core beliefs about their right to be happy and be treated well by others. It also underpins their belief in their abilities to cope with challenges and solve problems. People with high self-esteem are more resilient to setbacks and better able to face challenges. High self-esteem is linked with success in life and with good mental health. On the other hand, having constantly low self-esteem undermines a person's ability to cope with everyday challenges and increases the risk of mental health problems such as anxiety and depression.

Both self-respect and self-confidence can fluctuate. For example, anyone's self-confidence can take a knock if they are made redundant and have difficulty finding another job. However, having a wide range of roles and characteristics from which to derive a sense of worth helps protect self-esteem; strong areas can compensate for perceived weaknesses. Achievements, social standing, attractiveness and belonging to groups can all protect self-esteem.

## Social comparison

One of the ways people form judgements about themselves is by comparing themselves to others. If a person sees themselves as lower than others on any attribute this can lower self-esteem. This is particularly likely to happen if the aspect found wanting is something that is important to the person.

Sometimes people increase their self-esteem by actively looking for comparisons that can make them feel superior. This process is called 'downward comparison'. Downward comparisons may also include denigrating others similar to themselves or denying their membership of a group that is seen as not socially valued. For example, someone with a mild physical disability may compare themselves to wheelchair users saying *'I'm not a useless cripple'* and refuse to engage with activities for people with physical disabilities. While this may boost their self-esteem, it comes at a cost to the person; it may isolate them from people who might otherwise be able to support them and undermines them developing a positive attitude towards their own disabilities.

# Self-image and self-esteem in individuals with personality disorder

Difficulties with self-image are a diagnostic characteristic of a number of personality disorders. Some examples are given in Box 2.2.

Issues with how the individual sees themselves are implied by some other criteria. For example, in antisocial personality disorder individuals do not take responsibility for their behaviour or respect rules. This implies distorted beliefs about the self, relating to being untouchable and above rules. Likewise, disregard of the needs or feelings of others may arise from a sense of entitlement or superiority to others.

Difficulties with self-image are characteristic of individuals with borderline personality disorder. As a result of their experiences growing up, they frequently have an unhealthy self-image and low self-esteem. They may have a strong sense of being flawed, damaged, dirty or bad. They often feel that they are unlovable and do not deserve to be treated well. This can lead to them unconsciously seeking people who will treat them badly or accepting situations that most people would find

Intellectual Disabilities and Personality Disorder: An integrated approach
© Pavilion Publishing and Media Ltd and its licensors 2014.

intolerable. They may send out powerful unconscious messages that put pressure on even the kindest people to behave badly towards them. Even if individuals have some insight into the contribution their attitude makes to their difficulties they lack the self-confidence and optimism needed to try to resolve the problems. These issues can make it very difficult for them to seek help and engage with services.

---

### Box 2.2: Difficulties with self-image in personality disorders

**Paranoid personality disorder**
- Disproportionate sense of personal rights
- Think only of themselves and how situations impact on them, talk about themselves and assume things overheard must be about them

**Borderline personality disorder**
- Disturbances in and uncertainty about self-image, aims and personal preferences

**Narcissistic personality disorder**
- Grandiose sense of self-importance, expects to be recognised as superior
- Belief that they are special and can only be understood by or should mix with other special or high status people or services

**Avoidant personality disorder**
- Inhibited in social situations because of feelings of inadequacy
- Sees self as socially inept, unattractive or inferior to others

---

Sometimes people with borderline personality disorder may feel that they have no real existence at all. They cling to other people as the interaction proves that they are real and may panic when alone for fear of disappearing altogether. This feeling can underlie some of the more extreme behaviours individuals sometimes show, such as acts of self-harm.

Other individuals with borderline personality disorder may have an unstable sense of self. They experience sudden and dramatic changes in their view of themselves. This will show in changes of dress and hairstyles, choice of job, leisure activities and friends. There may be changes in opinions and sexual identity. To staff supporting them it can sometimes feel as if these individuals are not one person but several different people.

People with some personality disorders (eg. borderline, avoidant) often experience the effects of low self-esteem such as being overly self-critical, sensitive to criticism, irritable and pessimistic. They are often insecure; seeking constant reassurance but seemingly unable to accept and hold onto any positive comments.

## Self-image of victimisation

If a person with personality disorder has experienced abuse this may have shaped their sense of self. Some people who have been abused develop a self-image of victimisation. This way of being is characterised by feelings of loss of control, helplessness and hopelessness, guilt, shame and self-blame. Seeing themselves as 'a victim' can make individuals more vulnerable to abuse in the future.

## Stigma

Having a diagnosis of personality disorder can sometimes add to an individual's difficulties with self-image. Personality disorder is not something that is valued in society. Many professionals still think that it is untreatable and will seek to exclude such individuals from services. This adds to the individual's sense of being unwanted and feelings of hopelessness.

# Self-image and self-esteem in individuals with intellectual disabilities

Many individuals with intellectual disabilities will have a poor self-image and low self-esteem as a result of the challenges arising from their disabilities. Having intellectual disabilities exposes individuals to many negative life experiences and reduces the range of positive opportunities. It is likely that individuals with intellectual disabilities will experience frequent failure. They will struggle with tasks that those around them find easy and are often the least competent person in their family circle. As they grow up they may not move through valued life stages at the same rate as their peers and siblings; for example, finding a job, finding a partner, leaving home and having a family. Failing to achieve these important milestones is likely to have a negative impact on their self-esteem and reduce access to things that can protect self-worth; for example, a wide social network, rewarding work and strong close relationships.

In addition to the direct consequences of struggling with intellectual disabilities, individuals are exposed to how others view those disabilities. Having a disability is not valued by western society. This is reflected in how individuals with intellectual disabilities are treated. They are vulnerable to bullying at school and may be picked on in their local community. Many individuals with intellectual disabilities take on society's view of them and develop a sense of being different and inadequate. They may also use downward comparison as a means of boosting their self-esteem. Individuals with mild intellectual disabilities may call others with this disability names such as *'stupid'* and refuse to access local services because *'I'm not one of them'*.

Very occasionally, having intellectual disabilities may lead to an individual having a sense of being special and above the rules that apply to other people. This can occur when individuals are not held accountable for their actions and are protected from the consequences that would usually be associated with inappropriate behaviour.

## Self-image and self-esteem in individuals with intellectual disabilities and personality disorder

When an individual has both intellectual disabilities and personality disorder it is likely that they will have many issues with self-image and self-esteem. Some may have an over-inflated sense of their importance or that they are above the law. These issues are explored more fully in Chapter 7. However, it is much more common to find individuals with low self-esteem and a poor self-image. These individuals are likely to have grown up in a family that was unable to give them unconditional positive regard. They will have had to cope with all the negative experiences that are linked to having intellectual disabilities without the support of a loving family. They may also have experienced abuse within the family, through being bullied for their disabilities or through exploitation.

Like more able individuals with personality disorder, they may have a strong sense of being flawed, damaged, dirty or bad. Feelings of being unlovable and undeserving of good treatment will shape their responses to others. This makes them vulnerable to further abuse or neglect, which further reinforces their negative self-image. Box 2.3 gives examples of some of the negative core beliefs that may be held by individuals with intellectual disabilities and personality disorder.

Feelings of worthlessness can also lead the individual to self-neglect. This may take the form of poor personal care and untidy appearance. However, it may take a more serious form when the individual completely neglects their physical health. This can result in serious tooth decay, infected wounds, extreme weight loss or gain, and non-compliance with treatment for illnesses such as diabetes or colitis. These severe forms of self-neglect are explored more fully in Chapter 10.

---

## Box 2.3: Negative core beliefs about the self

### Different/defective

I am stupid, inferior, not good enough, defective

I am not like other people, not like my brothers and sisters

### Helpless, dependent

I am ineffective, incompetent, unable to cope, powerless, out of control, trapped, vulnerable, needy, weak, a failure, useless, no good at anything

I don't measure up, fail no matter how hard I try

### Unlovable

I am unlovable, unlikeable, unwanted, undesirable, unattractive, different, defective, not good enough to be loved by others, ugly, boring

I will be rejected, abandoned, always alone

I have nothing to offer

### Worthless

I am bad, irresponsible, worthless, dangerous, toxic, evil, inhuman

### Undeserving

I can't have what I want

---

# Self-esteem

Individuals with intellectual disabilities and personality disorder often have very low or very fragile self-esteem. This has a wide-ranging impact on their interactions with other people and their approach to life. Some of these consequences are given in Box 2.4.

Low self-esteem can lead to apparently opposite behaviours in different individuals depending on their underlying personality traits. For example, an impulsive person may react to low self-esteem by rejecting help but a more cautious individual may react by becoming overly dependent on others. In fact, low self-esteem is linked with all the areas of difficulty addressed in the subsequent chapters of this book. It either contributes directly to the problem area or impacts on intervention by making it difficult for individuals to engage with services and accept support or advice.

Intellectual Disabilities and Personality Disorder: An integrated approach
© Pavilion Publishing and Media Ltd and its licensors 2014.

## Box 2.4: Possible consequences of low self-esteem

**Highly self-critical**

Being continually dissatisfied with many aspects of themselves.

**Distorted view of abilities**

Exaggerating their weaknesses and underestimating their strengths.

**Selective attention to feedback**

Focusing on negative comments or experiences and not registering positive comments or compliments.

**Hypersensitive to criticism**

Taking the slightest comment as criticism, triggering an intense emotional reaction and anger.

**Excessive guilt**

'Over-reacting' to often minor errors or 'sins'. These are seen as far worse than most people would consider them, are remembered for much longer and the person is often unable to forgive themselves.

**Perfectionism**

Putting pressure on themselves for everything to be done perfectly without any mistakes. Being unforgiving of (own/others') mistakes and experiencing high levels of frustration when events and people do not live up to expectations.

**Low expectations**

Lacking the self-belief that they can achieve good outcomes or that life will offer them anything positive.

**Pessimism**

Lacking hope about themselves, life and the future which makes it difficult to get any enjoyment out of life. This extends to relationships: expecting everyone to treat them badly or let them down.

**Irritability**

Having a sense of disappointment and lack of satisfaction about everybody and everything leads to explosions over tiny things.

**Indecision**

Finding it difficult to make choices out of fear of making mistakes and lack of confidence in their judgements or uncertainty about what they really want.

Continued...

---

**Excessive will to please**

Going along with things they do not want to do and being unable to say no because they fear upsetting others.

**Putting others down**

Making negative comments about other individuals or groups.

**Fear of failure**

Lacking the confidence to try new activities or go to new places.

**Lack of persistence/perseverance**

Giving up too easily with anything challenging or difficult.

**Over-dependence**

Unwilling to try things on their own.

**Over-independence**

Finding help and support humiliating and hence trying to do everything alone.

---

Low self-esteem is particularly important when looking at mental health problems, especially depression. In the most extreme situation it can be associated with suicidal thoughts and actions. These are explored more fully in Chapters 9 and 11.

# Improving self-image and self-esteem

The pervasive nature of problems with self-image and self-esteem mean that this area needs to be considered whatever problems an individual presents with. However, working to help an individual build a positive self-image, self-esteem and confidence is a long-term process. It is unlikely that a few sessions of individual therapy (however good the therapist) will change an individual's long-term view of themselves if all the other contacts in their life fail to challenge (or even actively reinforce) their negative view of themselves. Consequently, when looking to improve self-image and self-esteem it is important to consider how these issues can be actively addressed in every area of the individual's life. While this initially appears a daunting prospect, considering how therapeutic interventions work can make this an achievable objective.

Any therapeutic or support activity has two important components; what is done and how it is done. Most attention is usually given to what is done or the content of any intervention. However, how it is done or the process of the intervention is in fact as important, if not more important, than the content, if the intervention is to succeed.

Carl Rogers explored the process of intervention and identified a number of therapist characteristics that helped individuals feel better about themselves and have the confidence to change. These are given in Box 2.5.

---

**Box 2.5: Characteristics of the therapist that create an environment that helps individuals to understand, accept and change themselves**

- Warmth – kindness, compassion, care
- Being non-judgemental – accepting the person without negative judgement of their core worth
- Empathy – understanding how the person is feeling
- Offering unconditional positive regard – positive support is offered whatever the individual does or says
- Genuineness – the above must be real feelings not an 'act' put on

---

This work was done specifically in the context of psychotherapy and was used to develop an approach called person-centred counselling. However, the characteristics identified are relevant to all types of support and care. Even the simplest of actions such as helping someone tidy a bedroom can be done in ways that convey powerful messages about how the member of staff views the individual. It can give the message that the member of staff cares about the individual, understands that they feel too low to do this alone, and that this does not make them bad or lazy. Alternatively, the staff member can convey that this is a waste of their precious time, that the individual is lazy and inconsiderate, and that the individual's feelings are exaggerated or silly. The first approach will help build self-esteem, the second will confirm the individual's view that they are not worthy of help because they are a bad person.

If attention is given to the process/'how' of support and care then self-image and self-esteem can gradually be improved by absorbing these positive messages, experiencing positive feedback from others and achieving personal successes. This may be termed 'positive support' and is explored more fully in the next section. Once the positive support process is in place it may be helpful to consider more traditional therapeutic activities (content) that may improve self-image and some suggestions for these are also given.

# Positive support

Positive support shows interest in the individual and sensitivity to their needs and forms one element of the 'authoritative' support style that is explored more fully in Chapter 5. It is a combination of positive attitudes and actions that aim to create an environment in which an individual can begin to develop a more positive sense of self and work towards changing their behaviour. Some of the characteristics of this approach are given in Box 2.6.

| Box 2.6: Characteristics of positive support | |
| --- | --- |
| **Positive attitude** | **Positive actions** |
| ■ Non-judgemental | ■ Having fun |
| ■ Respectful | ■ Praise and compliments |
| ■ Hopeful, long-term view | ■ Constructive criticism |
| ■ Realistic expectations | ■ Goal setting |
| ■ Persistence and consistency | ■ Encouragement and support |
| | ■ Calm and balanced reaction to setbacks |

# Positive attitude

## Being non-judgemental

Adopting a non-judgemental approach avoids reinforcing the individual's negative view of themselves. However this is not always easy to do. Individuals with intellectual disabilities and personality disorders can show some extreme behaviours and can be very hurtful to those around them. It is easy to react to these behaviours with anger and criticism. Phrases such as 'How could you do that to yourself/me?' can spring to mind. It is a short step from these thoughts to wanting the person to be punished for what they have done. Such reactions confirm the individual's belief that they are bad and do not deserve to be treated well.

The reasons for extreme and hurtful behaviours and how to manage both the behaviours and staff reactions to such behaviours will be explored more fully in later chapters. However, it can be helpful for staff to hold in mind that such behaviours arise from overwhelming feelings that the individual's negative life experiences have left them ill-equipped to resolve; they are coping in the only way they can. It can be helpful to think back to what is known about the individual's past and imagine how difficult it must have been for them as a small child. In this way staff may be able to avoid condemning the individual, however they feel about the behaviour.

Intellectual Disabilities and Personality Disorder: An integrated approach
© Pavilion Publishing and Media Ltd and its licensors 2014.

## Respect

Treating an individual with respect tells them they matter and are worthy of good treatment. Box 2.7 lists some respectful behaviours and compares them to disrespectful behaviour.

| Box 2.7: Comparison of respectful and disrespectful behaviours | |
| --- | --- |
| Respectful behaviours | Disrespectful behaviours |
| Being polite | Being rude |
| Being punctual | Being late |
| Using someone's preferred name | Not remembering someone's name |
| Listening to what they have to say | Thinking about other things |
| Answering questions honestly | Not saying the truth |
| Giving someone time | Cutting interactions short |
| Believing what they say | Disbelieving what is said |
| Doing what is promised | Making false promises |
| Apologising for mistakes | Pretending mistakes did not happen |
| Using a warm, friendly tone of voice | Using a bored or sarcastic tone of voice |

This may look like stating the obvious. However in busy, high pressured services it is often very difficult to maintain respectful behaviour towards individuals with intellectual disabilities and personality disorder because of the way they may behave towards staff. Such behaviours might include interrupting conversations, asking repeated questions, turning up late or not at all, not keeping their word, blaming staff for things they have not done and not telling the full truth. These behaviours often make staff feel that they are being treated disrespectfully.

Anyone can respond to politeness with respect but it takes hard work, insight and self-control to continue to respond respectfully in the face of repeated inconsiderate behaviour. Again, it can be helpful to keep considering the individual's perspective; often they are so overwhelmed by their own needs that they do not consider the impact of their behaviour on others. Also, their ability to imagine what others are feeling may be impaired, meaning they have little awareness of the impact of their behaviour on the other person. If it is thought that the individual is aware of and takes some satisfaction in the impact of their behaviour on staff it may be helpful to think about the traumatic things that might have happened to them to create the need to put others down and treat them poorly. (More ideas on how to understand and manage staff's personal reactions to individuals are given in Chapters 13 and 14.)

Maintaining respect in the face of all challenges gives a strong message that staff think that the individual with intellectual disabilities and personality disorder matters.

## Hope

The importance of hope is being increasingly recognised in mental health services. Even when someone has given up on themselves, it is important that those supporting them maintain hope that change is possible and that things will get better. Again this is easier said than done; it can be difficult to maintain hope in situations where change seems impossible. At the darkest times it can be helpful to hold on to the knowledge that stability is an illusion. In the same way that good things cannot go on for ever, bad things also have an end. In reality things are always changing but sometimes the pace of change is so slow that it is difficult to spot. A particularly helpful phrase at times when things seem stuck is *'This too will pass'*.

## Realistic expectations

People with intellectual disabilities and personality disorder often set themselves unrealistic goals, for example, *'I will never self-harm again'* when they have been self-harming frequently for many years or *'I'm going to get a full-time job'* when they are spending all day in bed and have never sustained even part-time work. Words such as *'never'* and *'always'* give clues that expectations are unrealistic. When they meet a setback, as they must if the goal is over ambitious, it confirms their sense of being useless and they will abandon their efforts to achieve the goal. Every time this happens it is a setback for their self-esteem, making it harder for them to try again in the future.

It is easy for staff to fall in with such goals as they often reflect things they long for the individual to achieve. This adds to the individual's sense of letting others down when things go wrong. Rather than get caught up in the enthusiasm of a great goal, it is helpful to be quietly optimistic. Low key responses might be: *'It's great you want to do that but it will be hard work.' 'That's fantastic but remember, Rome wasn't built in a day, let's have a look at what you will need to do'*. The aim is not to pour cold water on the idea but to set the scene for some realistic goal setting. This is easy to do first time round but needs to be maintained even if it is the fifth time someone has tried to change something and they have abandoned it every previous time.

### Persistence and consistency

Individuals with intellectual disabilities and personality disorder are likely to have grown up with people whose reactions were inconsistent. It is important that those who support them maintain a calm, consistent approach whatever they are confronted with. This can sometimes take a lot of determination as a person's behaviour and reactions will often have the effect of pushing staff to behave like all the other people who have let them down.

## Positive actions

### Having fun

One of the most powerful ways of helping individuals to feel better about themselves is to do things that they enjoy. Having fun, laughing, joking, playing games or dancing create a positive atmosphere and give the message that the individual is someone worth spending time with. Actions speak louder than words.

### Praise and compliments

Praise and compliments from others are usually pleasant experiences that make us feel good about ourselves. Giving praise and compliments is very important. However, people with intellectual disabilities and personality disorder have often had very little experience of praise or compliments and can find them hard to accept. It can feel like wasted breath as comments such as *'You look great today'* or *'This room looks so clean'* are repeatedly ignored or contradicted. Despite these reactions the person will still hear the compliment. Gradually they will find compliments and praise easier to accept and will begin to accept that they have positive qualities and successes that others think well of.

Individuals with intellectual disabilities and personality disorder will often be reluctant to try new things and will give up easily. It is therefore important to praise effort rather than just achievement. For example, if someone tries but it did not quite work say *'Well tried, you keep working like that and you'll soon get the hang of it'*.

Praise and compliments need to become an automatic part of any interaction and staff should always be looking for opportunities to give positive feedback. However the praise must have a genuine basis and be given with real feeling. Individuals are quick to pick up if something is said without meaning it.

## Constructive criticism

Giving praise and compliments does not mean that individuals should only be told positive things. However, staff are often wary of giving feedback because of the intensity of many individuals' reactions to anything approaching criticism. It is therefore important to think about ways feedback can be given to increase the likelihood of it being positively received.

One important principle is to ensure there is always a balance between positive and negative comments. A useful rule of thumb is to give at least six positive comments for one negative. It can also be helpful to precede a negative comment with a positive statement. For example, *'You've done a really good job of vacuuming the carpet but there is still some dust on the shelves'*. Criticism should also be specific and tell the person how they could do things differently. For example, compare *'your bedroom is filthy'* with *'your room will look great if you put those dirty clothes in the laundry basket and vacuum the carpet'*.

## Goal setting

Goal setting is a useful technique for turning unrealistic expectations or distant goals into achievable short-term steps. Turning something impossible or very long-term into lots of small tasks creates many opportunities to succeed and consequently, to build self-confidence.

It can be helpful to draw a ladder with a lot of rungs, putting where someone wants to be at the top and where they are now at the bottom. Working together, the individual and staff member can then identify a number of small steps that would let them know if the individual was making progress towards their goal. This makes the goal seem more achievable, helps create an action plan and also makes it easier to evaluate the seriousness of any setbacks. Each step can then be developed into a more detailed action plan. Once one step is achieved a detailed action plan can be made for the next step. It is also possible that the individual will make it part of the way up the ladder and will be happy to stop there. Some example ladders are given in Boxes 2.8 and 2.9. Each individual's ladder will be unique to them and their goal.

## Box 2.8: Example 1: Safe alternatives to self-harm

Goal: Give up self-harm – only use safe alternatives

Mostly able to use alternatives to self-harm

Sometimes able to use alternatives to self-harm

Self-harm less frequent/less severe

Delaying self-harm

Practice using alternatives to self-harm

Identifying alternatives to self-harm – making a crisis box

Exploring the pros and cons of self-harm. What function does it serve?

Starting point: Severe and frequent self-harm

## Box 2.9: Example 2: Having a full-time job

Goal: Having a full-time job

Developing job-seeking skills eg. interview skills

Sheltered employment/work experience

Basic skills course at college

Part-time voluntary work in related area

Getting up earlier (may be several steps)

Identifying realistic job options; job centre interview

Exploring the pros and cons of working. What does a full-time job mean?

Starting point: Staying in bed until midday, no structured activities at all

## Encouragement and support

It is hard for anyone to stay motivated all the time in the face of a big challenge. Gentle encouragement and support can make a huge difference. Reminding someone of how far they have come, how good it will feel if they do have a go and listening when it feels too difficult will all make a difference. Let them know you believe in them even when they don't believe in themselves. More ideas on motivating individuals are given in Chapter 6.

## Reactions to setbacks

It is important for staff to prepare themselves and the individual for the inevitable setbacks. Individuals with intellectual disabilities and personality disorder are likely to be very upset by even small setbacks and will easily give up. It is important for staff to acknowledge how bad the setback has made the individual feel (see Chapter 3 for how to validate emotions) but to be calm and completely unfazed themselves.

Just how bad is this setback? Imagine a ladder:

■ Are they back at the beginning or have they just slipped a few rungs?

■ Are the steps still too big – should the ladder have more rungs?

■ Does the action plan need changing?

Staff need to show that setbacks are a normal part of any attempt to change and that, while painful, they are just a message to look at the plan again and see if it needs improving. Make it clear that the setback does not change how staff see the individual or the belief that they will make progress in the end. If the individual cannot yet accept this and gives up on the goal, staff need to accept their choice but make it clear they still believe the individual has done well by trying and that they will be there if they change their mind.

If the individual enjoys board games it can be helpful to play snakes (chutes) and ladders. This gives a concrete example of how a goal can be achieved despite multiple setbacks. Playing the game can make a safe space in which to talk about the individual's efforts to achieve seemingly impossible goals.

# Therapeutic activities

Once a healthy environment has been created by using positive support, more traditional therapeutic activities may be considered. There are many options and self-esteem may be addressed as part of dialectical behaviour therapy (DBT) or cognitive behaviour therapy (CBT). DBT is a wide-ranging approach developed specifically for individuals with borderline personality disorder involving both individual therapy and group work. CBT is a more focused approach looking at how to change unhelpful thoughts, feelings and behaviours. Both CBT and DBT need to be delivered by professionals who are trained in the approach and are also skilled at adapting it to the needs of individuals with intellectual disabilities. Consequently, the individual would need to be referred to their local intellectual disabilities or mental health services.

Two approaches that do not need specialist therapy training and are particularly helpful are given in the following sections.

## Good memories book

Dealing with low self-esteem can be particularly difficult when someone is alone; for example, if they wake in the middle of the night and are unable to get back to sleep. A good memories book can be helpful for such times. This involves working with the individual to create a visual record of their achievements, positive personal qualities and happy experiences. At times when they are feeling down, the book will remind them of better times and their better qualities.

Work on the book needs to be done when the person is calm and settled. Staff need to take opportunities to talk to the individual about themselves and their past. As the individual finds pleasant thoughts or memories, staff help them find ways to record them. This might be words (an account or poem), personal photographs, images from the internet, drawings or souvenirs such as ticket stubs. It is important to take time creating the pages and make it fun. This way, the process of making the book will also be associated with positive memories. Maybe someone could take a photo of the work in process. Possible topics are given in Box 2.10. If the individual is unable to come up with ideas for some pages it may be helpful to ask other people to tell them something nice.

---

### Box 2.10: Memory book contents

- My achievements
- My favourite things/activities/places/pets/people
- My good qualities
- Looking my best
- Great days out
- Wonderful holidays
- People who care about me
- Nice things people have said about me

---

It is important to be aware that if the individual is feeling very down they may destroy the book. This should be discussed openly with them and ways of reducing the impact of this should be identified. For example, it might be better to take a photo of a treasured ticket stub for the book while keeping the original in a box where it is difficult to access. Art work can be photocopied or scanned into the computer for safekeeping. This way the book can be recreated after a setback. It may also be helpful to have multiple copies of the book, each in different settings that the individual uses. In this way there will still be a copy available elsewhere. The setback will also not seem so bad as it had been anticipated and planned for and special keepsakes have not been destroyed.

The memory book should never be finished as new experiences and achievements can be added as they happen.

## Self-esteem group

Group work offers individuals the chance to work together to help each other. There are opportunities to give and receive feedback to give emotional support and to share practical solutions. A well-run group creates the opportunity for individuals to realise that they are not alone and that other people have had similar experiences. It gives the opportunity to learn with and from other people in a safe setting. A group may also give individuals the opportunity to explore and challenge the views that society holds of them.

Self-esteem and empowerment groups have been successfully run for individuals with intellectual disabilities. Such groups usually explore how self-esteem and self-image develop, give individuals space to think about what influenced their self-image, the chance to share negative experiences such as bullying, and to develop skills such as being assertive. They may create resources to help the individual outside the group setting, such as making a 'strengths card' (a credit card sized list of good qualities that they can carry with them). They may also work to identify automatic negative thoughts about themselves and work to challenge these thoughts (see Chapter 7). Role-play can be used to help individuals see how their responses may influence how other people respond to them.

These groups can be adapted for individuals with intellectual disabilities and personality disorder. For this to be successful the group leaders need to be skilled at resolving interpersonal conflict. The group needs to start by identifying and agreeing to stick to clear rules about behaviour in the group. The rules should be revisited at the start of every session and referred to when there is a need to address the behaviour of individuals. In particular it is important to have rules about taking turns, what to do if someone does not let others speak, how to give feedback and what to do if an individual finds the content of the session too distressing. It can be helpful to negotiate a clear agreement with individuals on their own before the group starts. This might look at increasing their motivation by talking about how attending the group might fit with their personal goals, how many sessions they are expected to attend and what will happen if they miss a session. Some individuals with personality disorder strongly resist attending any groups; for them it is better to focus on individual work. However, many individuals find groups enjoyable as well as helpful and often find it easier to learn from their peers than from a therapist.

# Key learning points

- Self-image is the mental picture a person has of themselves, including their evaluation of themselves or self-esteem.

- Healthy self-image and self-esteem promote good mental health and give people the inner resources to face life's challenges.

- Individuals with intellectual disabilities and personality disorder often have a damaged sense of self and low self-esteem. They may have a strong sense of being flawed, damaged, dirty or bad. Feelings of being unlovable and undeserving of good treatment may shape their responses to others.

- A damaged sense of self and low self-esteem can lead to a range of problems including hyper-sensitivity to criticism, reluctance to try anything new, self-neglect and depression.

- Improving self-image is a long-term project that requires staff to think as much about how they do things as about what they do.

- By adopting positive attitudes (non-judgemental, respectful and hopeful) and positive actions (such as having fun, goal setting, giving praise, compliments and feedback) staff can create an environment that fosters a positive sense of self.

- Some individuals may also benefit from further individual or group interventions to help them to build a positive sense of self and develop helpful skills.

# Further reading

Dagnan D & Sandhu S (1999) Social comparison, self-esteem and depression in people with intellectual disability. *Journal of Intellectual Disability Research* **43** (5) 372–379.

Field L (2001) *Creating Self-esteem: A practical guide to realizing your true worth.* London: Vermilion.

Lindsay W & Kasprowicz M (1987) Challenging negative cognitions: developing confidence in adults by means of cognitive behaviour therapy. *Journal of the British Institute of Mental Handicap* **15** 159–62.

Mearns D & Thorne B. (2007) *Person-centred Counselling in Action.* London: Sage. (For information on Carl Rogers' approach.)

Szivos S & Griffiths E (1992) Coming to terms with learning difficulties: the effects of group work and group processes on stigmatised identity. In: A Waitman & S Conboy-Hill (Eds) *Psychotherapy and Mental Handicap.* London: Sage.

Whelan A, Haywood P & Galloway S (2007) Low self-esteem: group cognitive behaviour therapy. *British Journal of Learning Disabilities* **35** 125–130.

# Chapter 3: Emotional distress

This chapter explores what emotions are and how emotional distress is expressed. It looks at how the experience of emotions and emotional distress may be influenced by personality disorder and intellectual disabilities. It looks at the challenges emotional distress presents for both individuals with intellectual disabilities and personality disorder and the staff supporting them, and explores how these challenges may be addressed.

## Key topics

- Emotions

- Managing emotions

- Emotions and individuals with personality disorder

- Emotions and individuals with intellectual disabilities

- Emotions and individuals with intellectual disabilities and personality disorder

- Supporting individuals who have difficulty managing their emotions

## Emotions

For something that is a universal part of human experience, emotion is remarkably difficult to define and there are many different theories about what happens when an emotion is experienced. An emotion may be described as a spontaneous state of mind that arises in response to internal events (such as thoughts or physical sensations) or external events (such as other people's behaviour). An emotion is usually a short-term experience. When an emotional state persists for any length of time it is usually referred to as a 'mood'.

There are six basic emotions: anger, disgust, fear, sadness, happiness and surprise. These seem to be 'hard-wired' into the human system. These emotions have a wide variety of expressions, from mild to intense and there is an extensive vocabulary to reflect these differences (for example, 'sadness'; low, down, upset, depressed, distraught). The basic emotions can also be influenced by social experience to create more complex emotions such as jealously, embarrassment, grief, shame, guilt and remorse.

## Components of emotion

There is general agreement that emotions comprise a number of different components, although every theory has a slightly different view on what the components are and how they interact. The most commonly suggested components are given in Box 3.1.

---

### Box 3.1: Components of emotions

- **Expression:** External signs of the emotion eg. facial expression, changes to voice, posture and body language.
- **Subjective experience:** How the individual experiences the emotion (in contrast to what may show to others through expression of emotion).
- **Action tendencies or motivation:** The desire to act eg. run away, attack, approach.
- **Physical reactions:** Physiological changes eg. heart rate, breathing, circulation, sweating.

---

Some approaches include physical reactions and thoughts about the situation as part of emotion. Others view these as separate from the emotion but closely involved in the overall experience of emotion.

## Functions of emotions

It is sometimes suggested that emotions serve no useful function for modern humans, that they disrupt and disorganise behaviour and that they are illogical. While it is true that emotions can be messy, they do in fact serve a range of useful functions. Some of the most frequently suggested functions are given in Box 3.2.

---

**Box 3.2: Functions of emotions**

- Maintain social systems eg. form attachments, maintain co-operative relations
- Communicate with/influence others: tell others how someone is feeling and hence how to react to them – comfort someone who is sad, avoid someone who is angry
- Communicate information about the situation to the person experiencing the emotion eg. awareness of danger, 'gut feeling'
- Prepare for action – through links with the flight-fight response to prepare body for action
- Avoid physical threats and danger (particularly fear)
- Motivate to act eg. to overcome obstacles
- Prioritise actions: help people decide what they want to do and what is most important to them
- Help encode key information about a situation – events are remembered more clearly if linked to powerful emotions

---

## Emotions and thoughts

Emotional responses are closely related to thoughts. Emotional distress is partly caused by external events but also by how those events are interpreted. Two people may respond to the same situation with completely different emotions because of differences in the way that situation was interpreted. Interpretation also influences responses to the physical sensations that accompany emotional reactions. If these are misinterpreted, for example, as being a heart attack, the emotional response will be intensified. The influences of thoughts on behaviour and emotion are explored more fully in Chapter 7.

## Emotions and behaviour

The relationship between emotions and behaviour is complex. Emotions can create a drive, motivation or impulse to behave in a certain way. However, people may or may not act on that drive. Behaviour that is driven purely by emotion is often an 'instinctive', rapid response to an immediate situation. This is often helpful in an emergency but it is less helpful in everyday life. Mostly reactions are more thought through with the emotion felt being only one of the issues that a person considers as they choose to act. The process of controlling impulses is explored more fully in Chapter 6.

# Effects of emotion on information processing and memory

A person's mood or emotional state influences what they pay attention to, how events are interpreted, what is laid down as a memory and what memories can most easily be recalled. For example, when someone is feeling unhappy they are more likely to notice 'put downs' than when they are feeling cheerful. Events linked with strong emotions are more likely to be encoded in memory.

Once an event is encoded in memory a person will be most likely to remember that event when in a mood similar to the mood they were in at the time the memory was laid down. Whatever mood a person is in or emotion they are experiencing, they are more likely to recall events that have a similar emotional content. Hence when happy a person will find it easiest to recall happy events from their past. However if they are feeling depressed they will recall sad events and if angry will recall past annoyances.

## Biology of emotions

The experience of emotions is supported by a complex physical system involving a number of structures in the brain, a range of neurotransmitters (chemicals released by brain cells), the autonomic nervous system and a number of hormones such as adrenaline. The emotions of anger and fear are accompanied by the physical sensations of the 'fight-flight response'. This hard-wired physical response prepares the body for violent action by changing pulse rate, breathing and blood flow (this is explored more fully in Chapter 12).

## Individual differences

While all humans experience the six basic emotions, there are considerable differences between people in the pattern of their emotional experiences. There are differences in the ease with which emotions are triggered and resolved, the time they are experienced for, the strength of emotions, how much they fluctuate and what is the predominant emotion or mood. People also differ in their ability to tolerate and manage unpleasant emotional states. These differences are influenced by the individual's biology (such as genes, brain structure and hormones), their personality, their experiences growing up and their present circumstances.

# Managing emotions

In order to manage emotions a person needs to be able to recognise the emotion as their own, separate their emotions from those of people close to them and understand why they might be feeling that way (mentalising). They then need to be able tolerate the emotion while they think through how they will react, and be aware of a range of options for dealing with that feeling.

# Emotional validation

Early childhood experiences are thought to have a great impact on the ability to recognise, understand and manage emotions. Initially children are unaware of what emotions are called and cannot control them. Parents help the child learn about emotions through a process called 'validating'. For example, if a child is upset a parent may ask them why they are unhappy and try to comfort them. This gives the child a name for the emotion and makes it clear that the feeling belongs to the child. It also tells the child that their parent thinks the feeling is real and has offered help. As similar experiences are repeated the child gradually learns to recognise and manage their own emotions independently of their parents. This process is shown in Box 3.3.

---

### Box 3.3: Validating emotions

- Parent acknowledges the child's emotion
- Parent names the emotion for the child
- Parent responds to the child's emotion as a real and genuine response to the situation
- Parent accepts that the child's emotion must run its course
- Parent calmly offers support and comfort to the child while the emotion runs its course (emotional containment)
- Parent shows that whatever emotion is expressed does not change the way they view the child (unconditional positive regard)

---

Where emotions are consistently validated and contained, the child will come to understand their emotions and will gradually be able to manage them independently.

However, some families are unable to help their children learn about emotions. In some families the child's experiences are not acknowledged and they may receive the message that their feelings are not real. For example, a parent may be unable to cope with the pain of knowing that their child is unhappy and may therefore continue to behave as if nothing is going on. The child then has no name for the feeling, gets the message that they should be feeling differently and receives no help managing the emotion. Emotions may be met with disbelief (*'don't be so silly'*) or punishment (*stop that or I'll give you something real to cry about'*). Families may impose their interpretation on the child (*'he's not really upset, he's just playing up'*). This makes the child confused about whether their feelings are real. Some families are unable to separate themselves from their child's emotions; if the child is upset, they become upset, if something upsets a parent they behave as if it has also upset the child. This leaves the child frightened and overwhelmed by the emotion.

Some families are unable to give their children unconditional positive regard; rather they respond positively to the child only when they show acceptable emotions and reject them if they are unhappy, angry or fearful. In this situation the child comes to see themselves as bad or evil for having strong emotions.

## Responding to emotions

As well as validating the child's experience of emotion, the family plays an important part in shaping appropriate responses to emotions. If family members listen to and take action to help when the child asks for help, or notice and respond to early signs of distress and ask what is wrong, the child will learn that help will be given when they need it. However, if family members ignore, or do not notice the need for help, the child's response will escalate until it cannot be ignored. In this way a child is taught that only extreme responses to emotions will gain adult attention.

## High expressed emotions

Some families run on an even keel, sharing feelings and expressing their emotions in a contained way. Others are highly volatile; emotions are easily triggered and are given free rein. This is termed 'high expressed emotion'. Families where there are high expressed emotions are less able to help children learn to manage and tolerate emotions.

The consequences of growing up in an invalidating family environment where emotions are not tolerated or contained are given in Box 3.4.

> ## Box 3.4: Impact of growing up in an invalidating environment
>
> A child may not learn:
> - to recognise emotions
> - the names or labels of emotions
> - that distress can be tolerated
> - to trust their own emotions and will therefore need to look to others to tell them what they are feeling
> - to distinguish their own emotions from those of the people who are close to them
> - to soothe themselves until the strong emotion has passed.
>
> A child may learn that:
> - emotions are confusing, overwhelming and intolerable
> - others cannot recognise or help with these emotions
> - only extreme behaviours will get them care and attention
> - that they are only loveable when they express the emotions.

## Impact of abuse or trauma

Some people have experiences that are extremely distressing, completely beyond their control and inescapable. These may take the form of abuse or other traumas. The person may have responded to such situations by instinctively withdrawing into themselves and distancing themselves from the feelings caused. They behave almost as if they were not there or the experience was happening to someone else. In this way they are able to survive horrendous situations that they are powerless to escape or avoid. When this happens it is called a 'dissociative state'. Some people may then develop a pattern of responding to any strong emotion or reminder of past trauma by 'dissociating'. For these individuals dissociating can prevent them from resolving issues and from learning more positive ways of coping with difficult situations.

## Emotions and individuals with personality disorder

Difficulties with emotions are a feature of all personality disorders although different disorders show different problems. Some examples are given in Box 3.5.

## Box 3.5: Characteristics of personality disorder relating to emotion

**Paranoid personality disorder**
- Excessive sensitivity to setbacks and rebuffs
- Experiences characterised by intense and unreasonable fear and jealousy

**Antisocial personality disorder**
- Very low tolerance of frustration, quick to anger
- Failure to feel guilt or remorse

**Borderline personality disorder**
- Outbursts of anger
- Frequent sudden and unpredictable changes in mood

**Histrionic personality disorder**
- Exaggerated expression of emotion
- Rapidly shifting and shallow expression of emotion
- Continually seeking excitement

**Narcissistic personality disorder**
- Envious of others
- Avoidant personality disorder
- Experience of fear and shame in relation to social relationships

# Borderline personality disorder

Difficulties with emotion are central to the most common diagnosis, borderline personality disorder. Some of the problems experienced by individuals with borderline personality disorder are now given.

## Intense and volatile emotions

Many individuals experience highly volatile emotions; their emotions are easily triggered, reach a high level of intensity and may be slow to calm down. Individuals may swing rapidly from elation to depression or from boredom to anger. They may feel anxious, ill at ease or irritable. Mood changes are often short-lived; rarely lasting more than a few days and often happening several times in one day. Changes may be triggered by small events or may seem to happen out of the blue. These moods are intense, giving the impression that the person lives on an emotional roller-coaster.

## More frequent negative emotions

Individuals with borderline personality disorder experience more negative emotions than individuals with healthy personalities. They experience more sadness, anxiety, anger and jealousy, but less happiness.

## Difficulties understanding and tolerating emotions

Individuals with borderline personality disorder often lack understanding of their emotions and the skills to regulate them. Some individuals may lack awareness of their emotions to the extent that they may deny feeling a particular emotion despite their behaviour clearly acting out that emotion. For example, an individual might say they are not angry while they are shouting and swearing with their face contorted with emotion. They may have a low tolerance of negative emotions and believe that they should always feel happy. Individuals may rapidly feel overwhelmed and go into crisis, or they may try desperately to blot the emotions out, taking desperate measures to try to end the situation.

Individuals with borderline personality disorder often find it difficult to think rationally about situations when they are feeling emotional. They may accept their emotional interpretation of events as reality and may then act in ways that seem extreme or inappropriate to others who are looking at the situation in a more objective manner. For example, if they feel angry they may assume that there must be something to be angry about; they will not grasp that it is their interpretation of the situation that has triggered the feeling. Some individuals may go into a dissociative state when they experience strong emotions.

## The cycle of invalidation

The emotional responses of individuals with personality disorder may be completely incomprehensible to those around them. The responses seem to come from nowhere and seem out of all proportion to any possible triggers. This can lead those around them to challenge the validity of the emotion. The individual may be seen as 'over reacting', 'attention seeking', being 'manipulative' or using 'emotional blackmail'. Such interpretations mean that the individual does not get the support they need and also repeats the childhood pattern of emotions not being validated.

## Causes

It is thought that a combination of biological and social factors lead to the difficulties individuals with personality disorder experience with emotions. Difficulties regulating mood tend to run in families, suggesting there may be a genetic element to this problem. Differences in brain structure and function may also make controlling emotions more difficult for individuals with personality disorder. When individuals with this biological vulnerability grow up in an invalidating environment they are likely to find managing emotions extremely difficult.

# Emotions and individuals with intellectual disabilities

Individuals with intellectual disabilities experience the same range of emotions as other people. Like other people, individuals with intellectual disabilities also vary in the intensity and volatility of their emotions and their ability to control them. How individuals with intellectual disabilities experience and express emotions will also be influenced by their biological make up and their experiences while growing up.

## Impact of intellectual impairment

As a result of their intellectual impairment individuals may not have learnt names for emotions and may have greater difficulties working out the connections between thoughts, behaviours and feelings. The more severe an individual's intellectual impairment, the more likely they are to express their emotions through their behaviour rather than being able to put them into words. Individuals with intellectual disabilities are also likely to misinterpret the physical symptoms of emotion as bodily illnesses. So, for example, 'butterflies' in the stomach as the result of anxiety will often be reported as stomach ache.

## Impact of stereotypes

There are a number of stereotypes or assumptions about individuals with intellectual disabilities that may make it difficult for those around them to see what the individual is really feeling. For example, there is a belief that individuals with Down's syndrome are 'happy'. Such views make it less likely that the individual's emotional experiences will be validated by others. Many staff do not understand that, like everyone else, individuals with intellectual disabilities will express emotions in response to life events. For example, everyone is upset by the death of someone close to them and it is recognised that the grief process takes about a year to resolve. However, if a person with intellectual disabilities is 'still' upset three months after a death it is highly likely that they would be referred for 'grief therapy' or labelled as showing challenging behaviour. Such responses mean that the emotional reactions of individuals with intellectual disabilities are frequently misunderstood or ignored and they do not receive the support and comfort that they need. This may lead to them showing challenging behaviour as the only way to express their feelings.

# Emotions and individuals with intellectual disabilities and personality disorder

Individuals with intellectual disabilities and personality disorder are likely to have a biological predisposition to experience intense and volatile emotions. They are also likely to have grown up in an invalidating family environment. They will have had further invalidating experiences beyond their family because of the stereotypes and assumptions that surround having intellectual disabilities and will experience the impact of intellectual impairment on their ability to process and understand situations. The combination of these factors means that individuals with intellectual disabilities and personality disorder have great difficulty understanding and managing their emotions. Some of the difficulties experienced are given in Box 3.6.

---

### Box 3.6: Emotional difficulties and related problems experienced by individuals with intellectual disabilities and personality disorder

- Experiencing intense and volatile emotions: easily triggered, high levels of arousal, slow to calm down, rapid changes of mood state
- Frequently experiencing powerful emotions such as anger, jealousy, despair, fear and hatred
- Frequently experiencing emotions that undermine their self-esteem such as guilt and shame
- Experiencing emotions as confusing, overwhelming and intolerable
- Inability to self-soothe or distract themselves when distressed
- Emotions are expressed in socially unacceptable ways eg. shouting abuse, fighting
- Emotions are managed in ways that bring short-term relief but cause damage in the long-term to the individual and their relationships with family, friends and services eg. repeated phone calls, visits to A&E, use of drugs and alcohol
- Intolerable emotions are managed through extreme behaviours such as self-harm and suicidal behaviour
- Experiencing a dissociative state when experiencing strong emotions
- Difficulty recognising, naming and talking about emotions
- Inability to 'explain' their emotions and actions
- Difficulty distinguishing their own emotions from those around them eg. becoming acutely distressed because other people are upset

Continued...

---

- Seeing strong emotions as wrong or sinful and punishing themselves for having such feelings
- Being swamped with negative memories when experiencing strong emotions
- Living a chaotic and confusing lifestyle as behaviour is driven by emotional needs and reactions rather than rational thought
- Having repeated emotional crises that can lead to relationship breakdowns, placement breakdowns, mental health problems and hospital admissions
- Emotional reactions appear disproportionate leading to invalidation by friends, family and staff, which in turn increases emotional distress

## The cycle of invalidation

Individuals with intellectual disabilities and personality disorder often become trapped in the 'cycle of invalidation'. Their emotional responses are seen as disproportionate by those around them and they may be dismissed as 'over-reacting' or 'attention seeking'. Consequently they do not get the support and emotional validation that they need. As a result of this the individual's distress is intensified and their behaviour becomes even more extreme.

## Emotional contagion, the 'whirlpool of distress'

Even where those around the individual recognise the emotional distress, this does not always help the situation. Emotions are contagious; it is hard to stay calm if other people are angry, excited or frightened. There is a risk that family, friends and staff may be sucked into the intense experience and also become overwhelmed by the emotion. In such situations those around the individual also experience the situation as unbearable, hopeless and impossible to manage. They are then unable to help the individual contain their emotions. A vicious circle or 'whirlpool of distress' develops with the person's distress intensifying as they realise others are also overwhelmed by the feelings.

## Sinking into chaos

The experience of, and failure to understand or manage intense emotions often contribute to individuals with intellectual disabilities and personality disorder leading chaotic lives. They have no consistent routine and their behaviour is often out of control; they do what they want, when they feel like it and don't do anything they don't enjoy. This often means that their home is squalid, their personal care is neglected and they engage in emotionally-driven behaviour that is harmful to themselves or other people. This chaos has the effect of triggering more negative emotions, which in turn increases the chaos.

# Supporting individuals who have difficulty managing emotions

There are a number of elements that need to be in place in order to help individuals with intellectual disabilities and personality disorder work towards managing their emotions. These comprise:

- creating an emotionally competent environment
- creating a feeling of safety
- creating an ordered lifestyle
- containing the individual's emotions
- promoting the individual's understanding of emotions
- teaching the individual to relax and self-soothe
- therapeutic activities.

## An emotionally competent environment

The emotions of individuals with intellectual disabilities and personality disorder often appear so extreme, unjustified and irrational that it is easy for staff to respond in unhelpful ways, such as rejecting, ignoring or judging the individual. To prevent such unhelpful responses it is important that individuals with intellectual disabilities and personality disorder are supported by emotionally competent staff. This builds onto the positive support approach explored in Chapter 2.

To be emotionally competent staff must be able to understand and manage both their own and other people's emotions. Some key skills needed for this are given in Box 3.7.

---

### Box 3.7: Key skills for emotional competence

**Own emotions**

■ Recognise, accept and understand own emotions

■ Able to express emotions appropriately (low expressed emotion)

■ Able to contain own emotions

■ Self-aware, thoughtful, able to seek help and use supervision

**Others' emotions**

■ Recognise and understand wide range of emotions in others

■ Validate others' emotions

■ Contain others' emotions

■ Offer unconditional positive regard whatever the other's emotional state

---

It is important that staff understand the impact of both intellectual disabilities and personality disorder on an individual's ability to recognise and manage emotions. The booklet 'Understanding emotions in people with learning disabilities' (Surrey & Borders, 2012) explains the natural or 'reasonable' emotional reactions of individuals with intellectual disabilities and gives a good grounding.

However, the emotional reactions of individuals with intellectual disabilities and personality disorder will often seem disproportionate or 'unreasonable'. It is therefore important that staff have a good understanding of the factors that create the emotional volatility and intense distress individuals experience. They also need to understand how to avoid the 'cycle of invalidation' and the 'whirlpool of distress'. Once staff have an understanding of these factors it will be much easier for them to remain calm and positive when faced with intense emotions.

## Low expressed emotions

People with intellectual disabilities and personality disorder are often used to living in settings where people have short fuses and intense emotions are given free rein; people may shout, scream, throw things, bang doors and storm out. If one person shouts, others will shout back. Such behaviour is seen as normal. This is known as 'high expressed emotion' and such environments have a negative impact on people's mental health. They escalate distress and make extreme behaviours such as overdoses more likely.

When supporting someone whose emotions are out of control it is important to aim for 'low expressed emotions'. In this approach strong emotions are accepted as part of life, they are acknowledged, expressed and resolved with the minimum of fuss. Perhaps this is best understood as a warmer, kinder version of the traditional British 'stiff upper lip'. Most importantly, those around the person who is distressed do not join in the shouting or sobbing but react to events in a calm, kind and matter of fact way.

## Staying calm

Staff who are supporting individuals with intellectual disabilities and personality disorder need to be calm, confident, unshockable and unflappable. Staff need to be able to 'contain' the individual's emotional reaction. This means recognising the individual's distress but staying calm themselves. This gives the message *'I see you are afraid / upset / angry, that's OK, I will help you, but they are your feelings not mine, they won't overwhelm me'*.

## Creating a feeling of safety

The world is often a frightening place for many individuals with intellectual disabilities and personality disorder; they are not able to manage alone and are not able to trust others to help them. Creating a sense of safety and stability helps to calm individuals and bring them to a state of mind that allows them to begin thinking about and changing their behaviour. When looking at creating a sense of safety it is important to consider both the physical and social aspects of the individual's environment.

## Physical environment

The impact of the physical environment on how safe someone feels is often overlooked. However, this is of great importance to individuals who have had negative life experiences. For example, they may be unable to sleep (for fear of being assaulted) if they cannot securely lock doors and windows. Consequently, individuals will need private space and will often want to be able to keep others out. Where someone is likely to self-harm the need for privacy may conflict with the need to keep close observation. These issues will be discussed more in Chapter 11. However, with thoughtful and creative risk management, these aims need not conflict. Risk assessment and risk management are beyond the scope of this book but the approach recommended by Carol Sellars is particularly useful in such situations (see Further reading).

Individuals will also need somewhere safe to keep their personal belongings. When individuals have had difficult lives they will often have experienced money or possessions being taken by others (often people who had first won their trust) and they will not be able to relax unless they are certain their property is safe. Having a personal safe for money and valuables and being able to lock their door when out will help with this. Where individuals have been homeless they may not feel safe to leave valuables under any conditions and may carry many bags around with them. This needs to be dealt with sympathetically; with support the individual will gradually be able to leave items in a safe place.

The physical condition of the environment can also contribute to a sense of safety. The building needs to look as if it is well cared for: to be clean, freshly decorated and well maintained. If a service cannot look after its buildings, what will it do with people? It should also have a clear layout and good signposts so that it is difficult to get lost even if feeling very confused.

## Social environment

A sense of safety also comes from the people in a setting. It is not sufficient just to ensure that the individual is supported by an unflappable staff team. It is also important to think about the other people the individual comes into contact with. Is there anyone who might threaten their safety? Individuals with intellectual disabilities and personality disorder can be very vulnerable to bullying, abuse and exploitation. These are explored more fully in Chapters 4 and 15. Taking measures to minimise the risk of bullying, physical, emotional, sexual and financial abuse are an important part of creating a sense of safety.

## Creating an ordered lifestyle

Creating and implementing boundaries is the second dimension of the authoritative support style introduced in Chapter 1. Introducing structure and consistency to an individual's lifestyle helps them to feel emotionally contained and also improves their physical and mental health.

## De-cluttering

Many individuals with intellectual disabilities and personality disorder seek to fill a sense of emptiness with 'stuff' or to overcome loneliness with lots of items to cuddle. Consequently, they fill their rooms or homes with clutter. They will constantly buy items of clothing, soft toys and knick-knacks. They may also hoard worn-out and broken items and rubbish because throwing things away triggers feelings of abandonment. Staff often allow individuals to build up vast amounts of clutter, thinking that individuals have the right to spend their money how they wish and live how they choose. However, clutter is a great source of stress; nothing can be found and cleaning becomes a daunting task. Just looking at the mess can induce feelings of anger or despair. Creating a (fairly) tidy living area is a good first step to reducing stress and creating calm. Some ideas for clutter-busting are given in Box 3.8.

---

### Box 3.8: Clutter-busting ideas

- Throw out X (agreed number) pieces of rubbish a day
- Spend X (agreed number of) minutes a day throwing out junk
- Spend X (agreed number of) minutes a day tidying cupboards/wardrobes
- Tidy one drawer or shelf a week
- Take X bags of clothes/soft toys to a charity shop each week/month
- Implement a 'one in one out' rule: buy a shirt – throw out an old one
- Have a 'quota system eg. maximum of five stuffed toys, 10 pairs of (fit to be worn) shoes
- Take items to be recycled
- Have a car boot sale
- Make de-cluttering fun eg. play favourite music, rope in a friend
- Create 'homes' for items – that way it is easier to be tidy and to find things later

---

## Daily routine

A predictable daily routine is essential. This starts with getting up in the morning (not the afternoon!). There should be three balanced meals a day with additional coffee and tea breaks and a relaxing drink before bed. There needs to be a mix of activities including physical exercise with a quiet period in the evening preparing for bed. Finally, there should be a sensible bedtime (eg. 10pm–midnight rather than 4am).

Routine is important for a number of reasons. People with intellectual disabilities and personality disorder have often experienced chaos as young children. A casual routine, that allows them to choose when to get up, eat and so on, mirrors this chaos. This resurrects childhood fears about being neglected and feeling out of control and uncared for. In contrast, a clear routine brings a sense of order and a feeling of being cared for.

An inconsistent routine or total lack of structure also undermines physical and mental health. Inconsistent sleeping patterns mix up the body's natural clock creating a feeling like jetlag. Such changes can trigger relapses in problems such as bipolar affective disorder. Erratic sleep patterns also make it difficult to fit into everyday life; appointments are missed and getting a job becomes impossible. Ideas for promoting a healthy sleeping pattern are given in Box 9.1.

The lack of engagement in activities has a number of negative effects. Individuals miss out on the benefits of physical activity, they have little to distract them from negative thoughts, being at a loose end creates temptation to engage in inappropriate activities and they miss out on the opportunities to socialise, build skills and self-worth that come from working.

Erratic eating patterns, especially high consumption of sugary snacks and drinks that are high in caffeine (such as colas, sports drinks and special coffees) can create physical highs and lows that feed into wildly fluctuating emotions.

Clearly it is not possible to force someone to follow a structured routine. Indeed to do so would be counter-productive as it would make them feel angry and over controlled. However it can be promoted by positive and consistent encouragement with the message that following the routine will be beneficial.

Routines are sometimes criticised as being 'institutional' or as a 'breach of human rights'. However routines themselves are an important part of all our lives. Healthy routines are highly person-centred with the individual expressing a range of preferences as to the timing of activities. It is when the routines are designed to suit the organisation and staff rather than help the individual that they become institutional. For example, a routine that makes everyone go to bed before 8pm so that fewer night staff are needed is institutional.

## Boundaries, limits and rules

In addition to the daily routine, it is important to have other boundaries in place. These should cover areas such as how people treat each other and limit certain unhelpful behaviours. These must be clear with known, enforceable consequences and must not be overly restrictive. Examples might include:

- clean your bedroom once a week – if not someone will clean it for you
- no physical aggression – if you are aggressive the police will be called
- no recreational drugs – if found the police will be called.

It is important that the consequences are real and can be imposed. For example, some people would object to the consequence for room cleaning and would say that this would encourage 'laziness' as the person would simply leave it for others to clean. However, it is not possible to force someone to clean a room (or at least not within the law). Imposing a 'punishment' such as not going shopping might make staff feel there was a negative consequence for 'laziness'. However the room would still be dirty and the individual might become more angry or depressed as a result of missing a favourite activity. They would be even less likely to clean the room as a result of this. In contrast, cleaning the room for the person ensures the aim of the rule is met (that the room is sufficiently clean to avoid attracting vermin or causing disease). It is emotionally neutral and creates an opportunity to gradually encourage the person to join in the cleaning. After a few sessions like this they may well be willing to clean the room.

It is important that all members of a staff team understand and impose the agreed boundaries. Individuals with intellectual disabilities and personality disorder test teams for consistency and quickly find the person who will give in. This can cause tension and conflict in the staff team; a process called 'splitting'. This is explored more fully in Chapter 14.

Do not expect individuals to appear pleased by boundaries. They will usually argue against them, challenge and test them. It is important to avoid getting into arguments about the boundaries or being pushed to justify the reasons. There should be a simple reason for a rule for example, 'to prevent mice' for no food in bedrooms. Individuals will often argue against the rule saying things like *'it's not fair'*, *'I don't do that at home'*, *'no one else has to do that'* or even *'I like mice'*. These should be responded to calmly with comments such as *'I'm really sorry you don't like (the rule)/think it is unfair'* and then aim to change the subject. If on reflection staff think a rule is too restrictive, this should be discussed as a team and a planned change made. In this situation tell the individual that the team has listened to their arguments and has decided on the change. However, do not be surprised when the individual then challenges the new rule. Part of challenging rules is to test if staff care enough about the individual to enforce the rules.

Sometimes staff are tempted into not enforcing a rule. This may be because they agree with the individual but do not have the confidence to challenge the team or because they cannot bear to see the individual upset. It is important for staff to understand the harmful consequences of such behaviour. Not only will the individual not experience the benefits of a consistent routine and structure but they will see the member of staff breaking the rule as untrustworthy and dishonest. They will receive the message that this member of staff does not respect rules. This can lead to the thought *'If they are willing to break this rule, what other rules might they break? Might that include breaking rules about not mistreating me?'*

## Containing the individual's emotions

Being in a safe and containing place with a person-centred routine and clear boundaries will help individuals with intellectual disabilities and personality disorder to calm down, but it is likely that there will still be outbursts of intense feelings. These incidents need to be resolved for individuals until they develop the skills to do this for themselves. This involves a balanced approach that is neither too relaxed nor over controlling. It requires the ability to resolve interpersonal conflicts (see Chapter 4) and de-escalate emotional reactions. It may sometimes require the use of restrictive physical interventions. This is also an area where medication can sometimes be helpful. The aim is to respond quietly but effectively in a way that validates the individual's emotional experiences but does not over-react or join in the distress.

## De-escalation techniques

The early signs of over arousal need to be spotted and defused. This is often termed secondary prevention or a reactive strategy (see Chapter 10). There are a number of techniques that may be helpful in de-escalating situations and some are given in Box 3.9.

Intellectual Disabilities and Personality Disorder: An integrated approach
© Pavilion Publishing and Media Ltd and its licensors 2014.

## Box 3.9: De-escalation techniques

- Give the person physical space
- Remove on-lookers/relocate to a quiet place
- One staff member leads the interaction (but have another nearby in case the situation escalates)
- Use active listening: give undivided attention, be non-judgemental, focus on feelings rather than facts, allow silence, use restatement to clarify messages (see Chapter 10)
- Be respectful and polite
- Validate the individual's emotional experience
- Accept that the content of anything they say is true for the individual at that time even if you feel it is inaccurate eg. *'You feel that everyone else is being treated better than you'*
- Use positive and helpful statements eg. *'Tell me about it, I want to help'*
- Use calm, attentive body language; looking at the person, making eye-contact, relaxed body posture, turned towards the person
- Move slowly and gently
- Distract the individual; chat to them about their favourite topic, offer a fun activity, put on some calming music
- Re-focus the individual on positive aspects eg. if they are worried about not getting better remind them of the progress they have made
- Use gentle humour to lighten the mood (if it is known that they respond well to this)
- Give simple choices eg. *'I know you're upset about your family not visiting but we could go to the cinema or play a game of pool'*
- Suggest taking three deep breaths and shaking out the tension

However, individuals differ in which techniques are most helpful for them; what calms one person may wind another person up even more. It is therefore essential for staff to have a repertoire of de-escalation techniques and to monitor closely the impact of the approach they have chosen to use. In this way, if they see signs that the technique is making things worse they will be able to try a different approach.

All individuals need to feel that they are being respected and attended to. However, individuals differ in how helpful it is to spend time talking about the details of what is distressing them. Some individuals seem to be best helped by having the chance to talk in depth about what is bothering them; it brings emotional release and the feeling that they are not alone. However, for others the more they talk about something the more out of control their emotion becomes.

Where this is the case it is still important to validate their emotion but it is then much more helpful to distract them with more pleasant thoughts or activities until the emotion subsides.

Where the emotion is related to interpersonal conflict it is important that conflict resolution techniques are also employed. These are discussed in Chapter 4.

As well as thinking about techniques that de-escalate situations, it is important for staff to be aware of some of the responses that frequently lead to a situation escalating. Emotional responses are likely to escalate if responded to with invalidation. This might include any response that that does not recognise the emotion expressed, sees it as an over-reaction, questions its justification or judges the individual. This may seem obvious but it is very easy to slip into this trap. Box 3.10 gives some examples of common responses that are likely to escalate a situation if they are said to an individual with intellectual disabilities and personality disorder.

---

### Box 3.10: Common invalidating responses

- 'Calm down'
- 'It's not worth making a fuss about'
- 'Cheer up, it's not the end of the world'
- 'Never mind, you'll get another chance'
- 'S/he was only …'
- 'It was only…'
- 'You've got the wrong end of the stick'
- 'No good crying over spilt milk'
- 'Goodness, is that all? Anyone would think that the world was coming to an end!'
- 'Don't worry'
- 'You'll soon feel better'
- 'You're just tired'
- 'You don't really mean that'

---

## Managing emotional outbursts

It will not always be possible to prevent situations from escalating; individuals may try to harm themselves, others or staff. In these situations staff need to be able to respond quickly, calmly and effectively. Chapter 12 explores what to do if the situation escalates into a crisis. However, the following suggestions may be helpful in managing 'everyday' emotional outbursts.

Sometimes it can be enough to simply clear the area; all staff and other individuals leave quickly and quietly and let the individual get things out of their system. If doing this, it is important to keep a discrete watch to make sure the individual is not at risk of seriously harming themselves. If this is not possible, the use of restrictive physical interventions may be required to manage the situation. The techniques used should always be the least restrictive ones that can safely resolve the situation and be used for the shortest length of time. This is very important, not just because of the rights of the individual but because over control is a known cause of self-harm. An overreaction can increase the intensity of the behaviour it is intended to stop.

BILD (2002, 2006) provides guidelines to help ensure that restrictive physical interventions are used appropriately. Restrictive physical interventions should only be used by trained staff in the context of a positive behavioural support plan that includes preventative strategies. These are discussed in Chapter 10. Wherever possible, staff should work with the individual in a collaborative way to highlight when such techniques may be used. When calm, an individual will often be able to tell staff the impact of the restrictive physical intervention, what was helpful and what wasn't helpful. Using a collaborative approach to plan the response to emotional outbursts can have a significant, positive impact on the quality of the individual's life. The individual will feel understood, safe and contained and will understand that the restrictions are to keep them safe not to punish them.

Where services are not able to use restrictive physical interventions it may be necessary to call the police. Wherever possible this should be carefully thought through in advance so that everyone, including the individual, knows at what point behaviour becomes unacceptable and when action will be taken. Sometimes a situation will escalate to become a full-blown crisis. Responding to crises is explored fully in Chapter 12.

## Role of medication

'As required' medication can have a role in managing emotional outbursts. It is most helpful if given relatively early in the build-up of emotions: it can be dangerous to try to give medication to individuals once they are very distressed and the medication is then much less likely to be effective (see Further reading). However, this needs skilled assessment and monitoring to ensure it is helping rather than hindering the process. Where staff, or the individual, think 'as required' medication might help manage emotional outbursts, the individual will need to be referred to a psychiatrist by their GP. Where 'as required' medication is used there need to be guidelines that clearly spell out what should be tried first and when the medication should be given. Again, this plan needs to be developed in collaboration with the individual. If they do not see the usefulness of the medication, they are most unlikely to take it at a time when they are already upset.

Regular medication can also play an important role as a short-term aid to reduce emotional symptoms at difficult times; for example, to help someone get out of an episode of depression. Medication may also play a role in helping to stabilise mood.

However, using medication is not a straightforward process. First, there is no single effective medication. Different medications may need to be tried until the right one is found for each individual. If this process is not managed effectively the person may end up on large amounts of medication (both high doses and multiple medications). This is because once a medication has been started it can be hard to give it up for fear that the symptoms will become even worse. Taking large amounts of medication can muddle people's thinking, making it hard for them to work on other ways of managing their feeling. Having large quantities of pills around at a time that a person is distressed also increases the risk of them taking an overdose.

Second, there is a risk that people will misunderstand the role of medication and think that it can offer a cure for personality disorder. If an individual thinks they just need to find the right medication and all will get better they are unlikely to put in the huge amount of hard work that is involved in overcoming personality disorder.

If medication is used, the individual needs to be supported to work with their psychiatrist. They will need help to take the medication regularly, as prescribed and for at least two weeks to know if it will be any help. They must be helped to stop a medication if it does not appear to be working. The individual must also be helped to understand that the medication will not cure personality disorder; it is just to help with some symptoms. If this can be achieved, medication can help an individual reach a state where they are able to engage with work to help them understand and manage their emotions (see Further reading). There are useful guidelines for psychiatrists on the most effective approach to using medication with individuals with intellectual disabilities and personality disorder (Willner, 2005; Webber & Farrell, 2008).

# Promoting the individual's understanding of emotions

Managing emotional situations effectively is important but it leaves the individual dependent on others and is costly in time and resources. It is therefore important to help individuals move towards managing their own emotions. Remember, early experiences are likely to have left them with no names for what they are feeling, unsure of where these feelings have come from and with no idea how to control them. Therefore, the first steps to this are to help them recognise, name and understand their emotions.

# Validating emotions

As discussed earlier in this chapter, validating emotions is the process of responding in a way that gives the individual the message that their emotions are real, belong to them and that it is alright to feel that way. Validating emotions is important as it creates a situation in which an individual is able to name and accept their own emotional reactions. The steps of emotional validation and the types of comments staff might make to an individual with intellectual disabilities and personality disorder are given in Box 3.11.

---

**Box 3.11: Validating an individual's emotions**

Step 1: Identify and acknowledge the emotion

'You are feeling really angry' (If they have said they are angry)

'You seem really angry' (If they haven't named the emotion) 'Have I got that right?'

Step 2: Identify the source of the emotion

'Can you tell me what upset you?'

'What made you feel like this?'

'Something made you angry, can you tell me what happened?'

Step 3: Accepting the emotional reaction as real

'You're feeling angry because your mum kept you waiting. She didn't mean to be late, her train was cancelled. But I can understand that waiting would make you angry.'

---

It is important to remember that validating emotions will not make them go away. It usually helps to stop the emotion from escalating. However, it may still be necessary to use other de-escalation techniques to help the individual calm down.

Staff often find it difficult to validate emotions when they disagree with the individual's interpretation of the situation or feel that their emotional reaction is unwarranted or excessive. Staff may feel that they are reinforcing the individual's inappropriate behaviour or that they are giving the message that such behaviour is acceptable. However, validation does not mean agreeing with or approving the thinking behind the emotion or its behavioural expression. It is simply the recognition that the individual is feeling in a particular way and that you recognise that the emotion underlying the response is genuine.

Emotional validation is important for the individual but it is also very helpful for staff in the process of trying to understand why an individual behaves in unhelpful ways. Making the effort to identify what an individual is really feeling and to accept that feeling as real can be the starting point for staff beginning to explore why the individual might react so strongly to certain situations. This in turn can lead to information that can help identify better ways of helping the individual.

## Learning about emotions

Validating emotions at the time they are experienced lays the foundation for individuals to begin understanding their emotional reactions. However, this is just the starting point. It is also important to create an environment in which it is seen as healthy and safe to talk about emotions. At a time when the individual is calm it may be helpful to talk gently about recent incidents and speculate with the individual about what they may have been feeling. Staff will need to use their knowledge of the individual and their own skills at mentalising to guess what feelings might lie behind the individual's behaviour.

Some individuals may be able to cope with questions such as *'I wondered if you were feeling angry when you shouted at X?'* For others this will be too direct and may be taken as criticism. If this is the case it can be helpful to explore how some other person might feel in a similar situation or chat about a time you have felt similar feelings.

It can be helpful to have lots of pictures of people showing different facial expressions and to talk about what emotions they may be feeling and what might have caused these. This makes a neutral starting point and creates the opportunity for the individual to talk about their own reactions if they feel comfortable to do so.

# Identifying triggers

As individuals become more comfortable talking to staff about emotions it may be possible to work with them to spot what situations trigger these difficult feelings. It may help to keep a feelings diary – noting the emotion and what they were doing at the time. Most individuals with intellectual disabilities and personality disorder will not manage to do this alone. It can be helpful for staff to create a quiet, relaxed time in the evening, perhaps over a cup of camomile tea, when they can chat to the individual and fill the diary out together. Then once a week make time to go over the diary entries and explore more about the situations; who was there, what was happening, did it go as planned? Some of the situations will be ones which the person cannot do much to change; for example, a planned fun outing being cancelled or a much loved but unreliable family member failing to call at the promised time. It can help to work with the individual to find ways in which they can care for themselves at these times.

# Teaching individuals to relax and self-soothe

The ability to relax and self-soothe are important if individuals are to begin to manage their own emotions.

# Relaxation

Learning to relax is an important skill as it allows individuals to begin to regulate their level of physical arousal. There are a range of relaxation techniques (see Box 3.12) and staff need to help the individual find which techniques are most helpful for them.

---

### Box 3.12: Relaxation techniques

- Deep breathing
- Progressive muscle relaxation (tensing and relaxing different muscle groups)
- Visualisation and guided imagery (eg. imaging lying on a beach in the sunshine)
- Meditation
- Yoga

---

If someone is having a lot of difficulty with worrying thoughts it is important to avoid approaches to relaxation that involve clearing the mind. Such approaches just make more room for the worrying thoughts and can trigger 'psychotic' experiences (see Chapter 7). Instead, choose an approach that gives the individual something to focus on.

Relaxation needs to be practised regularly to be effective and is best if it is build into the individual's daily routine. There are a wide variety of DVDs that can help individuals to learn these techniques. Many of the techniques mentioned in other chapters of this book can also be relaxing including mindfulness exercises and distraction techniques (see Boxes 7.14 and 7.15).

## Self-soothing

Individuals with intellectual disabilities and personality disorders often depend on others to manage their distress. Developing the ability to calm themselves down builds their confidence and reduces the fear of being alone. Self-soothing means finding ways to comfort, care for and relax oneself, and to feel better. This usually involves physical, sensual things that are pleasant and calming for the body and mind. An example might be going for a walk in a pretty garden, listening to the birds and smelling the flowers. Each person will find different things that work for them. Some suggestions are given in Box 3.13.

Dialectical behaviour therapy (DBT – see Chapter 2) suggests thinking about the five senses: vision, hearing, smell, taste and touch. Staff could sit with an individual with pictures representing each sense and talk about what things they enjoy for each sense. Another sense, that is often important for individuals with intellectual disabilities and personality disorder, is proprioception or feeling movement. Many people find rhythmic motion very soothing.

Individuals may also be able to soothe themselves by drawing on religious or spiritual beliefs and positive memories or relationships. Where an individual has religious beliefs it may be helpful to work with someone of that faith to find prayers, texts or other symbols that might be helpful for them in times of distress. Such work should always be driven by the individual's beliefs; staff should not try to influence or impose religion on the individual.

It can be very helpful to have a portable 'self-soother'. This might take the form of a necklace (cross, crucifix, locket with photographs), key ring with photos, a cue card with special phrases, a scented handkerchief, or music on a portable player. This means that whenever difficult feelings occur the individual has something to hold on to, look at, read, listen to, or smell.

## Box 3.13: Self-soothing activities

- A warm, scented bath
- Listening to classical music
- Listening to a relaxation tape
- Doing some yoga exercises
- Going for a walk in the park
- Smelling flowers, fresh coffee, bread baking, cooking
- Listening to birds sing, water flowing or the sea
- Feeding the ducks
- Watching a favourite DVD
- Singing
- Walking and looking at lovely sights
- A cup of tea, coffee or hot chocolate
- Eating a special meal or favourite treat
- Looking at pictures or paintings
- Curling up with a hot water bottle or favourite soft toy and a duvet
- Taking the dog for a walk
- Stroking a cat/dog or a silky scarf
- Rubbing in cream or moisturiser
- Saying a prayer, singing a hymn or reading a verse from a religious text
- Holding a religious symbol such as a cross
- Saying positive statements 'I can survive this' 'I'm worth caring for'
- Looking at a photo of a special time or person
- Looking at a cartoon that has a special message for the person
- Rocking in a rocking chair
- Going on a swing
- Dancing slowly
- Taking 10 slow, deep breaths

It is important to remember that the individual will initially find it difficult to use these techniques; they may not recognise that they are becoming upset and once upset may find it difficult not to fall into their unhelpful response pattern. It is therefore important to practice these approaches when the individual is not upset. Staff also need to be vigilant for early signs of distress. They can then gently prompt the individual to try their self-soothing approaches. This needs to be done sensitively, in a way that validates the emotional response and respects individual choice. For example, staff might say *'It looks like you're a bit upset? Have I got that right? Would a cup of tea or a warm bath help?'* Teaching coping skills is explored more fully in Chapter 12. Box 12.13 gives a structure that can be used for teaching new coping skills and embedding them in the individual's behavioural repertoire.

## Therapeutic activities

Individuals with intellectual disabilities and personality disorder will often be referred for therapy to help them manage their emotions. However, they are unlikely to be able to benefit from the therapy unless they feel safe and are supported by family carers or staff who understand, validate and contain their emotional reactions. If the cycles of invalidation and whirlpools of distress are not recognised and addressed they will undermine the positive effects of therapy. Even with positive support, change is likely to be slow and may take much longer than the usual length of interventions such as CBT. It is important to remember that the difficulties individuals are experiencing have taken a lifetime to develop and that the individual is likely to lack even the most basic skills such as naming their emotions. Many individuals will continue to need ongoing support or additional support at stressful times, in order to be able to manage their emotions successfully.

It is also important to remember that therapy does not remove memories of difficult or traumatic events. When an individual is feeling low, bereft, angry or frightened, the emotion will trigger memories of events with a similar emotional content. These memories may be recalled vividly and will add to the individual's distress. This may make those around them think that the individual needs therapy for those events. However, once the emotional reaction is over the negative events will no longer be vividly recalled. The important issue is to manage the acute emotional state; therapy will only be needed for those memories that persist and pervade everyday life.

Once individuals are in an emotionally competent environment, feel safe, feel contained and are emotionally validated, more traditional therapeutic activities are much more likely to succeed. Some individuals may be able to engage in therapy to help them further understand and manage their emotions. Both CBT and DBT approaches, adapted for use with individuals with intellectual disabilities, may be helpful. If individuals wish to learn how to manage emotions more constructively and change their behaviour, they can be supported to make a referral to local services for therapy. For some individuals CBT and DBT may be too difficult to grasp. For this group, simply learning relaxation techniques may be very helpful. Sometimes an individual may not perceive therapy as being relevant to them. For such individuals it may be helpful to look at the Trans-theoretical Model of Change given in Chapter 12 (Box 12.7). By identifying where they are on the change cycle techniques can be selected to help individuals recognise and address their difficulties.

# Key learning points

- An emotion may be described as a spontaneous, short lived, state of mind that arises in response to internal events (such as thoughts or physical sensations) or external events (such as other people's behaviour).

- The six basic emotions (anger, disgust, fear, sadness, happiness and surprise) seem to be 'hard-wired' into the human system. These emotions have a wide variety of expressions. They can be influenced by social experience to create more complex emotions such as jealously, embarrassment, grief, shame, guilt and remorse.

- Managing emotions is complex. To manage emotions a person needs to recognise the emotion as their own, separate their emotions from those of people close to them and understand why they might be feeling that way. They then need to be able tolerate the emotion while they think through how they will react, and be aware of a range of options for dealing with that feeling.

- Managing emotions is a core difficulty for individuals with intellectual disabilities and personality disorder. Many individuals develop worrying ways of coping with intense emotions, such as self-harm.

- Individuals need to be supported by an emotionally competent staff team who are able to validate and accept intense emotions.

- It is important that individuals are helped to feel safe and that emotional outbursts are contained and managed by those around them.

- As the individual gains confidence they can be helped to understand their emotions and learn to self-soothe.

- Some individuals will benefit from a referral for therapy, for example DBT or CBT.

# References

BILD (2002) *Easy Guide to Physical Interventions: For people with learning disabilities, their carers and supporters*. Birmingham: British Institute of Learning Disabilities.

BILD (2006) *Code of Practice for the Use and Reduction of Restrictive Physical Interventions*. Birmingham: British Institute of Learning Disabilities.

Surrey & Borders Partnership NHS Foundation Trust (2012) *Understanding Emotions in People with Learning Disabilities*. Hove: Pavilion Publishing and Media Ltd.

Webber M & Farrell J (2008) Pharmacotherapy of borderline personality disorder. *Psychopharm Review* **43** 83–90.

Willner P (2005) The effectiveness of psychotherapeutic interventions for people with learning disabilities: a critical review. *Journal of Intellectual Disability Research* **49** 73–85.

# Further reading

Alexander R, Tajuddin M & Gangadharan S (2007) Personality disorder in intellectual disabilities: approaches to pharmacology. *Mental Health Aspects of Developmental Disabilities* **10** (4) 129–136.

Bell L (2005) *Managing Intense Emotions and Overcoming Self-destructive Habits: A self-help manual*. Hove: Routledge.

Esbenson A & Benson B (2003) Integrating behavioural, psychological and pharmacological treatment: a case study of an individual with borderline personality disorder and mental retardation. *Mental Health Aspects of Developmental Disabilities* **6** (3) 107–114.

Elliott C & Smith L (2009) *Borderline Personality Disorder for Dummies*. Indianapolis, Indiana: Wiley. (Chapter 20: Considering medication for BPD)

Fonagy P, Target M & Gergely G *et al* (2003) The developmental roots of borderline personality disorder in early attachment relationships: a theory and some evidence. *Psychoanalytic Inquiry* **23** 412–459.

Fruzzetti, A, Shenk C & Hoffman P (2005) Family interaction and the development of borderline personality disorder: a transactional model. *Development and Psychopathology* **17** 1007–1030.

Keltner D & Gross J (1999) Functional accounts of emotion. *Cognition and Emotion* **13** (5) 467–480.

Kroese B, Dagnan D & Loumidis K (1997) (Eds) *Cognitive-Behaviour Therapy for People with Learning Disabilities*. London: Routledge.

Livingstone K (2009) *Understanding Dissociative Disorders*. London: Mind.

National Collaboration Centre for Mental Health (2009) *Borderline Personality Disorder: The NICE guideline on treatment and management*. Leicester & London: The British Psychological Society & Royal College of Psychiatrists.

Sellars C (2011) *Risk Assessment in People with Intellectual Disabilities* (2nd edition). Chichester: BPS Blackwell.

Wilson S (2001) A four stage model for management of borderline personality disorder in people with mental retardation. *Mental Health Aspects of Developmental Disabilities* **4** 68–76.

# Chapter 4: Difficulties in interpersonal relationships

This chapter explores the nature of healthy relationships and how social behaviour is learnt. It explores how relationships may be influenced by personality disorder and intellectual disabilities. It focuses on the difficulties individuals with intellectual disabilities and personality disorder may have in relating to those they live with. It explores how these difficulties may be addressed both through providing the most helpful style of support and through individual interventions.

## Key topics

- Healthy relationships
- Learning social behaviours
- Relationships and individuals with personality disorder
- Relationships and individuals with intellectual disabilities
- Relationships and individuals with intellectual disabilities and personality disorder
- Inappropriate and inconsiderate social behaviour
- Promoting appropriate and considerate interpersonal behaviours
- Difficulties with relationships and conflicts
- Stabilising relationships and resolving conflicts
- Bullying
- Resolving bullying
- Therapeutic activities

# Healthy relationships

Humans are, by nature, social beings and have a drive to seek others and form relationships. People live in complex social networks and are biologically designed to work together for survival. Some relationships are close and intimate such as those between partners. Others are very superficial such as between a shopper and a cashier at a supermarket. The number and, more importantly, the quality of relationships a person has are important factors in their health. Positive, supportive relationships give a sense of purpose and belonging, reduce stress and help people cope with trauma. They also increase happiness, contribute to a healthy identity and boost self-esteem. Positive relationships can create pressure to change unhealthy habits and behaviours. Those with positive relationships have better physical and mental health, recover more quickly from illness, and live longer.

Human relationships are immensely complicated and influenced by a wide range of factors. Some of these factors are given in Box 4.1.

---

### Box 4.1: Some factors influencing the number and quality of relationships

- **Personality:** An extravert will have a wider social circle than an introvert (Chapter 1)
- **Status:** Marital and occupational status influence the number and type of social contacts
- **Economic status:** Money has an influence on the number and type of social interactions
- **Geography:** Isolation and limited travel opportunities reduce social contacts
- **Culture and religion:** Influence the pattern and quality of relationships and shape social networks
- **Access to electronic resources:** Computers, mobile phones etc create different patterns of friendship and interaction
- **Self-image and self-esteem:** Low self-esteem can reduce social confidence (see Chapter 2)
- **Core beliefs about other people:** Negative beliefs about others reduce the motivation to make friends (Chapter 6)
- **Attachment style:** Influences the ability to trust and form close relationships
- **Social cognition, the ability to 'mind read' or 'mentalise':** Difficulty understanding own and other people's feelings impairs the ability to respond appropriately (Chapter 3)

Continued...

---

- **Prejudice and stigma:** Reduce opportunities of those discriminated against
- **Physical attractiveness:** Looks influence how much other people find someone attractive and the assumptions they make about a person's qualities
- **Personal presentation:** Clothes, hair, personal hygiene can influence who people are likely to be approached by
- **Social capital:** The extent to which an individual shares and cares for others and hence 'earns' sharing and caring in return
- **Social skills:** Poor social skills reduce the ability to make and retain friends

Many of these factors are self-evident and do not need further explanation, some are explored in other chapters of this book. However, some key factors including attachment styles, mentalising, 'social capital' and social skills are explored in more depth here.

## Attachment styles

Chapter 1 explored the impact of early experiences, particularly parenting, on the nature of a child's attachment to their parents. Subsequent relationships can entrench or ameliorate the impact of these early relationships. Depending on the nature of their experience, adults develop either healthy, secure attachments or unhealthy, insecure attachments. Adults who make secure attachments tend both to view themselves as being worthy of love and to view other people as potentially loving. Further characteristics of a healthy or 'secure' attachment style are given in Box 4.2.

### Box 4.2: Secure attachment style

People with secure attachment styles tend to:
- feel worthy of being loved
- be comfortable with intimacy, inter-dependence and independence
- be able to become intimate but also to give the other person space
- expect relationships to be positive and do not worry much about them
- have trusting, long lasting relationships
- cope well with break-ups
- be comfortable sharing feelings with partners
- be willing to seek out social support.

People who form insecure attachments may have negative views of themselves as unworthy of love or may view other people as unloving. Some may hold negative views of both themselves and other people. These underlying perceptions lead to a number of unhelpful patterns of behaviour that can make it difficult to sustain relationships, put the person at risk of being abused by others or being abusive themselves. People with insecure attachments are less able to draw emotional comfort from their relationships and may not be able to support their partner in return. One way of conceptualising insecure attachments, based on the ideas of Bartholomew and Horowitz (1991), is given in Figure 4.3.

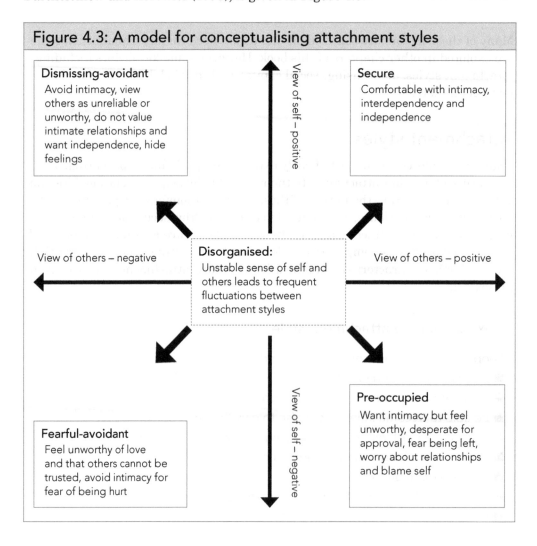

Figure 4.3: A model for conceptualising attachment styles

**Dismissing-avoidant**
Avoid intimacy, view others as unreliable or unworthy, do not value intimate relationships and want independence, hide feelings

**Secure**
Comfortable with intimacy, interdependency and independence

View of self – positive

View of others – negative

**Disorganised:**
Unstable sense of self and others leads to frequent fluctuations between attachment styles

View of others – positive

View of self – negative

**Fearful-avoidant**
Feel unworthy of love and that others cannot be trusted, avoid intimacy for fear of being hurt

**Pre-occupied**
Want intimacy but feel unworthy, desperate for approval, fear being left, worry about relationships and blame self

Attachment style is not fixed and people may, at times, show behaviours characteristic of different attachment styles. However, a person's relationships will tend to be characterised more by one style than the others. Where a person has very unstable views of themselves and others they may fluctuate frequently between different attachment styles depending on their views at any one time. This may be termed 'disorganised' attachment style.

## Mentalising

The development of mentalising is discussed in Chapter 1. In adults the ability to understand what other people may be thinking and feeling is important to healthy relationships. If a person cannot mentalise they are unable to imagine the impact their behaviour has on the other person. They are also unable to imagine how other events or experiences might make someone feel. Hence they are less likely to be able to offer support or to experience sympathy or empathy and their behaviour is likely to be inconsiderate.

## Social capital

Healthy social relationships tend to be reciprocal; there is give and take on both sides. Sometimes a person will give more than they take and at other times take more than they give. However, over time these will tend to balance out. The giving can take many forms such as: spending time, listening, giving emotional support, sharing helpful information, lending money or possessions. When a person gives more than they take it can be thought of as building up social capital. When they take more than they give this may be seen as using up this social capital. While it is over simplistic to think of these interactions as if money was changing hands, it is possible for someone to reach the end of their 'emotional credit limit'. Other people will become reluctant to help them because they know the person will never return the favour (or the money).

People may fail to build up social capital or go over their emotional credit limit for a number of reasons. Some people may lack the mentalising skills needed to recognise other people's feelings and needs. Often people may be too pre-occupied by their own needs to think about others. Some people may also feel a sense of entitlement; that others should look after them. Many individuals will have grown up in dysfunctional settings where caring and sharing were not part of everyday behaviour and hence will not have had the opportunity to learn that it is important to give as well as take.

## Social skills

Whatever a person's social opportunities, social skills play a significant factor in making and maintaining relationships. Social skills comprise a variety of verbal and non-verbal skills including: eye contact, body language, voice tone and the words spoken. They also include such skills as being able to initiate and maintain a conversation, take turns, pay compliments and make requests. Most people acquire these skills naturally through their life experiences as part of the social learning process described below. However, social skills can be formally taught and improved. A person's ability to mentalise will influence their ability to use the right social skill at the right time. This is much harder to teach or change as it requires a complex thinking process.

## Learning social behaviours

The foundations for relationships and social behaviour are laid down in the parent–child bond (attachment). As the child moves through life they gradually acquire a repertoire of social behaviour. This is learnt informally; it is rarely taught specifically.

The Social Learning Model (developed by Albert Bandura) is a particularly useful way of understanding this informal learning process. This approach suggests that people learn new ways of behaving by observing the behaviour of others. People are more likely to copy or imitate behaviours if they see other people being rewarded for those behaviours. The factors needed for an individual to adopt a new behaviour are given in Box 4.4.

---

### Box 4.4: Factors needed for an individual to adopt a new behaviour

- See it modeled by another person
- Pay attention to that behaviour
- Remember the behaviour
- Have the ability to carry out the behaviour themselves
- Have a good reason (motivation) for behaving in that way

---

This model is useful as it directs attention to what a person sees happening around them, not just at the consequences applied to their own behaviour. It highlights that people can absorb positive or negative behaviours depending on the behaviors that are modeled and rewarded around them. It suggests that, for

Intellectual Disabilities and Personality Disorder: An integrated approach
© Pavilion Publishing and Media Ltd and its licensors 2014.

people to show healthy social behaviour and have positive relationships, they need to have experienced others behaving in that way and have seen that behaviour being rewarded.

# Relationships and individuals with personality disorder

Difficulties with interpersonal relationships are central to the diagnosis of a number of personality disorders. Some of the characteristics of relationships associated with different diagnoses and characteristic attachment styles are given in Box 4.5.

---

## Box 4.5: Relationships, attachment styles and personality disorders

**Paranoid personality disorder:** Relationships will be distorted by suspicion, misinterpretation, blame and jealousy – fearful-avoidant attachment style.

**Antisocial personality disorder:** Show a lack of concern for other people and will disregard social rules and conventions. Are able to make but not maintain relationships – dismissive-avoidant attachment style.

**Borderline personality disorder:** Have unstable relationships which often lead to emotional crises. They are likely to fear being abandoned and make great efforts to try to avoid this happening or end relationships at the slightest let down to avoid being rejected themselves – disorganised attachment style.

**Histrionic personality disorder:** Seek always to be the centre of attention, show flirty, seductive behaviour – preoccupied attachment style.

**Dependent personality disorder:** May be clingy and unable to tolerate separation/independence – preoccupied attachment style.

---

A common theme through the different types of personality disorder is that relationships are unhealthy and lack reciprocity. Frequently those around individuals with personality disorder feel confused, used, manipulated or abused. Individuals may engage in a range of interpersonal behaviours that other people find difficult or distressing without having any idea of the impact their behaviour is having on the other person. They may also fail to respect the usual boundaries in relationships, becoming overly involved and intrusive.

However, individuals with personality disorder are also often vulnerable to abuse. They may stay in difficult or abusive relationships for fear that being alone is worse. They may also be drawn to people who use them emotionally or financially or who bring out the worst aspects of their behaviour. Individuals with some personality disorders may put themselves at risk by engaging in extreme behaviours, such as suicide attempts, in efforts to stop other people leaving them or to elicit the care and contact that they crave.

## Causes

Like difficulties with self-image and managing emotions (discussed in Chapters 2 and 3), the difficulties individuals with personality disorder have with relationships are thought to have their origins in a combination of biological predisposition and early experiences. Difficulties within the child–parent relationship and the style of parenting may cause unhealthy attachment styles in the child. The difficulties in the child–parent interaction are also likely to impair the development of mentalising skills, meaning that the child has difficulty understanding other people's emotions or the reasons for their emotions. If the child continues to be exposed to negative interpersonal interactions as they grow up, the unhealthy attachment style will continue into adulthood. Individuals with personality disorder are also unlikely to have had the opportunity to observe appropriate patterns of interpersonal behaviour and where these were observed it is likely that the appropriate behaviour was not rewarded. Individuals with personality disorder often show patterns of distorted thinking (Chapter 7). This can lead to them seeing other people in a distorted way or flipping between extreme perceptions of that person (see Chapter 14).

This means individuals with personality disorder are likely to have:

- unhealthy attachment styles
- lack the ability to think about how other people may feel
- have a narrow repertoire of, mostly inappropriate, interpersonal behaviours (see Chapter 14 – reciprocal roles)
- have distorted perceptions of the people they relate to.

# Relationships and individuals with intellectual disabilities

Individuals with intellectual disabilities can form healthy relationships and develop secure attachment styles. Individuals with mild or moderate intellectual disabilities show the same range of attachment styles as the general population. Where individuals with intellectual disabilities show insecure attachment styles they may be more vulnerable to showing challenging behaviour or experiencing depression.

Individuals with intellectual disabilities face a number of challenges when learning about and trying to form relationships. Their intellectual disabilities can make them dependent on others, making it hard to learn healthy independence. It can also restrict their social circle both directly (for example, by having limited ability to travel independently) and indirectly (for example, attending a special school that is a long way off means fewer friends near home).

## Abuse

Individuals with intellectual disabilities are vulnerable to abuse and are frequently subject to bullying because of their disabilities. Anxiety about such treatment and worries over the individual's ability to function independently can lead many parents and carers to be over-protective. The resulting unnecessary restrictions further reduce opportunities to make friends and practise social skills.

## Intellectual impairment

Limited intellectual skills can also directly impede the development of social skills; social situations are complex and difficult to understand. Individuals may be confused about the distinctions between relationships; for example, seeing the girl they sit next to on the bus as their girlfriend. In addition, healthy brain development underpins the ability to mentalise. For individuals with atypical brain development, particularly those on the autistic spectrum, learning to mentalise may be next to impossible.

## Dependency

Some adults with mild intellectual disabilities are able to lead completely independent lives. However, many individuals continue to need support with some aspects of daily living throughout their adult lives and many also continue to live with their parents, long after typically developing young adults usually leave home.

## Disempowerment

Many individuals with intellectual disabilities are disempowered by those around them. They are often seen as being unable to make decisions for themselves. Often other people will make choices for them, thinking that they know better than the individual. Consequently, individuals with intellectual disabilities frequently experience being ignored or being excluded from interactions. These experiences can distort their relationships; they may become passive, helplessly accepting others taking power or they may become aggressive and try to meet their needs through challenging behaviours.

# Relationships and individuals with intellectual disabilities and personality disorder

Individuals with intellectual disabilities and personality disorder are likely to have the same type of difficulties with relationships as more able individuals with personality disorder. However, these will be compounded by the difficulties that result from having intellectual disabilities including cognitive deficits (such as difficulties with memory, problem solving, planning or organisation) limited opportunities, the impact of bullying and abuse and the need for long-term support with aspects of daily living. Their disabilities may have contributed to disempowerment. For example, they may have very little choice about the people they live with. Their complex needs may mean that individuals with intellectual disabilities and personality disorder are surrounded by highly complex systems that may include family, friends, partners and paid carers.

As a result of these factors, individuals with intellectual disabilities and personality disorder are likely to experience many difficulties in their interpersonal relationships. This chapter explores their relationships with the people they live with. Other aspects of relationships are addressed in subsequent chapters:

Chapter 5: Relationships with staff
Chapter 13: Engaging with services
Chapter 14: Tensions and conflicts within staff teams
Chapter 15: Issues with families

Some of the difficulties experienced by individuals with intellectual disabilities and personality disorder with those they live with are given in Box 4.6.

> ## Box 4.6: Problems experienced by individuals with intellectual disabilities and personality disorder in relationships with people they live with
>
> - Inappropriate and inconsiderate social behaviour
>   - Lack of awareness of what appropriate behaviour is
>   - Lack of appropriate role models
>   - Poor social skills including difficulties with assertiveness
>   - Being rude and inconsiderate
>   - Lack of understanding of others' feelings
>   - Inconsiderate of others/selfishness 'me, me, me…'
>   - Inability/unwillingness to share or take turns
> - Difficulties with relationships and conflict
>   - Unstable, frequently changing patterns of friendship
>   - Intense distress when a relationship breaks down
>   - Impulsive relationships eg. instantly falling in love
>   - Personality clashes
>   - Difficulties resolving conflicts
>   - Not taking responsibility for their role in interpersonal conflict
>   - Multiple placement breakdowns because of clashes
> - Bullying
>   - Bullying others
>   - Being bullied
> - Fear of being alone (see Chapter 5)
>   - Inability to tolerate being alone
>   - Clinginess and dependence on others

The following sections explore some of these difficulties in more detail and give suggestions as to how they may be addressed.

# Inappropriate and inconsiderate social behaviour

Many individuals with intellectual disabilities and personality disorder do not seem to be aware of how to interact appropriately with other people. They may seem to disregard many of the unspoken rules of social interaction such as politeness and taking turns. They frequently appear insensitive to the needs of others, behaving in ways that seem demanding, ungrateful, unkind or even, cruel. They often appear to take everything they can from others but offer nothing in return, exhausting their social capital. They also often have great difficulty sharing objects, activities or the attention of people they like, and struggle with taking turns.

Such behaviours generally offend other people and make them respond unsympathetically or angrily towards the individual. As the individual is often unaware of the impact of their own behaviour, they may attribute these reactions as proof that other people dislike them, pick on them or are unkind. This creates a vicious circle, with the individual then behaving unpleasantly towards people they think dislike them.

## Causes

It is easy for staff to assume that individuals with intellectual disabilities and personality disorder choose to behave in these ways and, by implication, that they know how to behave appropriately. However, given their life experiences this is rarely the case. Box 4.7 summarises some of the factors that can lead to inappropriate or inconsiderate behaviours.

---

### Box 4.7: Factors that can lead to inappropriate or inconsiderate behaviour towards others

- Parents behaving inconsiderately or cruelly towards them as children
- Limited/no opportunity to learn appropriate behaviour
  - Appropriate behaviour not modelled by others
  - Appropriate behaviour not rewarded
- Overwhelming need to behave inappropriately eg. intense emotions
- Inability to recognise the needs of others
- Inability to recognise the impact of their behaviours on others
- Cognitive distortions
  - Feelings of entitlement: their needs are most important and must be met
  - Immature concept of 'fairness' (everyone should get exactly the same regardless of need)

---

# Promoting appropriate and considerate interpersonal behaviours

When working to promote appropriate and considerate interpersonal behaviours, check that the approaches suggested in Chapters 2 and 3 are in place. These build the foundations for developing more healthy relationships by improving self-esteem and containing extreme emotions.

## Setting and upholding standards

Where the individual lives in a shared residential setting, it is important to ensure that they are made aware of the behaviours expected and are supported to show these behaviours. The steps in this process are given in Box 4.8.

---

### Box 4.8: Setting the scene to enable individuals to learn new, appropriate interpersonal behaviours

Staff should:

- give clear, explicit, visible statements of the behaviours expected eg. codes of conduct, behavioural contracts
- model the expected behaviours (ie. staff need to behave appropriately)
- promote personal responsibility for behaviour
- name examples of appropriate behaviours
- reward appropriate behaviours
- not reward inappropriate behaviours
- create opportunities for peer-group discussions of behaviour and managed peer feedback.

---

## Setting standards

Staff should start by making explicit the standards of interpersonal behaviour that are expected. Behavioural standards might include: being polite and kind, respecting others' possessions and private space, sharing, taking turns, and behaving considerately in shared areas of the building. The standards might suggest that arguments should be resolved calmly between individuals but that if this could not be done, staff should be consulted. These standards should be backed up by the boundaries discussed in Chapter 3. For example, 'be polite' would be supported by rules that shouting and swearing are not allowed and that anyone doing so will be asked to leave the area until they have calmed down.

# Personal responsibility

It is important that a service acknowledges that individuals are responsible for their own behaviour. This approach accepts that provocation is never an excuse for inappropriate behaviour; however severe the provocation an individual always has options. This means that inappropriate behaviour is never acceptable and always needs to be addressed. It does not lower standards because 'they can't help it'.

Advocating personal responsibility is not the same as blaming the individual. Blaming involves a critical judgment of the individual's behaviour and is often linked to punishment. In contrast, personal responsibility recognises that individuals may struggle to control or change their behaviour. Rather than criticising the individual for the gap between how they actually behave and the expected standards, this approach tries to support the individual to work towards showing acceptable behaviour.

# Feedback

It is important that staff recognise when the standards are achieved and give individuals clear feedback. For example:

*'I noticed you **shared** your sweets with X, that was **generous** of you.'*
*'I noticed you **thanked** Y for helping you. That was **polite**'.*

Such comments make clear that the person has behaved appropriately. They also give words for the appropriate behaviour so that the person knows what this behaviour is called. As discussed in Chapter 2, such feedback also helps to build self-esteem and a positive self-image.

Feedback should also be given about inappropriate behaviour. This might be done as part of the conflict resolution and anti-bullying approaches discussed later in this chapter or in a calm discussion using the rules for constructive criticism discussed in Chapter 2.

# Consistency

Staff need to consistently apply the standards to all individuals. If some individuals are perceived as being allowed to behave inappropriately or as 'getting away with it', others are likely to copy those behaviours rather than show the behaviours staff are trying to promote. This may present challenges when some individuals are more unwell or significantly less able than others and hence are unable to reach a higher standard of behaviour. In these situations staff need to give a clear and consistent message to the individual. For example, *'Fred is very unwell at the moment and that makes him rude and grumpy. You're well, so we need to work on you being polite to other people'*.

## House meetings

Standards of behaviour and whether they are being met can be a helpful item for discussion in house meetings. This provides the opportunity to remind individuals of the standards and rules, explore why they are needed, and what problems have been encountered during the week. These meetings need careful chairing to ensure that they do not become a moaning session or degenerate into bullying weaker individuals. A structured agenda can be very helpful. For example, ask people to share times they have seen others behaving appropriately and giving praise to each other before exploring any problems. Hearing directly from peers about the impact of behaviour is often much more powerful than being told by staff and can motivate individuals to change their behaviour.

## Understanding social behaviours

For the many individuals who struggle to see why behaviour change is needed, it may be helpful to both teach them why certain behaviours are important and also to work on the development of mentalising skills.

## Social Stories™

One helpful approach, originally designed for individuals with autism, is the use of Social Stories™ or 'social articles' developed by Carol Gray (1994, 2010). These are positive stories that describe a situation, skill or concept in terms of the relevant social cues, people's perspectives and common responses. They give information about the how's and why's of behaviours in a way that is easily understood. They aim to help individuals improve their understanding of situations, become aware of other people's reactions and develop more realistic expectations of what might happen. They do not tell individuals how to behave but may influence their behaviour by changing their understanding and expectations. An example is given in Box 4.9.

---

## Box 4.9: Example story

### Swearing

Swear words are words that are rude or insulting. Swearing is when someone says these rude words.

Everyone swears sometimes.
Sometimes my dad swears.
Sometimes my brother swears.

People may swear when something goes wrong.
People may swear when they are angry.
People may swear when they have an argument.

These are some of the swear words I use: _____

I swear when I am angry with other people.
I swear when my laptop doesn't work.
Swearing makes me feel better. It gets my anger out.

People do not like to hear swear words. It makes them feel uncomfortable.
People do not like it when someone swears at them. It hurts their feelings and makes them upset.

It is important to be kind to other people. If I talk politely to them they will like me and want to be friends.

There are other words I can use to get my anger out _____
They are not swear words and will not upset other people.

Adapted from Ling (2006)

---

It is important to think about how a story is written; if it is too directive or critical it is likely to be rejected and will consequently be of no help in increasing the individual's understanding. Box 4.10 gives some tips to increase the likelihood of a story being effective.

Intellectual Disabilities and Personality Disorder: An integrated approach
© Pavilion Publishing and Media Ltd and its licensors 2014.

---

## Box 4.10: Tips for writing stories

- Give the story a clear structure (beginning, contents, end).
- Check it answers the key questions (who, where, when, what, how and why).
- Write negative information in the third person, otherwise use the first person.
- Ensure that the overall message is positive.
- Make sure the story makes sense if it is interpreted word for word.
- Avoid using any words that are known to upset the individual.
- Make sure the story is within the individual's reading ability and attention span.
- Make sure any pictures used enhance the meaning of the story.
- Incorporate the individual's interests if at all possible.
- Check that the story has a patient and reassuring quality.

---

It is also very important that the story is used correctly or it is unlikely to have the benefits intended. There are a number of steps to this process, outlined in Box 4.11.

---

## Box 4.11: Using stories

- Select or write a story to address the area of concern.
- Create an opportunity to work through the story with the individual. This needs to be done in a relaxed and supportive way. It is an opportunity to learn about and explore social behaviour, not to tell the individual off.
- Go at the individual's pace and allow them time to ask questions.
- Check that the individual has understood each phrase of the story.
- Work jointly to re-write any parts of the story that are unclear, or are disliked by the individual.
- Check supporting pictures convey the intended meaning.
- Once the individual fully understands and is happy with the format of the story, make a final version and give it to the individual to keep.
- Where the individual has a number of difficulties (as is most likely), address each in a separate story. These can be compiled into a booklet.
- Go through the stories regularly to remind the individual of appropriate behaviour and also to create opportunities to talk about any ongoing issues.

---

## Mentalising

The development of compassion and empathy is important in improving relationships. Chapter 3 outlined how to help individuals begin to understand their own feelings through the process of staff validating their reactions. A similar process can be used for developing an understanding of others' feelings. Individuals can be supported to think about how other people might be feeling.

Where individuals have great difficulty in understanding other people's feelings it may be helpful to adapt some of the materials developed to help people with disorders on the autistic spectrum with 'mind reading' (another word for mentalising). These resources break the process into steps and identify the specific skills that are needed to 'mind read' (Howlin *et al*,1999).

## Cognitive distortions

Staff need to be on the look-out for cognitive distortions that may be influencing an individual's interpersonal behaviour. The approaches suggested in Chapter 7 can be helpful in addressing these issues.

# Difficulties with relationships and conflicts

Individuals with intellectual disabilities and personality disorder often appear unable to get on with anyone for more than a short period of time. They may be friends with someone one minute but be unable to stay in the same room with them a few hours later. Some of the factors that contribute to such difficulties are given in Box 4.12.

---

### Box 4.12: Factors contributing to difficulties in relationships and experiencing conflict

- Learning history and past experiences
- The replication of past patterns of behaviour (Chapter 13)
- Emotional volatility (Chapter 3)
- Thinking errors that distort their perceptions and expectations of relationships (Chapter 7)
- Inability to consider the other person's perspective
- Inconsiderate and inappropriate behaviour towards others
- Not taking responsibility for their own behaviour eg. *'S/he started it!'*
- Fear of being alone

---

These difficulties are closely linked to and have the same origins as inconsiderate and inappropriate behaviours and mean that individuals are more likely to experience conflict with others. Sadly they also lack the skills to resolve that conflict successfully. In a conflict situation individuals may aggressively seek to impose their wishes on others, may let others ride roughshod over them or may avoid talking about the situation and allow things to fester until they explode (approaches to conflict resolution are also discussed more fully in Chapter 14). Consequently, where there are disagreements between individuals, arguments often develop, sometimes accompanied by verbal abuse or physical blows. Given the difficulties individuals have with interpersonal relationships, it is perhaps surprising that they do not all choose to live alone and avoid other people. However, many individuals find being alone unbearable. This drives them to continue to seek relationships despite all the difficulties they experience. The reasons for the fear of being alone and ways of addressing it are explored in Chapter 5. Paradoxically, by teaching individuals to manage on their own, their relationships are likely to improve. This is because they are more able to give other people space and are likely to reduce the annoying, frustrating and sometimes harmful behaviours they resort to in order to avoid being alone.

Where individuals with intellectual disabilities and personality disorder avoid addressing conflict they may move or demand to move when they have fallen out with the people they live with. This can result in multiple moves as the individual takes their relationship style with them and soon falls out with people in the new setting.

## Stablising relationships and resolving conflicts

When two individuals constantly clash the most frequent response is to try to separate them as much as possible. This can prove an effective short-term measure to lower the emotional tension and create space in which to explore other solutions. However, this is not a long-term solution. Partly, this is because it is virtually impossible to ensure that people will not encounter each other at some point. More significantly, it does not address the underlying difficulties with resolving conflicts and co-existing with others. The individual is likely to fall out with other people and, if no other strategy is used, could end up virtually in solitary confinement. Hence it is important to look for ways to improve the individual's abilities to relate to others and resolve conflicts.

Relationship difficulties will often first become apparent as the result of a conflict or emotional outburst. It is important to realise that this is not the time to try to address the problems in the relationship. The emotional distress needs to be managed using the approaches described in Chapter 3. Once the situation has calmed down the underlying issues can be identified and attempts made to heal the ruptured relationships.

## Conflict or bullying?

Once the situation has calmed down the first step is to explore why the individuals are clashing. Talk to everyone who has witnessed incidents and find out their views on what was going on. In particular, it is important to establish whether an incident was just a 'falling out' or whether it constituted bullying. Resolving bullying is explored later in this chapter. The following approach should be used only when individuals 'fall out' with each other.

## Conflict resolution

The following is one possible approach to resolving conflicts. The steps are given in Box 4.13.

---

### Box 4.13: Conflict resolution

- Gather information eg. what each individual did and possible reasons for the conflict
- Meet separately with each individual:
  - Explore their perception of what happened
  - Use a problem-solving approach to look at how the issues can be resolved
- If individuals are willing, facilitate them meeting so that they can each share their ideas for resolving the conflict
- Make a shared action plan

---

## Information gathering

There is a huge list of potential reasons why people might row and why arguing might meet important needs for an individual. Some possible reasons are listed in Box 4.14. This list is not exhaustive.

Once some ideas about what is going on have been gathered, it is time to start helping the individuals to resolve their differences. Choose a time when the individuals are calm. The aim is to help the individuals resolve the conflict themselves rather than do

Intellectual Disabilities and Personality Disorder: An integrated approach
© Pavilion Publishing and Media Ltd and its licensors 2014.

this for them. However, bringing people together can risk, reigniting the conflict. It is usually better to work with each individual separately first to explore what has gone on and get their understanding of the conflict.

---

### Box 4.14: Common reasons for rows

- Individuals may be jealous of each other. (The more insecure a person is the more likely they are to be overwhelmed by jealousy.) They may feel that the other person:
  - is more popular
  - sees their family more often
  - has more money.
- Individuals may see the other person as a competitor. This might be for the attention of staff or the affections of a potential partner.
- The individual may feel that they have been treated unfairly to the benefit of the other person. This can happen if one person needs a lot more help than the other. The individual thinks only about the amount of help given without appreciating that the help is given because it is needed.
- Conflicting choices, for example, one individual wants quiet while the other wants loud music.
- Conflicts of need, particularly if both individuals make demands on staff at the same time.
- Individuals may discover that busy staff will take time out to resolve disputes; in this way the arguments act as a way of initiating interaction with staff.
- For some people the experience of being 'saved' or 'rescued' by staff who step in to resolve a dispute can be powerfully reinforcing. It tells them that staff care about them and want to keep them safe.
- Some individuals have unrealistic expectations of others and will become very angry if they feel let down.

---

## Individual discussions

It is important at this stage not to be drawn into discussions of blame or right and wrong. Individuals are likely to argue that their behaviour was justified because of something the other person did and that they had no alternative to the behaviour they showed. Shouting, swearing or hitting out are wrong, however much provocation occurred. This needs to be explained firmly but sensitively as there is a risk that the individual will decide that the member of staff is taking the other person's side and may get angry and storm out. It may help to keep reminding the individual that this work is intended to help them, that they are important and cared for and that their needs will be met. The approaches to de-escalation and validating emotions described in Chapter 3 will be very helpful in keeping the individual engaged in the discussion.

## Problem solving

Taking a problem-solving approach can help make individual discussions more productive. The steps of problem solving are given in Box 4.15.

---

### Box 4.15: Problem-solving approach

- Define the problem
- Generate alternatives
- Evaluate alternatives and select a potential solution
- Implement solution
- Evaluate outcome

---

Work with the individual to find out what the problem is. This will take careful use of questions to get beyond 'X keeps winding me up'. Use the ideas gathered from other people to gently suggest things that might be causing the tension. Once you have some clear ideas about the triggers for the conflict, start to explore what could be done to prevent further clashes. It is likely that the individual will only suggest things that the other person could do, which are sometimes not very complimentary or constructive. It is important not to become annoyed with this but continue gently exploring options and making suggestions that might help the individual. In particular, explore if it would be helpful to have a meeting with the other person to try to resolve the differences.

If the individuals choose to meet and talk to each other about what happened it can be helpful to work with each person to agree in advance and write down what they are going to say. This needs to explain how they felt, why they behaved as they did, what they are going to change and what they would like the other person to change.

## Meeting up

It is most helpful if there are two members of staff present when doing this. This avoids the risk that one member of staff will be seen as taking sides. The first step is to set the rules for the meeting. The basic rules are that each person should be polite and listen to the other. Individuals can share their 'statements' about the clash. Once each person has shared their statement they should be supported to negotiate a joint action plan. Be careful about pushing individuals to apologise to each other. Individuals can then get the message that they can behave as they like so long as they apologise afterwards. This is not a helpful way of thinking and can perpetuate hurtful behaviours.

## Evaluation

It is then important to monitor the progress of the relationship and whether the action plan has worked. In particular be aware that some individuals may find the problem-solving process reinforcing and might unconsciously trigger incidents so that they can talk about them with staff. If it looks like this is happening it may be useful to use the approaches discussed in Chapter 5 on managing interaction with staff.

## Other approaches

If it appears that everyone is clashing in a service it may be helpful to look at the approach taken by the staff team. It may be that staff are inadvertently reinforcing inappropriate behaviour, for example, arguing individuals may be split up, with each being offered a fun activity. There may also be too much emphasis on shared activities and becoming a 'family'. Everyone needs time to themselves and to get away from the people they live with. Look carefully at how activities are organised and try to make sure that everyone has time away and also regular times to chat to their key worker without interruptions from other people. It can also be helpful to look at how activities are timetabled. It is surprising how much relationships can improve if individuals find that extra outings are possible if they are able to 'put up with' someone they clash with also sharing the activity.

## Bullying

Sometimes individuals with intellectual disabilities and personality disorder can behave in very hurtful ways towards other individuals to the extent that the behaviour comprises bullying. Box 4.16 describes bullying.

## Box 4.16: Definition of bullying

Bullying occurs when individuals use their power to distress, hurt or exploit weaker individuals. It is targeted, repeated, and the perpetrators have more power than the victim.

Bullying may take a number of forms:

- name calling
- ignoring or excluding a person
- physical aggression (eg. pushing, hitting)
- taking money and possessions
- damaging property
- using modern technology such as text messaging, email and social networking sites to distress and intimidate the victim ('cyber bullying')
- spreading gossip or rumours about a person (indirect bullying).

There may be many different reasons for an individual to engage in bullying. Some possible motivations for bullying are given in Box 4.17.

## Box 4.17: Motivations for bullying

- To impress others
- To keep in with a crowd
- To appear tough
- As an outlet for jealousy
- A reaction to having been bullied
- An attempt to boost self-esteem
- To put others down and make the person feel powerful
- A response to perceived rejection
- To punish someone once an intense, very close relationship has ended unhappily
- An expression of prejudice related to a characteristic of the person eg. ethnicity, sexuality

Individuals with intellectual disabilities and personality disorder have often experienced bullying during their childhood. As adults, they often have a powerful need to fit in and impress others. This is often combined with complex emotional needs and insensitivity to the pain of others. These factors make them vulnerable to becoming bullies themselves. Many individuals will switch between the role of perpetrator and victim of bullying depending on their mood state and the people they are mixing with.

# Resolving bullying

Bullying is a serious issue within any service and requires a thoughtful and integrated approach. The power imbalance, intensity of the hurt caused and the persistence of bullying mean that it needs to be addressed differently from everyday conflicts.

## Policy

Every service should have an anti-bullying policy that outlines what bullying is, how the service will try to prevent it and what action will be taken when it occurs. How staff view and respond to bullying will shape the culture of the service. If bullying is seen as a part of life that individuals just need to come to terms with then the problem is likely to escalate. In contrast, if bullying is seen as unacceptable and there are well thought out strategies to prevent and resolve incidents, bullying is likely to be minimised.

## Balanced approach

It is important that the approach taken is not too heavy handed; this can have the effect of making bullies hide what they are doing more carefully. However, where bullying is extreme it is important to recognise when an offence may have been committed; for example, physical assault, sexual harassment or racist abuse. Such incidents must always be addressed through safeguarding procedures. Individuals should always be supported to report these behaviours to the police and to take legal action if they wish.

## Awareness

The service should create an atmosphere in which staff are alert to signs of bullying and where individuals feel comfortable telling staff about incidents that have distressed them. Staff should know how to respond to reports including reporting the incidents, offering support to the individual and exploring ways of ending the bullying.

## The no blame approach

For all but the most severe bullying the 'no blame' approach may be helpful. The 'no blame' approach is a seven-step process to resolving incidents of bullying that was developed for use in schools. It is based on the thinking that individuals will only give up bullying if they develop empathy and consideration for others. It aims to help the bully choose to give up the behaviour rather than try to stop bullying by policing behaviour and punishing bullying. The 'no blame' approach is readily adapted for use in other settings and for work with adults. The steps involved are given in Box 4.18.

Where the individual who is bullying others lacks empathy and struggles to mentalise, the techniques for promoting appropriate behaviours, discussed earlier in this chapter, may be helpful.

## Victim behaviours

Sometimes individuals will have behaviours that are not helpful and may encourage bullying. They may need help to explore the role of these behaviours in the bullying and to change them if this is what they choose to do. However, care should be taken to make sure that this help does not imply that they are responsible for being bullied.

# Therapeutic activities

Individuals with intellectual disabilities and personality disorder are often referred for therapy to help them with their relationships. A social skills group can be helpful for individuals who appear to lack the basic skills to form and maintain relationships. However, group leaders need to be alert to signs of anxiety, anger and jealousy between group members. These must be resolved quickly if the group is not to become victim to difficulties in the relationships between group members that it was trying to address.

Social skills groups will rarely be enough on their own. This is because they do not address underlying issues, particularly insecure attachment styles and lack of mentalising or 'mind reading' skills. They should therefore be used as part of a wider therapeutic approach. Some individuals may be able to engage in therapy to help them improve their relationships. The DBT approach mentioned in earlier chapters may be helpful. Another useful approach may be cognitive analytic therapy (CAT). CAT helps individuals identify repetitive, unhelpful patterns of behaviour and ways of relating to other people. The individual may be helped to draw this pattern and then to look for ways of changing their responses. Referrals for therapy will need to be made through the individual's GP.

## Box 4.18: The 'no blame' approach to bullying – seven steps

**Step one:** Interview with the victim. When staff find out that bullying has happened they start by talking to the victim about their feelings. The focus is not on what happened but about the impact on the victim and finding out who was involved and who may have helped or watched the bullying. Together they can create a way of showing distress to the group involved. This might be choosing or making a picture, a poem or some writing.

**Step two:** A meeting is arranged with the people involved (ie. the perpetrator(s) and witnesses. A group of six or eight people works well. This group is lead by a member of staff. The victim does not attend.

**Step three:** The problem is explained. The member of staff tells the people about the way the victim is feeling and uses the picture, poem or piece of writing to emphasise their distress. At no time does the member of staff discuss details of the incidents or allocate blame to the group.

**Step four:** Responsibility for the distress is shared with the group. The member of staff does not attribute the blame but states that they know that the group is responsible and can do something about it.

**Step five:** Each member of the group is encouraged to suggest a way in which the victim could be helped to feel happier. The staff member gives some positive responses but does not go on to extract a promise of improved behaviour.

**Step six:** The staff member ends the meeting by passing over the responsibility to the group to solve the problem.

**Step seven:** About a week* later the member of staff discusses with each person, including the victim, how things have been going. This allows the staff to monitor the bullying and keeps the people involved in the process.

(*If extreme bullying occurs during this period it should be addressed and not allowed to continue, however change can take time and it is also important not to jump in too quickly.)

# Key learning points

- Humans are social beings and have a drive to seek others and form relationships. People live in complex social networks and are biologically designed to work together for survival.

- Positive, supportive relationships promote good physical and mental health. They give a sense of purpose and belonging, reduce stress and help people cope with trauma. They also increase happiness, contribute to a healthy identity and boost self-esteem.

- Individuals with intellectual disabilities and personality disorder are likely to have wide-ranging difficulties in their relationships with the people they live with. Relationships may be unstable, overly intense and sometimes abusive.

- Individuals will struggle with many of the basics that sustain positive relationships; they may appear uncaring and self-obsessed. They may both bully others and be bullied themselves.

- Despite these difficulties individuals often fear being alone and will show extreme behaviours in an effort to avoid being abandoned.

- These difficulties are the result of a range of biological and social factors associated with both their intellectual disabilities and personality disorder.

- Individuals can be supported to have more positive relationships through a number of approaches including setting and maintaining standards, constructively managing conflict and resolving bullying.

- Some individuals will also benefit from therapy to address some of the issues that underlie their difficulties with relationships, including lack of skills, distorted thinking and insecure attachment styles.

# References

Bartholomew K & Horowitz L (1991) Attachment styles among young adults: a test of a four-category model. *Journal of Personality and Social Psychology* **61** 226–244.

Gray C (1994/2010) *The New Social Story Book*. Hammond Indiana: Horizon. (These stories are very childish and would not be suitable for adults without altering the illustrations and wording, however at the end of the book there is an excellent guide to writing Social Stories™.)

Howlin P, Baron-Cohen S & Hadwin J (1999) *Teaching Children with Autism to Mind-read*. Chichester: John Wiley. (This book is intended for use with children but the approach contained can be adapted for use with adults.)

Ling J (2006) *I Can't Do That! My social stories to help with communication, self-care and personal skills*. London: Lucky Duck, Sage. (This book is intended for use with children but some of the Social Stories™ can be adapted for use with adults.)

# Further reading

Adair J (2010) *Decision Making and Problem Solving Strategies: 66 (creating success)*. London: Kogen Page.

Agrawal H, Gunderson J, Holmes B, & Lyons-Ruth K (2004) Attachment studies with borderline patients: a review. *Harvard Review of Psychiatry* **12** (2) 94–104.

Denman C (2001) Cognitive-analytic therapy. *Advances in Psychiatric Treatment* **7** 243–252 doi: 10.1192/apt.7.4.243.

Kumpulainen K (2008) Psychiatric conditions associated with bullying. *International Journal of Adolescent Medicine and Health* **20** (2) 121–32.

Larson F, Alim N, Tsakanikos E (2011) Attachment style and mental health in adults with intellectual disability: self-reports and reports by carers. *Advances in Mental Health and Intellectual Disabilities* **5** (3) 15–23.

Lyddon W & Sherry A (2001) Developmental personality styles: an attachment theory conceptualization of personality disorders. *Journal of Counselling and Development* **59** 405–414.

National Collaboration Centre for Mental Health (2009) *Borderline Personality Disorder: The NICE guideline on treatment and management*. Leicester & London: The British Psychological Society & Royal College of Psychiatrists.

Robinson G & Maines B (2008) *Bullying: A complete guide to the support group method*. (Lucky Duck Books). London: Sage. (This book is intended for use with children but the approach can be adapted for use with adults.)

# Chapter 5: Difficulties in relationships with staff

This chapter explores the characteristics of constructive relations between staff and the individuals they support. It considers the way in which professional relationships differ from personal relationships. It examines interpersonal boundaries and how these are maintained. It looks at the challenges that staff may encounter when working with individuals with intellectual disabilities and personality disorder. It explores how these difficulties might occur when working with individuals with intellectual disabilities and personality disorder and discusses some ways of addressing those issues.

## Key topics

■ Professional relationships

■ Professional relationships and individuals with personality disorder

■ Professional relationships and individuals with intellectual disabilities

■ Professional relationships and individuals with intellectual disabilities and personality disorder

■ Promoting positive professional relationships with individuals with intellectual disabilities and personality disorder

## Professional relationships

Health and social care staff have a wide range of roles and undertake many different tasks ranging from complex medical treatments and intimate personal care, to helping an individual with their shopping. However diverse their responsibilities, all staff share the characteristic of being in a professional relationship with the people they treat or support. Professional relationships can often look very similar to personal relationships. For example, staff may chat and joke with the individuals they support. However, professional relationships differ from personal relationships in a number of important ways. Some of these are given in Box 5.1.

## Box 5.1: Differences between professional and personal relationships

| Characteristic | Professional | Personal |
|---|---|---|
| Behaviour | Regulated by professional and ethical codes | Guided by personal values and beliefs |
| Payment | Is paid to provide treatment and care | No payment for being in the relationship |
| Length of relationship | Time limited by length of time treatment or care is needed | No time limits – depends on decisions of individuals in the relationship |
| Location of relationship | Defined by the nature of the care/treatment | Places unlimited and undefined |
| Purpose of relationship | Goal directed – care/treatment/ | Pleasure, interest directed |
| Structure of relationship | Defined by nature of care/treatment | Spontaneous, unstructured |
| Boundaries of relationship | Defined by care/treatment, consistent | Continually evolving by mutual agreement, flexible |
| Power balance | Unequal – professional has more power through authority, knowledge, influence and access to privileged information | Generally equal in healthy relationships |
| Responsibility for relationship | Professional responsible for starting, maintaining and ending relationship | Shared/equal responsibility for relationship |
| Preparation for the relationship | Requires training for and induction into the role | No formal training or preparation needed |
| Time spent in relationship | Dictated by contractual agreements and care/treatment requirements | Personal choice, mutual agreement |
| Intimate contact | Dictated by care/treatment requirements, regulated by codes of conduct, given only with consent/best interests | Negotiated by individuals for mutual pleasure |

Intellectual Disabilities and Personality Disorder: An integrated approach
© Pavilion Publishing and Media Ltd and its licensors 2014.

As Box 5.1 shows, despite some surface similarities, professional and personal relationships differ on every dimension. Personal relationships are highly varied, flexible and wide ranging. In contrast, professional relationships seek to achieve mutually agreed goals through the appropriate use of power, from a basis of trust and respect, within a clearly defined framework.

## Working alliance

A key aspect of a professional relationship is that it exists to achieve certain tasks or goals. To be able to achieve these goals, staff need to build a working alliance with the individuals they treat or care for. The individual must feel comfortable with the member of staff and trust them. The importance and complexity of this connection varies with different professional roles. For example, GPs have only to convince a patient to tell them about symptoms that are already bothering the patient. In contrast, a psychotherapist has to create a situation in which the individual is confident to share their deepest concerns and fears and reveal intimate details of their life.

Establishing this connection is often called 'engagement' and is discussed fully in Chapter 13. A number of characteristics that help professionals connect emotionally with individuals are also discussed in Chapter 2.

The member of staff and individual also need to negotiate the tasks they will be attempting together and the work each of them will do. Again, these tasks will vary in complexity. Conflict can occur if this process is not carried out carefully as the individual and staff member may have different expectations of the purpose of the work and their roles within it.

This working alliance can be distorted by a number of psychological processes including projection, transference and countertransference. These processes are discussed in depth in Chapter 14.

## Professional boundaries

In order for staff to carry out their work with individuals safely, there needs to be clear boundaries to their role. These professional boundaries mark out how the professional relationship is different from a personal relationship. They protect the individual from abuses of power including the risks of physical, emotional, sexual and financial abuse by the member of staff. The boundaries also protect the member of staff's privacy and time, guard them against temptations to enter unprofessional relationships with individuals and provide some protection from misunderstandings or fictitious allegations of abuse. Some examples of the areas where professional boundaries are needed and how these are achieved are given in Box 5.2.

---

## Box 5.2: Examples of professional boundaries

### Contact

- Within working hours, not meeting individual when not on duty
- Time limited eg. one hour appointment, 7½ hour shift
- Punctual eg. starting and ending appointment on time, arriving and ending shift on time
- Out of hours availability eg. not available or clear agreement for specific tasks
- Only in specified locations eg. clinic room, individual's home, not professional's home (or in private practice seeing only in a designated treatment room/office)
- Limited ways of contacting eg. through work email, work telephone and mobile. Not sharing home address, personal phone numbers or email, not tagging as a friend on Facebook

### Relationship

- Task-focused and time-limited eg. for piece of work, duration of contract
- Tasks fall within professional's work remit and skills, not going beyond these
- Limited self-disclosure by professional eg. none at all or planned disclosure for therapeutic reasons
- Confidentiality: the professional will not disclose information (within agreed limits eg. risk to individual or others)
- Gifts: not accepted or limited to 'gestures' eg. cards, chocolates
- Money: not borrowing money from or lending to individual
- Not getting to know professional's friends and family
- Physical contact: limited to handshake unless clearly agreed with consent/best interest agreement for specific therapeutic tasks
- Negotiation: limited within certain strict limits eg. can choose an appointment time within 9–5pm on working days but not outside these hours

---

It is important that professional boundaries are in place for all staff who come into contact with individuals. The need for professional boundaries is usually taught as part of formal training for professions such as nursing, medicine and psychology. However it may sometimes be overlooked in roles that are learnt 'on the job'. This can mean that support workers, cooks and cleaners are left without guidance on where to draw the limits of their role.

# Professional relationships and individuals with personality disorder

Individuals with personality disorder most frequently have contact with staff in adult mental health services either to address their personality disorder directly or to obtain help with additional mental health problems (see Chapter 9). Those with additional physical health needs will have contact with medical specialists (see Chapter 8). They may also have contact with staff in A&E departments as a result of self-harm and with staff in crisis houses or inpatient units (see Chapters 11 and 12).

Individuals with personality disorder often have great difficulty engaging with services. The reasons for this are explored in Chapter 13.

Once engaged with services, individuals with personality disorder have great difficulty in accepting the boundaries of professional relationships. This is particularly characteristic of individuals with borderline personality disorder. Their intense needs, learnt patterns of behaviour and patterns of thinking lead them to have inappropriate expectations of what staff can offer. As a result, they behave in a range of ways that challenge professional boundaries and can draw staff into behaving in inappropriate, unprofessional ways. Some examples are given in Box 5.3.

These patterns of behaviour can be very difficult for staff to deal with and may trigger unhelpful reactions in staff. The reasons for this and ways of addressing these reactions are explored more fully in Chapter 14.

# Professional relationships and individuals with intellectual disabilities

The pattern of contact that individuals with intellectual disabilities have with services varies with the severity of their intellectual disabilities. Generally, the more severe their disabilities, the more regular contact they will have with support staff. Individuals with intellectual disabilities have poorer mental and physical health than the general population and consequently have more contact with services to address these needs. As a consequence of their intellectual disabilities and other health needs, many individuals with intellectual disabilities have long-term contact with a range of different services within health and social services and the private and voluntary sectors. They will therefore need to interact with a range of staff in a variety of roles. For many this will include the need for intimate personal care such as help with washing, dressing and managing continence. It can be difficult for the individual with intellectual disabilities to understand these complex situations and the nature of the relationships between them and the different staff and professionals they meet.

---

### Box 5.3: Ways in which individuals with personality disorder challenge professional relationships

- Forming an instant bond and sharing how other staff or services have let them down or have not understood them – drawing staff into 'rubbishing' other services.

- Giving incomplete or one-sided stories that make staff feel the individual has been neglected or badly treated by others – staff may become angry and try to rescue or protect the individual.

- Saying they have special needs and negotiating contact in a way that is not normally offered eg. early/late appointments/a different location.

- Not turning up or being late for appointments.

- Revealing important information at the end of sessions so that staff are tempted to extend beyond the agreed time.

- Becoming distressed at the end of sessions so that staff feel they need to extend the session to console the individual.

- Making frequent contact with staff, telephoning frequently often at the end of the day and in a state of great distress – taking up huge amounts of time.

- Seeking help with issues that are outside of the role of the member of staff or are beyond their skills and experience but *'only you can help me'* – drawing staff into overstepping their responsibilities.

- Behaving inappropriately towards staff, chatting to them as if they were friends, flirting or behaving seductively – drawing staff into a personal relationship.

- Seeking personal information about staff. For example, using the internet to track down home details or trying to make contact through social networking sites.

- Trying to make contact with staff outside of work by finding out where they go when off duty and then 'accidentally' bumping into them.

- Being overly interested in/sensitive to staff's moods – drawing staff into confiding inappropriate personal information.

---

Individuals with intellectual disabilities are often socially isolated and find it difficult to make friends or form intimate relationships. Consequently, they are vulnerable to becoming overly emotionally attached to staff and to seeking to form personal relationships with them. This risk is compounded by the impact of their intellectual impairment as this makes it harder for them to understand the differences between professional and personal relationships. The nature of the support role, whereby staff are friendly, kind, considerate and responsive to the individual's needs, increases the risk of individuals 'falling in love' with staff members. Some individuals will be sexually attracted to staff and might seek to have a sexual relationship with them.

The social isolation and loneliness of many individuals with intellectual disabilities can make staff feel very sorry for them and can tempt staff to try to compensate for this by letting the individual into their life. Staff may share information about their own lives, let the individual meet their family, include them in special events and outings. Staff may be distressed that the individual never receives a hug or cuddle from another person and hence may allow these behaviours to occur. These forms of contact are potentially beneficial. However, they can lead to misunderstandings or can lead on to behaviours that are totally inappropriate, if they are not thought through and managed.

Rather than outlawing all sharing or physical contact, most services for individuals with intellectual disabilities recognise that these present opportunities to enhance individuals' lives if performed in a professional manner. When staff teams identify that an individual enjoys or is comforted by physical contact, a team decision is made about what forms of contact are acceptable and when they can be used. This is then recorded in a care plan and the impact on the individual's well-being can be monitored and reviewed. Some of the differences between professional and unprofessional physical contact are given in Box 5.4.

## Box 5.4: Differences between professional and non-professional physical contact

| Professional | Non-professional |
|---|---|
| ■ Driven by individual's needs and preferences<br>■ Based on a team decision<br>■ Best interests discussion for individuals without capacity<br>■ Use recommended in care plan<br>■ Use recorded in progress notes<br>■ Impact monitored and reviewed<br>■ Complies with local policies eg. intimate care<br>■ Whole team, including manager and any professionals involved, are aware of what contact is being made<br>■ Contact initiated by individual or in response to a specific need<br>■ Type of contact is related to the need it is to fulfil:<br>  ■ comfort or greetings: handshake, high fives, holding hand, hand on shoulder, arm round shoulder<br>  ■ support with learning tasks: hand over hand, hand on shoulders<br>  ■ managing challenging behaviour: hand on arm, hand on shoulder<br>  ■ intimate care: contact minimum necessary for effective care<br>■ Staff have the opportunity to discuss their views and reactions to the physical contact in supervision<br>■ Individual has the opportunity to express their views on the contact | ■ Driven by needs of staff member<br>■ Isolated decision of staff member<br>■ No consideration of capacity<br>■ Not in care plan<br>■ Not recorded in progress notes<br>■ No formal monitoring or review<br>■ Based on views of individual staff member<br>■ Contact is secret to the staff member or to a sub-group of staff<br>■ Contact led by staff member<br>■ Contact related to perceptions of member of staff. May include contact unlikely to be agreed by team eg. full body hug, sitting on lap, cuddling on sofa, touching intimate areas when not involved in agreed intimate care, allowing individual to touch more intimate areas eg. head resting on staff member's lap or chest.<br>■ Unofficial nature means it is unlikely to be discussed in supervision<br>■ Individual has no channel to express their views |

Informed by Job G (2007) Handouts for 'creating and maintaining professional relationships and boundaries between staff and service users. Available at: www.cawt.com/Site/11/Documents/Publications/Disability/POVA/BehavingProfessionally.pdf (accessed April 2014).

# Professional relationships and individuals with intellectual disabilities and personality disorder

Individuals with intellectual disabilities and personality disorder have multiple issues with professional relationships. They share the intense needs, learnt patterns of behaviour and distorted patterns of thinking that lead individuals with personality disorder to have inappropriate expectations of professional relationships. However, these are influenced by the impact of their intellectual impairment and the social isolation associated with having intellectual disabilities. These mean that staff are likely to play a large role in individuals' lives. They may also have to offer more intimate care than would occur with more able individuals. As a result of this combination of factors, individuals experience a range of issues with the staff who support them on a daily basis. These relate to both the quality of the interactions and the amount of contact they seek. Some common difficulties are given in Box 5.5.

## Box 5.5: Day-to-day difficulties interacting with support staff

- Unhealthy relationships with staff:
  - 'Hating' and refusing to work with particular members of staff
  - Insisting on working with particular members of staff
  - Monopolising particular members of staff (eg. following them around)
  - Overly intense positive relationships eg. fixations, crushes and obsessions
  - Switching from 'loving' to 'hating' a member of staff
  - Repeatedly wanting to change workers ('sacking' staff)
  - Treating staff like friends, trying to form personal relationships eg. flirting, wanting to go on outings
- Calls on staff time ('attention seeking behaviour'):
  - Need for constant reassurance
  - Repeated, insistent, questions and demands
- Over dependence ('demanding behaviour'):
  - Repeated requests for 'unnecessary' help
  - Reluctance to do things independently
  - 'Exaggerating' their difficulties or the amount of help needed
- Behaviours that make staff feel 'manipulated' eg.:
  - Asking every member of a team until someone gives the answer the individual wants
  - Giving selected information that makes a situation look different eg. 'the GP said I need pain killers' (but not mentioning they also said to exercise as much as possible), 'X swore at me' (but not 'after I turned the TV over')
  - Using 'hook' words that make the situation appear more serious or pressing eg. 'I feel suicidal', 'I need to do X, it's urgent'.
  - Using expressions that make it appear that they have not been given help and support eg. 'I've never been offered…'
  - Creating false permission 'the doctor said I must…' 'X said I could…'
  - Misquoting other people eg. 'X said you didn't do it right last time'
  - 'Emotional blackmail' 'If you don't then I will…' 'If I can't then I will…' 'No one cares what happens to me, I'm going to end it all'
  - Escalating behaviours in response to 'no' – eg. individual wanted to go to hospital but was told an injury was too minor; they then make the injury worse
  - Doing something that disrupts situations in which other individuals are the centre of attention eg. self-harming during someone else's party
  - Unfounded allegations of abuse

There are several possible reasons why these behaviours occur. Unhealthy patterns of interaction may simply reflect the individual's attachment style (see Chapter 4). Some individuals rapidly form intense attachments to members of staff, seeing them as the 'perfect carer' and avoiding contact with others (see Chapters 7 and 14). Sometimes the individual will attach themselves to someone who is 'softer' and is more likely to give them things that they want. The flip side of this is refusing to work with someone after they have firmly enforced agreed boundaries. Sometimes the individual will have strong prejudices and will refuse to work with someone from a different ethnic group or because the staff member has some physical characteristic they dislike.

Sometimes it can feel that, however much is done for an individual, it is never enough. Some of the factors that can lead to individuals with intellectual disabilities and personality disorder needing a lot of input from staff are given in Box 5.6.

---

### Box 5.6: Possible reasons for needing frequent interactions with staff

- Major life event eg. bereavement, relationship breakdown, moving house
- Lack of appropriate activities or facilities to entertain self (eg. being on a ward with no day services)
- Reluctance to be alone:
  - Loneliness – social isolation
  - Fear of being abandoned
  - Feelings of emptiness or not existing
  - Intrusive unpleasant thoughts/memories/flashbacks
  - Have not learnt to amuse self
  - Boredom – high need for stimulation/low boredom threshold
  - Feeling they are missing out on something
- Reluctance to do things independently:
  - Fear that they cannot manage alone
  - Lack of confidence
  - Difficulties self-motivating
  - Difficulties remembering what they should do if there is no one to remind them

Continued...

---

- Need for reassurance:
  - Fears that hoped for positive events will not happen (impatience)
  - Worries about forthcoming negative events or possible events eg. 'what happens if my mum dies, my benefit cheque gets lost...'
  - Ruminations or 'over-thinking' about past negative events, their causes and consequences
- Inability to self-soothe or distract themselves
- Poor memory – needs repeated reminders as forgets key information
- Poor sense of time – do not realise how much time they are taking up, or how much time has (or hasn't!) elapsed since last interaction
- Lack of trust – do not believe they can rely on staff to look after them or remember the individual's existence
- Seeking perfect care – feel that staff must always be with them
- Jealousy and possessiveness – not wanting to share staff with other individuals
- Checking boundaries – testing out if there is any weakness in the team/way round the boundaries being imposed

## Impact on staff

These 'demanding', 'manipulative' and 'attention seeking' behaviours make great demands on individual staff members and can lead to them experiencing emotional exhaustion and a sense of failure. The individual's behaviour can also create friction and disagreements within the staff team, often leading to the team being unable to agree on or stick to a single course of action. This process is called 'splitting' and is explored fully in Chapter 14.

# Promoting positive professional relationships with individuals with intellectual disabilities and personality disorder

Creating and sustaining healthy professional relationships with individuals with intellectual disabilities and personality disorder places a lot of demands on staff. Box 5.7 lists some characteristics of staff and services that are able to do this successfully.

> ## Box 5.7: Characteristics of staff and team able to form healthy professional relationships with individuals
>
> **Staff**
>
> - Knowledge – of personality disorder, intellectual disabilities and helpful approaches
> - Skills – eg. active support style, active listening, de-escalation, emotional validation and containment
> - Attitude – positive, hopeful, confident, unshockable
> - Experience – worked with lots of different individuals
> - Reflection/self-awareness – open and thoughtful
>
> **Service** (see Chapter 14)
>
> - Team work – good communication and conflict resolution skills
> - Supervision – regular, supportive, knowledgeable
> - Post-incident support
> - Policies and procedures – in place, clear and accessible
> - Code of conduct – in place and used
> - Audit/quality assurance – problems identified and addressed

Most of these characteristics are explored in greater depth in other chapters of this book. The following section focuses on how staff can create an environment that promotes healthy professional relationships and how to deal with everyday difficulties in interactions between staff and individuals with intellectual disabilities and personality disorder.

It will look at:

- support styles
- promoting professional relationships with staff members
- managing calls on staff time
- over-dependence
- behaviours that make staff feel manipulated.

## Support styles

It is important to remember that building positive relationships is a two-way process. The way staff interact with individuals with intellectual disabilities and personality disorder will have a significant impact on the quality of that relationship and will help promote positive interpersonal behaviour. It is therefore important to think about the most effective way for staff to interact with individuals.

The way staff support individuals can be seen as varying along a number of dimensions. These are:

■ sensitivity to and interest in the individual

■ clarity and enforcement of boundaries

■ expectations of the individual.

Figure 5.8 shows how these dimensions combine to make four different support styles.

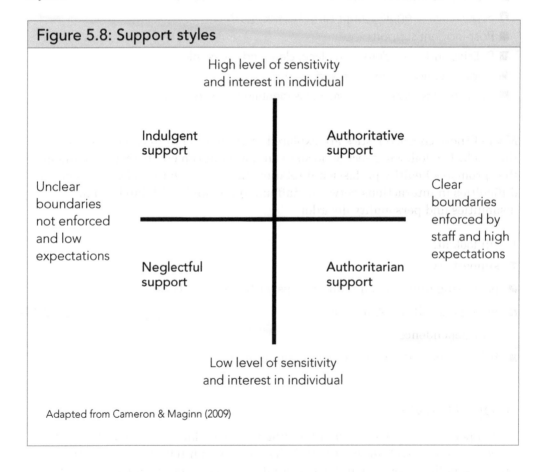

### Figure 5.8: Support styles

High level of sensitivity and interest in individual

Indulgent support

Authoritative support

Unclear boundaries not enforced and low expectations

Clear boundaries enforced by staff and high expectations

Neglectful support

Authoritarian support

Low level of sensitivity and interest in individual

Adapted from Cameron & Maginn (2009)

Intellectual Disabilities and Personality Disorder: An integrated approach
© Pavilion Publishing and Media Ltd and its licensors 2014.

Each of these support styles can be encountered in services for individuals with intellectual disabilities and personality disorder.

**Indulgent support** is often encountered. It is seen most often in new, enthusiastic but inexperienced services. Staff are kind, caring and hopeful for the individuals they support. However, the approach is overly friendly, avoids confrontation and staff have difficulties saying 'no' to anything. There is an over-emphasis on 'rights' and choice but under-recognition of responsibilities and the limitations on capacity to make choices. As a result, individuals with intellectual disabilities and personality disorder feel uncontained and may engage in risky behaviours. This support style leads to repeated crises or placement breakdown.

**Neglectful support** is seen much less often. This tends to occur in over-stretched, exhausted services. Here staff are too busy and tired to take an interest in the individual and lack the energy to enforce boundaries. They have generally given up hope of anyone improving and have low expectations of individuals. Staff focus on delivering basic care and leave the rest to chance. The lack of care and support may place individuals at risk of harm.

**Authoritarian support** is also rare but sadly can develop in services that are isolated (geographically or socially) from outside scrutiny. Here staff have little interest in the individual and have low expectations of change. The focus becomes controlling the individual's behaviour with an emphasis on punishment and physical restraint. This support style is abusive and traumatises the individuals it is intended to help.

**Authoritative support** is seen in the most effective services. Here staff are very interested in the individuals they support and are sensitive to their individual needs. They are hopeful and have high but realistic expectations for the individuals they support. However, staff also recognise the need for clear and well-enforced boundaries to promote positive behaviour and contain intense emotions and harmful or risky behaviours. This 'authoritative' approach is active, confident and caring but not over-controlling. Individuals with intellectual disabilities and personality disorder do best when the authoritative support style is used. This approach models kind but balanced behaviour. It makes individuals feel wanted, accepted and valued. Individuals are able to build trust because staff are consistent and predictable.

Figure 5.8 can be used to help understand the balance of qualities that an effective service needs. For example, it is necessary to show some flexibility in order to be sensitive to individual needs. Too much flexibility will lead to unclear boundaries and will contribute to an indulgent support style. Too little flexibility will lead to an authoritarian support style.

It can be difficult to maintain an authoritative support style. Often the behaviour of individuals with intellectual disabilities and personality disorder can push staff towards roles which are unhelpful (over-indulgent, over-controlling or neglectful). However, working within an authoritative support style provides a sound basis for addressing the problems that can arise between individuals with intellectual disabilities and personality disorder and staff who support them.

## Promoting professional relationships with staff members

Unhelpful relationships with staff members are so common that it is sensible to arrange support in such a way as to minimise the likelihood of the problems occurring. While strategies can also be put in place after problems have developed, it takes much longer to resolve issues.

### Team support

A helpful approach is to think in terms of 'team support'. This is explained in Box 5.9.

The team approach aims to reduce the intensity of the professional relationships formed and to ensure that trust is built with a number of staff members. In this way, it reduces the risk of over-dependence on one team member and makes the support system more resilient to planned and unplanned staff absences and turn-over.

This approach needs to be carefully managed to protect both the staff members and the individual with intellectual disabilities and personality disorder. It is important that the team understands that staff are protected by law from abuse. They have the right to contact the police if they are being abused by an individual and should be supported to do this if they wish. The team manager needs to ensure that all staff are behaving professionally and to take action if this is not the case. Complaints about staff should always be taken seriously, reported and investigated appropriately; individuals with personality disorder are vulnerable to abuse and sadly sometimes this is done by the people meant to be caring for them. However, the team approach should, in reality, reduce the risk of abuse occurring as the individual is less likely to become angry with any one member of staff and staff are less likely to be overwhelmed by the individual's needs.

---

## Box 5.9: The team support approach

- All staff are trained to understand and recognise the emotional needs of individuals with personality disorder.
- The individual is expected to work with every member of the team (residential services) or a small team of people (community services).
- Rotas/diaries are managed to ensure that the individual works with a range of staff.
- Professional relationships (eg. key-worker or named nurse) and roles are defined in terms of tasks rather than a special relationship.
- There are clear rules for changing key worker/named nurse related to the tasks not the quality of the relationship.
- As a pattern of preferences emerges the team work with this:
  - Preferred staff are allocated to work with the individual when the individual is doing things they do not enjoy
  - Less favoured staff are allocated to the individual's favourite activities. If the individual refuses to work with that member of staff the activity is postponed rather than changing the staff allocated to support the activity
- Where refusal to work with staff is motivated by prejudice, the teamwork to help the individual question their assumptions about people eg. by using Social Stories™ (see Chapter 4).
- The staff team are supported to be open about their (positive and negative) reactions to individuals and to use supervision as a safe place to explore these feelings (see Chapters 13 and 14).
- There is post-incident support that addresses the emotional distress that can be caused when individuals are verbally abusive to staff.
- The quality of staff interactions with individuals is carefully monitored by the team manager. Complaints are investigated to ensure that any genuine reasons for dislike are identified and addressed through supervision and, if necessary, disciplinary procedures and the safeguarding process.

---

# Maintaining professional boundaries

Individuals with intellectual disabilities and personality disorder challenge professional boundaries due to emotional needs and also their lack of understanding of the nature of professional relationships. It is therefore important that the approach taken is both containing and educating. Staff need to have a good understanding of professional boundaries and should be confident to maintain these. Some ideas are given in Box 5.10.

---

### Box 5.10: Maintaining professional boundaries

- Code of conduct in place that addresses specific issues of staff roles
- Clear guidance on confidentiality and sharing of information
- Training given on professional conduct including disclosure of personal information
- Staff encouraged to reflect on own and others' practice
- Supervision addresses professional behaviour
- Where an individual shows a pattern of challenging professional boundaries (eg. trying to date staff, contacting them online), these are addressed in their positive behaviour support plan
- Where an individual has intimate care needs the approach taken is clearly recorded in their care plan
- Where an individual enjoys and derives comfort from physical contact, permissible contacts are clearly described in the care plan and are carefully monitored
- Providing an individual with accessible information on how they can access support out of hours/for crises (see Chapter 12)
- Use Social Stories™ (see Chapter 4) to explain limits of professional relationships
- Support an individual to develop a wider social circle

---

Deciding how much personal information to share with an individual is particularly difficult when working with individuals with intellectual disabilities and personality disorder. If a member of staff does not disclose any personal information to the individual, the individual is likely to distrust them and fail to form a working alliance with that member of staff. The individual may have paranoid thoughts about that member of staff or may fill the gaps with their own ideas, most of which will be inaccurate and unhelpful.

However, individuals may draw staff into sharing too much information. For example, the member of staff might share that they too dislike a member of the team, or that they too have problems with alcohol. Such disclosures are unhelpful for a number of reasons. They are likely to create rows within the team as the individual will not 'respect confidentiality' and will share the information with others. They tell the individual that the member of staff is not to be trusted (if they say this to me, what are they saying about me to other people?). They may also put the individual in the position of feeling they need to support the member of staff. There are no fixed rules on what should be shared but some suggestions are given in Box 5.11.

---

## Box 5.11: Guidelines for self-disclosure by staff

- Never volunteer information.
- Do not share anything you are not happy for the whole world to know/that your colleagues and manager don't already know about you.
- Consider questions carefully before answering and give minimal information eg. Q 'Where were you last week? A 'I was on leave' not 'I went to Spain for a luxury holiday with my boyfriend to celebrate our engagement…'
- It may sometimes be helpful to share successfully resolved personal issues that relate to what an individual is going through eg. 'I used to have a problem with alcohol but going to AA helped me get back on track, I'm sure it a great idea to go'. Discuss this in supervision/with colleagues before sharing.
- Never share on-going personal issues eg. 'Yes, I know how you feel, I just split up with my girlfriend and I can't stop thinking about her…'
- Don't talk specifically about where you go when not at work eg. 'Yes, I love eating out' not 'My favourite restaurant's that Thai restaurant on the London Road'.
- Be confident not to share information that feels uncomfortable. Use assertiveness. Humour may take the sting out of 'rejection' eg. 'I can't answer that, I might get fired!'

---

This balanced approach to self-disclosure should let the individual feel that they know staff and can trust what they say, but not risk crossing boundaries.

## Managing calls on staff time

When looking to manage what feels like excessive demands on staff time, it is important to:

- identify the reason why the individual seeks so much contact with staff
- seek to address these underlying needs
- consider how the process of interactions could be more successfully managed.

If the underlying need is not addressed, the intervention is doomed to failure. However, this process may take some time. While the underlying issues are being explored and addressed it is important that staff support individuals in ways that promote trust and contain their behaviour.

## Addressing underlying need

Some suggestions on how underlying needs might be addressed are given in Box 5.12.

## Box 5.12: Ways to address underlying needs for interaction with staff

**Major life event:** Everyone needs more interaction at stressful times such as moving house or if a family member is ill, look for ways to increase contact until after the crisis has resolved.

**Lack of appropriate activities:** Find out what they enjoy and arrange more activities, build this into a busy daily routine (see Chapter 3).

**Loneliness:** Look for social activities that do not make too great demands on social skills eg. a line dancing class and try to keep the person busy, teach self-soothing skills, work on ability to maintain healthy relationships (Chapter 4).

**Fear of abandonment:** Take time to create a Social Story™ together that reminds the person why staff sometimes have to do other things but have not forgotten them (see Chapter 4). It may help to use a 'comfort object' such as a soft toy, quilt or heavy blanket to reassure the individual when they are alone.

**Feelings of emptiness or not existing:** Use approaches from Chapter 2 to begin to build a positive sense of self. Teach self-soothing (Chapter 3) and distraction techniques (Chapter 6), use 'comfort object', look at a 'memory book' (Chapter 2).

**Intrusive unpleasant thoughts/memories/flashbacks:** Teach distraction, grounding (Chapter 9) and self-soothing techniques. Remind the individual to use these.

**Have not learnt to amuse self:** Find out what they enjoy, do it together, then gradually introduce short periods of doing this alone, slowly increase time alone.

**High need for stimulation/low boredom threshold:** Review activity timetable and adjust the balance of number vs. length of time of activities.

**Reluctance to do things independently:** Build confidence, gradually reduce interaction when doing some things, praise and reward any independent activities.

**Fear that they cannot manage alone/lack of confidence:** (See Chapter 2) Make a prompt card with statements such as *'it's only 10 minutes, I can do this!'*.

**Difficulties self-motivating:** (see Chapter 6)

**Poor memory:** Write information down in a way that the individual can understand eg. prompt cards, timetables, diaries, checklists. Remind them to use these memory aids.

Continued...

Intellectual Disabilities and Personality Disorder: An integrated approach

**Need for reassurance**

■ **Looking forward to an event (impatience):** Use a visual calendar. Cross off days to show progress. Use a whiteboard to write out what is happening, fill the waiting time with other activities – keep the individual busy.

■ **Worrying about a future event:** Find out what they are worrying about and reassure them, consider a Social Story™, schedule something nice to happen straight after the worrying event, use distraction techniques (see Chapter 3).

■ **Worrying about an issue/ruminating about past events:** Be supportive, and reassure the individual. Look for ways to make them less worried. For example, remind them of times when things went well in the past, write a Social Story™, use distraction techniques. Teach mindfulness techniques to distract from ruminations (see Chapter 7), keep them busy.

**Poor sense of time:** Use a kitchen timer (but keep a check on the time too, in case of cheating!).

**Lack of trust:** Use honesty, patience and consistency to build trust, ensure answers to questions are consistent (it is much easier to be consistent when telling the truth). Do not use 'loose' phrases such as 'in a minute' or 'later'. It is much better to say something like *'When I have finished these phone calls, I should be about 10 minutes'*.

**Seeking perfect care:** Use Social Stories™ to explain why staff can't always be there.

**Jealousy and possessiveness:** Build trust, use Social Stories™ to explain emotions, teach distraction and self-soothing techniques (see Chapters 3 and 4).

**Checking/challenging boundaries:** This is sometimes called 'pester power'. Ensure there is good communication and that everyone knows what the rules are (see also section on 'manipulative' behaviour).

# Managing interactions with staff

There are a number of strategies that can help staff to contain interactions with individuals. These include:

■ scheduling interactions

■ ending interactions

■ containing repetitive questioning

■ reinforcing appropriate behaviour.

## Scheduling interactions

It may be helpful to keep a note of how often an individual seeks interaction. Once it has been established how often they currently need interaction, the team can work to gradually extend the time between contacts. Do not make the gap too long. If a person feels they need to speak to someone every five minutes, they are unlikely to be able to wait an hour. However, they might be able to cope for 10 minutes. Individuals are much more likely to cope if they are given something to fill the time. For example, *I'll speak to you after you have made your bed / had a cup of tea / got the washing out of the machine'*. If possible, staff should keep out of sight during this time to reduce temptation. It is essential that staff ensure they are then available at the agreed time.

Scheduling interaction is a particularly helpful technique for individuals who are unable to reduce their need for interaction (perhaps because the behaviours are too long-standing or they lack the cognitive skills needed). Providing clear boundaries and scheduling interaction can ensure that positive relationships are maintained with staff despite the persistence of the demands.

## Ending interactions

Sometimes it can be hard to end interactions; once the individual has someone's attention they will not stop talking. Depending on the nature of the interaction a number of strategies may be helpful. See Box 5.13.

## Managing repeated, insistent questions

Once underlying issues have been addressed, the most effective strategy to managing repeated questions is to set limits on the number of times a question will be answered, and stick to this. Staff should have a consistent response that makes it clear they will not answer the question again and directs the individual to where they can find the information or an activity that can take their mind off the subject.

## Reinforcing appropriate behaviour

Staff also need to ensure that they reward appropriate behaviour. This is often easier said than done in a busy setting. For example, having made a commitment to talk to someone after finishing a job it is easy for a member of staff to forget or be distracted by another person who is being more demanding. If anything occurs that stops the staff member from keeping their word (and hence rewarding the individual for coping for a short period of time) the individual is likely to revert to inappropriate behaviour to ensure staff do interact with them. Such experiences also confirm the individual's belief that they have been 'fobbed off', that staff are untrustworthy and will forget them unless constantly pestered.

It is also important for staff to remember that an individual learns both from how staff react to them and also their observations of how staff react to other individuals. If a staff team is not thoughtful about which behaviours it responds to it may find that individuals all 'catch' each other's inappropriate behaviours.

---

### Box 5.13: Strategies for ending interactions in a timely manner

■ Schedule the next interaction at the beginning of the conversation/appointment so the individual knows they will see staff again eg. *'I know you have lots to talk to me about, let's book another date now in case we can't do it all today/I'm very busy now, we may need to talk again after supper'.*

■ Structure the interaction:

■ State how long the interaction can be eg. *'I've got 10 minutes/this appointment is for one hour.'*

■ Make an agenda/tick list of items to discuss

■ Use the agenda to keep on track eg. tick items off or say *'we haven't talked about X.'*

■ If the individual brings up a new point, write this on a new list for next time rather than extending a session.

■ Give the individual a 'five-minute warning' that the conversation is going to end.

■ End on time, saying clearly *'We need to stop now, I have to do X. We can talk about the other things next time we meet'.*

■ Remind the individual of something pleasant they can do now the interaction has finished.

■ Use assertiveness approaches eg. 'scratched record technique' (Chapter 15) if the individual tries to extend the session.

■ Praise the individual when they co-operate.

---

## Overdependence

The term 'overdependence' is used here to refer to individuals who seem to seek more support with activities of daily living than appears necessary. However, working out the difference between dependence and overdependence can be very difficult when supporting individuals with intellectual disabilities and personality disorder. Individuals may need help with daily tasks for a number of reasons that may be related to their learning experiences, their intellectual impairment, their personality disorder or emotional needs. There is considerable overlap between the factors that lead to individuals seeking a high frequency of interaction with staff and those leading to 'overdependence'. Some of these reasons are given in Box 5.14.

---

## Box 5.14: Possible reasons for dependence

- Have not had the opportunity to learn the skill
- Do not understand the need to carry out the task
- Lack intellectual skills to complete the task eg. memory, organisation
- Lack the physical skills to complete the task eg. poor fine motor control
- Lack the confidence to carry out the skill alone
- Have not learnt to do the skill alone
- Low motivation
- Poor self-control
- Low mood
- Dislike the task and prefer if others do it for them
- Difficulties coping alone
- Need for high levels of interaction
- Find being 'nagged' reinforcing

---

It is important to untangle these underlying needs and establish how much help each individual needs. If the individual is not given sufficient help they may become disheartened and important needs will go unmet. However, if an individual is given more help than they really need this is a waste of scarce resources. It is also harmful to the individual in the long term, as they will lose confidence in their abilities and may even lose the skills through lack of practice.

Where an individual with intellectual disabilities and personality disorder appears to have a skill but does not use it, this is often attributed to 'laziness'. However, there is often an underlying emotional reason for their reluctance to engage in the task independently. Where an individual uses overdependence to meet emotional needs it is important to address these emotional needs rather than simply withdrawing the support. Without the emotional support that they are gaining from caring interactions around everyday tasks, the individual may have to resort to more extreme behaviours to manage this need.

Sometimes such emotional needs can be excluded and it becomes clear that the individual just wants other people to do the task for them. However, this should not be judged harshly. Rather it should be understood as just human nature; most people who dislike a task would rather someone else did it for them. In this situation the focus should be on building their motivation and developing insight into how their behaviour makes other people feel. Social Stories™ may be helpful with this (see Chapter 4).

Once the factors influencing an individual's need for support becomes clear it is possible to arrange support in a way that maximises their independence. Some tips for getting this right are given in Box 5.15.

---

### Box 5.15: Maximising independence

- Do things with someone and not for them, gradually shift the balance so that they do more and staff do less
- Focus on the positive – praise any small improvements
- Never nag – every reminder is:
  - a social interaction, which can be reinforcing
  - a potential knock to a person's self-esteem, which reduces motivation.
- Reward independence with interaction eg. *'when you've cleaned your room we can have coffee together'*
- Adjust support when someone's mood state changes
- Explore other ways of meeting the person's need to feel cared for eg. peer support groups, pampering sessions (nails, hair etc)
- Use Social Stories™ to explain why certain things need to be done
- Teach self-soothing strategies (see Chapter 3)

---

# Behaviours that make staff feel 'manipulated'

Individuals with intellectual disabilities and personality disorder are often described as being 'manipulative'. An extensive but not comprehensive list of such behaviours is given earlier in this chapter. Sometimes these behaviours are carried out calmly in a way that can give the impression that the individual is calculating. At other times the individual may appear to be overly emotional, as if they are putting on an act.

## Emotional reactions to feeling 'manipulated'

These behaviours can seriously damage the relationship between an individual and the staff supporting them. People in general dislike feeling that they have been manipulated and staff are no exception to this. Being on the receiving end of such behaviours can trigger strong emotional reactions in staff. Some of these are given in Box 5.16.

> ## Box 5.16: Possible emotional reactions to feeling manipulated
>
> - Feeling used and taken in
> - Feeling tricked into doing something that they would not have otherwise done
> - Feeling that their sympathy and kindness have been exploited
> - Feeling powerless and controlled
> - Feeling embarrassed and humiliated when the full situation becomes clear
> - Feeling angry with the individual
> - Rejecting the individual
> - Reluctance/refusal to work with the individual
> - Wanting to punish the individual
> - Wanting to control the individual and ensure they do not 'get their own way'
> - Fearful that they may lose their job or their good reputation

When staff believe an individual behaves in these ways to 'manipulate' staff they show less empathy and treat the individual less well than if they think the behaviours are due to another cause such as depression. If not managed appropriately, the urge to punish and control individuals can easily lead to abusive treatment.

## Motivations for 'manipulative' behaviours

To maintain positive relationships with individuals showing such behaviours it is important to understand both the individual's unconscious motivations and the process by which they may have learnt to behave in these ways. Some possible motivations are given in Box 5.17.

Individuals with intellectual disabilities and personality disorder have experienced very difficult lives. Consequently, they have developed behaviours that meet their needs in situations where the usual, acceptable approaches do not work. To cope with overwhelming needs they have learnt to do whatever helps them get through, without considering the impact on other people's feelings. Therefore it can be much more helpful to think of these behaviours as 'survival strategies'.

## Box 5.17: Motivations and reasons for 'manipulative' behaviour

- Do not know other ways of getting needs met
- Staff have not responded to more appropriate requests for help
- Individual experiences their need as intense and overwhelming
- Individual is unable to tolerate uncertainty
- Individual is unable to bear waiting
- Individual is experiencing mood-related recall from memory and has forgotten the times that they have been helped in the past/parts of the situation that do not fit with their mood (see Chapter 3)
- Individual's thinking about the situation is distorted (see Chapter 5)
- Individual feels controlled, powerless and not listened to, so seeks ways to challenge this and gain a sense of being in control
- Individual is testing boundaries to see if staff care enough to contain and protect them
- Individual has learnt that these behaviours get things they want to happen eg. for a staff member to be moved

If the individual is viewed as struggling to survive in the only way they know, it is much easier to respond to these behaviours in a calm and caring way. Thinking of these behaviours in this way also recognises that the individual will continue to behave in such ways until they have learnt new ways of meeting their needs. Once this calm and positive mindset is established, most of these behaviours are relatively straightforward to manage. Some suggestions are given in Box 5.18.

It is important to talk to the individual about what is being done, how the team will meet their needs and to negotiate some aspects of the guidance with them. Ironically, if this is not done sensitively, the process may make the individual feel powerless, controlled and manipulated by staff. This in turn will lead to an intensification of the behaviours the staff team was trying to reduce.

> ## Box 5.18: Strategies for managing survival behaviours (manipulation)
>
> - Identify underlying need and address that need
> - Use guidelines and contracts:
>   - Involve the individual in writing the guidelines
>   - Make sure these are clear and written down
>   - Make sure everyone knows what is in the guidelines
>   - Follow the guidelines
>   - Have a clear process for updating guidelines and letting everyone know about the changes
> - Maintain a questioning approach and check the evidence eg. Individual: *'X said I can … '* Staff: *'Did they?...I'll just check if the guidelines have been changed … I'm really sorry, that's not in the guidelines … I can't do it today but I'll check and get the guidelines updated if things have changed.'*
> - Check things out with other people, preferably including the individual. Take a neutral stance eg. *'Can we have a chat about X? Things seem to have got a bit muddled, I just want to get it straight.'*
> - Do not give in to 'pester power'

## Unfounded allegations of abuse

Some individuals unfortunately learn that unfounded allegations of abuse against staff are an effective way of getting rid of them. This is very worrying for staff and presents problems for managers as staff may need to be moved or suspended from duty during investigations. Despite these worries, **all allegations of abuse must be reported**. This is the case even if the team is confident that an allegation is unfounded; for example, the staff member accused was on holiday at the time of the alleged incident. It is important to remember that, however many unfounded allegations an individual has made, they are still vulnerable to abuse and their concerns must be investigated to keep them safe. Where an individual makes repeated unfounded allegations it is possible to work with the safeguarding process to find ways of managing this. It is important that this process does not result in guidelines being relaxed or other changes that might reinforce the behaviour. Where individuals repeatedly make unfounded allegations it may be helpful to use Social Stories™ to explain the impact of their behaviour on staff and the possible consequences for them (for example, staff not being able to spend time alone with them; legal action). Staffing may need to be organised so that staff are protected, including staff never interacting with the individual alone.

All of the above actions fit comfortably within the authoritative support style. If an approach appears not to be working it is important to revisit the issue of underlying needs to ensure these are being met. It is also important to review any interventions to ensure that they have the correct balance of sensitivity to, and interest in, the individual, clarity and enforcement of boundaries and appropriate expectations of the individual. It is easy to slide towards indulgent or authoritarian support without realising what is happening.

# Key learning points

■ Professional relationships and personal relationships are superficially similar but in reality differ on every dimension. These differences are essential to protect both the individual and the staff member.

■ Individuals with intellectual disabilities and personality disorder are likely to have wide-ranging difficulties in their relationships with the staff supporting them. They will challenge professional boundaries in ways that can make staff feel used and manipulated.

■ It is important to understand that individuals have developed these 'survival strategies' to meet their needs in situations where the usual, acceptable approaches did not work. To cope with overwhelming needs they have learnt to do whatever helps them get through, without considering the impact on other people's feelings.

■ To address these issues it is important that staff have a good understanding of the difference between professional and personal relationships and have the confidence to enforce professional boundaries.

■ As individual staff members are easily overwhelmed by the needs and demands of individuals, a team approach to support is essential.

■ The team needs to work in an 'authoritativo' style. This style provides the high expectations, clear and enforced boundaries, high sensitivity to needs and interest in the individual that are necessary for positive relationships to develop and be maintained.

# References

Cameron R & Maginn C (2009) *Achieving Positive Outcomes for Children in Care*. London: Sage.

# Further reading

Bell L (2005) *Managing Intense Emotions and Overcoming Self-destructive Habits: A self-help manual*. Hove: Routledge.

College of Registered Nurses of British Columbia (2006) *Nurse-Client Relationships*. Vancouver: CRNBC. Available at: https://www.crnbc.ca/Standards/Lists/StandardResources/406NurseClientRelationships.pdf (accessed April 2014).

Job G (2007) Handouts for 'creating and maintaining professional relationships and boundaries between staff and service users. Available at: www.cawt.com/Site/11/Documents/Publications/Disability/POVA/BehavingProfessionally.pdf (accessed April 2014).

Potter N (2006) What is manipulative behaviour, anyway? *Journal of Personality Disorders* **20** (2) 139–156.

# Chapter 6: Difficulties with self-control and impulsivity

This chapter explores impulses, impulsive behaviour, impulse control and impulsivity. It explores how having intellectual disabilities and personality disorder may affect the ability to control impulses and the problems this may cause individuals. It looks at the issues facing staff in supporting individuals who behave impulsively and approaches that may help to address these difficulties.

## Key topics

- Impulses and impulsive behaviour

- Impulse control

- Influences on impulse control

- Importance of impulse control

- Development of impulse control

- Impulsivity

- The right to behave in unwise ways

- Impulsivity and impulse control in individuals with personality disorder

- Impulsivity and impulse control in individuals with intellectual disabilities

- Impulsivity and impulse control in individuals with intellectual disabilities and personality disorder

- Assessment and identifying causes

- Managing impulsive behaviour

- Promoting the development of independent impulse control

# Impulses and impulsive behaviour

Impulses are sudden thoughts that urge immediate action. Impulses often come from basic drives. These might include the need for food, comfort, safety, affection, possessions, amusement and sexual gratification. They may also be in response to strong emotions, particularly anger. Impulsive actions are not thought through or planned; rather they focus on the immediate satisfaction of the urge without consideration of later consequences. It has been proposed that impulsive behaviours stimulate a pathway in the brain that is involved in creating feelings of intense pleasure.

Everyone acts on impulse at times; acting on impulse brings fun and excitement to life. However, life would get become totally chaotic if this were the only way people behaved.

# Impulse control

Impulse control is part of a group of abilities called 'executive functions'. These abilities help people behave in organised and purposeful ways. Impulse control can be understood as a process of choosing to behave in a particular way rather than simply reacting to a situation. This ability has been given a variety of other names including self-control, self-regulation, will power and delayed gratification. Impulse control is a complex process with a number of components. Some of these are listed in Box 6.1.

---

### Box 6.1: Components of impulse control

- Inhibiting action long enough to think about how best to respond
- Managing sensations caused by the underlying urge eg. hunger, anger
- Resisting temptation of intense pleasure from immediate action
- Thinking through the possible consequences of various actions:
  - Recalling what has happened in the past (memory)
  - Thinking what might happen in the future (a sense of time)
  - Linking causes to consequences that may not be immediate
  - 'Mentalising' or 'mind reading' how others might react to the behaviour
- Weighing up the various options and making a plan for how they will satisfy or manage the underlying impulse
- Paying attention, concentrating and staying focused long enough to consider all these issues
- Having the motivation to stop the impulsive behaviour
- Being positive, believing that controlling the impulse will achieve the more positive outcome imagined

---

# Influences on impulse control

The ability to control impulses is also influenced by a number of factors relating to the situation, how that situation is interpreted and the state of the person experiencing the temptation. Some of these factors are given in Box 6.2.

---

### Box 6.2: Factors that influence impulse control

- Presence/absence of tempting sights, sounds or smells
- Deprivation/satiation eg. being hungry vs. having just eaten
- Physical state eg. being tired/ill vs. well rested/healthy
- Mental state eg. being sad or angry vs. a positive mood
- Using/abstaining from disinhibiting substances eg. drugs or alcohol
- Social/peer pressure vs. social/peer support
- The perception of how likely it is that the behaviour will be punished
- Attitudes and values that condone/condemn the action

---

For example, the likelihood of someone speeding might be increased by driving a sports car, having had an alcoholic drink, seeing a clear straight road without a speed camera, having encouragement from a passenger and believing that speed limits are overly restrictive.

# Importance of impulse control

The ability to control impulses is important for a number of reasons. Impulse control allows the inhibition of behaviours that are not compatible with long-term goals, for example, resisting the temptation of an expensive holiday when saving for a deposit on a house. It is also important in maintaining relationships It means that people do not always say what first comes to mind; avoiding comments that might antagonise, shock or hurt other people. It can also help inhibit behaviours that would be damaging to intimate relationships, for example, a married person saying 'no' to an invitation from an attractive co-worker. Impulse control can also help to keep people safe and healthy. This might be through resisting the highly enjoyable but short-term 'fix' of a cigarette because of concerns about the long-term risks to health. Impulse control can also protect people from engaging in risky behaviour such as gambling away savings or having unprotected sex with strangers.

Impulse control also helps people comply with the rules of society. This ranges from obeying rules of polite behaviour such as not pushing to the front of a queue, to resisting the urge to commit serious crimes, such as murder.

# Development of impulse control

The ability to control impulses begins to develop in early childhood but is not complete until early adulthood. Impulse control develops as an interaction between the social world and the developing brain. Many parts of the brain are needed for these skills to develop successfully including the limbic system and the frontal lobes. The frontal lobes do not finish developing until early adulthood, hence the late age for the full development of self-control.

Interactions with parents are important in the development of impulse control. Initially parents need to control the child's impulsive behaviour. For example, grabbing a child to stop them running in front of a car, putting the lid on the biscuit tin or stopping a child from pulling the cat's tail. However, as the child grows, parents need to give the child increasing freedom in which to exercise self-control. This is a balancing act; too much parental control and the child will not have the opportunity to practice these skills, too little parental control and the child will not understand that it is necessary to control impulses (and might come to serious harm).

Parents also need to help the child learn how to manage the emotional distress caused by resisting an impulse. Again, initially the parent will comfort the child, often by giving cuddles and then offering fun distractions. Gradually the child needs to be supported to manage their reactions alone. If parents continue to jump in at the first sign of distress the child never needs to learn to manage their own feelings. If parents never offer comfort the child does not learn that such feelings can be managed at all.

Parents also provide examples of how to respond to temptations. If parents have a healthy balance between indulging harmless, fun impulses and resisting more harmful ones, children will see first-hand how such situations may be managed.

However, not all children react to situations in the same way. Some are naturally more impulsive while others are naturally more cautious. There seems to be a genetic basis for these differences. These differences in temperament interact with parenting style to create a range of response patterns to impulses, from over-controlled to highly impulsive.

# Impulsivity

By adulthood people develop a characteristic approach to situations where self-control might be required. For this reason some approaches to personality theory suggest that impulsivity is part of a personality trait called 'novelty seeking'. People scoring highly on this trait seek thrills and are impulsive, extravagant and disorganised. This 'novelty seeking' has also been associated with developing addictions.

Impulsivity may be understood as a tendency to react rapidly in an unplanned way without considering the negative consequences of the action. This may take a number of forms (see Box 6.3).

---

### Box 6.3: Forms of impulsivity

■ Positive urgency – the tendency to behave impulsively while in a positive mood.

■ Negative urgency – the tendency to behave impulsively while in a negative mood.

■ Lack of premeditation – the inability to anticipate the likely consequences of an action.

■ Lack of perseverance – the inability to see a task through to the end.

■ Sensation seeking – being attracted to risky behaviours.

■ Low boredom threshold – rapidly becoming bored, short attention span.

---

Impulsive people often seem unable to learn from experience. They will persist with risky behaviours despite these having resulted in negative consequences on previous occasions.

Previously self-controlled people may also become impulsive as the result of accident or injury. Traumatic brain injury, neurodegenerative diseases, infections such as meningitis and chemical poisoning can all lead to impulsive behaviour.

# The right to behave in unwise ways

Many impulsive acts may be considered unwise by more cautious people. However, adults have the right to behave unwisely if they choose; the law assumes that adults have the mental capacity to make such choices for themselves.

## The Mental Capacity Act (2005)

Mental capacity is the ability to make decisions and to act autonomously. All adults are assumed to have capacity unless it can be established that they lack capacity. The Mental Capacity Act (2005) was developed to address situations in which adults may lack the capacity to make some decisions. A person may be found to lack capacity to make a decision if they have 'an impairment or disturbance' that affects the way their mind or brain works and that the impairment or disturbance means that they are unable to make a specific decision at a specific time. Where an adult lacks capacity, those supporting them have a duty of care to make that decision for the adult on the basis of what would be in the adult's best interests. (For more information, see Further reading.)

# Impulsivity and impulse control in individuals with personality disorder

Individuals with personality disorder often behave impulsively and issues related to impulsivity comprise a number of key diagnostic criteria for personality disorder (see Box 6.4).

---

## Box 6.4: Impulsivity and personality disorder

**Antisocial personality disorder**
- Highly irresponsible behaviour with disregard for social norms, rules and obligations
- Very low tolerance for frustration
- Very low threshold for aggressive and violent behaviour
- Not learning from negative experiences
- Not taking responsibility for actions; blaming others or rationalising

**Borderline personality disorder**
- Argumentative especially when impulsive acts are criticised or thwarted
- Frequently acting without thinking about the consequences
- Frequent and uncontrolled outbursts of anger or violence
- Difficulty maintaining any action that does not offer immediate reward

**Histrionic personality disorder**
- Continually seeking excitement or seeking to be the centre of attention
- Inappropriate seductiveness in appearance or behaviour

---

Many individuals with personality disorder have chaotic lifestyles. They come across as irresponsible, impatient and acting for the moment. They may engage in behaviours that place themselves or others at risk and may bring them into trouble with the law. Individuals with personality disorder are also vulnerable to developing problems related to impulse control. Some of the most frequent difficulties arising from impulsivity and poor impulse control are given in Box 6.5.

## Box 6.5: Impulsive behaviours that can be problematic for individuals with personality disorder

- Drug and alcohol misuse
  - Binge drinking, heavy regular drinking
  - Illegal drug use
  - Misuse of prescription medication
  - Misuse of over-the-counter medication
- Sexual relationships
  - Unprotected sex
  - Sex with strangers
  - Being unable to say no
- Financial problems
  - Overspending, impulse spending, 'shopaholic' behaviour
  - Taking out loans, multiple credit cards
- Gambling
- Shoplifting
- Binge eating, poorly controlled eating leading to obesity
- Reckless driving
- Inappropriate behaviour in public

# Causes

As with many other characteristics of personality disorder the difficulties with impulsivity and impulse control seem to arise as a result of the interaction between biological and social factors. Individuals appear to inherit a biological tendency to behave impulsively. This may be reflected in structural or functional differences in the parts of the brain that control behaviour and manage emotions.

Individuals with personality disorder have often grown up in families where adults are unable to provide positive role models or support their children's development. Hence they have often grown up without experience of healthy restraint from adults; they will have been under or overcontrolled. They may also have witnessed adults behaving without restraint, for example, witnessing frequent episodes of drunken or drug-induced behaviour. This means that they do not learn healthy and effective ways to control impulses.

Most individuals with personality disorder can control impulses to some extent. However, Elliott and Smith (2009) vividly describe the ability of individuals with personality disorder to control impulses as being like having a golf-cart braking system on a five-tonne truck. There are a number of factors that make it harder for individuals with personality disorder to control impulses and change their impulsive behaviours. Some of these are described in Box 6.6.

---

### Box 6.6: Factors that make it hard for individuals with personality disorder to control impulses

- **Intense emotions:** They often experience intense emotions and may frequently become distressed. Such feelings make it much harder to control impulses.

- **Past experiences of abuse:** Intrusive memories and flashbacks to past abuse can lead to impulsive behaviours in an effort to blot out these highly distressing experiences.

- **Distorted thinking:** This can act both to increase the likelihood of behaving impulsively and to make it harder to change damaging patterns of impulsive behaviour once these are established. Individuals will often minimise the potential negative outcomes of their behaviour. For example, *'It won't happen to me'* or *'Doctors exaggerate the effects to scare people'*. They may also rationalise taking risks by thoughts such as *'What the heck, all my family die young, I might as well have fun while I can'*. (See Chapter 7)

- **Staff reactions:** Often other people try to protect the individual by pointing out the dangers of behaviour or by trying to prevent them from engaging in certain activities. This is likely to be misconceived by the individual as efforts to control them. They may persist with, or even intensify, behaviours as a way of asserting that others cannot control them, regardless of the costs to their well-being.

- **Peer group:** Individuals often associate with other people who engage in risky behaviours. This can make such behaviours appear more acceptable because others are frequently seen engaging in them. It also increases temptation and creates peer pressure to join in.

---

# Impulsivity and impulse control in individuals with intellectual disabilities

## Impulsivity

Having an intellectual disability does not necessarily mean that an individual will behave impulsively. Research suggests that about one in seven individuals with intellectual disabilities will have difficulties with hyperactive behaviour or impulsivity (Bradley & Isaacs 2006, Burbridge *et al*, 2010). However, the frequency of impulsivity is higher in individuals with some specific syndromes associated with having an intellectual disability. For example, as many as one in two individuals with disorders on the autistic spectrum will have difficulties with inattention, hyperactivity or impulsivity (Bradley & Isaacs, 2006). Higher rates of impulsivity are also found in conditions such as foetal alcohol syndrome (Mukherjee *et al*, 2006), Smith-Magenis syndrome (Martin *et al*, 2006) Fragile X syndrome and William's syndrome (Ozonoff & Jensen, 1999; Martens *et al*, 2008). Individuals with intellectual disabilities who show impulsivity are more likely to self-injure or be aggressive (Burbridge *et al*, 2010).

## Impulse control

Having an intellectual disability can make impulse control more difficult for a number of reasons. Impaired intellectual ability makes it more difficult for individuals to think abstractly; it is harder to problem solve and to link actions with delayed consequences. Individuals may also have difficulties with sequencing and planning, which can make it more difficult to turn alternative solutions into action. Individuals with intellectual disabilities also often have difficulties with understanding time concepts. This can make it difficult for them to think beyond the moment and hence to work towards some future goal. Finally, individuals with intellectual disabilities often have a reduced sense of self-efficacy as a result of multiple experiences of failure. This can make it difficult for them to believe that they might be able to control and change their behaviour and hence they may not even try to do this.

As a result of these difficulties, many individuals with intellectual disabilities who behave impulsively may be dependent on others to help them behave in ways that are not a danger to themselves or others. Overall, the more severe the individual's intellectual disabilities, the more likely they are to be unable to manage impulses independently.

## Impulsivity and impulse control in individuals with intellectual disabilities and personality disorder

Individuals with intellectual disabilities and personality disorder are likely to be highly impulsive and to have great difficulty with impulse control. The problems that they are likely to encounter are the same types of difficulties that are seen in more able individuals with personality disorder. However, the way in which the impulsivity is shown is shaped by the severity of their intellectual disabilities and also by their different lifestyles. For example, individuals with more severe intellectual disabilities are less likely to have access to illegal drugs but may have issues arising from addiction to nicotine. There is also likely to be a greater occurrence of minor inappropriate social behaviours such as impulsive comments or touching. Some of the most frequent problem areas are given in Box 6.7.

---

## Box 6.7: Problems arising from impulsivity in individuals with intellectual disabilities and personality disorder

- Low threshold for verbal and physical aggression
- Lack of motivation/interest in everyday activities (boredom)
- Losing interest/not seeing things through
- Acting only for immediate rewards
- Not thinking about long-term consequences of behaviour
- Financial problems eg. running up large debts, 'shopaholic' behaviour
- Risky behaviours eg. running into the road
- Inappropriate behaviours eg. sexual comments to attractive strangers, exposing self
- Substance misuse and addictions eg. alcohol, cigarettes, gambling, sex phone lines
- Risky sexual behaviours

---

These difficulties are likely to arise from the combined effects of their intellectual disabilities and personality disorder. This makes understanding and intervening with their difficulties much more complex than if they only had one or the other condition.

## Causes

An individual's impulsivity may have its origin in the combination of genetic vulnerability and upbringing that is thought to cause personality disorders. However, impulsivity may also arise from the factors that caused the individual's intellectual disabilities. Impulsivity that arises from intellectual disabilities or later brain damage tends to be more truly random and erratic than that arising purely from personality disorder. Impulsivity related to personality disorder is more patterned ie. an individual may respond with different levels of impulsivity in different situations. These patterns emerge as a result of the impulsivity being influenced by both internal and external factors.

Understanding that impulsivity may have different causes in individuals with intellectual disabilities and personality disorder is important as it has implications for intervention. Each individual will present with a unique pattern of impulsive behaviour, influenced by their brain structure, function and chemistry and their experiences and learning opportunities. Difficulties arising from having intellectual disabilities are very difficult to treat and may be considered to be 'hard-wired'. Instead they need to be understood and managed. In contrast, difficulties arising from personality disorder may sometimes be changed through therapeutic approaches.

## Mental capacity

Like all other adults, individuals with intellectual disabilities and personality disorder should be assumed to have the capacity to choose to act in impulsive ways unless it has been established that they lack capacity at any particular time. However, as a result of their intellectual disabilities and the presence of additional mental health problems, it is highly likely that at times individuals may lack the capacity to choose to engage in impulsive behaviours. Trying to understand whether or not an individual with intellectual disabilities and personality disorder has capacity adds another layer of complexity to supporting their impulsive behaviour.

## Impact on the staff team

Supporting individuals with intellectual disabilities and personality disorder who show impulsive behaviours can be very distressing and frustrating for staff. Staff may find some behaviours conflict with their own moral code and may find it hard not to be judgmental. Other behaviours can create fears for the safety of the individual, those they live with or the staff supporting them. Such fears can push staff to behave in controlling ways. Conversely, anxiety about protecting individual choice and not infringing the individual's human rights may leave staff feeling unable to take action.

It is important that staff are supported to address such emotional reactions and explore the impact they may have on their work with such individuals. This might be done through the supervision process (see Chapter 14). As with many of the other challenges presented by individuals with intellectual disabilities and personality disorder, staff will only be able to help them successfully if they are able to approach the problems individuals experience in a balanced and thoughtful manner.

# Managing impulsive behaviour

Managing impulsive behaviour can be a complex process and it is important that it is approached with the correct priorities. These are:

- risk management
- authoritative support style
- identifying the causes and functions of impulsive behaviours
- selecting and implementing appropriate practical strategies.

Only once these have been achieved should staff begin to explore whether the individual can be helped to change their behaviour.

# Risk management

A systematic approach to risk assessment and management is essential when trying to manage impulsive behaviours. The aim should be for the individual to be as safe as reasonably possible before work begins on helping them to manage or change their behaviour. This is not always easy, as, where an individual has the capacity to make decisions, the law allows them to make 'unwise' choices. To ensure that they are acting within the law, staff may need to seek help with assessing whether the individual has the capacity to make any given choice. This is because the same course of action could be lawful and respectful where an individual has capacity, but constitute neglect where capacity is lacking. In extreme situations, where the individual's behaviour is a danger to themselves or others, it may be necessary to consider the use of the Mental Health Act (2007) (see Chapter 12).

Making sound decisions in this area is difficult. It requires a good understanding of the law including the Mental Capacity Act (2005), Deprivation of Liberty Safeguards (DOLS) and the concept of 'duty of care'. A full exploration of these issues is beyond the scope of this book. The analysis of the issues and the systematic approach to risk assessment and management suggested by Carol Sellars (2011) may be helpful.

# Using the authoritative support style

When trying to support individuals who show impulsive behaviours it is important that a team approach is taken. The authoritative support style explained in Chapter 5 is very helpful in providing a framework for balancing concern for the individual with the need for clear boundaries.

## Boundaries

Staff need to work together to provide clear, consistent boundaries for the individual showing impulsive behaviour. These boundaries need to be sensitive to individual need and be enforced in an atmosphere of support for the individual, with high expectations that change is possible.

Boundaries are most helpful when they are explicit and transparent. This is best achieved by putting them on paper in a form that the individual can read. They should be drawn up in collaboration with the individual and there should be room for the individual to negotiate if they feel the boundaries are overly restrictive (see Chapter 3).

The security given by the authoritative support style will create an environment in which it is possible to begin understanding the causes of the impulsive behaviour and possible approaches to reducing its impact on the individual and those supporting them.

# Identifying the causes and functions of impulsive behaviour

Staff frequently make the assumption that an individual with intellectual disabilities and personality disorder could control their impulsive behaviour if they wanted to. Such beliefs can be damaging to the relationship between staff and the individual. They can also mean that the team does not explore how difficult it is for the individual to control impulses.

## Ability to control impulses

Understanding the extent to which an individual's impulsive behaviour arises from their intellectual disabilities is important when planning interventions. Trying to teach someone something they cannot learn is very distressing for all involved. It is likely to damage the individual's self-esteem and this may, in turn, increase their urge to behave in impulsive ways.

A helpful approach can be to look at the steps involved in impulse control and common factors that influence the ability to control impulses and identify which present problems for the individual. Some questions that may be helpful in this process are given in Box 6.8.

---

## Box 6.8: Assessing the ability to control impulses

Does the individual also have a condition that is known to influence impulse control? (eg. Fragile X, Smith-Magenis syndrome)

Does the individual have a mental health problem that might influence impulse control? (eg. bipolar affective disorder)

Can the individual:

- Inhibit action long enough to think about how best to respond?
- Manage sensations caused by the underlying urge eg. hunger, anger?
- Resist temptation of intense pleasure from immediate action?
- Think through the possible consequences of various actions?
    - Recall what has happened in the past (memory)?
    - Think what might happen in the future (a sense of time)?
    - Link causes to consequences that may not be immediate (logical thinking)?
    - 'Mentalise' how others might react to their behaviour?
- Weigh up the various options and make a plan for how they will satisfy or manage the underlying impulse?
- Pay attention, concentrate and stay focused long enough to consider all these issues?

Is the individual motivated to stop the impulsive behaviour or does it perform important functions for them?

Does the individual:

- Believe that controlling the impulse will achieve a more positive outcome?
- Believe that there will be no negative consequences for behaving this way?
- Hold attitudes and values that support the impulsive behaviour?
- Have distorted thinking that supports the impulsive behaviour?
- Take disinhibiting substances? eg. drugs or alcohol
- Mix with other people who also engage in the risky behaviour?

Does the behaviour occur more often when the individual is:

- In the presence of tempting sights, sounds or smells?
- In a state of deprivation? eg. being hungry, thirsty, tired, bored or lonely
- Experiencing intense emotions? eg. anger, sadness, distress, jealousy

---

For each difficulty identified, it may be helpful to think *'Is this hard-wired or soft-wired?' 'Can it be changed or does it need to be managed?'* Sometimes, assessment of impulse control will highlight that the individual has difficulties with the cognitive processes that underpin impulse control, for example, inhibition, memory, awareness of time or self-monitoring. If this is the case it can be helpful to arrange a comprehensive assessment of the individual's intellectual abilities including executive functioning and understanding of time concepts. The assessment will highlight the individual's intellectual strengths and weaknesses. Once these are understood it will be much easier to select approaches that will be helpful for the individual.

For other individuals the assessment may suggest that they have some ability to control impulses but appear not to be using these abilities. In these situations, the impulsive behaviour may be fulfilling important functions for the individual. This can make the behaviour very difficult to give up. Hence, it is also important to take time to think about why the individual might be engaging in the impulsive behaviour. A number of possible reasons are given in Box 6.9.

---

### Box 6.9: Needs and emotions that may increase the frequency of impulsive behaviours

- Social interaction
  - To feel close
  - To feel wanted/to get in with a crowd
  - To have someone's time and attention
- Pleasure
  - For excitement
  - To get a fix or feel high
- Escape
  - To relieve tension
  - As a focus to avoid thinking about other problems
  - To block out painful memories/flashbacks
  - To avoid feeling empty
- Emotional release
  - To punish self
  - To get rid of something bad inside (particularly vomiting/purging)
- To defy others (particularly to feel that they are making their own decisions)
- A combination of these – with different functions at different times

---

It is also helpful to look at when and where impulsive behaviours occur. Is it when the individual is alone, out with friends or after a row with their family? Is it when they are hungry, tired or stressed? Exploring these issues can sometimes identify situations where small changes to an individual's routine can make a huge difference to controlling impulses. It may be helpful to use the 'formulation' approach discussed in Chapter 10 to bring all this information together to give a coherent picture of the individual's difficulties and to highlight where intervention might be most effective. Box 6.10 gives an example of an assessment of impulsive behaviour.

---

### Box 6.10: Example assessment of impulsive behaviour while shopping

**Impulsive behaviours**

- Overspending – on clothes, jewellery and makeup
- Pushing to the front of queues
- Shouting, verbal abuse and physical assaults if encouraged to spend more wisely

**Results of assessment of impulse control and impulsivity**

**The individual:**

- has mild intellectual disabilities and borderline personality disorder but no other condition associated with poor impulse control
- does not currently have a mental health problem that might influence impulse control
- is unable to resist buying items (only stops when runs out of money)
- has difficulty controlling their anger in other situations
- appears unaware of the impact of their behaviour on others or the possible consequences of their behaviour
- seems unaware of the link between shoppers' anger at them and their pushing to the front of the queue
- is unable to tell the time and has difficulty waiting for other things eg. they get impatient waiting for meals
- has a short attention span and finds it difficult to distract themselves
- is not motivated to change the behaviour
- is concerned that staff have expressed the view that if this continues they will no longer be able to support the individual to go shopping
- believes that queuing is for 'losers' and that *'it's OK to jump the queue because I'm special'*; they comment that *'staff are always trying to stop me having fun'*
- does not use drugs or alcohol.

**The behaviours:**

- seem to perform functions for the individual including getting a 'buzz' out of buying items, escaping from or avoiding the boredom of queuing

Continued...

---

■ become more pronounced the more shops are visited and the longer the trip continues for

■ are worse when the individual is worried, stressed or jealous of others

■ are modelled by the individual's mother, who describes herself as a 'shopaholic' and is skilled at using her mild physical disability to jump queues.

**Formulation (see Chapter 10)**

The individual has some 'hard-wired' issues with impulse control eg. short attention span and difficulty with time concepts. These have been exacerbated by their learning history, their belief that their behaviours are acceptable and their lack of awareness of the potential negative consequences of their behaviour. The behaviours are also maintained by the physical buzz and escaping from an unpleasant situation. While the individual is not motivated to change their behaviour they are concerned that staff may stop supporting them on shopping trips.

(Practical strategies for managing this behaviour are given in the next section.)

# Practical strategies for controlling impulses

Once there is some understanding of the factors underlying difficulties with impulse control it is much easier to support the individual to control their impulsive behaviour.

Practical strategies for helping individuals control impulses include:

■ addressing the underlying need

■ managing temptation

■ managing 'trigger' activities

■ providing immediate rewards

■ structuring the environment

■ use of medication.

Using Elliot and Smith's (2009) analogy, these actions are the equivalent of reducing the weight of the truck rather than increasing the power of the braking system.

Each individual will need a unique combination of the practical strategies suggested below, depending on the factors identified in the assessment of their impulsive behaviour. These can then be drawn together into a positive behavioural support plan (see Chapter 10). The positive behaviour support plan might include ensuring that basic needs are met regularly (for example, food, drink, sleep, exercise and social interaction), providing a full timetable of enjoyable but not tempting activities, actively avoiding trigger situations, and a range of distractions for when temptation cannot be avoided. It is important to involve the individual as much as possible in the process of selecting the strategies and creating the plan to avoid creating a sense that staff are trying to control them.

# Addressing underlying needs

These strategies aim to reduce the intensity of the need to behave impulsively. Box 6.11 contains examples of such strategies.

---

## Box 6.11: Strategies for addressing the needs underlying impulsive behaviour

**Basic needs**

These strategies aim to make sure the underlying need is met regularly so that the urge does not become too intense. For example:

- Hunger
  - Having a small snack before going to a tempting setting eg. free buffet so not so hungry
  - Having a healthy eating plan with small meals and regular snacks and small treats
- Attention
  - Scheduling regular social activities, phone calls, text messages etc
- To feel needed
  - Work for a local charity, help care for animals
- To feel part of a group
  - Join groups working for a local cause, take up a group activity
- For excitement
  - Try to find a legal, safer activity that meets the same need eg. attending/ being involved in stock car racing rather than 'joy riding'

**Intense emotions**

(See Chapters 3, 9 and 11)

- Sharing – talking to others about concerns
- Relaxing diversions
- Self-soothing
- Accepting – learning not to be afraid of bad memories

Continued...

---

---

**Self-punishment**

■ Build self-esteem (see Chapter 2)

■ Address distorted core beliefs about self (see Chapter 7)

■ Alternative self-punishment strategies: activities that are unpleasant in the short-term but helpful in the long term eg.

   ■ Unpleasant chores – clean the toilet/oven

   ■ Intense physical activities – sit-ups, press-ups

---

# Managing temptations

Where it is not possible to reduce or remove the impulse it may be helpful to minimise the temptation that the individual experiences. This may be done directly by removing temptation or indirectly by distracting the individual's attention from the temptation. Some suggestions for doing this are given in Box 6.12.

---

## Box 6.12: Strategies for managing temptations

**Managing temptations**

■ Removing temptation eg.

   ■ Put things out of sight

   ■ Don't have temptation in the house

   ■ Have a pay-as-you-go-phone to limit calls

   ■ Choosing routes that avoid tempting places

   ■ Choosing time of day to avoid temptation eg. shop is shut

   ■ 'Jam jar' bank account so money not easily available

■ Adding distractions (see also Chapter 7) eg.

   ■ Playing music through headphones

   ■ Posters or photos that create positive thoughts/mood

■ Structure time to reduce opportunities eg. following an activity timetable

■ Change the scene eg.

   ■ Go out for a walk

   ■ Visit a friend

   ■ Go to the cinema

---

It can be more difficult to manage temptation if the impulsive behaviour is linked to being in the company of certain people. In this situation it is usually counterproductive to try to separate the individual from their 'friends'. Instead they need to be supported to develop a wider social network and take up different activities so that they spend less time with the 'bad influences'. It may be helpful to look in more depth at their ability to form relationships (Chapter 4). It is also important to build-up their self-esteem because when people feel better about themselves they will often choose friends who are more supportive of them (see Chapter 2). Where 'friendships' are seriously damaging it may be necessary to use safeguarding procedures (see Chapter 15).

## Managing trigger activities

Frequently, the activities that trigger impulsive behaviour cannot be avoided. Where this is the case the activity needs to be carefully planned with the individual. Staff need to clearly identify the problem behaviours and explore the issues of capacity, duty of care and risk. A problem-solving approach can then be used to work out how the activity can best be managed. The solution is likely to involve careful planning, some form of explicit contract for the activity and other activities to practice the correct behaviour.

Box 6.13 gives suggestions of how impulsive behaviour while shopping might be managed. This is based on the example assessment given in Box 6.10.

## Providing immediate rewards

Where individuals have great difficulty in making connections between immediate actions and delayed benefits it can be helpful to use a reward system (sometimes called a 'token programme'). In this approach a 'token' (money, sticker, counter, button in a jar) is given immediately after the desired action. Once a number of tokens have been collected they can be exchanged for an agreed treat. The token provides immediate, tangible evidence of success and helps to bridge the delay until the final reward is given.

However, such systems have a number of difficulties and need careful thought and planning. They can be difficult to apply consistently. Staff often resent using what is frequently called 'bribery'. These systems can easily become punitive as there is a great temptation to take away tokens for 'bad' behaviour. Individuals can become frustrated with the system and will often tear up stickers or throw out tokens during an angry outburst. These programmes can also raise difficult ethical issues about what an individual is entitled to by right and what has to be earned. Where it looks as if such an approach may be helpful it may be appropriate to discuss this with the service's ethics committee.

> ## Box 6.13: Example way of managing the impulsive behaviour while shopping described in Box 6.10
>
> Behaviours
> - Overspending
> - Pushing to the front of queues
> - Shouting, verbal abuse and physical assaults if encouraged to spend more wisely
>
> Issues
> - Capacity to make unwise decisions
> - Staff duty of care
> - Risks such as retaliation from public, getting in trouble with police, impact of debts
>
> Possible solution
> - Explain why behaviour is unacceptable and how people should behave when shopping (might need Social Story™ – see Chapter 4)
> - Agree contract that staff will support shopping trips if there is agreement to:
>   - a budget for shopping
>   - decide which shops to visit and what to buy before setting off
>   - to buy only the items on the shopping list
>   - be polite to staff when they remind individual to follow the list
>   - wait their turn in the queue.
> - Make accessible version of the contract
> - Before each trip read the contract and make a shopping list
> - Take only sufficient money for the list and leave cash card at home
> - Shop at quiet times when there are shorter queues
> - Identify distractions to help while waiting in queues eg. talk about favourite topic, game on mobile phone
> - Praise individual when trips go well
> - Use Social Stories™, role play or social skills group to practice new behaviours in a safe situation

## Environmental change

Thought should also be given to making changes to the environment. For example, if an individual is driven to eat all the food in the kitchen, stopping them from doing this may require frequent use of restrictive physical interventions. However, if the food cupboard and the fridge have secure locks the person may stop fighting to get in the kitchen. Locking things should never be undertaken lightly; there needs to be full discussion. The decision needs to be recorded in writing and should be reviewed regularly. Again, discussion with the local ethics committee might be helpful. In extreme situations actions may need to be taken that might be considered to deprive the individual of their liberty. Such actions should always be carefully considered. Where the individual lacks capacity this can be addressed by using the Deprivation of Liberty Safeguards (DOLS) process (see Further reading).

## Using medication

There is some limited evidence that medication may help some individuals with intellectual disabilities and personality disorder to control impulses. Medication may also be useful if impulsivity is linked to attention deficits (eg. if the individual also has a diagnosis of attention deficit hyperactivity disorder – ADHD). It is also possible that medication may be helpful where impulsive behaviour is linked to periods of emotional distress. The advantages and disadvantages of using medication discussed in Chapter 3 apply equally when considering using medication to help with impulse control. Medication should always be combined with other practical interventions; it is unlikely to be effective if used alone.

# Promoting the development of independent impulse control

For individuals who do not have significant intellectual deficits, the next step is to look at ways to help them develop better impulse control. It is important not to omit any of the earlier stages (risk assessment, authoritative support and practical strategies for managing impulses) as these will create a safe situation in which skills can be developed. It is particularly important to address underlying needs as this will greatly reduce the intensity of the impulses the individual is trying to manage. Returning to Elliot and Smith's (2009) analogy, having lightened the load on the truck as much as possible, it is now time to think about improving the brakes.

Approaches to promoting independent impulse control have a number of elements:

■ adapting the support framework

■ increasing motivation

■ changing behaviour

■ specialist therapeutic interventions.

# Adapting the support framework

Staff need to adapt the support given to the individual to allow them to test out new skills, to celebrate success and to manage failure. The approaches given below will help create a safe and supportive environment in which to take controlled risks.

## Positive risk taking

The risk management process described earlier in this chapter aimed to keep the individual as safe as possible while their impulsive behaviour was assessed. Once it has been agreed that the team are going to work with the individual on improving their impulse control, the risk management plan needs to be reviewed. It is not possible for the individual to practice new skills without taking some risks. For example, after working with an individual on issues relating to their spending patterns the individual might be supported to test this by shopping alone. The team must be willing to take positive risks and to see failure as a learning opportunity, not a disaster. It is totally unrealistic to expect that the individual will never give into temptation. Using a structured approach to risk assessment and management will ensure that risks are minimised during this process. For example, on the first shopping trip alone the individual might take twice the amount of money needed for their shopping list but leave their cash card at home.

## Managing lapses

As part of the positive risk taking process, the team should explore how they will respond to the inevitable lapses. It is very important that lapses are not punished; if individuals are anxious about how staff will react to their impulsive behaviour they will be reluctant to talk about it and may try to hide lapses from staff. This is counterproductive and greatly increases risk.

Each time the individual engages in the impulsive behaviour this should be viewed as a chance to learn. In a calm and non-judgemental way staff can explore why the person was not able to resist on this occasion. Box 6.14 shows how this might be done using the example of managing spending and behaviour during a shopping trip.

The team should use the information gathered to improve the support they are giving the individual and to update risk management strategies.

## Support

Whichever of the following approaches are used, it can be difficult for individuals to implement strategies on their own. Wherever possible, staff should try to work with the individual to practice using the skills. This could include role playing situations in which the skills might be needed; this builds up new patterns of responding at times when the urge is not overpowering. Staff might accompany the person to a challenging situation so that they can gently remind the individual to use the agreed strategies. For the shopping example, staff might (with the individual's agreement) shadow the individual on a trip, only stepping in if it looks like they need support to resist temptation. For some problems it may be possible to join a support group such as Alcoholics Anonymous or Gamblers Anonymous. For those who use computers there is a lot of support available online. However, it is important to work with the individual to find appropriate sites as internet sites are not regulated and may have content or contacts that will make the problem worse.

---

### Box 6.14: Example of reviewing lapses (see example assessment 6.10 and strategy 6.11–6.13)

- **Reassurance:** *It's OK, we knew it would be hard to resist the temptation to buy extra stuff, I'm not angry, don't be too tough on yourself!*
- **Help individual to see what went right:** *But you did great queuing to pay for it!*
- **Remind them of past successes:** *You've come so far, look how well you have been doing.*
- **Remind them of the goal they are working towards:** *We need to stick to this so that you can save for that dream holiday in Spain.*
- **Check they are willing to talk now:** *Is this a good time to think about what happened?*
- **Ask about the situation, their thoughts, feelings, what strategies they used and if these worked:** *Did something upset you? What went through your mind? How were you feeling? Did you use your distraction techniques?*
- **Explore what they might do differently next time:** *Do you think it would help if you had a card with a picture of Spain in your wallet? Would it be better to stay out of the chemists until you're more confident out alone? What do you think might have helped you?*

---

## Adjusting boundaries

As the individual progresses, staff can revise rules and expectations to reflect progress. This has a number of benefits. It makes it clear to the individual that they have made progress and that staff trust them to behave appropriately. This avoids the understandable resentment created by restrictions that are felt to be no longer necessary. It also ensures that they have opportunities to practise their new self-control skills. This can be done by regularly reviewing risk assessments and updating guidelines.

## Increasing motivation

Frequently, individuals with intellectual disabilities and personality disorder appear not to want to change their impulsive behaviour. If this seems to be the case, it may be helpful to explore where they are in the cycle of change (see Chapter 12). This may show that the individual does not see that they have a problem, holds very different views of the problem from staff or does not see the benefits of change. Where this is the case, the individual needs to be encouraged to think about the impact of their impulsive behaviour in a way that is not judgemental, damaging to their self-esteem or frightening. If the approach is judgemental or critical, it will be self-defeating. The individual's emotional reaction (for example, fear, shame or guilt) will increase the strength of the impulse and make them respond to staff as enemies rather than allies.

## Motivational interviewing

An approach called 'motivational interviewing' can be helpful in this situation. Motivational interviewing is a person-centred, collaborative approach that aims to strengthen an individual's motivation for and commitment to change. This approach recognises that the individual may have a very different view of what they want from life, how they see the 'problem' behaviour and what they want to do about it from the staff trying to help them change their behaviour. This can make the individual feel staff are trying to control them rather than trying to help them and leads to resistance. To address this, motivational interviewing aims to help the individual identify their own goals, to define the problem for themselves and to find their own solutions. The process of motivational interviewing is given in more detail in Box 6.15.

Using this approach staff need to work with the individual to identify their wishes and aims. They can then explore what gets in the way of achieving those aims and how these difficulties might be overcome. In this way staff and the individual can be on the same side; trying to achieve the individual's own goal by overcoming the negative consequences of the impulsive behaviour.

---

## Box 6.15: Motivational interviewing

- **Express empathy**: *'It must be very hard for you…'*, *'It sounds like…'*
- **Help self-reflection**: Open questions *'How do you feel?'*, *'What do you think about that?'*
- **Explore goals**: *'What do you want to do? 'How do you want to feel?'*
- **Develop discrepancy between 'Now' and goals**: *'What would need to change for that to happen? 'Is there anything about (behaviour) that bothers you?' 'What's the worst that could happen if you carried on ….?'*
- **Elicit motivation**: *'What concerns do you have?'*
- **'Roll with resistance'**: Don't confront, don't challenge, avoid arguments, de-escalate, dance together, don't wrestle. *'So it sounds like (behaviour) is a good thing to do?' 'So maybe it's OK if you never change/stop (behaviour)?'*
- **Invite exploration of new points of view**: *'What about…? 'What if…?*
- **Reflect ambivalence**: *'On the one hand you … on the other you…'*
- **Can do approach**: Support individual's belief that they can change *'What could work for you if you decide to change?' 'When have you succeeded in doing something you wanted to achieve?'*
- **Cost-benefit analysis**: Listing the pros and cons of the behaviours (see example below)

---

It is also important to explore the positive side of the impulsive behaviour as this will often explain why the individual finds the behaviour so difficult to control. Box 6.16 gives an example of the consequences an individual might identify for continuing or stopping smoking.

Some of the issues identified might surprise staff supporting the individual; it certainly makes clear why this particular individual would find it very hard to give up smoking. However, by making explicit what the individual really thinks and feels, this process also creates opportunities. Staff can work creatively with the individual to find other ways of meeting the positive consequences of the problem behaviour and to enhance the perceived benefits of change. For the example given above, actions such as teaching strategies for managing anger and anxiety, building self-esteem, exploring nicotine substitutes (such as patches or gum) and a full health check might help shift the balance in favour of giving up smoking. Once the balance has shifted in favour of giving up the problem behaviour, these discussions can be turned into a booklet or poster that the individual can use to motivate themselves when they are feeling discouraged.

Intellectual Disabilities and Personality Disorder: An integrated approach
© Pavilion Publishing and Media Ltd and its licensors 2014.

## Box 6.16: Example cost benefit analysis of smoking

Should I continue smoking?

| SMOKING | GIVE UP SMOKING |
|---|---|
| I enjoy smoking, it makes me feel great | Smoking is expensive – I will be able to afford the new clothes I want |
| I look cool and tough when I smoke | I will be left out when my friends smoke |
| I feel terrible when I want a cigarette and don't have one | Smoking makes me cough |
| Smoking helps me calm down when I am angry | I have been told that smoking is damaging my heart and lungs (but I can't feel anything wrong with them!) |
| Smoking helps me concentrate | I will live longer |
| Smoking helps when I am worried about things | My friends will laugh at me |
| | I might hit people when I am angry |
| | I will worry more |
| | I will be left out when my friends smoke |
| | I feel terrible when I want a cigarette and don't have one |

Some other strategies for increasing the motivation to change are given in Box 6.17.

## Box 6.17: Change strategies

**Increasing awareness** eg. through information, education, and personal feedback

Awareness of negative feelings; becoming aware of feeling fear, anxiety or worry arising from unhealthy behaviour

**Inspiration and hope:** Learning how others have changed their behaviour

**Changing self-image:** Realising that healthy behaviour is an important part of who they are and want to be

**Self-belief:** Building belief in their ability to change and making commitments and recommitments to act on that belief

Continued...

**Exploring impact on others:** Realising how their unhealthy behaviour affects others and how they could have more positive effects by changing. Where individuals appear unaware of the impact of their behaviour on other people, it may be helpful to use the approaches to improve mentalising skills such as Social Stories™ (see Chapter 4)

**Helping relationships:** Finding people who are supportive of their change

**Social impact:** Realising that society is more supportive of the healthy behaviour

**Swapping actions:** Substituting unhealthy ways of acting and thinking for healthy ways

**Reinforcement management:** Increasing the rewards that come from positive behaviour and reducing those that come from negative behaviour

**Stimulus control:** Using reminders and cues that encourage healthy behaviour as substitutes for those that encourage the unhealthy behaviour.

Adapted from Prochaska *et al* (1994)

# Changing behaviour

Once an individual has decided they want to try to change their behaviour a number of approaches can be helpful.

## Relationship between urges and behaviour

It can be helpful to explore with them the relationship between urges, feelings and actions. Many individuals do not realise that urges and emotions are not a good basis for action – most people don't do things just because they feel like it. The approaches suggested in Chapter 3 may be helpful in developing a more thought through approach.

## Relationship between thoughts and behaviour

For some individuals, distorted thinking seems to play a significant role in their impulsive behaviour. If this is the case it may be helpful to explore this more fully, taking the approaches given in Chapter 7.

## Practical actions

There are a number of practical things an individual can do at the point of feeling an impulse that can help them avoid behaving impulsively. Some examples are given in Box 6.18.

These actions work in a number of different ways. Some interrupt the sequence of behaviour for long enough for the individual to remember they are trying to stop behaving in that way. Others channel and disperse the build-up of physical tension and energy that often accompany impulsive behaviour. Others satisfy the urge to act but direct it in a way that is not harmful for the individual. Individuals should be supported to try a number of these approaches and to practice using them at times when they are not experiencing an impulse. They are likely to struggle at first to remember to use the strategies, or they may not be able to implement them successfully. The approaches suggested in Chapter 2 for setting goals and evaluating progress may be very helpful in encouraging individuals to persist in their efforts to use new approaches.

---

### Box 6.18: Practical actions for controlling impulsive behaviour

- Make time to think
  - Take three deep breaths
  - Count to 10
- Interrupt the physical sequence of the behaviour
  - Put hand over mouth (eg. to stop impulsive comments)
  - Clasp hands (eg. to stop self-harm or hitting others)
  - Put hands in pockets (eg. to stop smoking)
- Take physical exercise
  - Walk
  - Jog
  - Swim
  - Dance
- Do something different
  - Jump up and down on the spot
  - Tear up cardboard
- Do something incompatible with the behaviour
  - Rub body lotion into the body part that would have been harmed
  - Post money into a piggybank
  - Suck on a cigarette replacement

---

Box 6.19 gives an example of some of the approaches that might be used to help the individual described earlier in this chapter to manage their behaviour and spending on a shopping trip.

## Box 6.19: Example strategies for changing impulsive behaviour while shopping (see also Boxes 6.10, 6.13 and 6.14)

**Behaviours**

- Overspending
- Pushing to the front of queues
- Shouting, verbal abuse and physical assaults if encouraged to spend more wisely

**Current situation:** Behaviours are now under control when supported by staff on strict programme of short shopping trips following a list with a limited amount of money and no cash card. Individual has saved £200 towards their dream holiday.

**Goal:** Individual wishes to shop alone.

**Goal setting:** Individual works with staff to create ladder with 20 steps from current situation – shopping with two members of staff in local shops, to shopping alone in big, out of town shopping complex.

**Working on emotions:** Individual works with staff to understand more about anger and jealousy, what they are, the causes and how to manage these feelings.

**Working on self-esteem:** Individual works with staff to build a sense of worth that is not dependent on owning the latest clothes and lipstick.

**Working on thoughts:** Individual works with staff to explore their ideas about being 'special' and outside rules that apply to other people, exploring ideas of fairness and how others might feel when they push in queues or shout.

**Awareness of consequences:** Explore with staff what might happen eg. police called, not enough money for holiday.

**Social support:** Identify friends who support them in their new behaviour, avoid shopping with mum (go out for a meal instead). Send an encouraging text message to them while they are out shopping eg. 'U can do it!'

**Passing time in queues:** Setting up a fun game on mobile phone to pass the time.

**Resisting impulses:** Go out of the shop, walk round for five minutes, go back if really need to buy item. Saying 'Spain' 10 times to self before putting an item in the basket that is not on the list. Keeping card with picture of Spain in wallet over cash card so see it before getting money out.

**Rewarding appropriate behaviour:** Make time to listen to how things went, praise their behaviour. Create a money thermometer poster for wall showing how much they need to save for Spain, after each trip colour in red the amount they have saved.

## Specialist therapeutic interventions

Some individuals may have complex problems arising from issues with impulse control such as serious drug or alcohol misuse, other addictive behaviours or eating disorders. In these situations it is important to support them to seek specialist help for these difficulties. Specialist services can be accessed through the individual's GP or psychiatrist.

# Key learning points

- Impulses are sudden thoughts that urge immediate action and often come from basic drives. Impulsive actions focus on the immediate satisfaction of the urge without consideration of later consequences.

- Impulse control is part of a group of abilities called 'executive functions' that help people behave in organised and purposeful ways. Impulse control is the process of choosing to behave in a particular way rather than simply reacting to a situation.

- Impulsivity describes the tendency to react rapidly in an unplanned way without considering the negative consequences of the action across a wide range of situations. Impulsive people will persist with risky behaviours despite these having resulted in negative consequences on previous occasions.

- Impulsivity is influenced by both biological and social factors.

- Difficulties with impulse control are common in individuals with personality disorder.

- The picture is more complex where the individual has intellectual disabilities as a number of conditions that cause intellectual disabilities also influence the ability to control impulses. It is therefore important not to make assumptions about the causes of impulsivity and the ability to control impulses; instead these should be carefully assessed.

- When trying to manage an individual's impulsive behaviour, staff need to work closely together to manage risks and create a safe environment with clear boundaries.

- Staff members may also need the space to explore their emotional reactions to behaviours that they find upsetting.

- Once the individual is safe, their impulse control and the functions of their impulsive behaviours can be assessed. This information can then be used to address the underlying needs and to develop a positive behaviour support plan.

- For individuals with the potential to improve their impulse control, work can then begin on increasing motivation and developing skills.

- For individuals with complex problems such as addictive behaviour it may be necessary to support them in seeking specialist help.

# References

Bradley E & Isaacs B (2006) Inattention, hyperactivity, and impulsivity in teenagers with intellectual disabilities, with and without autism. *Canadian Journal of Psychiatry* **51** (9) 598–606.

Burbridge C, Oliver C, Moss J, Arron K, Berg K, Furniss F, Hill L, Trusler K & Woodcock K (2010) The association between repetitive behaviours, impulsivity and hyperactivity in people with intellectual disability. *Journal of Intellectual Disability Research* **54** (12) 1078–92.

Elliott C & Smith L (2009) *Borderline Personality Disorder for Dummies*. Indianapolis, Indiana: Wiley. (Chapter 20: Considering medication for BPD.)

Martens M, Wilson S & Reutens D (2008) Research review: Williams syndrome: a critical review of the cognitive, behavioural and neuroanatomical phenotype. *Journal of Child Psychology and Psychiatry* **49** (6) 576–608.

Martin S, Wolters P & Smith A (2006) Adaptive and maladaptive behaviour in children with Smith-Magenis Syndrome. *Journal of Autism and Developmental Disorders* **36** (4) 541–552.

Mukherjee R, Hollins S & Turk J (2006) Fetal alcohol spectrum disorder: an overview. *Journal of the Royal Society of Medicine* **99** (6) 298–302.

Ozonoff S & Jensen J (1999) Brief report: specific executive function profiles in three neurodevelopmental disorders. *Journal of Autism and Developmental Disorders* **29** (2) 171–177.

Prochaska JO, Norcross JC & DiClemente CC (1994) *Changing for Good*. New York: Avon Books.

Sellars C (2011) *Risk Assessment in People with Intellectual Disabilities* (2nd edition). Chichester: BPS Blackwell.

# Further reading

Barber B (Ed) (2002) *Intrusive Parenting: How psychological control affects children and adolescents*. Washington, DC: American Psychological Association Press.

Baumrind D (1991) The influence of parenting style on adolescent competence and substance use. *Journal of Early Adolescence* **11** (1) 56–95.

Fox N & Calkins S (2003) The development of self-control of emotion: intrinsic and extrinsic influences. *Motivation and Emotion* **27** (1) March 7–26.

Gilger J & Kaplan B (2001) Atypical brain development: a conceptual framework for understanding developmental learning disabilities. *Developmental Neuropsychology* **20** (2) 465–481.

Judd P (2012) Neurocognitive deficits in borderline personality disorder: implications for treatment. *Psychodynamic Psychiatry* **40** (1) 91–110.

Kazdin A (2001) *Behavior Modification in Applied Settings* (6th edition). Belmont, CA: Wadsworth.

Mencap (2000 /2002) *Am I Making Myself Clear? Mencap's guidance for accessible writing.* Available at: http://www.easy-read-online.co.uk/media/10609/making-myself-clear.pdf (accessed April 2014).

Rollnich S, Miller W & Butler C (2008) *Motivational Interviewing in Health Care: Helping patients change behavior.* New York: Guildford press.

Rowe J, Lavender A & Turk V (2006) Cognitive executive function in Down's syndrome. *British Journal of Clinical Psychology* **45** 5–17.

Van der Molen M, Huizinga M, Huizenga H, Ridderinkhof, Van der Molen W, Hamel B, Curfs L & Ramakers G (2010) Profiling Fragile X syndrome in males: strengths and weaknesses in cognitive abilities. *Research in Developmental Disabilities* **31** 426–439.

Walley R & Donaldson M (2005) An investigation of executive function abilities in adults with Prader-Willi syndrome. *Journal of Intellectual Disability Research* **49** 613–625.

Whiteside S & Lynam D (2001). The Five Factor Model and impulsivity: using a structural model of personality to understand impulsivity. *Personality and Individual Difference* **30** 669–689.

Woodcock K, Oliver C & Humphreys G (2009) Task switching deficits and repetitive behaviour in genetic neurodevelopmental disorders. *Cognitive Neuropsychology* **9** 172–194.

# Chapter 7: Unhelpful core beliefs and distorted thinking

This chapter looks at what thoughts and core beliefs are and how they influence and are influenced by emotions and behaviour. It explores thinking styles and thinking errors. It looks at the way individuals with intellectual disabilities and personality disorder may think, the problems that can be caused by distorted thinking and how these might be addressed.

## Key topics

- Thoughts
- Core beliefs
- Attribution style
- Thinking patterns
- The relationship between core beliefs, thoughts, emotions and behaviour
- Thoughts and individuals with personality disorder
- Thoughts and individuals with intellectual disabilities
- Thoughts and individuals with intellectual disabilities and personality disorder
- Problems related to unhelpful thinking
- Supporting individuals with unhelpful thinking

## Thoughts

Thoughts comprise ideas, beliefs and images that make up people's mental picture of themselves, other people, the world, the past and the future. They are the means by which people understand their experiences, solve problems and make decisions about how to act. At times people are very aware of the thinking process. For example, when struggling to learn something new and difficult. However, much of the time thinking is automatic and people rarely question why they viewed a situation as they did or chose to act in a certain way.

# Core beliefs

'Automatic thinking' is the result of the way the brain organises and uses information. Experiences, knowledge and assumptions are organised into core beliefs or 'schemata' about particular aspects of the world. People hold core beliefs about:

- themselves (such as, I am kind, I am a failure)
- relationships (such as, people are kind, people are untrustworthy)
- the world (such as, the world is safe, the world is an unhappy place)
- the future (such as, things will get better, nothing will work out).

Core beliefs may be positive and optimistic or negative and pessimistic. These core beliefs provide shortcuts for interpreting events and making decisions about how to behave in any particular situation. They effectively provide a guide to, and help us make sense of, the world. Core beliefs are the summation of a person's experience. Consequently, people rarely question the validity of their world view.

## Development

Core beliefs are built up during childhood and are shaped by major life-events. Chapter 2 explored how these experiences shape core beliefs about the self (self-image and self-esteem). In a similar way, experiences shape a person's view of other people, the world and the future. A person's core beliefs may be positive or negative; the more difficult someone's life has been, the more likely they are to hold negative beliefs. These beliefs are helpful when they accurately reflect the world the person lives in. For example, growing up in a war zone might create the core belief that the world is a dangerous place. This belief is helpful all the time that the war continues but once peace is achieved it might cause the person to be unnecessarily anxious, cautious and mistrustful.

## Stability and self-perpetuation

Core beliefs are very stable and tend not to change even when there is evidence that they are no longer accurate or helpful. This is the result of how core beliefs develop; they make sense in the context of the person's life experiences and hence are unlikely to be questioned. It is also the result of the way core beliefs act as filters for interpreting and responding to information. People are more likely to notice things that fit with their core beliefs and disregard contradictory information. Where a contradiction is noticed it will tend to be interpreted as the exception to the rule rather than evidence that the rule is wrong. In this way core beliefs can skew or distort reality.

Core beliefs can also lead people to act and react in ways that make their expectations come true. This can work in a number of ways. Core beliefs lead to the creation of rules for living, for example, *the world is a dangerous place so I must be on my guard and trust no one*. If the belief is faulty, the rules based on it can lead the person to make choices or take actions that are unhelpful or even damaging.

People may be drawn to other people or situations that conform to their core beliefs. They may also make faulty assumptions about other people's motives or thoughts and respond as if these were true. Finally, people may also behave towards others in ways that are likely to provoke the behaviour they expect. This can become a vicious circle; the reaction will be seen as proof that the core belief is true rather than a natural human reaction to the provoking behaviour. In these ways, core beliefs may undermine a person's efforts to lead a happy and successful life.

## Activating core beliefs

Core beliefs, especially negative ones, can lie dormant most of the time and only become activated when a crucial situation triggers them. This is thought to be one of the mechanisms that lead to people developing mental health problems such as depression. For example, if a relationship breaks down this may trigger the person's core belief that they are unlovable; despairing of finding another partner, they may fall into depression.

# Attribution style

Attribution, or explanatory, style refers to the way people explain things that happen in their lives. This is an important aspect of thinking as it influences factors such as how much responsibility a person takes for their behaviour, their beliefs about whether they can change and whether they take an optimistic or pessimistic view of the future. Any event may be appraised on three important dimensions: stability, specificity and locus (location) of control. These dimensions are explored more fully in Box 7.1.

---

### Box 7.1: Dimensions for appraising events

- Stability
  - Is the event seen as stable or unstable?
  - Will it change over time?
  - *'I always mess this up'* vs. *'I learn from my mistakes'*.
- Specificity
  - Is the event thought to impact on the whole of a person's life or only a small part of it?
  - *'I can't get anything right'* vs. *'I'm useless at …'*.
- Locus of control
  - Is the cause of the event viewed as internal or external to the person?
  - *'My hard work paid off'* vs. *'That was an easy test'*.
  - *'Wonder what I did to upset them?* vs. *'They're out to get me'*

---

These dimensions may combine to create optimistic or pessimistic explanatory styles. People with a pessimistic attribution style tend to blame themselves for negative events, believe that such events will continue and that they will affect all aspects of their life. In contrast, people with an optimistic attribution style tend to blame others for negative events, believe that such events will be short-lived and that they will not impact on many aspects of their lives.

The locus of control dimension appears to be related to control of behaviour and responsibility. Those who believe that they are able to influence events (internal locus of control) are more likely to exhibit control of their behaviour, take responsibility for their actions and may be more motivated to try to change their behaviour. As with core beliefs, people are rarely aware of their attribution style; it is so automatic that they are likely to think that this is just the way the world is.

## Thinking patterns

In addition to the effect of core beliefs and attribution style, people's interpretation of and reaction to situations are also influenced by their patterns of thinking. In particular there are a number of unhelpful ways of thinking that can distort reality. For example, people may exaggerate, jump to conclusions or take things personally. More examples of common thinking errors are given in Box 7.2.

## Box 7.2: Thinking errors

**Black and white thinking:** Also called 'all-or-nothing' thinking and 'splitting'. This allows no shades of grey or degrees. Something is good or bad, right or wrong, a total success or utter failure. A person is either a hero or a villain.

**Catastrophising:** Magnifies the likely negative outcomes of situations, *'It will be a total disaster'*, *'I'll never find another lover if he leaves'*.

**Exaggerating/over-generalising:** One instance is treated as if it is always the case. For example:

One person is rude = *'people ALWAYS treat me badly'*.
Girlfriend fails to reply to one text = *'she NEVER calls me back'*.
One person ignores you = *'NO ONE EVER listens to me'*.

**Jumping to conclusions:** Making assumptions about other people's thoughts and motives without any evidence. *'He did that to wind me up'*, *'There's no point getting up, it's going to be a bad day'*.

**Taking things personally:** Assuming general comments are aimed specifically at the person or taking the blame for things that had nothing to do with the person. *'It's my fault, if I had stayed at home it wouldn't have happened'*.

**Focus on the negative/discounting the positive:** If something nice is said or happens it is not noticed or invalidated in some way. If something negative occurs it is noticed and remembered. For example:

*'She's just saying that to make me feel better, she doesn't mean it'*.

**Fixed rules:** This way of thinking has rigid rules and harsh judgement for breaking them. These thoughts create feelings of failure, disappointment and guilt. *'I SHOULD be happy*, *'I OUGHT to be better by now'*, *'I MUST survive on my own'*, *'I CAN'T be the first one to call back'*

**Emotional reasoning:** Being blind to the difference between fact and feeling. *'I feel …(angry / upset /empty) so I must …(hit them/cut myself/get drunk)*. (This way of thinking can increase impulsive behaviour)

Everyone thinks in these ways at times, particularly when very stressed or distressed. However, when a person routinely thinks in these distorted ways it can contribute to a range of difficulties in everyday life and may also lead to mental health problems.

# The relationship between core beliefs, thoughts, emotions and behaviour

The relationship between emotions, thoughts, physical reactions and behaviour was discussed briefly in Chapter 3. One way of thinking about the complex interaction between these different components is shown in Figure 7.3. This diagram is based on one created by Padesky (1986) called 'the five aspects of your experience' (Beck *et al*, 1995). It is used a lot in cognitive behaviour therapy (CBT) and is affectionately referred to as the 'hot cross bun' because of the pattern it makes.

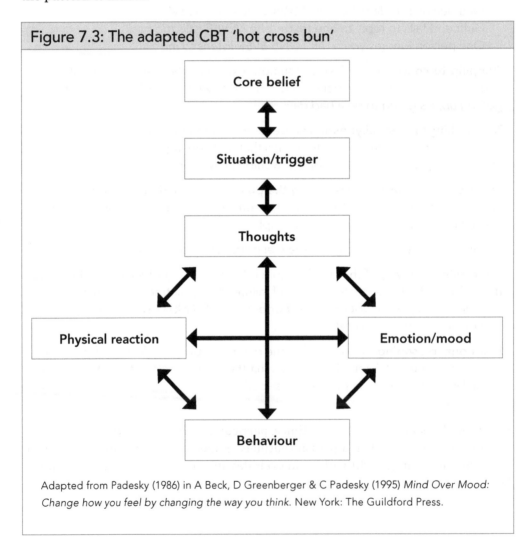

**Figure 7.3: The adapted CBT 'hot cross bun'**

Adapted from Padesky (1986) in A Beck, D Greenberger & C Padesky (1995) *Mind Over Mood: Change how you feel by changing the way you think.* New York: The Guildford Press.

The role of thoughts in this complex system is often the most difficult to identify. This is because of the way that thinking becomes automatic; people are often unaware of their thoughts. It is also the result of the way that core beliefs and thinking errors shape interpretation of events creating the impression that there is no other way of interpreting the situation. Also, as mentioned above, thoughts often shape behaviour in a way that is self-fulfilling and this creates the impression that the thought was correct.

In reality, the way a situation is interpreted can lead to completely different emotional reactions and behaviours. Box 7.4 gives an example of how holding different core beliefs can lead to completely different responses to the same situation.

## Box 7.4: Example of the influence of core beliefs and thoughts on behaviour

| Core beliefs: | I am likeable<br>People are trustworthy | I am not likeable<br>People cannot be trusted |
|---|---|---|
| Trigger situation: Friend cancels an outing saying she has a hospital appointment | | |
| Thoughts: | 'Poor X, I hope she's OK. She must be worried. I'll make sure I give her time to talk next time we get together.' | 'What a lame excuse, I always thought she didn't like me. I bet she found someone more fun to go out with.' |
| Emotion: | Calm, but a bit worried | Upset, sad, rejected or angry |
| Behaviour: | Sends friend a cheerful text suggesting coffee next week, goes for a walk in the park | Cries, self-harms, sends a text saying she feels let down |
| Consequence: | Friend feels valued, agrees to meet up, says thanks for the support and explains that it was nothing to worry about | Friend is upset and does not reply |
| | Confirms beliefs | Confirms beliefs |

Thoughts play a key role in creating some of the more complex and often unhelpful emotions such as guilt and shame. These are often the result of thoughts that start *'I should have…', 'I shouldn't have…', 'if only I had / hadn't…'.*

Thoughts are also often the part of the system that is most inaccessible to other people; behaviour may be seen and emotions guessed from facial expressions and body language. However, to guess at another person's thoughts needs careful consideration, taking into account their life experiences and their different perspective on events. If this can be achieved, what appeared at first as totally inexplicable behaviour suddenly makes sense.

The physical arousal associated with intense emotion can also have a strong impact on the thinking process, switching off rational thought and triggering more primitive, emotional thinking. This process is explored in greater depth in Chapter 12.

# Controlling thoughts

If thoughts are difficult to identify, they are even more difficult to control. It is very common to have difficulty focusing on boring tasks, to find it difficult to stop thinking about problems or to avoid daydreaming. It has been said that if bodies were as difficult to control as thoughts, no one would ever get down stairs without falling. Hence difficulty controlling thoughts is a part of everyday life. However, sometimes out of control thoughts can be very distressing. Box 7.5 gives information about some types of thoughts that can cause distress.

## Rebound effect of thought suppression

One common feature of these different types of thought is that the more worried a person is about the thoughts and the harder they try to stop them, the worse the thoughts become. It is recognised that trying not to think about something actually makes people think about that topic more. This has been called the 'rebound effect of thought suppression'. One way of experiencing this effect is to test what happens in response to the instruction 'Do not think about a pink elephant'. For most people this instruction results in a vivid picture of a pink elephant. The harder people try to block out the image of the elephant, the bigger and more vivid the image becomes.

Intellectual Disabilities and Personality Disorder: An integrated approach
© Pavilion Publishing and Media Ltd and its licensors 2014.

> ## Box 7.5: Distressing and out of control thoughts
>
> **Intrusive thoughts:** Unwelcome, unpleasant, involuntary thoughts, images or ideas which are difficult to get rid of. These thoughts may be aggressive, sexual, religious (blasphemous), or fears about health or loved ones. They may be thoughts of past experiences (flashbacks) or may seem to have no connection to the person's experiences.
>
> **Worries:** Concerns about bad things that might happen in the future. Often focuses on *'What if…'*
>
> **Ruminations:** Endless cycles of thoughts about something distressing that has happened, its possible causes and consequences. The person 'overthinks' or 'obsesses' about situations, life events or abstract questions such as *'Why do these things happen to me?'* or *'Why am I like this?'* Ruminating is associated with increased stress, more negative mood, less productive behaviour and more self-sabotaging behaviour.
>
> **Hallucinations:** Sensing things that are not really present. This may include seeing, feeling, smelling or hearing things. Hearing things is the most common experience.
>
> **Auditory hallucinations:** Hearing voices – these are experienced as if they occurred outside the person – as if spoken by someone not visibly present and beyond the control of the person hearing them.
>
> **Delusions:** Powerful beliefs that do not match the reality as experienced by other people eg. *'They are all plotting to bring me down'.*

# Building a positive relationship with thoughts

A number of approaches have been developed for building a more positive relationship with thoughts. Many of these have their origins in meditation, such as 'mindfulness', which is explored more fully later in this chapter. Others rely on the power of distraction to change the focus of thoughts and to fill the mind with other, more pleasant thoughts. It is also increasingly recognised that if thoughts are accepted rather than judged then they tend to become less intense and intrusive.

# Thoughts and individuals with personality disorder

Difficulties with thinking are common in individuals with personality disorder and comprise some of the diagnostic criteria; some examples are given in Box 7.6.

---

### Box 7.6: Diagnostic criteria related to thoughts and thinking style

**Paranoid personality disorder**

- Suspicious of others
- Misunderstanding actions of others as hostile or contemptuous
- Disproportionate sense of personal rights
- Think only of themselves and how situations impact on them, talk about themselves and assume things overheard must be about them
- Preoccupation with conspiratorial explanations of events
- Recurrent unjustified suspicions about faithfulness of partners

**Antisocial personality disorder**

- Blaming others or rationalising their behaviour

**Borderline personality disorder**

- Disturbances in and uncertainty about self-image, aims and personal preferences

---

Pervasive, distorted thinking is characteristic of individuals with paranoid personality disorder. These distortions are very stable and difficult to challenge. In contrast, individuals with borderline personality disorder often show very unstable patterns of thinking with their views seeming to switch from moment to moment, often with no apparent cause. Some individuals may also develop particular problems with thinking at times when they are highly stressed, resulting in them ruminating, worrying obsessively, experiencing hallucinations or having delusions.

## Core beliefs

Individuals with personality disorder frequently hold core beliefs which are negative and exert a powerful influence on their behaviour. These beliefs will relate to all aspects of their life: self, relationships with others, the world and the future. Individuals may believe themselves to be helpless, unlovable or worthless. Some will believe that they are undeserving and should not be treated well. In contrast, others will have a sense of entitlement and hence will expect special treatment.

These unhelpful core beliefs arise as the result of the experiences these individuals had in childhood. They may also have been shaped by traumatic events that happened later in life such as being assaulted or raped. These negative core beliefs make individuals with personality disorder vulnerable to developing mental health problems. They can also undermine their motivation to change or to engage with others; it is hard to commit to therapy when you feel hopeless, helpless or that others will seek to harm you.

## Attribution and thinking styles

Individuals with personality disorder are particularly prone to thinking in unhelpful ways. Their thinking style and thinking errors can make individuals with personality disorder more likely to respond to situations in overly emotional ways by rapidly becoming upset or angry. For example, thinking in an 'all-or-nothing' way can contribute to extreme behaviours. If a person thinks they are either totally in control or totally out of control they are likely to give up trying to control themselves at the first small signs of distress or anger as they see total loss of control as inevitable.

Individuals with personality disorder often have unhelpful attribution styles. Most frequently they will have an external locus of control. This makes it difficult for them to see the part they play in the difficulties they experience and makes it less likely that they will take responsibility for their behaviour.

## Difficulty mentalising

Chapters 3 and 4 explored the difficulties individuals with personality disorder have in understanding their own and other people's emotions and behaviour. Negative core beliefs and thinking errors make the process of mentalising more difficult as they predispose the person to make unhelpful assumptions about their own and other people's behaviour.

## Abnormal thinking when under stress

Individuals with personality disorder can experience a breakdown of thinking during periods of extreme stress. At such times they may become muddled or be unable to think at all. They may experience psychotic symptoms, become paranoid or dissociate.

## 'Psychotic symptoms'

When highly stressed, some individuals with personality disorder may experience hallucinations or delusions. These symptoms are sometimes referred to as being 'psychotic'. Psychotic symptoms are associated with major mental health problems such as schizophrenia. However, for most individuals with personality disorder, psychotic symptoms are short lived and only associated with periods of stress.

## Paranoia

Individuals with personality disorder often develop paranoid ideas when stressed. When experiencing paranoia, people suspect, without sufficient evidence, that others are deceiving, exploiting or harming them. They feel that they must always be on their guard, staying vigilant to protect themselves from others. They will be unable to trust others and will see threatening intentions behind the most innocent of behaviours or comments. Friends and loved ones are suspected of betraying them. Strangers are seen as hostile. This vigilance makes people see ordinary situations as menacing and they may react with anger or aggression. When feeling paranoid, individuals are likely to be unforgiving of perceived insults or slights and will hold grudges and seek revenge. It is often difficult to find out what the individual suspects or fears as they will be very reluctant to talk to others for fear that what they say will be used against them.

For some individuals this way of thinking is pervasive and occurs even when they are not stressed. These individuals are likely to have a diagnosis of 'paranoid' personality disorder.

## Dissociation

Finally, as discussed in Chapter 3, some individuals may react to highly stressful situations by going into a dissociative state. Their system reacts to overload by cutting off from the stressful situation. This severely disrupts their ability to think about and respond to that situation.

# Thoughts and individuals with intellectual disabilities

The account given above explaining thoughts, core beliefs and thinking errors is given in the context of the individual having typical intellectual development. By definition this is not the case for individuals with intellectual disabilities. Depending on the severity of their intellectual disabilities, their ability to think will be impaired.

# Development of thinking

The ability to think develops from birth to adulthood. Thinking begins with discovering the world through the senses, followed by the development of language, logical thinking and abstract reasoning. A number of stages in this process have been identified. These stages are explained in more detail in Box 7.7.

---

### Box 7.7: Developmental stages in thinking

**Sensorimotor** (birth–2 years): Experience the world though their senses and movement. Thoughts derive from senses and what is going on in the world. Child gradually learns that they are separate from the world.

**Pre-operational** (2–7 years): Thinking is not logical (magical thinking). Child has difficulty understanding time. Child can solve problems by manipulating objects. Language and symbols allow thinking about things that are not present. World centres around them.

**Concrete operational** (7–11 years): Developing logical thinking in relation to real life practical situations. Greater understanding of their position in the wider world.

**Formal operational** (11–adulthood): Abstract thought develops. Able to think about multiple possibilities and take different perspectives.

Based on Piaget. See Piaget J & Inhelder B (1969, 2000).

---

Few individuals with intellectual disabilities will progress through all these stages. Most will not have the ability to think abstractly. Time is a particularly difficult concept to grasp. Individuals are likely to have difficulties with telling the time, thinking back in time (such as when past events occurred) and will struggle to understand ideas relating to the future. Many will think in concrete ways; they are able to problem solve in a logical way but only in relation to real-life problems impacting on them at the time. Some may not have achieved the ability to think things through logically. Such individuals may make sense of the world by how things are associated together. For example, *'it hurt when I went to the dentist, the dentist is bad and I don't want to go there again'*. This misses out the logical thoughts that the dentist was trying to help them, tried her best to hurt them as little as possible and that bad teeth hurt much more if they are not treated. Thinking errors that arise from incomplete intellectual development can be regarded as 'hard-wired' and are difficult, or impossible to change.

## Understanding thoughts

Individuals with intellectual disabilities often do not have a clear understanding of what thoughts are and may have difficulty distinguishing thoughts from feelings. Even if they are able to understand the idea of thoughts they may have difficulty recognising and explaining what they are thinking. Some individuals will experience thoughts as if hearing voices speaking to them. This can lead to confusion as it can be mistaken for the auditory hallucinations experienced in psychosis.

Individuals with intellectual disabilities also have great difficulty thinking about other people's thoughts (mentalising) and may not be able to put themselves into someone else's position.

## Attribution and thinking styles

As a result of impaired development of thinking, individuals with intellectual disabilities are more vulnerable to developing unhelpful ways of thinking. Their difficulties in understanding and communicating about their thoughts also mean that it is much more difficult for them and others to explore how they see the world and what thinking errors they are making.

Their life experiences also make individuals with intellectual disabilities vulnerable to developing unhelpful attribution styles. Experiences such as dependence on others, over-protection, disempowerment and discrimination can lead to belief in external locus of control, a sense of pervading personal powerlessness and an acceptance that things cannot be changed.

# Thoughts and individuals with intellectual disabilities and personality disorder

Individuals with intellectual disabilities and personality disorder are likely to have many difficulties with thinking. Depending on the level of their intellectual disabilities they may have a limited ability to think abstractly (to think about different possibilities and perspectives), be very concrete in their thinking (only able to think logically about real-life problems) or lack the ability to think logically (jumping to conclusions based on associations, believing the world revolves around them). They are likely to find it very difficult to think about and understand their own and other people's thoughts (problems with mentalising).

The difficulties with thinking that arise from their intellectual disabilities are 'hard-wired', that is they are the result of incomplete or abnormal development of their brain. Consequently, they are usually not amenable to change.

Intellectual Disabilities and Personality Disorder: An integrated approach
© Pavilion Publishing and Media Ltd and its licensors 2014.

In addition to the 'hard-wired' difficulties, individuals with intellectual disabilities and personality disorder are likely to have had life experiences that contribute to unhelpful attribution styles, unhelpful core beliefs and thinking errors. Box 7.8 gives some example core beliefs that are often associated with having intellectual disabilities and personality disorder.

---

### Box 7.8: Core beliefs associated with having intellectual disabilities and personality disorder

**Self**

**Helpless/dependent core beliefs**

I am: ineffective, incompetent, unable to cope, powerless, out of control, trapped, vulnerable, needy, weak, a failure

I: don't measure up, fail no matter how hard I try

**Unloveable core beliefs**

I am: unlovable, unlikeable, unwanted, undesirable, unattractive, different, defective, not good enough to be loved by others, ugly, boring

I will be: rejected, abandoned, always alone

I have nothing to offer

**Worthless core beliefs**

I am: bad, irresponsible, worthless, dangerous, toxic, evil, inhuman

**Undeserving core beliefs**

I can't have what I want.

I don't deserve: happiness, love, pleasure

I am not important

I am: stupid, inferior, not good enough, defective

**Entitlement core beliefs**

I should always get what I want, restrictions/rules don't apply to me, I can't tolerate restrictions, my needs are more important than other people's, s/he is supposed to take care of me.

**Relationships**

I can't attract/keep a good person. I can't win so I might as well get even. Even if I try to explain, I won't be heard. I have to take what I can get. People I depend on will let me down. Women/men can't be trusted. People are out to get me. Men/women are tough, scary, angry, etc

Continued...

---

**The world**

The world is: hostile, an unhappy place, isn't a safe place, owes me a living.

Life is unfair.

**The future**

Nothing will: work out, get better, change.

There is no hope.

The difficulties with thinking and interpreting the world that arise from having a personality disorder may be amenable to change, although progress is likely to be slow.

## Concept of 'fairness'

Individuals with intellectual disabilities and personality disorder often struggle with the concept of 'fairness'. A frequent comment in a range of situations is likely to be *'it's not fair – no one else has to… / X is allowed to… / everyone else is…'* Such comments have their origins in an immature understanding of fairness and the impact of selective attention. Individuals with intellectual disabilities often believe that being fair means treating everyone exactly the same. They rarely understand that, in a mature approach to fairness, issues such as need and ability have to be considered. Hence they will feel aggrieved if someone else receives 'better' treatment than they do. However, they are also likely to be selective in their attention and will fail to notice times when they are the person that receives 'better' treatment. They are likely to believe that it is **always** them who misses out. Individuals with intellectual disabilities and personality disorder are also unlikely to have the mature acceptance that much of life is fundamentally unfair and there is very little that can be done about this.

## Problems related to unhelpful thinking

Difficulties with thinking contribute to individuals with intellectual disabilities and personality disorder experiencing a wide range of problems (see Box 7.9).

The list in Box 7.9 covers almost all the issues discussed in other chapters of this book. It is important to recognise that, whatever difficulties an individual has, staff need to think about how the problems have been influenced by the individual's difficulties with thinking. Staff need to consider whether these difficulties arise from the individual's intellectual impairment (hard-wired) and/or unhelpful core beliefs, thinking style and thinking errors that may be related to their experiences and personality disorder.

---

### Box 7.9: Problems related to unhelpful core beliefs and thinking errors

- Poor self-image and low self-esteem (Chapter 2)
- Intense emotional reactions (Chapter 3)
- Poor emotional regulation eg. difficulties managing anger (Chapter 3)
- Lack of trust in personal relationships (Chapters 4 and 5)
- Interpersonal conflict and relationship breakdown (Chapter 4)
- Difficulties with impulse control (Chapter 6)
- Verbal and physical aggression (Chapter 10)
- Poor stress management (Chapters 8 and 9)
- Experiencing 'psychotic symptoms' when highly stressed (current chapter)
- Mental health problems such as depression, anxiety and phobias (Chapter 9)
- Poor compliance with treatment for physical and mental health problems (Chapters 8 and 9)
- Difficulty engaging with services (Chapter 13)
- Hopelessness and low motivation to try to change (Chapter 12)
- Unreasonable expectations (current chapter)
- Being misunderstood or disbelieved by those supporting them (current chapter and Chapters 13 and 14)

---

The pervasive influence of difficulties with thinking is due to the way core beliefs and thoughts influence emotions and behaviour. The CBT 'hot cross bun' diagram, presented earlier in the chapter, shows the complex interactions that can take place in response to a particular trigger situation. Core beliefs and thinking errors act like distorting mirrors and filters. They change views and exclude any information that might contradict or disprove that view. These distortions make individuals behave in ways that seem irrational, erratic and incomprehensible to people who see the situation from a less distorted perspective. They also trap the individual in that maladaptive pattern of behaviour by undermining their self-esteem, motivation and any hope that things could ever be different.

## Impact on staff

Most staff hold very different core beliefs from individuals with intellectual disabilities and personality disorder. This can make it very difficult for them to understand an individual's behaviour and to support them in a positive way. Looking through the filter created by a staff member's core beliefs, the behaviour of individuals with intellectual disabilities and personality disorder may appear self-destructive, self-centred, ungrateful, inconsiderate, self-indulgent or manipulative. The processes that lead such distortions in staff perceptions of the individuals they support are complex, and are explored fully in Chapters 13 and 14. It is important to recognise that staff need to understand their own thinking before they are able to help the individuals they support. They then need to use their ability to mentalise to try to understand what the individual may be thinking and why they think in that way.

The following sections will give a general framework for exploring the impact of thoughts, whatever the specific nature of the problem the individual is experiencing.

# Supporting individuals with unhelpful thinking

There are a number of steps to supporting individuals with unhelpful thinking. These include:

■ identifying the individual's thinking errors, styles and core beliefs

■ assessing the causes of these thinking errors ie. do they arise from their intellectual impairment, their personality disorder or life experiences?

■ developing an understanding of the extent to which thinking errors may be 'hard-wired' or may be amenable to change

■ using this to inform the approach adopted:

   ■ supporting and compensating for thinking styles that cannot be changed or where the individual does not feel ready to work on change

   ■ exploring approaches that may help develop more healthy thinking patterns for individuals who may be able to change

■ how to support individuals at times of great stress when their usual thinking may breakdown.

## Identifying core beliefs, attribution style and thinking errors

Identifying problems with thinking is a difficult area. Individuals with intellectual disabilities and personality disorder are rarely able to tell staff what they are thinking at any particular time and may not even understand the concept of what a thought is.

## Staff approach

The first step is for staff supporting individuals with intellectual disabilities and personality disorder to have a thorough understanding of core beliefs, attribution styles and thinking errors, how these arise and how they may influence behaviour. Secondly, staff must challenge their own thinking style to stop them jumping to conclusions about why individuals might behave in a particular way. Staff need to develop and maintain an open, curious, non-judgemental mindset that is always asking 'why?' Once these are in place staff can start to explore how an individual thinks.

## Brainstorming and mentalising

A good starting point to identifying how an individual might be thinking is to find time to talk with colleagues and explore:

*'What would I be thinking and feeling for (unexplained behaviour) to seem like my only / best option?'*

It can be helpful to have a list of unhelpful core beliefs, attribution styles and thinking errors to help generate ideas. Thinking about what is known about the individual's past experiences may also help generate ideas. Questions might be:

*'How would that experience make me see myself / other people / the world / the future?'*

## Active listening

It is also important to make time to chat with the individual and to give them space to talk about what is going on in their life. By regularly chatting with the individual, using the active listening approach (see Box 11.14), staff will be able to identify themes in the individual's thinking. This will help in understanding their core beliefs and the type of thinking errors they are prone to. In turn, this is likely to help explain patterns of behaviour that on the surface may seem self-defeating.

## Exploring alternatives

Once staff have established a good rapport with an individual it may be helpful to use thoughtful questions to explore whether they are able to think about situations in different ways. These might introduce different views of the situation. For example, *'Maybe X was just having a bad day, she is usually nice to you'* or *'What if it was just an accident?'* By gently probing it may be possible to find out how entrenched the individual's views are. It can sometimes be helpful to use cartoon drawings of people and empty thought bubbles to show how people in a situation may be thinking different things.

# Looking at whether difficulties with thinking arise from intellectual disabilities or their personality disorder

It can be very difficult to distinguish between the problems with thinking that arise from having intellectual disabilities (hard-wired) and those that arise from having a personality disorder. However, this process is essential to avoid the misunderstandings, frustrations and disappointment that arise on all sides if 'hard-wired' problems are overlooked.

## Staff thinking errors

Interestingly, one of the barriers to doing this successfully lies in the common thinking errors staff make when estimating how able an individual is. Some examples are given in Box 7.10.

---

### Box 7.10: Common thinking errors made by staff about individuals' abilities

- 'S/he understands everything we say'
- 'S/he could do it if they wanted to'
- 'S/he is just lazy'
- 'S/he just likes the attention'
- 'S/he's really clever, they always know where I've hidden the chocolate'
- 'If s/he can do a 100-piece puzzle they can make their own bed'

---

Staff often attribute an individual's difficulties to motivational issues rather than difficulties with understanding or lack of skills. Staff also often overestimate general intelligence. They overgeneralise from one or two special skills or abilities or base their judgement on superficially good communication skills.

## Hiding difficulties

Another complication is that individuals with intellectual disabilities and personality disorder often find it painful to acknowledge that they do not understand or cannot do something. They may go to great lengths to hide their difficulties. Many individuals are skilled at nodding and smiling when in reality they do not know what is being said. If asked, individuals will often say they can do something that in reality they find difficult or need help with. They may have learnt not to challenge others and may just go along with what others suggest. This is sometimes called 'learned acquiescence'.

## Informal assessment

It is therefore important to give careful thought to the impact of the individual's intellectual disabilities on their thinking. It can be helpful to look at how well an individual copes with everyday practical tasks. Can they handle money, work out a bus timetable, use a mobile phone or use a computer? Individuals who can successfully do such tasks are likely to have relatively mild intellectual disabilities.

Most individuals with mild intellectual disabilities will have reached the concrete operational stage of thinking. This means that they are intellectually capable of logical thinking in relation to practical situations and are able to have some understanding of their relationship to the wider world. If individuals with mild intellectual disabilities show a range of unhelpful core beliefs and thinking errors, these will be in large part related to their personality disorder and difficult early experiences. While the process will not be easy, it should be possible to achieve some changes through sensitive support and therapeutic activities.

If an individual is having difficulties in all areas of their life it may be that they have a more severe intellectual disability. These individuals may have only reached the pre-operational stage of thinking. At this stage an individual cannot think logically but rather their understanding is based on association of events. Individuals at this stage have little awareness of the wider world, rather they are the centre of their own small universe. Individuals at the pre-operational stage of thinking will show many thinking errors as a result of their intellectual disabilities. They are likely to jump to conclusions, over-generalise, take things personally, use emotional reasoning and have great difficulty considering other people's needs. These difficulties may be exacerbated by the negative experiences associated with personality disorder but are 'hard-wired' and hence will be very difficult, if not impossible, to change.

## Formal assessment

If, after taking the time to look at their everyday functioning, there is any remaining confusion about an individual's abilities, it would be helpful for them to be offered a referral to a psychologist for an intellectual assessment.

## Supporting and compensating for thinking styles

Many individuals with intellectual disabilities and personality disorder will not be able to change their thinking patterns. Even those with the potential to change may not feel able to tackle these issues directly. Changing thinking patterns is very difficult and efforts to do this can sometimes be counterproductive; individuals may feel blamed for their thinking and may feel they have failed if they cannot change. Sometimes it may be more helpful simply to recognise how the individual thinks and to look for ways to ensure this does not get in the way of them achieving what they want from life. Later, as they become more settled and confident, individuals may decide they are ready to work on these issues. The motivational interviewing techniques explored in Chapter 6 may be helpful in this process.

## Practical and social support

The most important step that can be taken to compensate for unhelpful thinking is to ensure that individuals have the right level of practical and social support. This is because inadequate support increases the demands on the individual and results in high levels of stress. High levels of stress cause mental exhaustion and reduce an individual's capacity to think clearly. It is surprising how many problems related to unhelpful thinking can be resolved simply by reducing stress.

Once the individual is well supported, their remaining issues relating to thinking need to be managed. This can usually be done by following the positive behaviour support approach explored more fully in Chapter 10. It is particularly helpful to identify trigger situations and to look at how these can be avoided or minimised.

## Reducing misunderstandings

It is often possible to avoid triggering unhelpful thoughts by reducing opportunities for misunderstanding. It is easy for staff to assume that the individual understands why staff are doing something. However, this is often not the case. For example, simple statements such as *'I'm just going to answer that phone and then I will come back'* can avoid triggering thoughts of dislike or abandonment.

## Promoting positive emotions

Negative thoughts and thinking errors are often related to emotional states. Using the approaches in Chapter 3 to promote positive emotions is likely to reduce the impact of unhelpful thinking.

## Responding to unhelpful thoughts

Where situations cannot be avoided it is important to manage them in a way that minimises emotional distress and helps to promote more positive thoughts. The approach given in Box 7.11 may be helpful.

The key to success is not to confront or challenge the unhelpful thinking. Instead the unhelpful thought is accepted and the emphasis is placed on shifting thoughts on to other things.

---

### Box 7.11: Supporting individuals to manage unhelpful thoughts

- Listen to the individual and let them express their concerns (active listening).
- Accept that the content of anything they say is true for the individual at that time even if you feel it is inaccurate. *'You think that everyone hates you'.*
- Do not challenge their thinking.
- Put things on paper by writing or drawing.
- Remind the individual of facts they may have forgotten eg. if the individual is worried about hearing from their family, remind them *'Mum usually rings on Friday and it is Thursday today.'*
- Distract the individual; chat to them about their favourite topic, offer a fun activity, put on some calming music, offer a cup of tea (for more distracting activities see Box 7.14 later in this chapter).
- Try mindfulness exercises such as the birthday cake (see later in this chapter).

---

## Exploring approaches that may help develop more healthy thinking patterns

If staff and an individual with intellectual disabilities and personality disorder decide to work on thinking errors, there are a number of things that need to be in place.

## Understanding thoughts

Working on thoughts is very difficult if an individual does not know what a thought is. It can be helpful to work with the individual on understanding the differences between thoughts, emotions, physical sensations and behaviour. Box 7.12 gives an accessible explanation of what a thought is.

---

### Box 7.12: What are thoughts?

- **Thoughts** are words or pictures inside our heads. Other words for thoughts are ideas, beliefs, notions, images, mental pictures, views. Other people cannot see or hear our thoughts (but they may guess them from our behaviour, facial expression and body language).
- **Behaviour** is what we say and do.
- **Emotions** are feelings such as happiness or sadness.
- **Bodily sensations** are things like pain, tiredness, feeling hot or cold. They also include awareness of heart rate, breathing or sweating.

---

It is also important to help the individual understand more about thoughts. Some key concepts are given in Box 7.13.

Gaining a better understanding of thoughts and how they work often reduces an individual's anxiety about thoughts and makes it easier to explore how to accept and manage troublesome thoughts.

---

### Box 7.13: Important things to understand about thoughts

- Everyone has thoughts.
- These include pleasant and unpleasant thoughts.
- It is natural to think about things that we may think of as 'wrong' or 'bad'.
- Thoughts cannot hurt anyone.
- Thoughts cannot make anything happen in the world.
- For thoughts to have an effect in the world someone has to act on their thoughts.
- Thoughts come and go for no apparent reason.
- The harder anyone tries not to think about something, the more they will think about it.

---

## Identifying troublesome thoughts

Once an individual has a good understanding of what thoughts are they may be able to identify some of the thoughts that cause them problems. It might be helpful to begin with a conversation about what the individual believes. Staff might say something like *'It seems to me you think no one likes you?'* or *'You seem to worry a lot, what do you think might happen to your mum?'* Once the thoughts have been identified staff can explore with the individual if they want to try to change the thought or simply to reduce the amount of time they spend thinking it.

### Distraction

Using distraction is one of the easiest and most effective ways of dealing with unpleasant or worrying thoughts. It is also highly effective at breaking the vicious cycles that can develop between emotions, physical sensations and thoughts. Box 7.14 gives a selection of distracting activities.

It is important to have a variety of different distracting activities and to include some that can be done alone and others that can be done in company.

Tasks that are active and require a degree of concentration are most helpful as distracters. Passive pastimes such as listening to music, watching TV or DVDs can be distracting but they also allow the mind to wander and so may be less effective at dislodging unwanted thoughts. (However, well chosen films or music may be very effective at promoting a more positive mood state.) Likewise, physical

Intellectual Disabilities and Personality Disorder: An integrated approach
© Pavilion Publishing and Media Ltd and its licensors 2014.

activities are more effective as a distracter if it requires some concentration. Walking and jogging are helpful in promoting positive moods but do not require mental focus. Consequently, they are less effective at changing thoughts than, for example, following a dance routine.

---

### Box 7.14: Distracting activities

- **Mental exercises:** Counting/counting backwards, reciting poetry, listing objects that are red, yellow etc
- **Absorbing activities:** Reading, wordsearch, picture searches eg. 'Where's Wally?', spot the difference, crossing out the letter 'o' in a newspaper, crossword puzzles, knitting, cross-stitch, colouring
- **Games:** Noughts and crosses, Jenga, computer games, draughts (checkers), dominos
- **Physical activities:** Badminton, exercise class, exercise DVD, ballroom/Latin/line/sequence dancing, dance DVD, Zumba
- **Repetitive chores:** Weeding, vacuuming, sorting laundry, pairing socks, cleaning windows

---

## Mindfulness

The term 'mindfulness' is used to refer to developing a state of mind in which the individual is able, purposefully, to pay attention to their current experience on a moment-to-moment basis. This state of mind promotes awareness of thoughts, emotions and sensations in a non-judgemental and accepting way. Mindfulness has its origins in religion and is created through exercises based on meditation. Mindfulness techniques form part of a number of modern therapies including DBT and ACT (discussed later in this chapter). Mindfulness exercises can help individuals to remain in the present moment (manage their attention), reduce stress and build tolerance of distressing thoughts, feelings and sensations. The intuitive mindset induced by mindfulness is described more fully in Chapter 12.

The concepts of mindfulness are difficult for individuals with intellectual disabilities and personality disorder to grasp. However, one useful exercise that has been found to make mindfulness more accessible is 'the birthday cake'. The individual is helped to imagine and act out the process of blowing out the candles on a birthday cake. As they do this they are encouraged to focus on their breathing and to feel the air moving in and out of their body. The appearance of the cake is adjusted to appeal to the individual and the number of candles is adjusted to promote a long, slow breath. Once the most helpful appearance of the cake and the number of candles has been worked out this is made into a visual prompt for the individual to use at times when their thoughts are distressing them or at any time they want to reduce stress. A simplified version of a prompt is given in Box 7.15. However, they are most helpful when they are colourful and engaging to look at as this helps attract the individual's attention.

---

### Box 7.15: The birthday cake mindfulness exercise

- Think about a (colour) birthday cake [picture of the cake].
- Blow the candles out gently and smoothly [picture of someone blowing out candles]
- Blow out the candles one a time [picture of a row of candles]
- Try doing that three more times 1, 2, 3 [each showing the cake, someone blowing it out and a line of candles]
- If you start thinking about other things, think about the cake again and gently and smoothly blow out the candles [picture of cake]
- As you are thinking about the birthday cake, think about your breathing.
- There are two parts to breathing.
- Before you blow the candles out you breathe in.
- Air comes in your nose and mouth, goes down your throat to your lungs and your tummy moves out [pictures of where the air goes].
- Now think about breathing in.
- Can you feel the air going in your nose and mouth?
- Can you feel it going down your throat?
- Can you feel it fill your lungs?
- Can you feel your tummy move out?
- Try thinking about breathing in three times.
- The second part of breathing is breathing out.
- Your tummy moves inwards.
- Your breath goes out of your lungs, up your throat and out of your nose and mouth [picture of where the air goes].
- Can you feel your breath leaving your body?
- Can you feel your stomach move in?
- Can you feel your breath going up your throat?
- Can you feel your breath come out of your nose and mouth?
- Try thinking about breathing out three times.
- Now think about the (colour) birthday cake [picture of the cake].
- You breathe in before you blow the candles out.
- You breathe out to blow the candles out [picture of candles].
- Try thinking about breathing in and out as you blow the candles out.

Adapted from Rose & Webb, 2012. Developed in clinical work, unpublished, available from the 2nd author.

---

# Changing thoughts

Working to change thoughts is a difficult process and needs to be done patiently, sensitively and non-judgementally. An individual's problematic thoughts and thinking styles will have developed from a lifetime of experiences; they are not going to change as the result of one or two conversations.

The key is to choose times when the individual is calm and to create a warm and supportive atmosphere in which to question some of their assumptions. This might include explaining other people's actions in a way that challenges the assumptions arising from a core belief, highlighting events that challenge faulty thinking or gently questioning the individual to explore whether events might be seen differently. Where an individual's thinking appears to be influenced by unhelpful core beliefs it may be helpful to explain that there are different ways of seeing the world and to present some alternatives to their core belief. Box 7.16 gives suggestions for these approaches.

Key concepts in this process are explaining, exploring and giving feedback. The approaches to improving self-image and self-esteem given in Chapter 2 will also work to influence negative core beliefs about the self.

## Therapeutic approaches

For some individuals the impact of their unhelpful core beliefs and distorted thinking will have a severe negative effect on their physical or mental health and general well-being. In these cases, therapy may be helpful and it would be appropriate to support them to seek a referral to the local mental health or intellectual disabilities team.

There are a number of therapies that have been developed to help individuals identify and overcome the problems associated with negative core beliefs and faulty thinking patterns. Helpful approaches include cognitive behaviour therapy (CBT), dialectical behaviour therapy (DBT), acceptance and commitment therapy (ACT) and schema therapy. CBT and DBT have been discussed in earlier chapters.

ACT has developed from CBT. It uses a variety of techniques to help individuals make healthy contact with thoughts, emotions, physical sensations and memories that have been feared and avoided. It promotes a healthier approach that includes Accepting reactions and being present (mindfulness), Choosing a valued direction and Taking action. ACT was developed for the general population but can be adapted for individuals with intellectual disabilities and personality disorder. It might be particularly useful for individuals who are highly distressed by their thoughts.

---

## Box 7.16: Changing negative core beliefs

### Self

### Helpless/dependent core beliefs

Explain that no one can do everything, everyone needs help sometimes, feedback small steps towards independence that the individual has already made, remind the individual of times they have achieved things.

### Unloveable core beliefs

Explain that no one gets on with everyone, feedback likeable qualities: *'You've got such a good sense of humour'*, *'People love your smile'*.

### Worthless core beliefs

Separate the behaviour from the person. Explain that everyone does bad things sometimes but that does not make them a bad person. Explore forgiving and making new starts.

### Undeserving core beliefs

Explain that everyone deserves to be treated well and have their rights respected, people don't have to be perfect to have rights and making a mistake does not take away someone's rights.

### Entitlement core beliefs

Explain that rules apply to everyone – even princes get speeding tickets. Rights are balanced by responsibilities. We all depend on each other and must share and contribute.

### Relationships

Build trust, be reliable. Explain that other people are only human and are bound to make mistakes occasionally. Explain reasons: *'Sorry I was late, I had to take an urgent phone call, don't worry I will still be able to get everything done.'*

### The world

Explain that some places are safe, others less so. There are things that can be done to make it safer. Some people and places are hostile, others are welcoming and kind.

### The future

Explain that nothing stays the same, change is inevitable, if you try you might be surprised what can be achieved. Explore previous times when it seemed hopeless but things had come out well.

---

Schema therapy was developed for individuals with personality disorder to help individuals meet their emotional needs in a healthier manner. As part of this process it aims to explore and heal schemas (core beliefs) that make the individual vulnerable and to challenge punitive, overly critical or over demanding schemas and to build healthy schemas and modes of thinking. Schema therapy may require a higher level of intellectual functioning than ACT and hence may be most helpful for more intellectually able individuals.

## Helping individuals cope with abnormal thinking when under stress

The changes that can happen to an individual's thinking at times of extreme stress can be very frightening for the individual and for those who support them. It is important for staff to be aware of and to recognise signs that the individual's thinking has become detached from reality.

### Psychiatric support

Where psychotic symptoms, paranoia or dissociation are suspected it is important to support the individual to seek a referral to a psychiatrist for specialist assessment. The psychiatrist may suggest the use of medication to help manage symptoms. If the problems are severe they may also recommend that the individual has a short period of inpatient treatment. These issues are discussed more fully in Chapter 12.

### Day-to-day support

Staff need to take practical measures to identify the cause of, and wherever possible reduce the stress that has led to the individual to become so distressed. While this is happening staff need to support the individual in a calm and compassionate way that does not exacerbate their problems.

When an individual is acutely unwell they may be terrified of things that are unreal to staff. The instinctive response in this situation is often to try to convince the individual that what they fear is unreal and therefore there is nothing to worry about. Staff may feel that they should not 'collude' with the individual or that by recognising the individual's experience as real to the individual, they may make the situation worse. However, when an individual is acutely unwell any attempts to challenge their views or giving responses which make them feel disbelieved will increase their distress and sense of isolation. It is much more helpful if staff accept that the individual's perspective is real to the individual. Staff can then work to try to make the individual feel that they have been listened to and believed. Active listening is useful in this situation. Once the individual feels listened to, distraction techniques may be helpful.

For individuals who experience paranoia it is important for staff to think carefully about their everyday practices and how these might appear from the individual's perspective. Simple situations, such as staff chatting in the kitchen, a meeting about something else going on in the building or a person arriving to check the meter, can seem to the individual to be proof of conspiracy and plotting. Worrying about an individual feeling paranoid can also paradoxically lead staff to behave in ways that intensifies that feeling. For example, they may stop talking as they see the individual approach out of concern that the individual may think they are talking about them. It is important to continue to be open and honest with individuals while they are experiencing paranoia and to keep responses to distrust low key; the more staff try to reassure the individual and 'prove' that they are trustworthy, the more likely the individual is to distrust them.

Where individuals experience dissociative states, the grounding techniques described in Chapter 9 may be helpful.

## Key learning points

- Thoughts comprise ideas, images and beliefs. They are the means by which people interpret their experiences and solve problems.

- Much thought is automatic and people are unaware of how their core beliefs and patterns of thinking shape how they understand and respond to the world.

- The way someone thinks is influenced by both the development of their brain and by their life experiences. The ability to think can also be disrupted at times of severe stress. These processes apply both to individuals with intellectual disabilities and personality disorder and the staff who support them.

- Individuals with intellectual disabilities and personality disorder are likely to have difficulties with thinking that arise both from their intellectual disabilities and their personality disorder.

- The difficulties arising from intellectual disabilities are 'hard-wired' and are not amenable to change.

- In contrast, difficulties with thinking that arise from life experiences and personality disorder may be more flexible.

- In order to support individuals with these difficulties it is important that staff have a clear understanding of the difficulties that arise from the individual's intellectual impairment (hard-wired) and those that arise from their personality disorder and life experiences.

- Once staff have developed a clear understanding of the origins and nature of an individual's thinking style, there are a range of practical strategies that can help to support and compensate for thinking errors.

- For more able, motivated individuals there are also options that may help them develop healthier patterns of thinking.

# References

Padesky (1986) in Beck A, Greenberger D & Padesky C (1995) *Mind Over Mood: Change how you feel by changing the way you think*. New York: the Guildford Press.

Piaget J & Inhelder B (1969; 2000) *Psychology of the Child*. New York: Basic Books.

Rose A & Webb Z (2012) Birthday cake mindfulness exercise. Unpublished, available from the authors.

# Further reading

Bell L (2005) *Managing Intense Emotions and Overcoming Self-destructive Habits: A self-help manual*. Hove: Routledge. (Chapter 7: Investigating and modifying thinking habits and beliefs.)

Elliott C & Smith L (2009) *Borderline Personality Disorder for Dummies*. Indianapolis, Indiana: Wiley. (Chapter 20: Considering medication for BPD.)

Hayes S & Smith S (2005) *Get Out of Your Mind and Into Your Life: The new Acceptance and Commitment Therapy*. Oakland, CA: New Harbinger.

Hayes S, Strosahi K & Wilson K (2012) *Acceptance and Commitment Therapy* (2nd edition) New York: Guildford Press.

Linehan M (1993) *Skills Training Manual for Treating Borderline Personality Disorder: Diagnosis and treatment of mental disorders*. New York: Guildford Press.

Linehan M (1993) *Cognitive-Behavioral Treatment of Borderline Personality Disorder (Diagnosis & Treatment of Mental Disorders)*. New York: Guildford Press.

McGrath E (2003) The rumination rut. *Psychology Today*. Available at: http://www.psychologytoday.com/articles/200304/the-rumination-rut (accessed April 2014).

Scott E (2012) Rumination and how rumination affects your life. About.com Guide. Available at: http://stress.about.com/od/psychologicalconditions/a/rumination.htm (accessed April 2014).

Taylor J, Lindsay W, Hastings R & Hatton C (Eds) (2013) *Psychological Therapies for Adults with Intellectual Disabilities*. Chichester: Wiley-Balckwell.

Young J & Klosko J (2003) *Schema Therapy: A practitioner's guide*. New York: Guildford Press.

# Chapter 8: Physical health problems

This chapter looks at physical health and the factors that may contribute to poor health. It explores pain and the factors that influence how pain is experienced. It examines the physical health problems experienced by individuals with intellectual disabilities and personality disorder. It looks at some of the challenges facing staff trying to support individuals to improve their physical health and manage pain and suggests practical support strategies.

## Key topics

- Physical health

- Physical pain

- Physical health and personality disorder

- Physical health and intellectual disabilities

- Physical health and individuals with personality disorder and intellectual disabilities

- Supporting individuals with physical health problems

## Physical health

Health is more than simply not being ill. The World Health Organization describes it as being '*a state of complete physical, mental and social well-being*' (WHO, 1946). This definition recognises that the physical, mental and social aspects of a person are interwoven and do not work in isolation. Aspects of a person's social life may influence physical health and vice versa. Mental health is discussed more fully in Chapter 9.

Physical health is determined by a number of factors. These may be seen as falling into three groups: biomedical (factors within the body), environmental (external factors that the person has little or no control over) and lifestyle (factors over which the person has control). Some of these factors are given in Box 8.1.

---

## Box 8.1: Factors that can influence health

**Environmental**
Culture
Education and literacy
Social policy/discrimination
Social class and status
Social support networks
Income/poverty
Health care services
Housing
Pollution (air/water/soil)
Road safety
Employment
Work conditions
Sanitation
Immunisation

**Biomedical**
Gender
Nutrition in pregnancy and early childhood

**Lifestyle**
Substance misuse
Obesity
Stress
Diet
Exercise
Sleep

---

The impact of many of these factors is obvious. However, it is worth exploring some in more detail.

# Stress

The impact of stress on mental health is often recognised. However, stress also has significant effects on physical health. Stress causes the release of hormones, particularly cortisol. Long-term exposure to cortisol impacts on the body's immune, cardiovascular and nervous systems and contributes to a wide range of physical illnesses. Cortisol suppresses the body's immune response making it more likely that the person will catch infections.

Stress is a risk factor in high blood pressure, strokes and heart attacks. Stress also impacts on the digestive system, for example, contributing to stomach ulcers, increasing stomach aches and diarrhoea. Stress can exacerbate conditions such as asthma and eczema. It can also lead to headaches, back pain and neck pain. Prolonged stress can lead to the state of total physical and mental collapse described as burnout (see Box 14.10). Stress can also have an indirect impact on health by increasing high risk behaviours such as smoking, substance misuse and unhealthy eating.

Consequently, the amount of stress a person is exposed to and their ability to cope with it can have a significant impact on their well-being.

# Lifestyle

The choices a person makes about the way they live can have a significant impact on health. Some of the most important healthy choices are given in Box 8.2.

## Box 8.2: Health lifestyle

- Eating a healthy diet
- Maintaining a healthy body weight (not over or underweight)
- Drinking plenty of fluids (water, squash etc)
- Drinking caffeinated drinks in moderation (tea, coffee, cola, 'power drinks')
- Drinking alcohol in moderation
- Taking regular exercise (eg. 30 minutes a day)
- Sleeping well; the right amount (about 7 hours per night) and self-waking (rather than an alarm clock)
- Having a healthy life/work balance
- Managing stress positively eg. practicing yoga
- Making positive social contact eg. voluntary work
- Mental stimulation eg. crossword puzzles, quiz games
- Not smoking
- Not misusing drugs
- Self-care eg. attending regular check-ups/screening, cleaning teeth

Perhaps the most perplexing aspect of lifestyle choices is, given that so much is known about what actions lead to good physical heath, why do so many people continue to make unhealthy choices? There is no simple answer to this question but a number of factors may play a role.

First, healthy choices do not immediately make someone feel better, especially if they have long-established unhealthy patterns of behaviour. For example, taking up exercise can make muscles ache or cause painful minor injuries such as blisters. Healthy foods often do not taste as good as unhealthy foods to someone used to a diet high in sugar, fat and salt. They also do not give the immediate 'sugar rush' of less healthy foods such as cakes, chocolate or fizzy drinks. Psychological and physical dependency can also play an important role in the choices made. Chemicals found in cigarettes, alcohol, tea, coffee and chocolate all have pleasurable, immediate effects and can cause unpleasant withdrawal symptoms.

Attending check-ups and having screening tests involve tedious and often uncomfortable procedures at a time when the person does not feel unwell. They also make people think about unpleasant topics such as cancer or tooth decay.

Often lifestyle choices have to be made at times when the person is tired or stressed. It can be difficult to leave work on time if there is urgent work to do. It is also hard to find the motivation to go to a yoga class to manage stress when smoking a cigarette is so much easier.

Making healthy choices therefore involves:

■ acting on the basis of logical thinking rather than meeting emotional needs/ satisfying physical cravings

■ understanding the long-term consequences of choices

■ putting long-term results ahead of immediate pleasurable consequences (delaying gratification)

■ being willing to undergo immediate minor discomfort to avoid possible greater discomfort in the future

■ being prepared to put in the extra mental and physical effort needed to carry out the healthy option.

This can be difficult enough when life is going well. It can seem almost impossible when faced with challenges such as negative life events or mental health problems.

# Physical pain

Pain is an unpleasant sensation caused by stimuli that are very intense or cause damage to the body. Pain alerts the person that damage is likely or is actually occurring. It motivates them to withdraw from the stimuli, to protect that area until any damage has healed and to avoid similar damaging situations in future. The word 'pain' covers a number of different unpleasant sensations that are the result of different tissues being damaged (eg. nerves, joints, muscles, internal organs), different types of damage (eg. burns, cuts) and the involvement of different types of nerves that convey pain messages.

While it might appear that pain is a purely physical experience, the perception of pain is influenced by psychological and social factors. These factors can influence both the perceived intensity of the pain and the extent to which is it experienced as unpleasant. For example, excitement and distraction may block the perception of pain, while mindfulness and meditation techniques may reduce the extent to which pain is experienced as unpleasant. Good social support can reduce the impact of pain, while isolation and depression or anxiety can increase it.

People differ in the extent to which they can cope with pain. This is sometimes described as having a high or low 'pain threshold'. While some people are born with nervous systems that do not feel pain or do not experience it as unpleasant, this is extremely rare. Mostly differences can be accounted for by the psychological and social factors discussed above. The concept of pain thresholds can be unhelpful and can contribute to poor care. For example, pain control techniques may be neglected if professionals perceive a person as having a 'high pain threshold' while the pain of someone with a 'low pain threshold' might be seen as not in need of treatment as it is out of proportion to the procedure being carried out.

Pain usually resolves when the intense stimulation stops and the damage has healed. However, some people are left with ongoing pain as the result of long-term conditions such as arthritis. For others, pain persists after physical damage has mended. These situations are often referred to as 'chronic pain'. Pain can also occur in the absence of any identifiable physical cause. This is often called 'psychogenic pain'. People who experience pain in the absence of treatable physical causes are often poorly supported by both the medical profession and wider society because such pain is seen as 'psychological' and therefore 'all in the mind'. In fact, such pain is just as 'real' and unpleasant as pain from a physical cause and the lack of belief by others only increases the person's distress.

# Physical health and personality disorder

Individuals with personality disorder often have poor physical health. The nature of these problems and some of the possible causes are explored next.

## Life expectancy and chronic illness

Individuals with personality disorder (or other serious mental health problems) have a shorter life expectancy than people who do not have such problems (Ward, 2010). Some of this difference may be accounted for by the increased risk of suicide. However, there is evidence that these individuals are also at greater risk of developing physical illnesses (such as cancer, liver disease and septicaemia) and of having more complications and poorer outcomes for those illnesses.

A number of factors may be responsible for these differences in life expectancy and vulnerability to chronic illness. Individuals with personality disorder are more likely than the general population to engage in risky behaviours that may result in an increase in accidental death or serious injury. Some medications prescribed for mental health problems increase the risk of some physical illnesses, particularly diabetes and heart disease. They may also have an indirect effect on health by increasing appetite and therefore the risk of obesity. 'Self-medication' with cigarettes, alcohol or drugs may increase the risk of certain illnesses such as lung and liver disease. It is also thought that individuals with serious mental health problems are less likely to take medication prescribed for physical illnesses or may take it incorrectly.

## Stress

Individuals with personality disorder often have chaotic lives which expose them to high levels of stress. They also experience wildly fluctuating and very intense emotions. It is therefore likely that they are exposed to high levels of stress hormones with the consequent negative impact on their physical health.

## Lifestyle choices

Individuals with personality disorder often find it very difficult to follow a healthy lifestyle. They frequently develop dependencies on cigarettes, alcohol or drugs. They may also rely on foods such as chocolate and drinks that are high in caffeine or sugar for 'quick fixes' to get them through the day. They often take little exercise, have unhealthy sleeping patterns and do not take good care of themselves.

A number of factors work together to make it very difficult for individuals with personality disorder to make healthy choices. Unhealthy patterns have often been established in childhood; individuals have never had the example of how to live healthily or been encouraged and praised for making healthy choices. Impulsivity and thinking errors (see Chapters 6 and 7) make it difficult for individuals with personality disorder to make logical rather than emotional decisions, to resist temptation and delay gratification. Unhealthy behaviours are often rewarded by attention from others (family, friends, staff and health care professionals) who may work hard trying to persuade them to choose more healthy options. Being ill can also be rewarding for some individuals.

## Secondary gains

The unintended benefits of being physically ill are often called 'secondary gains'. At first it can be difficult to think of benefits from being unwell. However, on closer inspection there are a number of benefits that might meet the needs of individuals with personality disorder. Being unwell, particularly with vague or unusual symptoms, can mean repeated trips to the GP and trips to hospital to see specialists or undergo tests. Throughout this process the individual is the centre of attention. People around them ask questions and express interest and concern. This can meet an individual's need to feel special.

People in general are kind, sympathetic and patient with people who are physically unwell. This contrasts strongly with the intolerance and impatience which is often shown to individuals with mental health problems. When someone is physically ill they are cared for; others take responsibility for paying bills, they do not have to go to work, cook, clean or do the laundry. People may visit them in hospital, bringing cards, presents and flowers. These responses can meet the need some individuals have to feel totally cared for, protect them from the emptiness they feel when alone and allow them to escape the demands of adult life that they often find overwhelming.

These secondary gains can reduce an individual's motivation to get well and contribute to poor compliance with medical treatments. For some individuals these gains are so powerful that they can lead to what is called 'factitious illness' or 'Munchausen's syndrome'. This is where the individual deliberately fakes illnesses in order to be treated in hospital. Having a personality disorder is recognised as a risk factor for this rare condition.

## Depression

Individuals with personality disorder are vulnerable to experiencing depression. Individuals with depression can neglect their physical health for a number of reasons. They may lose their appetite and consequently not eat or drink enough and they may not have the motivation to carry out self-care activities. Individuals may also have strong negative feelings about themselves. They may feel that they do not deserve to be well and that they deserve to be in pain. Consequently, they may punish themselves by neglecting chronic illnesses, not taking medication correctly and failing to attend appointments consistently. Co-morbid depression is explored more fully in Chapter 9.

## Physical pain

Individuals with personality disorder appear more likely to have problems with chronic pain and are at risk of developing dependence on pain control medication. The reasons for this are not fully understood. However, it is possible that this is linked to the low and unstable mood states often experienced by individuals with personality disorder. In particular, depression and anxiety may make it more difficult for an individual to cope with pain and also make it more difficult for them to take actions that might reduce the pain, such as engaging in mentally absorbing activities to provide distraction.

This contrasts with the view, sometimes put forward to explain self-harming behaviours, that individuals with personality disorder have high pain thresholds.

This view is often used to justify using less than optimum pain control strategies when treating self-induced injuries. Individuals with personality disorder often use self-harm as a way to manage intense emotional pain (see Chapter 11). It is possible that in times of intense emotional distress physical pain may be experienced as less intense because of the adrenaline in the individual's system. However, as physical pain is often used to distract the person from intense and overwhelming emotional pain, it is likely that the physical pain is experienced intensely if it effectively blots out the emotional pain. This suggests that there is no reduction in pain sensation at the time of self-harming.

Whatever changes, if any, occur to an individual's perception of pain in the moment of self-harm, these resolve quickly and the individual then returns to being vulnerable to experiencing pain intensely.

# Physical health and intellectual disabilities

Historically, individuals with intellectual disabilities have experienced very poor physical health. In the 1930s average life expectancy of an individual with intellectual disabilities was less than 20 years. This has increased dramatically to 58–74 years now, depending on the severity of the individual's disabilities. However, this still remains below the life expectancy for the general public. Individuals with intellectual disabilities continue to have poorer health than the general population and are more likely to have conditions such as epilepsy.

Individuals with intellectual disabilities are also less likely than the general population to receive good health care. Investigations following a number of deaths in hospitals of individuals with intellectual disabilities suggest that health care professionals do not value the lives of such individuals as much as those of members of the general population. This leads to a failure to recognise and meet their needs. There may be poor communication, delays to diagnosis and treatment and a failure to recognise and treat pain. When in hospital, individuals with intellectual disabilities may not receive the extra support they need with basic self-care such as washing and eating.

## Physical pain and intellectual disabilities

Individuals with intellectual disabilities feel pain in the same way as other people. However, as a result of communication difficulties they may have difficulties putting this into words and may express pain through their behaviour and body language. It is therefore necessary for staff to look for signs of pain and make the extra effort to communicate with individuals with intellectual disabilities if pain is to be managed well. Sadly, this is often not done because there is an entirely false but widespread belief among health professionals that people with intellectual disabilities have a higher pain threshold than the rest of the population. Consequently, individuals with intellectual disabilities often go without the pain control that would be offered to other people.

## Impact of cognitive deficits

Difficulties with problem solving and abstract thinking can impact on the ability of individuals with intellectual disabilities to understand the need to follow a healthy lifestyle and comply with medical advice. They will often need a lot of skilled support to help them understand the need for actions that are important to keep them healthy.

## Health action plans

As a result of the concerns about the poor health of individuals with intellectual disabilities, the Department of Health (2001; 2009a; 2009b) recommends that every individual has a health action plan (HAP). This is a document that includes the actions needed to maintain and improve the individual's health and any help they need to accomplish these actions. The HAP is intended to provide a link between the individual and the range of services they need for their physical and mental well-being. The plan is intended to be jointly made by health professionals and the individual and should be in a format that the individual is able to understand and use.

## Care passports

Care passports (originally called hospital passports) were developed as a result of concerns about staff in hospitals not knowing how to communicate with or support individuals with intellectual disabilities. The passports have evolved to be used to support individuals going into any setting where staff are unfamiliar with the individual. There are a number of different formats for care passports but all versions bring together key information about the individual and how to communicate with and support them in a form that is well organised and easy to read. They also include information about current medication, allergies, dietary and religious requirements and important contact numbers. The link to a good example ('this is me') is given in the Further reading section. Care passports have been positively received by general hospital staff and go some way to preventing some of the misunderstandings that arise as to the type of care and support individuals need.

# Physical health in individuals with intellectual disabilities and personality disorder

Individuals with intellectual disabilities and personality disorder seem particularly vulnerable to developing physical health problems, perhaps because they have the additional vulnerabilities that come with each condition. They sometimes seem to live their lives on the basis of doing the opposite of every aspect of a healthy lifestyle. It is not unusual to find that an individual eats nothing but fast food, drinks large quantities of cola and strong coffee, smokes, misuses alcohol, has a reverse sleep/waking pattern, takes very little exercise and spends most of their time watching TV and feeling bored. Poor personal hygiene means that they often have tooth and gum disease leading to problems with pain and abscesses. If they have skin problems such as eczema or psoriasis, these may develop secondary infections.

Many individuals seem to be ill all the time, often with vague ailments that move around their bodies; as one problem is resolved another seems to develop. They often need pain relief and may end up on high doses of powerful painkillers. Where they have a chronic illness such as diabetes, colitis, or celiac disease, it will often be poorly controlled. Individuals with epilepsy may present a complex picture of poorly controlled seizures and also non-epileptic seizures.

Individuals with intellectual disabilities and personality disorder often seem to be an unreliable source of information about their health problems. They may be in a state of panic about a particular symptom one day but seem to have forgotten it the next. Often they will attend a doctor's appointment arranged to address a particular health problem only to return with medication for something completely different. When at the doctor's they may use dramatic language, show intense emotional distress and intense reactions to physical examinations. This can cause the doctor to suspect serious illness and consequently to prescribe strong medications and request further testing. Alternatively, an individual may present as completely mystified as to why their symptoms have occurred. For example, someone with diabetes and high sugar levels may purport to be following a strict diet. This may lead the doctor to prescribe higher doses of drugs such as insulin rather than helping them address their (undisclosed) unhealthy eating.

On their return from the appointment, the information an individual shares about the action the doctor has suggested often sounds unlikely when staff think about what is usually prescribed for a particular problem. For example, an individual with diabetes may tell staff that the diabetic nurse has told them to drink cola regularly to maintain their sugar levels. In fact the health professionals are often misquoted to allow the individual to continue with aspects of an unhealthy lifestyle which have powerful benefits for them.

Even when it is clear what has been prescribed, individuals with intellectual disabilities and personality disorder often struggle to follow the advice. Medication may be taken inconsistently, forgotten or the prescribed dose exceeded. Advice about diet, exercise, smoking or other lifestyle issues is often completely ignored. The individual will often return to the doctor complaining of the problem persisting and may not share the information about their inconsistent compliance with the doctor's previous advice. This can result in the prescription of stronger or additional medications and more investigations. Unwanted side effects from these can lead to further medications being prescribed. Consequently, individuals can end up on multiple medications while still feeling physically unwell.

Where they are also experiencing depression, individuals with intellectual disabilities and personality disorder can neglect their physical health to an extent that it puts their lives at risk.

## Supporting individuals with physical health problems

Supporting individuals with intellectual disabilities and personality disorder who have physical health problems can be frustrating and distressing for staff. Staff often feel powerless in the face of someone who is unwell and appears to be making themselves worse. However it is possible to help individuals meet their physical health needs. There are a number of steps to this process:

- A holistic assessment of the individual's behaviour; physical health needs to be considered in the context of the individual's intellectual disabilities, personality disorder, mental health and their social context.

- Assessing the individual's capacity to make decisions about their physical health.

- Understanding and addressing the conflicts that can arise within and between staff teams supporting individuals with intellectual disabilities and personality disorder (splitting).

- Creating a health action plan (HAP) that addresses the unmet needs driving the unhelpful behaviours.

# Holistic assessment of physical health and health related behaviours

Making sense of an individual's health-related behaviour requires thorough assessment. Box 8.3 suggests some areas that it is useful to explore.

---

## Box 8.3: Factors to consider when assessing physical health

**Accuracy of physical assessments:** Check that individual has not been able to distort results eg. drinking cola before taking a 'fasting' blood sugar test

**Current medication:** Number, dose, side-effects and interactions – is this causing the health problem?

**Compliance with medication:** What is actually being taken (rather than reported to be taken)?

**Compliance with other medical advice:** What was actually recommended by the doctor? What is the individual doing (as opposed to saying they are doing)?

**Physical/psychological dependence:** Is the medication(s) associated with dependence? Does the individual have a history of dependence eg. drugs, alcohol?

**Risky behaviours:** What are they? Links to impulse control?

**Intellectual deficits:** Does the individual have a concept of time/future and the ability to understand that events have delayed consequences? Memory – can the individual retain and accurately recall what they have been told? Are they able to understand their health problems and the need for certain actions?

**Communication deficits:** Do they have the ability to communicate physical and emotional pain?

**Stress:** How stressed is the individual? What support/skills do they have to deal with this stress?

**Emotional needs:** Intensity and instability of emotional reactions, their ability to meet these appropriately. Does physical illness meet these needs or help manage the emotions?

**Mental health:** Does the individual also have a mental health problem eg. depression or anxiety?

Continued...

---

---

**Functions of the unhealthy behaviour:** Does the behaviour arise from unmet needs or have powerful immediate benefits (secondary gains)? For example:

- immediate physical rewards/pleasure eg. smoking, caffeine
- avoiding immediate pain/discomfort
- avoiding unpleasant ideas or thoughts
- gaining attention/sympathy
- being the centre of concern/feeling special (*'The doctors don't know what's wrong with me'*)
- being cared for/being dependent
- being treated by ambulance/paramedics
- going to hospital/accessing hospital care
- avoiding responsibilities/activities because of illness
- blotting out emotional pain
- inflicting pain on self/self-punishment/self-destruction
- creating a sense of powerlessness in others
- proving they are not controlled by others/defiance.

---

Sometimes staff can feel deskilled by the fact that the problems relate to physical illness and think that they should leave sorting these problems to physical health care professionals. However, physical health professionals are often unskilled at supporting individuals with intellectual disabilities or mental health problems and, with rare exceptions, tend to expect those supporting the individual to address any difficulties.

In fact, once physical causes such as side-effects of medication have been eliminated, it can be helpful to assess and manage health-related behaviours in the same manner as other behaviours described as 'challenging'. It is particularly helpful to consider what purpose or function the behaviour may be serving for the individual. The techniques of functional analysis developed for exploring challenging behaviours can be very helpful (see Chapter 10).

## Capacity, choice and human rights

Often individuals appear to be happy with their unhealthy behaviour and seem not to want to change this pattern. In such situations staff may say that the individual has made a choice and that it would be an infringement of their human rights to try to change that behaviour. It is certainly true that most members of the general public make unhealthy choices several times every day.

There is no reason why individuals with intellectual disabilities and personality disorder should be deprived of the right to occasionally eat cream cakes or take the lift rather than walking up stairs. However, when behaviour has potentially very serious or life-threatening consequences it is important to consider if the individual has the capacity to make that choice.

Capacity must be assessed sensitively and in a non-judgemental way to encourage the individual to be open and honest about their behaviour. The assessment needs to explore what the individual knows about their illness, the impact of their behaviour on their present and future health, and their reasons for behaving in the way that they do.

If the individual does not understand their health problems and is unaware of the consequences of their behaviour, it does not necessarily mean that they lack capacity. Attempts must be made to help them understand. If, despite all efforts to inform them, they do not understand, this may be an indication that they lack capacity and decisions must be made for them following the principles of best interests.

Individuals who are aware of the consequences of their behaviour may still not be making a positive choice to behave in a harmful way. They may want to avoid the negative effects of their behaviour but be unable to resist emotional pressures and short-term enjoyment. They may understand the benefits of regular tests but be afraid of the discomfort involved. They may have been discouraged by the repeated failures of their efforts to manage their own behaviour and have given up on themselves. They may be suffering from depression and feel that there is no point or that they deserve to be ill. By exploring the reasons for their behaviour with them it may be possible to find a constructive way of working with the individual to change their behaviour.

Only where the individual fully understands the consequences of their behaviour and would be able to behave appropriately if they wished, but actively chooses to behave in ways that are harmful to their health, can staff consider that this is an informed choice. Even in this situation staff have a duty of care towards the individual. This would allow staff, for example, to say 'It is true that we cannot tell you what to drink when you are out alone. However we must encourage you to only drink sugar-free cola here, because of your diabetes'. Staff would still need to explore the factors driving the unwise choices and continue to work to promote healthier choices. Where an individual is making unwise choices staff teams should also think carefully about their own behaviour and whether they are inadvertently rewarding the individual's unhealthy behaviours. If this is found to be the case then staff need to identify ways in which they can switch the balance so that rewards are given for healthier choices.

# Splitting

Physical health care often involves a number of different teams and services, for example; GPs, hospital consultants, nurse practitioners, community nurses and care staff. Given the emotive nature of many health problems it is not surprising that disagreements and tensions can occur between teams. It is important that these issues are resolved if the individual's health needs are to be successfully addressed. How these tensions arise and ideas for addressing them are explored fully in Chapter 14.

# Creating and following a HAP

It can be very helpful to pull all the information about an individual's health needs together in a HAP. The process of working together with the individual to develop the plan can be very productive as they can be supported to explore how their emotional needs and cognitive deficits are impacting on their physical health. This can become a resource for the individual to use and also a means of promoting consistency within and between staff teams. In developing the plan it is important that staff draw on accurate information about any health conditions an individual has rather than accepting at face value what an individual may tell them. However well drawn up a HAP is, an individual with intellectual disabilities and personality disorder is unlikely to follow it without support from staff. Hence drawing up the plan together is only the first step in the process of working towards a healthier lifestyle. Some ideas for promoting adherence to the plan are given now.

## Understanding specific health problems

Building up a sound knowledge of the individual's health problems and the recommended treatments can be very helpful in reducing conflict within and between teams. It also helps to ensure that individuals receive a consistent message about what they should be doing to look after themselves. This consistent message in turn makes it more likely that the individual will follow the HAP. When exploring any health problem, it is particularly important to think about the mind–body links and how these might be influenced by the individual with intellectual disabilities and personality disorder.

Two conditions that are relatively common and often difficult to manage are diabetes and seizures (epileptic and non-epileptic). These are explored more fully in Boxes 8.4 and 8.5.

---

## Box 8.4: Diabetes

There are two types of diabetes.

**Type 1/insulin dependent:** Controlled by regular insulin injections and diet. Sugar levels can go too high (eating too much sugar) or too low (imbalance between dose of insulin and food eaten or exercise taken). Frequent tests of blood sugar are needed (finger prick tests). If sugar levels drop too low it is necessary to quickly consume a small amount of something sugary to raise levels to avoid losing consciousness.

**Type 2:** This is controlled by diet and oral medication. Sugar levels can go too high (eating too much sugar) but do not go too low. Blood sugar levels are only checked at intervals.

### Supporting individuals with diabetes

Individuals with diabetes can present a range of challenges for staff. Individuals with type 2 diabetes often do not understand the difference between that and type 1 diabetes. They may insist that they need lots of sugary snacks to 'keep up' their sugar levels and may want to check their blood sugar several times a day. Individuals with type 1 diabetes are often unreliable informants about their diet and insulin injections. They will often end up on high doses of insulin that still do not control their sugar levels. Staff need a good understanding of how these illnesses work in order to give consistent advice and support. Often supposedly difficult to control, diabetes turns out to be very manageable once the individual is supported to do what they are meant to be doing rather than telling staff they have done one thing and doing another.

---

## Promoting a healthy lifestyle

Healthy lifestyles can be encouraged by a number of approaches. Staff need a good knowledge of, for example, diet and exercise so that they can answer questions and suggest healthy alternatives. It is also helpful if staff model healthy behaviours. It is important that teaching materials are accessible and also fun to complete. Individuals may also enjoy attending health promotion groups.

## Reducing temptation

Where an individual wants to follow a healthy lifestyle but has problems maintaining their motivation it can be helpful to work with them on ways of reducing temptation. These might include shopping from a list, shopping with a friend who supports their attempts to improve their health, always having a supply of healthy snacks and joining support groups. Other ideas on managing impulses are given in Chapter 6.

---

## Box 8.5: Epileptic and non-epileptic seizures

**Epileptic seizures**

These occur as a result of disorganised electrical activity in the brain. There are different types including tonic-clonic (loss of consciousness and jerking of limb), partial complex and absence seizures. Prolonged tonic-clonic seizures can be life-threatening. Seizures may be partially or completely controlled by medication. They may have environmental triggers and can be influenced by factors such as arousal/excitement.

**Non-epileptic seizures**

These are not linked to electrical activity in the brain. Rarely, they may be the result of other medical conditions including muscle disorders. More often they are psychological in origin. They can co-exist with epileptic seizures or occur alone. They are more common in individuals who have experienced abuse.

**Supporting individuals with seizures**

Supporting individuals with seizures can be very worrying for staff as prolonged epileptic seizures can be life-threatening. Epilepsy often improves dramatically if staff are able to support the individual to accurately follow medical recommendations. Non-epileptic seizures can be very difficult to manage, particularly if the individual also has epilepsy. However, if staff have a good understanding of both conditions it is often possible to distinguish between the types of seizure and to ensure that each receives the correct treatment. Where epilepsy is severely out of control, this may require inpatient assessment.

---

## Reinforcing healthy behaviour

As a general principle it is helpful to aim to notice and praise healthy behaviours but to be very low key in responding to unhealthy behaviours. This can be difficult to do in practice as often individuals will flaunt their unhealthy behaviours in front of staff as they are looking for a reaction. It can be helpful to show recognition of the fact that staff cannot control the individual. Responding with *'It's your body'* and changing the subject can be helpful with some individuals.

Where individuals find health care reinforcing it can be helpful to look at ways of minimising this reinforcement. Individuals should always receive good physical care, however it may be helpful to minimise 'pampering' or 'cosseting'. The treatment should be treated in a matter-of-fact way. Discussions during hospital visits might focus on all the fun things that can be done once the individual is better.

## Support and monitoring

Many health problems can be resolved by encouraging individuals to accept greater support. For example, jointly preparing for a visit to the GP or specialist, writing down the current problem, symptoms, and worries can help ensure that important issues are not overlooked at the appointment. Individuals should be encouraged to let a trusted member of staff accompany them to appointments so that they are able to hear the advice given. If there are concerns that medication or other treatments are not being accurately followed, individuals should be encouraged to accept closer support for at least a few weeks to see if they are accurately taking medication. Staff may be able to help individuals keep a log of symptoms and responses to medication to provide the doctor with more accurate information. Techniques for helping individuals engage with and form positive relationships with services are explored more fully in Chapter 13.

## Meeting underlying needs

Unhealthy behaviours should not be viewed in isolation from the individual's other needs. Actions to promote emotional well-being will often help address physical health problems and vice versa. Where a functional analysis has identified that the health-related behaviours are serving important functions for the individual, these behaviours will not change until those needs are met in another way.

## Knowledge of pain management approaches

It is helpful if staff are aware of and able to use pain management techniques that can complement and reduce the need for pain-controlling medication. These can include looking at seating and positions, use of hot or cold compresses, creams and rubs, and gentle exercise. Distraction techniques and mindfulness exercises (see Boxes 7.14 and 7.15) may also be helpful.

# Preparing for potential hospital admission

It is also helpful to ensure that the individual has a hospital/care passport. Staff can work with the individual to ensure that key information needed by general hospital staff is included in the passport. Work on preparing the passport can also be helpful in motivating the individual to follow their health action plan. Thinking about what it will be like in hospital may bring home the potential consequences of unhealthy behaviours.

By promoting good physical health the approaches above help individuals with intellectual disabilities and personality disorder feel better about themselves and increase their resources for addressing their emotional issues.

# Key learning points

- Health is more than simply not being ill. It is a state of complete physical, mental and social well-being. The physical, mental and social aspects of a person are interwoven and do not work in isolation.

- Physical health is determined by a number of factors. These are biomedical (factors within the body), environmental (external factors that the person has little or no control over) and lifestyle (factors over which the person has control).

- Pain is an unpleasant sensation caused by stimuli that are very intense or cause damage to the body. While it might appear that pain is a purely physical experience, the experience of pain is influenced by psychological and social factors.

- Individuals with personality disorder have poorer physical health and shorter life expectancies than the general population. They are more likely to have conditions such as epilepsy. They are also less likely than the general population to receive good health care. Individuals with both conditions are very likely to have poor physical health.

- To help individuals with intellectual disabilities and personality disorder look after their physical health and lead healthier lifestyles it is necessary to take a holistic approach.

- Unhealthy behaviours will often be linked to underlying intellectual deficits and unmet emotional needs. They may be performing important functions for the individual. Physical health will often improve it these underlying needs are met.

- Health action plans and care passports are helpful in promoting well-being and ensuring the individual's needs are met.

- Clarity about mental capacity and close team work can help resolve the confusion and disagreements that often arise in teams about how problems relating to physical health and unhealthy behaviours should be addressed.

# References

Department of Health (2001) *Valuing People: A new strategy for learning disability in the 21st century*. London: Department of Health.

Department of Health (2009a) *Valuing People Now: A three-year strategy for people with learning disabilities*. London: Department of Health (Chapter 3: Having a life).

Department of Health (2009b) *Health Action Planning and Health Facilitation for People with Learning Disabilities: Good practice guidance*. Available at: http://webarchive.nationalarchives. gov.uk/20130107105354/http://www.dh.gov.uk/en/Publicationsandstatistics/Publications/ PublicationsPolicyAndGuidance/DH_096505 (accessed April 2014).

Ward J (2010) *Life Expectancy in Mental Illness* [online]. Available at: http://psychcentral.com/ news/2010/07/13/life-expectancy-in-mental-illness/15502.html (accessed April 2014).

World Health Organization (1946) *Preamble to the Constitution of the World Health Organization as adopted by the International Health Conference, New York*. Available at: www.who.int/about/definition/ en/print.html (accessed April 2014).

# Further reading

Clarity (2002) *Health Action Plans. What are they? How do you get one? (A booklet for people with learning disabilities)*. London: Department of Health.

MacManus S & McGuire B (2010) *Feeling Better: A practical handbook for carers working with people who have an intellectual disability and chronic pain*. Brighton: Pavilion publishing.

Healthcare Commission (2007) *A Life Like No Other*. Available at: www.publications.parliamentuk/pa/ jt200708/jtselect/jrights/40/40i.pdf (accessed January 2014).

Mencap (2004) *Treat Me Right! Better healthcare for people with a learning disability*. Available at: www.mencap.org.uk/document.asp?id=316 (accessed April 2014).

Mencap (2007) *Death by Indifference: Following up the Treat Me Right! report*. Available at: www. mencap.org.uk/document.asp?id=284 (accessed April 2014).

Mencap (2012) *Death by Indifference: 74 deaths and counting. A progress report five years on*. Available at: http://www.mencap.org.uk/sites/default/files/documents/Death%20by%20Indifference%20-%20 74%20Deaths%20and%20counting.pdf (accessed April 2014).

Surrey Health Action (2014) *This is Me – My care passport*. Available at: www.surreyhealthaction.org/ downloads/hospital%20passport%20surrey.pdf (accessed April 2014).

Tragesser S, Bruns D & Disorbio J (2010) Borderline personality disorder features and pain: the mediating role of negative affect in a pain patient sample. *The Clinical Journal of Pain* **26** 4348–4353.

# Chapter 9: Mental health problems

This chapter looks at mental health and mental health problems. It looks at the type of additional mental health problems that may be experienced by individuals with intellectual disabilities and personality disorder. It looks at some of the issues arising from individuals having additional mental health problems and how staff may support individuals with these difficulties.

## Key topics

- Mental health

- Characteristics and causes of mental health problems

- Common mental health problems

- Treatment approaches

- Mental health problems and individuals with personality disorder

- Mental health problems and individuals with intellectual disabilities

- Mental health problems and individuals with intellectual disabilities and personality disorder

- Supporting individuals with additional mental health problems

## Mental health

The World Health Organization (2010) describes mental health as '*a state of well-being in which the individual realises his or her own abilities, can cope with the normal stresses of life, can work productively and fruitfully and is able to make a contribution to his or her community*'. Hence mental health goes beyond the simple absence of mental health problems to include achievements, resilience and social functioning. Mental health or mental well-being/'wellness' suggests a state in which a person does not have any significant difficulties with their thinking, emotions or behaviour and in which they are able to function well, both individually and within society.

The World Health Organization also sees mental well-being as a core component in general health. This recognises the interconnection between physical and mental well-being. All the factors identified in Chapter 8 as influencing physical health are likely to, either directly or indirectly, influence mental health.

# Characteristics and causes of mental health problems

A person may be seen as having mental health problems when they become distressed, or experience deterioration in their functioning, as a result of changes to their usual patterns of thoughts, emotions or behaviour. When these changes are significant and sustained the person may be considered to have a 'psychiatric disorder' or 'mental illness'. There is on-going debate about whether mental health problems should be seen as 'illnesses' and whether using terms such as 'illness' and 'disorder' is stigmatising. These issues are beyond the scope of this book; however it is important to be aware of the fears, anxieties and prejudices that surround these difficulties and to be sensitive and thoughtful when talking about mental health issues.

## Causes

The causes of mental health problems are still not fully understood. However, it appears that some people are more vulnerable to experiencing mental health problems. There appears to be a genetic element to this risk. The development of mental health problems has also been linked to the level of stress a person is exposed to and to major life events such as bereavement, physical illness or loss of a job.

## Common mental health problems

There are a huge number of mental health problems or disorders listed in the two international classification systems (ICD-10 and DSM-5). Some are extremely rare and others are very common. Some of the most frequently encountered mental health problems are described next.

## Anxiety disorders

Anxiety is a state comprising four components: emotion, thoughts, physical sensations and behaviours. The person experiences feelings of nervousness, uneasiness or dread. Their mind is occupied by worrying or frightening thoughts.

Intellectual Disabilities and Personality Disorder: An integrated approach

They may experience a range of physical sensations such as racing heart, butterflies in their stomach, sweating or rapid breathing. Their behaviour pattern may change; they may run away from, or avoid, certain situations. They may have difficulty falling asleep.

Anxiety is a natural reaction to stress but if it becomes excessive it may lead to an anxiety disorder. There are a number of anxiety disorders. Generalised anxiety disorder occurs where a person is highly anxious for a long period of time without any specific focus for their concerns. Other anxiety disorders include phobias, for example, agoraphobia where someone is afraid to leave home and social phobia where they fear social situations. Obsessive-compulsive disorder, where the person feels compelled to complete elaborate rituals and is preoccupied by anxious and distressing thoughts, is also classified as an anxiety disorder.

# Mood disorders

The term 'mood disorders' is used to refer to a group of mental health problems where the most prominent feature is disturbance to the person's mood or emotional state. However, these disorders will also impact on the person's thoughts, physical sensation and behaviour. There are a number of problems within this group including depression, mania and bipolar disorder.

## Depression

When depressed, people experience feelings of sadness, helplessness and hopelessness. They may become irritable and snappy. Their minds are occupied with negative thoughts about themselves, other people and their lives. They may think that life is not worth living and have thoughts about harming themselves or ending it all. They may feel tired all the time, find it difficult to do anything and may lose interest in things they usually enjoy. Others may be restless and unable to settle to anything. Their appetite may change so that they eat a lot more or less than usual. This will be reflected in weight gain or loss. Some people may have difficulty sleeping despite feeling tired or may wake up much earlier than usual. Others may sleep a lot more than usual. Some may attempt to kill themselves.

## Mania/hypomania

Mania is characterised by feeling euphoric. People experiencing mania have high energy levels and find it difficult to stay still; some may stop eating because they cannot sit still long enough to finish a meal. They will have difficulty sleeping; some may go without sleep for several days. They are likely to talk continually at a fast rate and sometimes it will be very difficult to make sense of what they are talking about; they may jump from one topic to another. People will find their thoughts racing and some may experience psychotic symptoms (see Chapter 7 and below). Hypomania is a milder version of mania.

## Bipolar affective disorder

In bipolar disorder people experience episodes of depression. However, they also have periods of mania or hypomania. Usually they will experience mood phases that last several weeks and will have periods between phases when they are neither high or low in mood. However, people vary greatly in their pattern of mood swings.

# Psychosis

Psychosis is used to describe mental health problems that stop people from thinking clearly and telling the difference between reality and imagination. These problems can cause severe disruption to perception and emotions. They can lead to a person behaving in ways that seem very strange to others.

Schizophrenia is one type of psychotic illness. In schizophrenia people experience a range of psychotic symptoms and a change to their emotional responding. The psychotic symptoms may include strange or paranoid thinking (delusions) or experiencing things that are not really there (hallucinations). Everyone can experience psychotic symptoms at times of stress but in schizophrenia these symptoms are much more pervasive and persistent. The person may truly believe that they are being pursued by enemy agents or that they are being controlled by aliens. They may experience voices talking about them or telling them to do things. These experiences feel 'real' to the person. They may be frightened or upset by their experiences and may become angry with people who challenge their beliefs or disbelieve their experiences. As a result of their experiences the person's behaviour may become very odd and their speech may be difficult to understand.

People with schizophrenia may also experience a loss of interest in things, reduced motivation and difficulties with concentration. They may withdraw into themselves and try to avoid contact with other people.

Most people with schizophrenia are not aggressive and are much more at risk from others than a risk to themselves. However, sometimes people, while in a severely psychotic state, may attack or even kill another person. The randomness and horror of such attacks means that they gain a great deal of media attention and this distorts public understanding of schizophrenia.

Schizophrenia used to be viewed as likely to lead to long-term, severe impairment of functioning. However, with better treatments and early intervention this view is being challenged and many people who experience psychosis go on to make good recoveries and lead full and active lives.

# Post-traumatic stress disorder

Post-traumatic stress disorder (PTSD), also called post-traumatic stress syndrome, is a collection of symptoms that may develop in response to a traumatic event. The condition may arise as a result of experiencing violent crime, physical or sexual assault, road traffic accidents, conflict situations or natural disasters. Children who have been abused are also vulnerable to developing PTSD. Symptoms may develop some time after the trauma, sometimes triggered by the occurrence of another trauma or a stressful period. Everyone will experience some symptoms in response to trauma but in PTSD these symptoms persist longer than a month or have a negative impact on the person's well-being. There are a number of symptoms of PTSD that include reliving the trauma, avoiding things associated with the trauma and increased arousal or anxiety. These symptoms are described more fully in Box 9.1.

The causes of PTSD are not fully understood. Some people are more resilient to trauma than others and it is known that people who had previously experienced mental health problems are more vulnerable to developing PTSD. Some events are more likely to cause severe and lasting reactions. Deliberate acts of violence or exploitation seem more damaging than natural disasters. Being the victim of deliberate acts may damage a person's trust in others, particularly if the aggressor is someone they have been close to.

---

### Box 9.1: Symptoms of PTSD

Reliving aspects of the trauma

- Flashbacks (feeling that or acting as if the trauma is happening all over again). The person may remain in touch with reality or may re-experience the events as if they were happening again in the present time.

- Intrusive thoughts and images – however hard the person tries they cannot get these thoughts and pictures to go away.

- Nightmares – these may be re-experiencing the traumatic event or may be about other frightening situations.

- Intense distress in response to anything that brings back memories of the trauma.

Continued...

---

Avoiding memories

- Keeping very busy – not allowing time to think
- Avoiding situations that trigger memories or thoughts of the trauma
- Repressing memories (being unable to remember aspects of the event)
- Feeling detached, cut off and emotionally numb
- Being unable to express affection
- Feeling there's no point in planning for the future

Over-arousal

- Being easily upset
- Quick to anger
- Difficulty falling asleep
- Disturbed sleep
- Irritable and aggressive behaviour
- Lacking concentration
- Extreme alertness – hyper-vigilance
- Panic response to anything associated with the trauma
- Being easily startled

# Eating disorders

Eating disorders are a group of illnesses that involve eating habits that damage the person's physical and mental health. These habits may involve restricting the intake of food by dieting, or trying to avoid the absorption of food after eating. For example, by vomiting, taking laxatives, diuretics or abusing insulin and burning off food by excessive exercise. They may also involve overeating, either bingeing when large amounts of food are consumed at one time or regularly overeating throughout the day. Certain combinations of symptoms have been given names (see Box 9.2), however, in reality people often show a combination of behaviours that cross the named conditions or move from one condition to another over time.

The causes of eating disorders are complex and they are associated with Western societies where food is freely available and there is a culture that is obsessed with beauty and slimness. As with many conditions, some people seem to have a vulnerability to developing eating disorders. It is also understood that people may use unhealthy eating patterns as a way of coping with difficult situations or emotions. Unhealthy eating habits may arise from low self-esteem. They may fill time if the person is bored or may be used to try to overcome an emotional feeling of emptiness. They may be a way of coping with anger, anxiety, loneliness, sadness or shame. Dieting and restricting food intake may create a sense of control. Both men and women can develop eating disorders but they are more common in women.

---

## Box 9.2: Eating disorders

**Anorexia nervosa:** Keeping body weight below healthy levels by dieting, exercise or excessive use of laxatives or diuretics.

**Bulimia nervosa:** Eating binges are followed by behaviours that aim to prevent the food from being absorbed eg. dieting, exercise, vomiting, excessive use of laxatives or diuretics (often called 'purging'). Weight may be normal for height, masking the condition.

**Binge eating:** Episodes of uncontrolled overeating (binges) without behaviours that aim to prevent the food from being absorbed.

**Compulsive overeating:** Overeating but without the bingeing.

---

There are a number of serious risks associated with eating disorders depending on the behaviours engaged in. These include physical problems such as damage to teeth and bones, damage to internal organs including kidneys, fertility problems, increased risk of heart attacks with an increased risk of death. Eating disorders are also associated with a risk of self-harm, suicidal thinking and attempting suicide.

# Alcohol and drug-related conditions

Excessive use of alcohol or drugs can lead to a number of problems. People are considered to have a disorder where their use of a substance leads to physical and mental health problems and impacts on their social functioning. At this level the problem will be described as alcohol or drug 'misuse' or 'harmful use'. Other people will develop a physical and psychological addiction to drugs or alcohol. This is described as having drug or alcohol dependence. People who are dependent on a substance will show a range of symptoms including; a strong desire to take the substance, difficulty controlling its use, giving a higher priority to using the substance than to other activities, increasing tolerance to the substance (needing to increase the amount used), experiencing withdrawal symptoms if they stop taking the substance and persisting despite the negative consequences of the behaviour. Such people are also at risk of engaging in criminal activity to fund their dependence.

# Treatment approaches

There are a number of elements to the treatment of mental health problems. These include:

■ specific treatments for particular problems,

■ overarching models for how treatment should be delivered such as the Recovery Model

■ programmes or packages aiming to implement these models

■ systems for structuring and monitoring care eg. Care Programme Approach (CPA).

# Specific treatments

It is beyond the scope of this book to explore the treatment of mental health problems. However, the treatment of mental health problems in the general population is increasingly well researched. The National Institute for Health and Care Excellence (NICE) evaluates the research evidence and issues guidance on the recommended treatments for a wide range of mental health problems. The full guidance and accessible summaries can be downloaded from the NICE website (see Further reading). This advice covers medication, psychological and social interventions.

# Overarching models of treatment

In addition to treatments focused on specific problems there some general approaches to addressing mental health needs that are being recognised as particularly helpful. These approaches emphasise a positive, collaborative relationship between a person and their mental health services. One example is the Recovery Model, which has been widely adopted both in the US and the UK.

## The Recovery Model

This approach aims to support each person's potential for recovery and sees 'treatment' as an individual journey rather than aiming for a set outcome or 'cure'. It recognises that recovery does not necessarily mean getting back to where someone was before they became ill and that while someone may never have full control over their symptoms, they can still have control over their life. Recovery is seen not as 'getting rid of' the illness, but as seeing beyond it, to help the person to recognise and develop their abilities, build on their interests and achieve their dreams. This approach has a number of elements, which are described in Box 9.3.

## Box 9.3: Elements of the Recovery Model

**Hope:** Having hope for a positive future living with mental health problems, whatever the end of the journey

**Security:** Having basic needs met eg. stable home, financial security

**Sense of self:** Having a positive sense of identity beyond the mental health problem

**Supportive relationships**
- Having positive relationships
- Mutual help/peer support
- Being supported by staff who care and value the individual

**Empowerment**
- Having knowledge of own mental health problem and the most effective treatments
- Recognising each person as an 'expert' on their own experiences
- Being an active user of services and directing own treatment (self-determination)
- Having rights upheld and respected by services
- Identifying and building on strengths
- Having a sense of control over own life and a sense of self-agency

**Social inclusion:** Being involved in and part of the larger community

**Coping skills**
- Developing new skills
- Self-management of symptoms and avoiding relapse (self-regulation)

**Meaning**
- Having a positive sense of the meaning of life
- Being involved in meaningful activities
- Developing spirituality

## Programmes based on the recovery model

A number of programmes have been developed as ways of helping people realise the objectives of the Recovery Model. These approaches are often described as 'self-management' systems. Self-management programmes aim to provide information, develop self-management skills, enhance hope and empower people. They take a holistic approach, encouraging people to move beyond just managing symptoms to building a meaningful life. One of the most widely used systems is Wellness Recovery Action Planning (WRAP ®). People are supported to create their own WRAP, setting out their goals, what help they need to reach the goals, what keeps them well and what puts their mental health at risk of deteriorating. They are supported to identify their personal resources and to use these as their 'wellness toolkit'. In developing the wellness toolkit people might be encouraged to look at areas such as healthy eating, building positive relationships, improving their sleep, taking up physical and social activities, managing their finances and their use of alcohol and cigarettes. A WRAP also includes a crisis plan and advanced directives for what should happen if the person's illness makes them unable to make decisions safely for themselves.

These approaches are relatively new but there is growing evidence that they are effective and well-liked by those who participate in them.

## Systems for structuring and monitoring care

The need for a more systematic and structured approach to supporting people with severe mental health problems was identified through a number of investigations into serious incidents. These incidents included occasions when, for example, a person with mental health problems killed a member of the public. These investigations identified a common theme of people slipping through the net and hence not receiving the treatment that would have prevented the serious incident. This highlighted the need for there to be systems in place to ensure that people received treatment and support. As a result, the UK government introduced the Care Programme Approach (CPA), making it mandatory for people with complex mental health needs.

The CPA does not dictate what treatment approach should be used. Rather it aims to ensure that a person's strengths and needs are identified, and that care is co-ordinated and delivered as it is described in the care plan. It also requires that people with complex needs have a relapse prevention and crisis management plan. The CPA is intended to be person-centred and to promote the involvement of the person in planning their care. The government's list of characteristics for health professionals to consider when deciding if a person should be supported by CPA is summarised in Box 9.4.

When a person is supported through the CPA they are allocated a 'care co-ordinator'; an experienced professional who is responsible for overseeing their care.

## Box 9.4: When CPA is needed

- Severe mental disorder (including personality disorder) with high degree of clinical complexity
- Current or potential risk(s), including:
  - suicide, self-harm, harm to others (including history of offending)
  - relapse history requiring urgent response
  - self-neglect/non-concordance with treatment plan
- Vulnerable adult; adult/child protection eg.
  - financial, sexual, physical or emotional abuse
  - child protection issues
- Current or significant history of severe distress/instability or disengagement
- Presence of non-physical co-morbidity eg. substance/alcohol/prescription drugs misuse, intellectual disability
- Multiple service provision from different agencies, including: housing, physical care, employment, criminal justice, voluntary agencies
- Currently/recently detained under Mental Health Act or referred to crisis/home treatment team
- Significant reliance on carer(s) or has own significant caring responsibilities
- Experiencing disadvantage or difficulty as a result of:
  - parenting responsibilities
  - physical health problems/disability
  - unsettled accommodation/housing issues
  - employment issues when mentally ill
  - significant impairment of function due to mental illness
- Ethnicity (eg. immigration status; race/cultural issues; language difficulties; religious practices); sexuality or gender issues

# Mental health problems and individuals with personality disorder

Individuals with personality disorder frequently experience additional mental health problems. Some estimates suggest that everyone diagnosed with a personality disorder is likely to have at least one episode of mental illness during their lifetime. The mental health problems most frequently associated with personality disorder are anxiety, depression, bipolar disorder, post-traumatic stress disorder (PTSD), eating disorders such as bulimia, and substance-related problems (drugs or alcohol). When individuals with personality disorder experience these problems they have the same symptoms as members of the general population who have that illness (see descriptions earlier in this chapter).

## Diagnosis

Having a personality disorder means that individuals often experience changes to their thoughts, emotions and behaviour that distress them or impair their functioning. This can make it very difficult to spot if they are developing an additional mental health problem. The single most helpful way of distinguishing features of personality disorder from additional mental health problems is the duration of the symptom. Symptoms arising from personality disorder rapidly fluctuate. In contrast, those related to mental health problems are more persistent.

## Vulnerability to mental health problems

Individuals with personality disorder appear to be at high risk of developing additional mental health problems. This may be because the conditions that lead to the development of personality disorder also contribute to the development of other mental health problems. This is particularly so for anxiety, depression and PTSD. Many individuals with personality disorder will have experienced abuse. Having experienced abuse is known to make individuals vulnerable to developing mental health problems.

Individuals with personality disorder often lead chaotic lives, have poor physical health and experience high levels of stress. These can all increase the risk of developing mental health problems.

Individuals with personality disorder may also be at risk of developing other conditions as a result of their efforts to address some of the difficulties they experience. This is particularly so for eating disorders, harmful substance use and dependence disorders. Individuals with personality disorder frequently lack self-confidence and have low self-esteem. This can lead them to seek happiness and self-worth in unhelpful ways. For example, in Western cultures being slim (or thin) is associated with happiness. This can lead people to extreme dieting in the belief that weight loss will solve their problems. Dieting can also bring a sense of control if the rest of their life feels out of control. Dieting, bingeing, exercise and purging may help block out intrusive memories. They may also address negative feelings about the self by creating the feeling of getting rid of something bad or as punishment for 'sins'. Bingeing can help create a physical sense of fullness to compensate for emotional feelings of emptiness. Drugs and alcohol can similarly provide an apparent short cut to happiness, numb intense feelings and block out intrusive memories. Difficulties with impulse control can make it hard for individuals with personality disorder to manage their use of drugs or alcohol, making it more likely that recreational use turns into a more significant problem.

### Treatment

Individuals with personality disorder often do less well in treatment programmes for additional mental health problems. They are more likely to drop out, may struggle to comply with treatment requirements and may need longer treatment. However, they can and do benefit from the range of treatment options available. It appears that the relationship with the therapist (therapeutic alliance) is particularly important if individuals with personality disorder are to benefit from treatment.

# Mental health problems and intellectual disabilities

There is some debate about the frequency of mental health problems in individuals with intellectual disabilities. This arises because of differences in the populations assessed (community or hospital based) and the type of mental health problems investigated. What is clear is that individuals with intellectual disabilities can experience the full range of mental health problems. These occur at similar or slightly higher rates to those in the general population. There is some evidence that individuals with mild intellectual disabilities are more vulnerable to developing schizophrenia than the general population.

A number of factors may make individuals with intellectual disabilities vulnerable to developing mental health problems. Some of these are given in Box 9.5.

> ## Box 9.5: Vulnerability factors for developing mental health problems
>
> **Biological**
>
> ■ **Genetic:** A number of conditions that cause intellectual disabilities also increase risk of developing mental health/behavioural problems eg. Fragile X syndrome
>
> ■ **Brain structure:** Structural abnormalities may lead to symptoms such as disinhibition
>
> ■ **Physical and sensory disabilities:** May contribute indirectly by increasing stress levels
>
> ■ **Medication:** Symptoms may be caused by medication prescribed for other problems
>
> **Psychological**
>
> ■ Poor stress management
>
> ■ Poor self-image and low self-esteem
>
> ■ Poor problem solving skills
>
> ■ Dysfunctional coping mechanisms
>
> **Social**
>
> ■ Under or overstimulating environments
>
> ■ Experiencing abuse
>
> ■ Lack of social support
>
> ■ Reduced life opportunities eg. work, social network
>
> Deb *et al* (2001)

# Diagnosis

It can be more difficult to spot the development of mental health problems in individuals with intellectual disabilities. There are a number of reasons for this. Communication difficulties can make it harder for individuals to describe what they are experiencing. Sometimes the symptoms will be noticed but may be thought to arise from the individual's intellectual disabilities and hence go untreated. Also, the presentation of mental health problems can be slightly different in individuals with intellectual disabilities. If people are not aware of these differences the problems may not be correctly identified. Some of these differences are given in Box 9.6.

In recognition of these differences and difficulties the two main systems for classifying mental health problems (ICD and DSM) have been adapted for use

Intellectual Disabilities and Personality Disorder: An integrated approach
© Pavilion Publishing and Media Ltd and its licensors 2014.

with individuals with intellectual disabilities (CD-LD and DM-ID). These bring together what is known about differences in presentation and suggest how diagnostic criteria should be adapted for use with this population.

However, there is also a risk that behaviour patterns that are associated with an individual's developmental level may be mistaken for a mental health problem. For example, having an 'imaginary friend' might be misunderstood as a hallucination. It is therefore important that the individual's usual functioning and developmental level are clearly understood before any diagnosis is made.

---

### Box 9.6: Different presentations of mental health problems in individuals with intellectual disabilities

**Anxiety:** Individuals may be more likely to report the physical symptoms of anxiety eg. saying they have a 'tummy ache' when experiencing butterflies in the stomach. This makes it more likely that anxiety will be mistaken for a physical illness.

**Depression:** Individuals may present as more irritable when experiencing depression (rather than the expected sadness). They may also become agitated and restless. Depression may also present a sleep problem (excessive sleeping) or as an eating problem (over or under eating).

**Hypomania and mania:** Individuals may show the behavioural signs of mania (lack of sleep, high levels of activity and restlessness) but this may be accompanied by irritability and aggression rather than an elated mood state.

**Bipolar affective disorder:** Rather than showing the expected changes from euphoria to sadness, individuals with intellectual disabilities may present as irritable both in episodes of mania and depression.

**Psychotic symptoms:** Delusions tend to be simpler eg. claiming to be able to do some every day activity that they cannot in reality do (and hence more difficult to spot).

---

## Treatment

Individuals with intellectual disabilities are often explicitly excluded from general research trials and research specifically with individuals with intellectual disabilities is limited. This can make identifying the most effective treatments more difficult. However, there is growing evidence that a range of approaches are helpful for this group provided adaptations are made for the impact of their intellectual disabilities (eg. simplifying wording, greater use of pictures). Useful techniques include CBT, DBT and relaxation techniques.

It is recognised that individuals with intellectual disabilities are more likely to have adverse reactions to medication prescribed for mental health problems and it is recommended that the doses used should be lower and should be reviewed more often than for the general public.

The Recovery Model fits comfortably with many of the values embedded in services for individuals with intellectual disabilities including choice, promoting independence and being person-centred. Self-management packages such as WRAP® are beginning to be adapted for use with individuals with intellectual disabilities.

# Mental health problems and individuals with intellectual disabilities and personality disorder

Individuals with intellectual disabilities and personality disorder are likely to be very vulnerable to experiencing additional mental health problems. The presentation of these mental health problems is likely to be influenced by their intellectual disabilities.

## Diagnosis

Diagnosing additional mental health problems in individuals with intellectual disabilities and personality disorder can be complex. For any symptom it is necessary to understand if it arises from their intellectual disabilities, their personality disorder, an additional mental health problem or some other cause such as a physical health problem, reaction to life events or the side-effects of medication. When trying to make sense of an individual's pattern of symptoms it is also important to be aware of both typical and unusual presentations of the mental health problems suspected. Approaches to diagnosis are explored in the following section.

## Treatment

Treatment for individuals with both intellectual disabilities and personality disorder is an under-researched area. It is likely that individuals will struggle to engage with and complete treatments. They are also likely to need approaches to be adapted to compensate for their intellectual disabilities. Approaches to supporting individuals are discussed in the following section.

# Supporting individuals with additional mental health problems

Supporting individuals with intellectual disabilities and personality disorder who develop additional mental health problems can be very difficult for staff. The individual may be very distressed and confused by their symptoms. Staff may also be confused about what is happening to the individual and may not be sure how to support or reassure them. However, taking a systematic, step-by-step approach can help support individuals to achieve a clear diagnosis and an effective support package. This should include:

- **seeking help** – supporting the individual to access specialist assessment

- a **holistic assessment** of the individual's symptoms; mental health needs to be considered in the context of the individual's personality disorder, physical health, intellectual disabilities and their social context

- using **the Recovery Model** within the framework of CPA to promote mental health and prevent or manage relapses

- **positive support** for dealing with symptoms, engaging with treatment and promoting mental well-being.

The approach below is intended for use where the individual's symptoms are not severe and the individual is engaging with the assessment and treatment process.

Where the mental health problem is resulting in challenging behaviours such as aggression it will also be important to look at the approaches discussed in Chapter 10. Approaches to supporting individuals showing suicidal behaviour and self-harm are explored fully in Chapter 11. Supporting individuals in crisis is addressed in Chapter 12 and Chapter 13 explores why an individual may have difficulties engaging with services.

## Seeking help

Sometimes individuals with intellectual disabilities and personality disorder will realise that they have additional problems and will seek help. At other times people who know the individual well may spot the symptoms and realise that they are behaving out of character. It is important to support the individual to seek a medical opinion as accurate diagnosis is essential and medication may be very helpful in some episodes. It is important to seek help in a timely manner as an individual's mental health may deteriorate rapidly and some episodes may require admission to hospital (either an acute adult ward or a specialist intellectual disabilities unit).

If an individual does not recognise that they may have mental health problems or does not want to seek help they should not be pressurised to accept a referral. Individuals may have had negative experiences with mental health services in the past, may be frightened by the thought of mental health services, or fear that they are 'going mad'.

Staff can use a number of approaches to help individuals explore their distress and difficulties and encourage them to seek help. Some helpful approaches are explored in other chapters of this book (see Box 9.7).

### Box 9.7: Approaches that may facilitate individuals recognising the need for help with mental health problems

- Active listening (Box 11.14)
- SET communications – Support, Empathy, Truth (Box 13.5)
- Motivational interviewing (Box 6.15)
- The Trans-theoretical Model of Change (Box 12.7)

Completing an assessment tool such as the Mini PAS-ADD (Moss & Estia Centre, 2001) with the individual. The Mini PAS-ADD (Psychiatric Assessment Schedule for Adults with Developmental Disabilities) is a screening tool developed to help staff spot mental health problems in individuals with intellectual disabilities. It is useful because it compares how the individual is thinking, feeling and behaving at the current time with how they felt at a previous time. This can help an individual to recognise that there have been changes to their thoughts, emotions and behaviour. Once this is recognised, they might be more willing to seek help.

However, if the individual's mental health deteriorates, it may then be necessary to follow the advice in Chapter 12 on using the legal framework to access the help the individual needs.

## Holistic assessment

When trying to clarify what is influencing the individual's thoughts, feelings and behaviour it is very important to have a clear picture of what exactly has changed, in what way and when. If the 'symptoms' arise from an individual's personality disorder they will come and go quickly with a lot of variation and fluctuation.

In contrast, symptoms arising from an additional mental health problem will be much more consistent and persistent but will not have been present for all their adult life. If the 'symptoms' are in fact aspects of their intellectual disabilities these will have been present over a long period of time; most will have developed in childhood or adolescence. 'Symptoms' that are a natural emotional response to life events such as bereavement or trauma will usually be closely linked to those events or some other smaller loss or trauma that reactivated difficult memories and unresolved feelings.

It is important that assessments are thorough and do not jump to conclusions on the basis of a few symptoms or the absence of one feature thought to be essential to the diagnosis of a particular mental health problem. It is particularly important to identify changes in all areas of the individual's lifestyle, social, psychological and physical functioning and to look at how these changes have interacted. Some areas to consider are given in Box 9.8.

## The Recovery Model and the CPA

Once the individual's mental health problems have been understood it is important to think about how care will be delivered. Delivering care based on the Recovery Model within the framework of CPA has a number of advantages when working with individuals with intellectual disabilities, personality disorder and additional mental health problems. This approach is person-centred and respectful. It empowers the individual and makes them central both to decisions about their care and also in leading efforts to improve their mental health. This helps avoid the individual slipping into a passive role of waiting for doctors to 'cure' them. It also reduces reasons for 'rebelling against' or 'resisting' treatment that feels as if it is being imposed on the individual. Using the terminology of motivational interviewing, this approach allows staff to 'roll with resistance'. Rather than 'You must take your antidepressants or you won't get better,' this approach would suggest the response 'OK, you don't want to take medication, how else can we work together to beat this depression?'

The clarity of roles and clear structure of the CPA process helps prevent splitting occurring within and between teams supporting the individual. It also gives one key point of contact in the CPA co-ordinator. The requirement for regular meetings to review progress also helps keep track of the individual's needs and makes sure that they do not slip through the net, for example, by repeatedly missing appointments and consequently being discharged from services.

The CPA aims to ensure that the individual has a comprehensive, multidisciplinary, multi-agency assessment covering the full range of needs and risks. It aims to promote safety through risk assessment and safety/contingency/crisis plans (see Chapter 12). The contingency and crisis plans should include arrangements so that the individual and the staff supporting them can contact the right professional/ service if they need to at any time.

---

## Box 9.8: Factors to consider when assessing symptoms suspected to arise from a related mental health problem

### Timeline of events

■ When did symptoms start?

■ When did other significant events occur?

■ Has this ever happened before?

Accurate information on the sequence of events is essential for understanding the relationship between events eg. did losing a job trigger the symptoms or was the job lost because symptoms resulted in poor job performance?

### Biological

■ **Genetic:** Does the individual have a condition or syndrome that is linked to an increased risk of developing mental health/behavioural problems? eg. Fragile X syndrome

■ **Brain structure:** Does the individual have known structural abnormalities that may lead to their symptoms?

■ **Physical and sensory disabilities:** Does the individual have any additional disabilities that may be contributing to their difficulties?

■ **Physical health:** Does the individual have any physical health problems that might be causing the symptoms? eg. poorly controlled diabetes can produce erratic behaviour and irritability

■ **Medication:** What medication is the individual taking? Symptoms may be caused by medication prescribed for other problems. Check also that they are taking the medication as prescribed. Has any medication been changed or stopped?

■ **Changes to usual bodily functioning:** Has the individual's sleep pattern changed? Are they eating more/less? Have they lost/gained weight? Are they more/less active? Are they going to the toilet more/less?

### Lifestyle and life events

■ What life events has the individual experienced?

■ Have there been any changes to their lifestyle/daily routine?

■ Does their lifestyle increase the risk of mental health problems?

■ Have they stopped doing things they used to enjoy?

Continued...

---

Intellectual Disabilities and Personality Disorder: An integrated approach
© Pavilion Publishing and Media Ltd and its licensors 2014.

**Psychological**

- **Stress:** How much stress is the individual experiencing? Has this changed? Do they have stress management skills? Do they have dysfunctional stress management techniques?

- **Self-image and self-esteem:** Does the individual have a poor self-image and low self-esteem? Has this changed?

- **Emotional regulation:** Does the individual have difficulty managing emotions? Has this changed? If so, when?

- **Intellectual disabilities:** How do the symptoms relate to the individual's cognitive deficits/developmental level?

**Social**

- Abuse/bullying – Is the individual currently experiencing or have they experienced abuse in the past?

- Has their social environment changed? Do they have less support? Do they see friends less often?

- Have important relationships changed/broken down?

**Risky behaviours**

- Have risky behaviours increased?

- Are there new risky behaviours?

## Positive support

It is important that individuals continue to receive positive, containing, 'authoritative' support (see Chapter 5) from staff during periods of mental health problems.

### Staff

Supporting individuals with additional mental health problems can be stressful for staff. It is important that staff look after their own needs while supporting an individual through acute mental health problems. This will help to prevent exhaustion and burnout (see Chapter 12). The extra stress should be taken into account when planning shifts and rotas. Staff will need breaks within a shift and also to have their usual days off and holidays, (it is easy for these to disappear if the individual needs additional support). Teams need to be able to talk to each other about their own feelings and reactions to the situation. Where individuals are re-experiencing traumatic events this may trigger difficult memories for some staff. There should be access to work-based counselling and a workplace atmosphere that is supportive of staff using that service.

Once the staff team have ensured their own ability to cope with the situation there are a number of things that they can do to support individuals and to help improve their mental well-being.

## Routine and structure

It is important to maintain, as much as possible, the individual's usual, personalised routine. This should continue to incorporate regular meal and snack times, waking and bed times, a range of activities including gentle physical exercise, household chores and social activities. These may have to be adapted to what the individual can cope with at any time but should not be abandoned altogether as this can slow recovery by building unhelpful and unhealthy habits such as sleeping during the day and long hours of inactivity. Where an individual feels down and is reluctant to do anything, it is important to encourage and even cajole but not to push to the point of bullying. A relay of smiling faces jollying the person on is usually better than a single person who can rapidly become demoralised themselves. Where an individual is restless or overactive it is important to try to channel this safely rather than try to contain them. Regular short walks and changes of scene may be helpful.

## Medication

If medication is prescribed it is important to support the individual to take the medication consistently and as prescribed. It is particularly important to be vigilant that the individual is not hoarding tablets with thoughts of taking an overdose. It is also important to observe for both therapeutic effects and side-effects so that these can be reported to their doctor. The individual should also be supported to carry out any other advice given by doctors.

It may be helpful to discuss with the individual if they would be happy for a trusted member of staff to accompany them to appointments. This has a number of benefits. The member of staff may have information that is helpful for the doctor. They will also be able to ask questions the individual may not have thought of or support them to ask questions they might not be able to ask alone. The member of staff will also be able to help them to remember all the doctor's advice.

## Attending appointments

It is very important that individuals consistently attend any appointments offered. Therapy is unlikely to work well if many appointments are missed. The individual may also be at risk of being excluded from services if they miss even a small number of appointments. It is therefore important that staff encourage and support individuals to attend and this may need tact and vigilance. Individuals may 'double book' themselves as a way of avoiding appointments, may forget to tell staff about the appointment or may lose appointment letters. If an individual is very reluctant to attend appointments, the approaches explored in Chapter 13 may be helpful.

## Emotional support from staff

Staff need to make time to listen to an individual's concerns, anxieties, thoughts, feelings and experiences. This needs to be done patiently as it can feel like the individual is endlessly repeating the same information and that no progress is being made. Staff should allow the person the space to express distress and be non-judgemental about what the person may tell them. Staff may need to encourage the individual to learn the skill of endurance. This means patiently bearing something until it passes. This is not easy but expressing a steady belief that it will pass and things will get better can start to inspire hope. The distraction approaches discussed in Chapter 7 may also be helpful.

## Peer support

Individuals may also find it helpful to make contact with other people who have had similar experiences. It may be helpful for them to attend support groups or make contact via one of the many websites that exist to offer support. Alcoholics Anonymous may be helpful for those with drink-related difficulties. Individuals should be encouraged to involve staff in the process of selecting groups or websites as some groups may be detrimental. This is particularly the case for eating disorders. There are a number of websites where individuals with anorexia swap tips on how to lose weight and reinforce each other's distorted ideas about extreme dieting.

## Social networks

It is also helpful to try to build a network of supporters for the individual so that they are not just dependent on staff or a few friends. This may need some creative thinking and might include local faith groups, paid or voluntary befrienders, helplines and drop-in centres.

## Promoting mental well-being

Healthy living groups have been found to be an enjoyable and effective way of helping individuals with intellectual disabilities and additional problems, including personality disorder and mental health problems, to learn about ways to improve their well-being. These groups use games and quizzes to help individuals understand more about the effects of diet, sleeping habits, relationships, drinking and smoking, money management and daily routines on their well-being. The group setting also facilitates the development of supportive peer relationships and builds self-esteem as individuals can see their progress through the results of the quizzes and in the certificates of attendance.

## Promoting healthy sleep

A feature common to many additional mental health problems is insomnia (problems sleeping). Box 9.9 gives some suggestions for promoting better sleep.

## Box 9.9: Suggestions for promoting good sleep (sleep hygiene)

- Have a regular bedtime – 7 days a week
- Have a regular getting up time – 7 days a week
- Spend 7–9 hours in bed
- Do not nap during the day
- Do not go to bed hungry or after a heavy meal
- Exercise daily (early in the day) as this improves sleep
- For three hours before bed, avoid caffeine, alcohol, smoking, and exercising (all are stimulating and will delay sleep)
- Create a relaxing bedtime routine eg. relaxing music or calm TV programme, milky drink, warm bath
- Ensure a comfortable and quiet bedroom – check the bed, have good blinds/curtains, no TV/computer, ensure room is neither too warm nor too cold

## Help for specific mental health problems

Some more specific suggestions for commonly encountered mental health problems are given in Boxes 9.10–19.

## Box 9.10: Suggestions for supporting individuals with anxiety or depression

There are a number of activities that can be considered 'antidotes' to anxiety and depression.

- Laughing – watch comedy programmes on TV. Buy/rent DVDs of favourite shows and films. Read favourite cartoon strips or funny stories. Laughter releases physical tension. It also reduces the levels of stress hormones such as cortisol and adrenaline. It is linked to the release of endorphins (the brain's natural painkillers) and hence can help reduce physical pain.

- Singing – sing-along to music on the radio or CDs – (Abba is popular) or DVDs of favourite musicals such as Mamma Mia. Choose songs that are cheerful and well known. Singing has similar effects to laughter but it also promotes healthy breathing. This can be very helpful for individuals with anxiety-related problems.

- Inspiration – find out what inspires the individual. Do they have favourite poems, pictures or pieces of music? Do they have a religious faith? Support the individual to access the things that inspire them. This might be a trip to an art gallery, a walk in beautiful countryside or attending a church service. However, it is important staff do not impose their ideas or faith on the individual.

- Exercising – can be as effective as medication at resolving mild depression and can be good for releasing tension when individuals are anxious. It is also good for physical health and can help make new friends.

Work on building self-esteem (Chapter 2) and managing emotions (Chapter 3) will also be helpful.

## Box 9.11: Suggestions for supporting individuals with manic symptoms

**Hypomania, mania and manic episodes** (bipolar mood disorder)

Managing acute episodes

- Create a calm, supportive and relaxing atmosphere eg. soothing music not loud pop music
- Offer calming, relaxed activities eg. long walk rather than going for a run
- Ensure the individual is drinking enough – offer small cups of favourite (decaffeinated) drinks frequently (use plastic or paper cups if there are concerns about throwing)
- Offer frequent snacks of high calorie fingerfoods if individual will not sit down to a meal
- Use de-escalation and distraction techniques to manage risky behaviours
- Support individual to continue to take their regular medication BUT seek urgent review if this includes an antidepressant as these should be stopped during a manic episode
- If prescribed, use 'as required' medication if behaviour is getting out of control (quick dissolving tablets may be helpful for individuals who find difficulty swallowing pills when unwell)
- Support good sleep hygiene behaviours
- If prescribed, use medication to promote sleep
- Encourage individual to reduce intake of caffeine (offer decaffeinated versions) or other stimulants and to reduce alcohol intake
- Encourage use of any relaxing techniques individual knows well
- Encourage individual to delay important decisions

Prevention

- Promote regular routine with sufficient sleep, good diet and gentle exercise
- Teach about the condition – plan for if they become extremely manic
- Promote stress management eg. teaching relaxation techniques
- Organise finances so it is more difficult to over-spend during a manic episode
- Identify warning signs and monitor thoughts, behaviour and feelings – take action on warning signs
- Give extra support when individual is experiencing high levels of stress/life events
- Encourage joining local support groups

Work on managing emotions (Chapter 3) may also be helpful.

## Box 9.12: Suggestions for supporting individuals with PTSD

- Reassure them that the worst is over – the event is in the past
- Encourage the individual to talk to, and gain support from, other survivors
- Discourage them from getting into a pattern of avoiding situations that remind them of the trauma; work with them to develop coping strategies for these situations
- If they experience nightmares, flashbacks or hear the voice(s) of their abuser(s), help the individual recognise that these are natural reactions. Explain what is happening. The person may fear that these experiences may become real or that they are sign that they have 'gone mad'.

### Nightmares

- Promoting a relaxing night time routine to encourage peaceful sleep (see section on insomnia)
- Developing a 'settling' routine for when the individual is woken up by nightmares. This might include breathing exercises, cuddling a soft toy or pillow, having a soothing drink, listening to relaxing music.
- Helping them to write down or draw the nightmare so that they can share it with their doctor or therapist. It may be helpful to work with them to create a new and happier end to the nightmare.

### Flashbacks

Helping the individual to learn 'grounding techniques'. These aim to help the person stay in the present moment and not cut off from the situation or slip back into the past. Grounding techniques involve doing things that connect the person with current reality by using their senses (sound, touch, smell, taste and sight).

- Sound – turn on loud jarring music so attention is directed to the noise
- Touch – grip an ice cube – the extreme cold helps keep in the person in the present
- Smell – something strong and not associated with the flashback (smell is often a part of the experience) eg. peppermint or lavender
- Taste – bite into a lemon/something very sour – this brings attention to the present
- Sight – focus on the objects in the room name them and perhaps describe them eg. *'bed with a pink cover, photos of family, wardrobe…'.*

**Hearing voices**

■ Explore with the individual what the voices are saying to them (this may help understand why they are behaving in certain ways).

■ Explore with the individual what approach(es) they would find most helpful. It could be:

▪ distracting self – with eg. with music, humming, singing, counting

▪ answering back – shout at the voice to go away

▪ creating images, statements or cue card – eg. *'it's over, you don't rule me now'*.

Work on unhelpful thoughts (Chapter 7) may also be helpful.

## Box 9.13: Suggestions for supporting individuals with eating disorders

■ Ensure that there is good observation and support around eating and drinking – individuals are unlikely to be reliable informants about how much they have (or have not) eaten if they have an eating disorder.

■ Monitor drinking. Stopping drinking rapidly leads to serious health problems. The individual may need admission to hospital for rehydration.

■ Develop a 'healthy eating' pack with the individual. This should have three meals a day, three healthy snacks and plenty to drink (water, herbal teas and decaffeinated drinks). The aim should be to include all food groups for a balanced diet. No foods should be forbidden. The aim is to never be very hungry and never to overeat.

■ If a person needs to binge, encourage them to wait for even a few seconds before giving in. Support them to gradually wait a bit longer each time. Often people find that the urge will disappear if they wait just a few minutes.

■ Work on building self-esteem – see Chapter 2

■ Work on managing emotions – see Chapter 3

■ Work on building motivation and controlling impulses – see Chapter 6

■ Work on unhelpful thoughts – see Chapter 7

---

**Box 9.14: Suggestions for supporting individuals with substance-related problems**

- Encourage the individual to access specialist support eg. drug and alcohol services and attend self-help/support groups such as Alcoholics Anonymous
- Support them in attending meetings/appointments
- Encouraging the individual to keep busy
- Work on building self-esteem – see Chapter 2
- Work on managing emotions – see Chapter 3
- Work on building motivation and controlling impulses – see Chapter 6

---

## Suicide risk

It is important to be aware that experiencing an additional mental health problem may increase the risk of an individual attempting suicide. This may be obvious if an individual is depressed. However, this risk also applies to the other mental health problems discussed in this chapter. Managing suicide risk is discussed in Chapter 11.

## Outcome measures

Using the approaches mentioned previously should help resolve additional mental health problems as quickly as possible and help reduce the risk of them escalating into a crisis. However, where progress is slow, an individual is very pessimistic or there is a two-steps-forward, one-step-backwards progression, it can be easy to miss changes. One way of addressing this is by the use of outcome measures. These are tools that help identify areas where progress has or hasn't been made. They can also identify areas that have been overlooked and not addressed and hence suggest possible new interventions. The Health Equalities Framework or HEF is a tool that might be particularly helpful (Atkinson *et al*, 2013).

# Key learning points

■ Mental health or well-being is a state in which a person does not have any significant difficulties with their thinking, emotions or behaviour and in which they are able to function well, both individually and within society.

■ A person may be seen as having mental health problems when they become distressed, or experience deterioration in their functioning, as a result of changes to their usual patterns of thoughts, emotions or behaviour.

■ Individuals with intellectual disabilities and personality disorder are vulnerable to developing additional mental health problems including anxiety and mood disorders, eating disorders and problems with drugs or alcohol.

■ It is important that staff are aware of the symptoms of these conditions and are able to support the individual to seek specialist help.

■ Mental health problems need holistic assessment and treatment within the framework of the recovery model and CPA approach.

■ Individuals will need support to attend appointments and consistently follow medical advice.

■ There is a range of things staff can do to help individuals address the problems they experience and improve their mental well-being including offering non-judgemental support through active listening, running healthy living groups, promoting healthy sleep and helping individuals to manage specific symptoms.

# References

Atkinson D, Boulter P, Hebron C, Moulster G, Giraud-Saunders A & Turner, S (2013) *The Health Equalities Framework: An outcomes framework based on the determinants of health inequalities* [online]. Available at: www.ndti.org.uk/uploads/The_Health_Equality_Framework.pdf (accessed November 2013).

Deb S, Matthews T, Holt G & Bouras N (2001) *Practice Guidelines for the Assessment and Diagnosis of Mental Health Problems in Adults with Intellectual Disability*. Pavilion: Brighton.

Moss S & Estia Centre (2001) *Mini PAS-ADD Handbook*. Brighton: Pavilion Publishing.

World Health Organization (2010) *Mental Health: Strengthening our response* [online]. Available at: http://www.who.int/mediacentre/factsheets/fs220/en/ (accessed January 2014).

# Further reading

Copeland M (undated) *Wellness: Recovery Action Planning*. Available at: http://www.mentalhealthrecovery.com/ (accessed January 2014).

Department of Health (2008) *Refocusing the Care Programme Approach: Policy and positive practice guidance*. Available at: http://www.nmhdu.org.uk/silo/files/dh-2008-refocusing-the-care-programme-approach-policy-and-positive-practice-guidance.pdf (accessed January 2014).

Handley E, Southwell O & Steel J (2012) Recovery and intellectual disabilities. *Advances in Mental Health and Intellectual Disabilities* **6** (4) 192–198.

National Institute for Health and Care Excellence (2004) *CG9: Eating Disorders*. Available at: http://publications.nice.org.uk/eating-disorders-cg9 (accessed January 2014).

National Institute for Health and Care Excellence (2005) *CG26: Post-traumatic Stress Disorder*. Available at: http://publications.nice.org.uk/post-traumatic-stress-disorder-ptsd-cg26 (accessed January 2014).

National Institute for Health and Care Excellence (2006) *CG38: Bipolar Disorder*. Available at: http://guidance.nice.org.uk/CG38 (accessed January 2014).

National Institute for Health and Care Excellence (2009) *CG78: Borderline Personality Disorder*. Available at: http://publications.nice.org.uk/borderline-personality-disorder-cg78 (accessed January 2014).

National Institute for Health and Care Excellence (2009) *CG90: Depression in adults: the treatment and management of depression in adults*. Available at: http://publications.nice.org.uk/depression-in-adults-cg90 (accessed January 2014).

National Institute for Health and Care Excellence (2009) *CG82: Schizoprenhia*. Available at: http://publications.nice.org.uk/schizophrenia-cg82 (accessed January 2014).

National Institute for Health and Care Excellence (2007) *CG51 Drug Misuse: Psychosocial interventions*. Available at: http://publications.nice.org.uk/drug-misuse-psychosocial-interventions-cg51 (accessed January 2014).

National Institute for Health and Care Excellence (2011) *CG115: Alcohol Dependence and Harmful Alcohol Use*. Available at: http://guidance.nice.org.uk/CG115 (accessed January 2014).

National Institute for Health and Care Excellence (2011) *CG113: Generalised Anxiety Disorder and Panic Disorder*. Available at: http://publications.nice.org.uk/generalised-anxiety-disorder-and-panic-disorder-with-or-without-agoraphobia-in-adults-cg113 (accessed January 2014).

NIMHE (2003) *Personality Disorder: No longer a diagnosis of exclusion: policy implementation guidance for the development of services for people with personality disorder*. Available at: http://www.personalitydisorder.org.uk/assets/resources/56.pdf (accessed January 2014).

Pitonyak D (2011) *Supporting A Person Who is Experiencing Post-traumatic Stress Disorder*. Available at: http://www.dimagine.com/PTSD.pdf (accessed January 2014).

Prosser H, Moss S, Costello H, Simpson N, Patel P & Rowe S (1998) Reliability and validity of the Mini PAS-ADD for assessing psychiatric disorders in adults with intellectual disability. *Journal of Intellectual Disability Research* **42** 264–272.

Rose A, Breen O & Webb Z (2014) An inpatient healthy living group. *Advances in Mental Health and Intellectual Disabilities,* in press.

# Chapter 10: Challenging behaviours

This chapter defines what is meant by the term 'challenging behaviour' and explains the concept of behaviours serving functions. It looks at factors that make individuals vulnerable to developing challenging behaviour and how such behaviours may arise in individuals with intellectual disabilities and personality disorder. It looks at the approach to assessing and managing challenging behaviour often referred to as 'positive behavioural support' and how 'formulation' may be used to understand challenging behaviour. The chapter also gives some suggestions for managing some challenging behaviours frequently encountered in individuals with intellectual disabilities and personality disorder.

## Key topics

- Challenging behaviour
- Positive behavioural support
- Challenging behaviour and individuals with personality disorder
- Challenging behaviour and individuals with intellectual disabilities
- Challenging behaviour and individuals with intellectual disabilities and personality disorder
- Assessment and formulation of challenging behaviour in individuals with intellectual disabilities and personality disorder
- Positive behaviour support for individuals with intellectual disabilities and personality disorder
- Specific behaviours (self-neglect, verbal aggression and physical aggression)

## Challenging behaviour

Challenging behaviour is a term that originated in services for individuals with intellectual disabilities. It was created in an effort to move the focus from the person showing the difficult behaviour to the setting in which they lived and the services that supported them. This was in recognition that difficult behaviours often arise from the interaction between a person and the environment around them rather than being a feature of the person alone. The following is a frequently used definition of challenging behaviour.

*'Behaviour can be defined as challenging when it is of such an intensity, frequency or duration as to threaten the quality of life and/or the physical safety of the individual or others and is likely to lead to responses that are restrictive, aversive or result in exclusion.'* (RCPsych, 2006)

# Positive behavioural support

The concept of challenging behaviour developed within a particular approach to understanding human behaviour, originally called 'behaviourism' or 'behaviour modification'. This approach is now more commonly called 'positive behavioural support'. Positive behavioural approaches look at the interaction between the person and their underlying human needs, their environment and the people around them. Behaviours such as physical aggression or self-harm are seen as meeting needs that have not been met by the service supporting the person or as arising from a mismatch between the person, the environment and the type of support given. This approach seeks to understand these interactions and then find ways of meeting needs and supporting the person that promote positive rather than challenging behaviours or minimise the impact of the challenging behaviour on the person and those who support them.

Positive behavioural support requires staff to look beyond the surface of behaviour and to really explore what is going on in the person's life. It questions the competence of the services supporting the person and asks them to explore the role that their actions may play in triggering and maintaining the challenging behaviour.

## Functions of behaviour

The positive behavioural support approach suggests that all behaviour has a meaning or function (purpose) and does not occur in isolation. Difficult behaviours may arise as ways of meeting underlying needs. These needs include:

- initiating/accessing social interaction

- accessing things the person needs or greatly enjoys (such as food, drink, money)

- escaping situations that the person finds unbearable

- avoiding situations that the person finds unbearable

- creating pleasurable sensations

- releasing tension.

These functions are explored more fully in Boxes 10.1 and 10.2.

## Box 10.1: Functions and messages of challenging behaviours (part 1)

**Social interaction (*'I'm lonely', 'being alone is unbearable'*)**
All humans need social contact. For most people their need for interaction, social skills and social opportunities balance and they are able to meet this need through appropriate behaviour. However, some people are unable to meet their needs appropriately as a result of issues such as:

■ high level of need
■ low boredom threshold
■ limited communication skills
■ poor self-occupation skills
■ limited opportunities.

They may learn that certain behaviours are a reliable way of attracting others' attention, even if the attention is negative (eg. being told off). Sometimes such behaviour is described as 'attention seeking'. This is unhelpful as it carries the judgement that the person is choosing to behave this way or is taking more than their share of attention.

**Access to things (*I'm starving', 'I feel empty'*)**
The desire for certain things eg. food, drink, objects or activities, can drive behaviour. It is natural to want these things. If these needs are not met (hunger, thirst, deprivation, poverty) a person may learn unacceptable behaviours to access things (eg. stealing). Other people may have high levels of need. For example, those with Prader-Willi sydrome always feel hungry no matter how much they eat. Sometimes the need for physical things may be driven by a psychological need. For example, a feeling of emotional emptiness may lead to compulsive eating.

**Escape (*'I'm powerless', 'no one listens to what I want'*)**
Everyone has things that they do not enjoy; certain activities or perhaps certain people. Most people have choices that allow them to avoid things they do not like, skills to politely leave situations they find unpleasant, a level of tolerance for such situations if they are unable to leave and the understanding that the situation will end soon. Where people have:

■ little choice
■ lack skills to excuse themselves
■ have limited tolerance
■ have no understanding that the situation will end

Continued...

they may learn inappropriate ways of escaping a situation. Sometimes the person may be trying to escape their own internal world eg. overwhelming distress or painful memories. If they lack the skills to manage these sensations they may resort to inappropriate behaviours such as harmful alcohol use.

### Avoidance ('I can't cope', 'I'm frightened')

Once people know that they do not like a particular situation, person or activity, they often avoid it. This is done appropriately by exercising choice and communicating this to others. Where a person is denied choice, is unable to communicate that choice or has a low tolerance for stress they may develop inappropriate behaviours as a way of avoiding that situation. For example, someone might fake illness to avoid going to a job they hate. People also avoid situations they fear or feel overwhelmed by.

---

## Box 10.2: Functions of challenging behaviours (part 2)

### Pleasurable/intense sensations ('I'm bored', 'I can't bear these feelings')

There are some activities people do because of the sensations created eg. listening to music, looking at artwork, smelling flowers, going on fairground rides and sexual activities. Such behaviours are described as 'self-reinforcing' ie. what is happening around the person (externally) is not so important as what is happening inside them. Everyone needs to engage in these activities at times. Most people are able to meet these needs through appropriate behaviour. However, some people with:

- a need for intense stimulation
- limited choice
- limited opportunities

may develop inappropriate ways of meeting their need for stimulation. The creation of intense sensations may also be a coping strategy to block out unbearable events, either external or internal.

When considering pleasurable sensation as a motivation for behaviour it is important not to be blinded by a narrow view of what is personally pleasant. People vary greatly in what is pleasant or unpleasant to them. For example, fitness fanatics often live for the 'buzz' or 'high' created by sustained exercise. The unfit give up very quickly as a result of the unpleasant sensations of breathlessness and muscle fatigue.

### Emotional release ('I can't take any more', 'this is too much')

Sometimes behaviours may be the result of the build-up of tension, stress or over-arousal. The behaviour acts to release the tension and bring the person back to

Continued...

---

Intellectual Disabilities and Personality Disorder: An integrated approach
© Pavilion Publishing and Media Ltd and its licensors 2014.

a calmer state. Behaviours serving this function are often active eg. shouting, running, throwing things, hitting out, but also include 'self-medication' such as drinking alcohol. Most people have adaptive ways of calming themselves down in such situations. However, some people may have:

■ a low stimulation threshold

■ a low tolerance for intense emotions such as anger

■ lack appropriate ways of calming themselves.

It is important to recognise that stressful does not just mean unpleasant. Some people will be over-aroused by pleasant events such as a birthday party and may 'explode' when it ends. This can make those who support them particularly upset as the person appears 'ungrateful' and it seems to have rebuffed the staff's efforts to please them.

The positive behaviour support approach suggests that, where a person has needs that are not met by the situation in which they find themselves, they will develop behaviours that lead to the need being met. If efforts are made to stop a behaviour without exploring the function that behaviour is serving, they are unlikely to be successful; either the behaviour will escalate or it will be replaced by a new (often worse) behaviour that achieves the needed result.

It is important to understand that there is no simple relationship between a behaviour and the function(s) it may serve. The different types of relationships possible are explored in Box 10.3.

It is always necessary to look below the surface of the behaviour to explore the purpose it serves and its relationship to the environment the person is living in.

This approach is very different from the medical model where specific behaviours are seen as 'symptoms' and assessment looks for the clusters of symptoms that are characteristic of particular physical or mental health problems.

## Development and maintenance of challenging behaviour

The positive behaviour support approach recognises a distinction between the situation that may have given rise to a behaviour and the factors that cause the behaviour to continue. Behaviours may occur for a wide range of reasons, for example, in response to physical pain, copying the behaviour of others or as an instinctive reaction to events. However, these behaviours will only become established in the person's behavioural repertoire if they achieve an outcome that is positive for the individual in some way (that is, they come to serve a function for the person).

---

### Box 10.3: Relationships between behaviours and functions

■ The same behaviour shown by different people serves a different function for each eg. getting drunk:
Person A gets drunk to escape unpleasant memories
Person B drinks to release pent up tension

■ Very different behaviours shown by different people serve the same function eg.
Person A gets drunk to escape unpleasant memories
Person B cuts their arms to escape unpleasant memories

■ Very different behaviours shown by one person may serve the same function for that person eg.
Occasion 1: Person A gets drunk to escape unpleasant memories
Occasion 2: Person A uses very loud music to block out unpleasant memories

■ A particular behaviour may serve different functions for the same person at different times eg.
Occasion 1: Person B cuts their arms to escape unpleasant memories
Occasion 2: Person B cuts their arms to access the comfort of someone else treating the wound

---

## Vulnerability factors for developing challenging behaviour

A number of factors have been identified that may make people more vulnerable to the development of challenging behaviours. These factors arise from the person's genetic make-up, personal characteristics and experiences. They act to intensify needs, limit the ability to communicate or reduce the ability to cope with situations. These are presented in more detail in Box 10.4.

## Box 10.4: Factors contributing to the development of challenging behaviours

**Physical health:** Discomfort, pain (eg. headache, sore throat, arthritis), physiological disturbance (eg. under or overactive thyroid, poorly controlled diabetes), infections (eg. urine infection)

**Mental health:** Mood disorders (eg. depression, bipolar affective disorder) anxiety, psychosis, obsessive-compulsive disorders

**Neuro-psychiatric disorders:** Epilepsy, Tourette's syndrome, attention-deficit hyperactivity disorder (ADHD), dementia

**Pervasive developmental disorders:** Autism, Asperger's syndrome

**Genetic conditions:** Prader-Willi syndrome, Lesch-Nyhan syndrome, Williams syndrome

**Psychological trauma:** Reaction to abuse or loss

**Communication difficulties:** Hearing loss, unclear communication, insufficient vocabulary or means of expression, difficulties understanding communication of others

**Enduring abnormalities of personality:** eg. borderline, paranoid or antisocial personality disorder.

# Characteristics of services that create and maintain challenging behaviours

The positive behaviour support approach also recognises that some services are more likely than others to lead people to behave in challenging ways and to be less able to respond constructively when this occurs. Some of these service characteristics are given in Box 10.5.

> ### Box 10.5: Service characteristics that create and maintain challenging behaviours
>
> - Inability to respond to individual need (eg. lack resources, inflexiblity, lack creativity, are not person-centred)
> - Believe that the causes of challenging behaviour lie solely in the person showing that behaviour (ie. strict medical model)
> - Lack relevant training (eg. not trained in positive behaviour support, how to prevent challenging behaviour, how to promote positive behaviour, choice and participation)
> - Over-emphasis on learning reactive strategies (ie. restrictive physical interventions)
> - Over-reliance on reactive strategies (eg. restrictive physical interventions)
> - High staff turnover
> - Poorly organised staff teams with lack of clarity about priorities of work
> - Lack of teamwork leading to inconsistent care
> - Poor record keeping (making it difficult to find out what has been happening)
> - May be over-controlling
> - May be chaotic and lack organisation or structure
> - Difficulties working with external 'professionals' – see professionals as not understanding the demands of their job. See themselves as unable to implement guidelines as these do not recognise the practical limitations of the staff's situation
>
> Summarised from Royal College of Psychiatrists, British Psychological Society and Royal College of Speech and Language Therapists (2006)

These issues may combine to form the unhelpful support styles discussed in Chapter 5, that is; indulgent, neglectful or authoritarian support.

# Challenging behaviour in individuals with personality disorder

Individuals with personality disorder can present a wide range of difficult behaviours that may meet the definition of challenging behaviour including self-neglect, aggression and misuse of services.

These behaviours are often seen as 'symptoms' of personality disorder, that is; being solely caused by having a personality disorder. This can leave staff feeling powerless to help the individual change their behaviour. It can also result in over dependence on medication to 'treat' the behaviours or even to individuals being excluded from mental health services as 'untreatable'.

Adopting ideas from the positive behavioural support approach immediately opens up more possibilities for change. Such behaviours are viewed as conveying important information about the individual, their quality of life and the way they are being supported. Many of these challenging behaviours are motivated by extreme need or intense emotion. By exploring vulnerability factors, the function of the behaviour and the consequence that it results in, it may be possible to help the individual meet their needs more appropriately. It may also help health and support services to turn the spotlight onto their own role in creating and maintaining the individual's problem behaviours. For example, if an individual has a strong need for contact with services but is discharged every time they appear to be improving the individual will need to become unwell again to have this need met. Thoughtful planning of alternative ways of meeting this need might reduce relapses.

## Challenging behaviour in individuals with intellectual disabilities

Individuals with intellectual disabilities are very vulnerable to developing challenging behaviours; any one individual will often have a significant number of the vulnerability factors noted earlier in this chapter. Individuals with intellectual disabilities and challenging behaviour frequently have very difficult lives and are vulnerable to being abused. It has been highlighted that these individuals are often marginalised, stigmatised, disempowered and excluded from mainstream society.

Within the field of intellectual disabilities the focus has tended to be on how to support individuals with more severe intellectual disabilities who show challenging behaviour. There is an extensive literature on this population and an exploration of this area is beyond the scope of this book.

# Challenging behaviour and individuals with intellectual disabilities and personality disorder

Individuals with intellectual disabilities and personality disorder are likely to present with a wide range of challenging behaviours as a result of the characteristics that are associated with both these conditions. Some of the most frequently encountered challenging behaviours are given in Box 10.6.

---

**Box 10.6: Challenging behaviours sometimes shown by individuals with intellectual disabilities and personality disorder**

- Self-neglect
- Verbal aggression
- Physical aggression
- Damage to property
- Theft
- Overuse of services (999 calls, GP, accident and emergency departments, specialist services)
- Inappropriate sexual behaviour
- Self-harm and suicide attempts

---

Some of these challenging behaviours are likely to bring the individual into contact with the police and the legal system as they may constitute offences eg. shop-lifting, actual bodily harm. This is reflected in the large numbers of individuals with personality disorder in forensic services for individuals with intellectual disabilities.

Some of the behaviours discussed in earlier chapters may also be regarded as challenging behaviours. These might include emotional outbursts, angry behaviours, interpersonal conflict, behaviours that elicit staff interaction ('attention seeking'), 'manipulative' behaviours and non-compliance with medical or other advice.

## Ways of thinking about challenging behaviour

Making sense of challenging behaviours can be very complicated. This is partly because of the inherent complexity of individuals' needs. However, it is also complicated by the need for staff to be able to work with two, often conflicting,

Intellectual Disabilities and Personality Disorder: An integrated approach
© Pavilion Publishing and Media Ltd and its licensors 2014.

ways of thinking about human behaviour. It is important that staff are able to think about behaviours both as possible symptoms of mental or physical health problems (medical model) and as possibly serving functions or having a purpose for the individual (positive behavioural support model). If staff are only able to work with one of these approaches, difficulties may arise.

If a strict 'behavioural' approach is taken there is a risk that the significance of the individual having a personality disorder may be missed. While it is now recognised that a thorough assessment of challenging behaviour should explore issues relating to personality disorder, this has not always been the case. Until recently there was a lack of emphasis on the possible role of personality factors in the development and maintenance of challenging behaviours. This meant that the presence or influence of personality disorder was often overlooked. If the role of personality disorder is overlooked, then important factors influencing an individual's needs may be missed. This will then result in less than optimum responses to their challenging behaviours.

However, there are also difficulties with applying a strict 'medical' model. As discussed in the section about personality disorder, this carries a risk that all behaviours will be seen as 'symptoms' of personality disorder. This means that 'treatment' approaches offered will be limited and are likely to be ineffective. In particular, health and support services may overlook the role their own behaviour and responses may play in creating and maintaining the individual's challenging behaviours.

## Assessment and formulation of challenging behaviour in individuals with intellectual disabilities and personality disorder

Supporting individuals with intellectual disabilities and personality disorder who show challenging behaviour can be very difficult. The individual may be very distressed, their quality of life is likely to be impaired and they may have been subject to interventions that are restrictive, aversive or exclude them from activities or services. Staff may fear for the safety of the individual, other people or themselves. Staff may also have been verbally abused or physically assaulted by the individual they are trying to support. However, taking a systematic, step-by-step approach can help to achieve a clear understanding of the individual's challenging behaviour and lead to the development of a positive behavioural support package. The process is very similar to that suggested in Chapter 9 for addressing mental health problems but involves thinking about the situation from a different perspective.

- **Seeking help:** supporting the individual to access specialist assessment.

- A **holistic assessment** of the individual's challenging behaviour. Challenging behaviour needs to be considered in the context of the individual's personality disorder, physical health, mental health, intellectual disabilities and their social context.

- Using a **'formulation'** to draw together and make sense of all the information from the assessment. This is used to generate ideas about how the behaviour developed, what functions it may serve for the individual, what factors precipitate and maintain the behaviour and possible points of intervention.

- Developing **positive behavioural support** that creates an environment that promotes positive behaviour and effectively manages challenges.

A holistic assessment for challenging behaviour can be a lengthy process and is not appropriate if the individual is in crisis. Where the situation has reached crisis point the approach given in Chapter 12 should be followed and detailed assessment should be delayed until the situation has stabilised.

A generic process for assessing and developing interventions for challenging behaviours is given below. In addition, some specific examples applying the approach to some commonly encountered challenging behaviours are given later in the chapter.

## Seeking help

Assessing and intervening with challenging behaviours is complex and it is likely that the individual will need to be referred to specialist services. This work often needs the involvement of a number of different professionals including psychologists, psychiatrists and specialist nurses. The individual may also need input from a speech and language therapist or occupational therapist. It is therefore important that the individual is referred to their local specialist team.

Most individuals with intellectual disabilities and personality disorder will understand that their behaviour is unhelpful for them and for other people and hence they are likely to be willing for a referral to be made. This is important because the more the individual is involved in, understands and supports the plans to prevent and manage their challenging behaviour, the more effective the intervention will be. However, a number of individuals will not understand the need for change and may refuse to seek help. This can paralyse staff teams if they think that to intervene without the person's consent infringes the individual's human rights.

## Capacity, consent and duty of care

It is therefore essential that staff understand fully the legal framework around capacity, consent and duty of care. In the UK this includes the principles of the Mental Capacity Act (2005) and the Mental Health Act (1983, amended 1995 and 2007). These acts provide a framework for assessing capacity, acting in the best interests of individuals who lack capacity and also make clear when treatment and care can be given without consent. Where an individual has capacity and refuses intervention but the behaviour does not come under the Mental Health Act it is also important to understand that there are still options that are open to staff teams. All services have a duty of care to the individuals they support and responsibilities for meeting service standards. These allow them to set limits and uphold basic standards of behaviour expected of those who live in or use the service, even if the individual does not see their behaviour as problematic. Many individuals will live in rented properties. Where this is the case their tenancies are likely to set some basic standards. These can be used to highlight to the individual that if their behaviour does not change it may lead to eviction.

# Assessment

The starting point for tackling challenging behaviour is a comprehensive assessment. This will look at a number of areas including historical information and a detailed understanding of the individual's current situation.

## History

Ideally, assessment should start by gathering as much information about the individual's life as possible. This process might include looking at old records and reports, talking with everyone who works with the individual, conversations with the individual themselves and (with the necessary permissions) members of their family. This information should include early development, schooling, work, family and life experiences. Look for traumatic events and losses (deaths or moves). If any such events have occurred, try to find out the time of year they happened as individuals with personality disorder often become unwell or show disturbed behaviour around the anniversaries of painful events. It is also important to find out about any physical or mental health problems they have experienced in the past. The assessment approaches given in Chapters 8 and 9 should be helpful with this. A full history will be helpful in understanding the individual's intellectual disabilities, their personality disorder, mental and physical health and their challenging behaviour.

## Current situation

It is also important to have a full picture of the individual's current situation. The individual will need a physical and mental health check. This might include investigations for any suspected genetic disorders, physical illnesses or additional mental health problems. Their current social situation also needs to be understood including; where and with whom they live, what support they have, their relationships, their occupations and activities. The assessment should explore recent and current life difficulties including personal and financial difficulties. It is essential to find out about the individual's current living arrangements and the support they are being given. This would include looking at service characteristics such as staffing levels, training and approach used. It would also include building an understanding of how those who support them currently view the individual's behaviours and what action is currently being taken.

It can be particularly helpful to ask the questions:

- 'What kind of life is this individual leading?'

- 'How would I feel if I were living their life?'

- 'How would I behave in their situation?'

- 'Why is this a problem now?'

## The individual

It is also essential to understand, as fully as possible, the individual as a unique person including exploring their strengths, weaknesses, vulnerabilities, coping strategies, likes, dislikes, aspirations, hopes and fears. It may be helpful to complete what is often called a 'reinforcement inventory' with the individual to explore this in detail. A good reinforcement inventory will cover everything from what the person's favourite food is, to whether they like reading poetry. If the individual's preferences are not understood assumptions may be made about their quality of life that may lead to important factors in motivating or maintaining challenging behaviour being overlooked. For example, someone who enjoys living in a busy town might assume that a flat in the centre of town near all the amenities is the perfect place for the individual they support. However, the individual might find it stressful, noisy and too near to tempting pubs and betting shops. This process can also be helpful in establishing whether the individual has unmet needs or if the service does not give opportunities for them to meet needs in appropriate ways.

It is important to have a good understanding of what happens to the individual during an episode of challenging behaviour. It can be helpful to explore their physical sensations, emotions and thoughts. It may be helpful to think about the core beliefs that might underlie the thoughts and emotions they experience in response to trigger events. The approaches explored in Chapter 7 may be helpful with this.

Intellectual Disabilities and Personality Disorder: An integrated approach
© Pavilion Publishing and Media Ltd and its licensors 2014.

It may also be helpful to have a profile of the individual's skills and abilities. Assessment by a speech and language therapist will be helpful in identifying expressive and receptive communication problems. An intellectual assessment may help by identifying difficulties with verbal or perceptual reasoning, memory or executive functioning. An occupational therapy assessment may be helpful in identifying difficulties with aspects of daily living, social and occupational skills, engagement and motivation, and sensory processing. These specialist professional assessments may highlight subtle but important gaps that may not be immediately obvious when interacting with the individual.

## The behaviour

It is also important to look at the challenging behaviour in detail. What exactly is the individual doing? How often is it happening? How long does it last? How severe is the behaviour? Where does it happen? What fears and associations does this behaviour hold for the individual and the staff supporting them? Often close observation will show there is an escalating sequence that leads to the challenging behaviour. For example, the individual may start by becoming restless, then progress through a sequence of talking loudly, slamming doors and then finally hitting out at others. For other individuals there may not be a sequence but there may be subtle physical signs, for example, going pale or red in the face, making or avoiding eye contact, becoming more or less talkative. Understanding the pattern will help identify points where it may be possible to intervene to de-escalate the situation.

## The function

It is also important to explore what function the behaviour might be serving for the individual. Box 10.7 gives one possible sequence for thinking about functions.

> ### Box 10.7: A screening sequence to explore the motivation of a behaviour
>
> Does the individual have a genetic disorder or syndrome that is associated with their challenging behaviour? If unknown, arrange a screening.
>
> Does the individual have any physical health problems/physical pain? If unknown, arrange a physical health check.
>
> Does the individual have any mental health problems/emotional pain? If unknown, arrange a mental health check.
>
> Does the behaviour increase under one or more of the following circumstances:
> (a) When the behaviour is attended to?
> (b) When the individual is in company (rather than alone)?
> If yes, motivation may be access to social interaction.
>
> Does the behavior result in the individual gaining access to things?
> If yes, motivation may be **tangible reinforcers**.
>
> Does the behaviour occur primarily when demands or other aversive stimuli are present?
> If yes, motivation may be **escape or avoidance**.
>
> Does the behaviour occur primarily when there are no activities available and/or the environment is barren?
> If yes, motivation may be **self-stimulation**. This may be boredom or lack of other external distractions from an unpleasant internal state eg. hearing voices.
>
> Does the behaviour occur primarily at times of high arousal such as after a party or when there are stressful life events?
> If yes, the motivation may be **release of physical or emotional tension**.

It can also be helpful to look at incidents using 'ABC' analysis. This considers what happens before (antecedents = A), the behaviour (B) and its consequences (C).

Exploring the antecedents of behaviours can help identify possible triggers. When looking at the ABC data, it can also be helpful to try to look at the situation both objectively and through the individual's eyes. Consider the thinking errors explored in Chapter 7. Could the individual perceive threats or insults where none were intended? It is also helpful to look at situations in which the behaviour does not occur as this can be useful in identifying ways of reducing the problem.

Exploring consequences helps to understand what the behaviour may be achieving for the individual. It is important to think about both external and internal consequences. For example, an apparently 'out of the blue' assault on another individual may appear to have achieved nothing externally but may have satisfied the individual's need to have revenge on that person for some previous (real or perceived) insult.

Where a behaviour appears totally unpredictable it may be helpful to look at the time (hours, days and sometimes weeks) leading up to the event and consider the individual's level of arousal. Much behaviour that looks initially as if it is totally unpredictable turns out to be functioning to reduce over-arousal. The metaphor of the straw that broke the camel's back is useful in understanding these events. The 'trigger' event may have occurred many times without resulting in challenging behaviour. The behaviour only occurs when the individual is so stressed that they cannot cope with another stressor, however small. If this is suspected it may be helpful to come up with a simple rating of stress for the individual eg. a scale of 1 to 5. Staff can then be asked to rate the individual's stress prior to and after the incident. If the challenging behaviours frequently occur when there is a high stress rating, and not when the rating is lower, arousal may be a key factor in triggering the behaviour.

## Formulation

Individuals with intellectual disabilities and personality disorder are complex. Sometimes it can be overwhelming trying to make sense of all the information gathered during the assessment process. 'Formulation' is a structured way of trying to make sense of this information. A good formulation will highlight any gaps in the assessment, suggesting questions that need to be answered before an intervention can be developed. Formulation brings together the results of assessments in a way that generates ideas about how a behaviour developed, what triggers it, the individual's motivation for behaving in that way and what maintains that behaviour. It should give predictions of how the individual might behave in future situations. A good formulation will also identify whether important factors are amenable to change or need to be managed and will generate suggestions for intervention.

There are many different formats for formulation. Some are linked to specific treatment models and others aim to be applicable across different treatment models. The Five Ps is a general model for formulation that can be helpful in thinking about challenging behaviours (see Box 10.8).

> ## Box 10.8: The Five Ps model for formulations
>
> **Presenting problem:** the behaviour that is seen as challenging.
>
> **Predisposing:** characteristics that make the individual vulnerable to developing that problem.
>
> **Precipitating:** how the problem started, its triggers or antecedents.
>
> **Perpetuating:** things that maintain the problem, what keeps it going, the consequences of the behaviour.
>
> **Protective:** factors that stop the problem occurring, reduce its severity or could be used to help address the problem. These might include characteristics of the individual, the situation, or the people and services around them.

Formulations may be written but they are more often presented as diagrams as these are helpful for illustrating sequences or vicious circles. As every individual and problem is unique, diagrams can be created to specifically illustrate those unique circumstances. However, it is often more helpful to use an initial format (even if this is adapted later) as this helps structure the information and generate ideas about how factors might interact. Using a standard diagram can also be a helpful way of identifying areas that have not been fully assessed. If there is nothing in a particular box, does that mean that it does not apply to this problem or that this area was forgotten in the assessment? Sometimes there may be gaps because it has not been possible to assess that area. When this happens it may be helpful to 'brainstorm' what might be happening in that area and see how these ideas might alter the interpretation of the information that could be found. It is important to remember that a formulation diagram is supposed to be a flexible aid to thinking and not a formal assessment that must be strictly adhered to.

## The extended hot-cross bun

An example of a formulation diagram that might be helpful with individuals with intellectual disabilities and personality disorder is given in Figure 10.9.

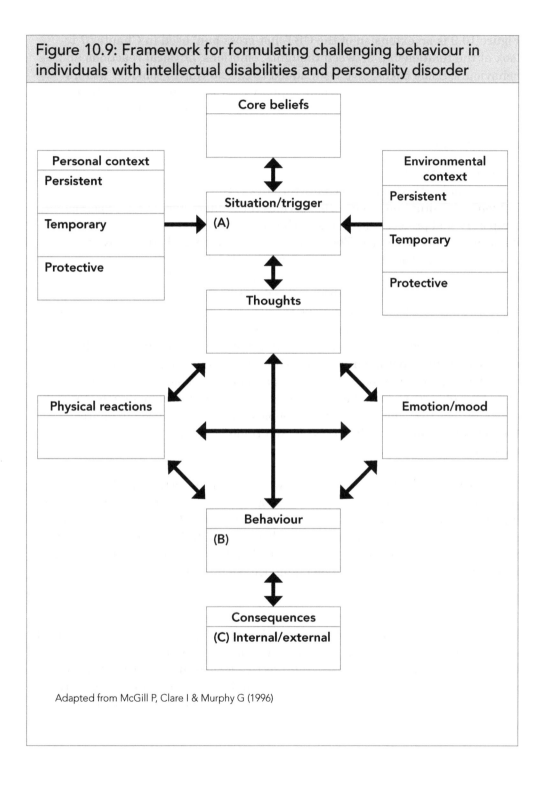

Figure 10.9: Framework for formulating challenging behaviour in individuals with intellectual disabilities and personality disorder

Adapted from McGill P, Clare I & Murphy G (1996)

Figure 10.9 is an extension of the CBT 'hot-cross bun' used in Chapter 7 to look at the relationship between thoughts, emotions, physical reactions and behaviours. Some boxes have been added to extend this to consider factors important in the positive behaviour support approach and the Five Ps model. These boxes look at the personal and environmental context of the behaviour and its consequences. The figure also shows where the information gathered from ABC charts would be entered.

## Personal context

The personal context refers to characteristics of the individual that might influence the situation. Figure 10.9 divides these characteristics into persistent, temporary and protective. Persistent characteristics are long-term and difficult, if not impossible, to change. These will need to be managed effectively or compensated for. They might include cognitive deficits, physical or sensory impairments, epilepsy or a high need for social contact and reassurance. These characteristics might be described as 'hard-wired'. Temporary characteristics are short-term factors that might resolve themselves or more flexible characteristics that might be amenable to change. These might include an episode of depression, a bereavement reaction or a deficit in a skill the individual could learn. Protective factors are things that might work to reduce the frequency or seriousness of the problem or might be harnessed to prevent the problem. These might include positive personal qualities such as a good sense of humour, motivations or aspirations to change, interests or hobbies that might be used to improve the individual's quality of life or skills that could be used to engage them in meaningful activities.

It is important to think carefully about which box a characteristic should be placed in. Are assumptions being made about how easy or difficult certain factors might be to change? If there is nothing in the protective factors box, this can be an indication that the team has been sucked into a totally negative picture of the individual. Every individual will have some helpful, positive characteristics, no matter how intractable their challenging behaviour may seem.

## Environmental context

The environmental context refers to characteristics of the situation the individual is in. This might include their living situation, working and social lives, financial situation and the staff and services that support them. Again, the diagram divides these into persistent, temporary and protective factors. It is important to look for protective factors that might help the individual. These might include positive relationships with particular staff members or good quality services that they could access.

## Core beliefs and thoughts

These may be the most difficult areas to access and the assessment may not produce any direct evidence from the individual to put in these boxes. Their presence in the formulation is, however, essential as they act as a reminder to consider events from the individual's perspective and not to make assumptions about their thoughts or motivations.

## Consequences

The consequences box will include what happens to the individual as a result of the behaviour. These consequences might include physical processes such as wounds being treated and social consequences such as how other people react to them. It is important to remember that the behaviour will also have internal consequences for the individual in terms of emotions, thoughts and physical sensations.

Once the Figure 10.9 has been filled in, actions that might prevent or minimise the behaviour often become apparent. It can be helpful to highlight these points by underlining, putting in bold or using different colours. This helps ensure that all the key points are integrated into the positive behaviour support plan. Some examples of formulations and positive behaviour support plans are given later in this chapter.

Completing a formulation provides the foundations for systematic and planned intervention, rather than a trial and error approach.

# Positive behaviour support for individuals with intellectual disabilities and personality disorder

This section will first look at a general framework for intervention that applies to all challenging behaviours including:

■ capable environments

■ positive behaviour support plans.

It will then look at some common challenging behaviours and give some specific suggestions that might be helpful in addressing those behaviours. This section includes example formulations and positive behaviour support plans.

Note that self-harm and suicidal behaviour are explored in depth in Chapter 11 because of the complexity of these behaviours and the anxiety they provoke.

# Capable environments

One of the essential elements of the positive behavioural support approach is the emphasis on the role support services may have in triggering and maintaining challenging behaviours. An important step in implementing this approach is for services to think carefully about how they can work to actively promote positive behaviour and effectively manage challenging behaviour.

The phrase 'capable environments' has been used in the challenging behaviour literature to highlight the importance of services in preventing, minimising and managing challenging behaviours. Capable environments are knowledgeable, creative, consistent, structured but flexible and person-centred. They will have staff with a good understanding of the factors that make individuals vulnerable to developing challenging behaviours, the functions that challenges may serve and an understanding of how to promote positive behaviours.

Capable environments for individuals with intellectual disabilities and personality disorder will be able to offer both consistency and flexibility. These reflect the two dimensions of the authoritative support style explored in Chapter 5.

## Consistency

To be effective, positive behaviour support plans need to be implemented consistently. This is essential to gain the trust of the individual; it can be very frightening and confusing for the individual if they are unable to predict how staff will respond to them. Frightened and confused individuals are likely to show more, rather than less, challenging behaviour.

Consistency is also important to avoid the risk of unintentionally creating situations that make the challenging behaviour worse. Research shows challenging behaviour that is successful some of the time but not all of the time is much more difficult to change. Inconsistent responses tend to give the message that the behaviour still works but needs to be done more often, for longer, or made more severe to get results.

## Sensitivity and flexibility

Strategies must also be implemented intelligently and flexibly. No plan can account for all situations. The staff implementing the plan need to understand the individual and the reasoning behind the strategies. In this way they can act in the spirit of the plan in the absence of specific guidance for a new situation.

# Positive behaviour support plans

A positive behaviour support plan brings together a number of elements aimed at preventing or managing the challenging behaviour, reducing the impact of that behaviour on the individual and others, and promoting a high quality of life for the individual. An effective positive behaviour support plan might contain the following components:

- proactive strategies: these are aimed at preventing the challenging behaviour from occurring

- reactive strategies: these are aimed at resolving the challenging behaviour as quickly and safely as possible

- risk assessment and management plan: this is aimed at identifying potential risks associated with the behaviour and its management, and minimising the risks to the individual, other people and the staff supporting the individual.

The starting point for developing a positive behaviour support plan must be the formulation. This will ensure that the strategies selected will address the unique circumstances, needs and wishes of each individual. It is often effective for the staff supporting the individual to meet as a team, to share the formulation and then brainstorm ways of responding to the behaviour and the situation that triggers it. Staff members will all have views on what might be helpful and will also be able to spot possible pitfalls in suggestions. This process also helps ensure that everyone is aware of the contents of the plan and reduces resistance to its implementation because staff have had an opportunity to express their views. Wherever possible the formulation should also be shared with the individual so that they can comment on it and can contribute their own ideas on the best ways of helping them address their difficulties.

The priority should be to prevent the behaviour from occurring. However, it is rarely possible to stop challenging behaviours completely. Hence it is also important to have a planned response for when the behaviour does occur. The approach should also take into account the wishes and aspirations of the individual. In this way the proactive and reactive strategies will be person-centred and can form part of the individual's 'person-centred plan'. The proactive and reactive strategies should be supported by proactive risk assessment and risk management (see Further reading).

Where physical health issues play a role in the challenging behaviour the individual's health action plan should be integrated in this process (see Chapter 8). Where an individual has additional mental health problems and is supported using the Care Programme Approach (CPA) (see Chapter 9) these strategies can be integrated into the CPA care plan.

## Role of medication

As discussed in earlier chapters, medication has a limited but important role in managing some aspects of personality disorder. Where medication is used, especially on an 'as required' basis, its use should be integrated into the positive behaviour support plan.

## Proactive strategies

Proactive strategies identify what to do on a day-to-day basis, to help minimise the likelihood that an individual will engage in the challenging behaviour. This is termed 'primary prevention' as it aims to prevent the behaviour occurring at all. Proactive strategies consider all aspects of the person's life. They should aim to enhance the individual's quality of life and to make the reactive plan redundant in the long term. Some examples of proactive strategies are given in Box 10.10.

---

### Box 10.10: Proactive strategies

**Individual factors**

**Specific conditions** – clear information on the implications of the condition and how it should be managed, accessible for individual and staff.

**Physical health** – strategies to promote health and reduce/manage physical pain (see Chapter 8)

**Mental health** – strategies to promote mental health and reduce/manage emotional pain (see Chapters 3, 7 and 9)

**Creating a meaningful life** – build on strengths, interests, wishes and aspirations to develop meaningful activities and positive lifestyle. This might include:
Building a positive self-image (see Chapter 2)
Managing emotions (see Chapter 3)
Improving relationships (see Chapter 4)
Managing impulsive behaviour (see Chapter 6)

**Communication difficulties** – develop a 'communication passport' to ensure everyone working with the individual is able to communicate effectively with them

**Intellectual deficits** – make accessible information so that the individual and those supporting them understand their limitations, develop compensation strategies for deficits eg. visual reminders for things that get forgotten, using mobile phone/ text messages for reminders

**Skills deficits** – develop compensation strategies for areas that cannot be changed and teaching strategies for those that can be addressed

Continued...

---

### Environmental factors

**Living arrangements** – support to find living arrangements that meet needs/ minimise triggers/temptations

**Support** – ensure support is sufficient and staff have correct skills to support individual

**Interaction style** – ensure individual is supported in the style that is most helpful for them (see Chapter 5)

**Structure, routines and boundaries** – ensure that the individual feels safe and emotionally and physically contained using positive, person-centred structure (see Chapter 3)

**Modifying, minimising and avoiding triggers** – eg. be out or engaged at trigger times, have clear strategies for dealing with problematic situations eg. waiting for appointments

### Addressing specific functions served by the challenging behaviour

**Social interaction** – schedule regular interaction, build social networks, build ability to tolerate being alone (see Chapter 5)

**Access to tangible items** – schedule regular access, minimise temptation (see Chapter 6), work on increasing tolerance for delays/sharing etc (Chapter 4)

**Escape** – refer for help with any underlying fears (eg. social phobia), be person-centred – does the individual really need to be in these settings? Find alternatives that are acceptable to the individual, respond to polite requests to leave

**Avoidance** – as for escape, for important areas look at using motivational interviewing (see Chapter 6) and the use of small steps (see Chapter 2 – ladders) to build tolerance

**Pleasurable/intense sensations** – build acceptable alternatives into routine for pleasurable sensation seekers, teach acceptable alternatives where sensation is used to block unwanted thoughts or sensations (distraction/grounding techniques), teach acceptance of negative thoughts and feelings

**Preventing the build-up of physical and emotional tension** – structure time to minimise over or understimulation, build in regular opportunities to let off 'steam' or vent emotional frustrations eg. running, kicking a ball, swimming, jogging or dancing. Build in relaxing activities eg. listening to music

As Box 10.10 highlights, proactive strategies are to be found in every chapter of this book. This is because primary prevention is about getting the individual's life right for them. When looking to select proactive strategies it is important to look at the formulation of the individual's challenging behaviour as this will identify specific areas where their life is not currently meeting their needs.

Sometimes the actions necessary to prevent challenging behaviours from occurring can feel uncomfortable for staff teams. For example, when challenging behaviour is motivated by gaining access to one-to-one staffing support, this should be given early on, before the individual has to resort to the challenging behaviour. However, staff may feel that this is 'feeding' an unhealthy need for staff input and is doing nothing to change the behaviour in the long term. In this case 'giving in' should be seen as a 'holding response'. That is, it reduces the challenging behaviour and gives a breathing space for the team to explore how this need could be met in more acceptable ways and to identify other strategies to reduce the intensity of the need. As these actions are identified they would also be included in the positive behaviour support plan.

## Reactive strategies

Reactive strategies may be divided into secondary and tertiary prevention. Secondary prevention describes what to do in response to the warning signs or early stages in a behavioural sequence. It aims to prevent these from developing into the challenging behaviour. Tertiary prevention is action taken once the behaviour is occurring to resolve it as quickly and safely as possible and to minimise the risk of it escalating.

### Secondary prevention

Some examples of secondary prevention strategies are given in Box 10.11.

---

**Box 10.11: Secondary prevention strategies**

**Individual factors**

**Physical health:** Timely use of painkillers or pain management techniques (see Chapter 8).

**Mental health:** Timely use of 'as required' medication to manage symptoms/ arousal level, active listening, use of familiar distraction/relaxation techniques (see Chapters 7 and 9).

**Emotional arousal:** Use de-escalation techniques (see Chapter 3), timely use of 'as required' medication.

Continued...

---

**Environmental factors**

**Physical environment:** Make changes eg. switch music/TV on or off, open/close windows, remove objects

**Location:** eg. change rooms, go outside/come inside, go to a quiet area

**Social environment** eg. asking people to leave the area, sitting and chatting with the individual, increase interaction/decrease interaction

**Specific functions**

**Social interaction:** Increase support level, engage individual

**Access to tangible items:** Give items as soon as possible then use de-escalation/distraction

**Escape:** Use of familiar relaxation/distraction techniques, timely use of 'as required' medication to help tolerate situation, leave the situation in a calm and orderly manner, reduce contact with staff

**Avoidance:** Reduce demands/staff contact, use familiar relaxation/distraction techniques and agreed motivational comments, allow to avoid situation in a calm manner

**Pleasurable/intense sensations:** Offer agreed stimulating activity, use familiar distraction/grounding techniques

**Emotional release:** Use familiar techniques for venting emotions eg. running, kicking a ball, popping bubble wrap, tearing paper or card, writing down their concerns

(see also Chapter 11 – alternatives to self-harm)

The number of reactive strategies in a positive behaviour support plan will be much smaller than the number of primary preventative strategies. This is because they are aimed at addressing specific early warning signs rather than improving the overall quality of the individual's life. It is essential that secondary preventative strategies are identified from the formulation and not selected on an ad hoc basis. This is because what helps to calm one individual may push another individual into the challenging behaviour it is intended to prevent. Also, randomly trying techniques to calm an individual is likely to make them feel insecure and hence increase the risk of them showing distressed and potentially challenging behaviours.

There is one important and deliberate omission from the list of secondary preventative strategies and that is 'ignoring' the behaviour. 'Ignoring' is often suggested as an approach for responding to 'attention-seeking behaviour'.

However, teams should be very wary of including ignoring or not responding to a behaviour as part of the reactive plan. There are several reasons for this. Firstly, people seem to find ignoring things very difficult. Much, so-called, 'ignoring' involves more interaction than paying attention to the behaviour. For example, someone might say *I'm not having anything to do with you while you are behaving like that, when you calm down I'll talk to you*'. This is a longer interaction than asking *'What's the matter?'* a phrase that might be seen as 'paying attention' to the individual. Secondly, where there is a strong drive to access something most individuals will escalate their behaviour in response to being ignored. Hence the individual is likely to go on to behave in a way that cannot be ignored. In this way 'ignoring' teaches the person to engage in more and more risky or dangerous behaviours. Finally, to be effective, 'ignoring' requires that every member of the staff team, other individuals using the service and visitors all ignore the behaviour, every single time it occurs. This level of consistency is rarely found even in highly specialised challenging behaviour services.

## Tertiary prevention

Tertiary preventative strategies are used when the challenging behaviour actually occurs. It is important to recognise that by this stage there is nothing that can be done to stop the behaviour. The response should aim to let it run its course as safely as possible and to avoid doing anything that would intensify or extend the incident. Effective tertiary strategies make the individual feel safe and cared for, provide physical and emotional containment, keep staff and other people safe and build the foundations for positive working together once the incident has been resolved. Chapter 12 explores in detail how to identify reactive strategies that are effective for each individual. Again, having a good assessment and formulation will help generate ideas about what strategies will be most helpful for each individual.

Sometimes tertiary prevention will involve the use of restrictive physical interventions. If included, restrictive physical interventions should always represent the least restrictive response to the challenge presented. As highlighted in Chapter 3, their use should comply with national guidance and restrictive physical interventions should only be used by appropriately trained staff.

Tertiary strategies should comprise the smallest part of the positive behaviour support plan. If this section is longer than the other parts of the plan it indicates that insufficient attention has been paid to meeting the individual's needs and improving their quality of life.

Intellectual Disabilities and Personality Disorder: An integrated approach
© Pavilion Publishing and Media Ltd and its licensors 2014.

# Specific behaviours

The following sections will look in more detail at:

- self-neglect

- verbal aggression

- physical aggression.

The challenging behaviours are described together with suggestions for assessment and intervention. Each section gives an example formulation using the adapted hot-cross bun and an example positive behaviour support plan based on that formulation.

# Self-neglect

This refers to when an individual does not engage in behaviours that keep them healthy and safe. It can include neglecting personal hygiene, not eating or drinking enough, neglecting treatment of physical illnesses or tooth decay (see Chapter 8), neglecting care of their living environment such that conditions become hazardous to their health or failing to take basic precautions to keep themselves safe. It also includes failing to limit or control behaviours that are actively harmful to the individual, for example, living on junk food, continuing to eat high sugar food despite developing diabetes, continuing to overeat despite developing obesity-related health problems or consuming large quantities of caffeinated drinks despite having high anxiety levels.

The point at which low standards of personal care become self-neglect is difficult to define. Behaviours may be seen as on a continuum from ultra high standards (perfectionism) to dangerously low standards. While it is easy to agree on the severest levels of neglect it is less clear where the cut-off lies between low standards and neglect. This can present difficulties for teams supporting individuals as it can lead to disagreements and confusion. It is therefore important to explore these issues when trying to understand if an individual is neglecting themselves.

## Exploring standards

Minimum safe standards will vary according to factors in the individual's circumstances and the nature of the neglect. For example, for most people it may not impact on their health to go for several weeks without having a shower and washing their hair (although others may find the resulting body odour offensive). However, if the person has a skin condition it may be necessary to shower more often. Many people eat too much sugar, however, such a diet will have more immediate, and potentially life-threatening, consequences for individuals with diabetes. Many people do not drink the recommended amount of water a day; however, for individuals with kidney disease this can have serious consequences. It is also important to consider how quickly the situation becomes critical. For example, most healthy individuals can go for several days without eating and not come to any serious harm. However, stopping drinking completely is much more serious. It can be very helpful to consult with relevant professionals about the impact of the individual's current behaviour to determine at what point the behaviour becomes harmful.

Like all people, staff will have different personal standards as to what they consider comprises good personal hygiene, how clean and tidy they keep their home, what they consider a reasonable diet and what and how much they drink. The first step in addressing self-neglect is to come to an agreement as to the point at which relaxed personal standards cross into being harmful and what is the minimum change that would keep the individual healthy enough. It can be helpful to brainstorm these issues as a team before discussing them with the individual. This is because there are likely to be as many different opinions as there are people in the discussion. Staff can feel passionately about their own standards and can be evangelical in their wish to see others conform to those standards. It is essential to thrash out what people personally find unacceptable from what is putting the individual at risk. If these initial discussions take place with the individual present they are likely to be able to play on these differences and nothing will be resolved. Box 10.12 gives some questions that may be helpful in thinking about how harmful self-neglect might be for an individual.

---

### Box 10.12: Issues to consider when agreeing minimum standards for self-care

- Impact on physical health
  - Presence of physical health problems that will increase impact of the behaviour
  - Short-term impact
  - Long-term impact
- Impact on health of teeth
- Impact on mental health (eg. increasing feelings of worthlessness)
- Impact on relationships
- Impact on social interactions
- Impact on living arrangements (eg. risk of eviction)
- Impact on employment/other activities (eg. risk of being excluded)
- Impact on relationship with services (eg. being struck off specialist list for not attending appointments)

---

## Keeping the individual safe

Where it is apparent that the self-neglect is putting the individual at risk, immediate action should be taken to ensure they are safe. This should include a risk assessment and management plan. Actions might include putting in additional support hours, admission to hospital or even hiring a firm of cleaners to deep clean their flat. Where the individual is assessed not to be at immediate risk, monitoring should be put in place to alert services to any deterioration in the situation. Once it is clear that the individual is safe it is appropriate to begin exploring the reason for their self-neglect.

Responding to self-neglect can present a lot of challenges to services. It raises complex issues such as balancing choice and capacity, human rights and duty of care. There is a fine line between colluding with the neglect and being overly controlling.

# Assessment

Assessment of self-neglect should follow the general process given earlier in this chapter, including gathering information on the individual's history and current situation. The screening sequence and the use of ABC charts may be helpful in establishing the function(s) of the self-neglect.

The following sections give some specific suggestions about exploring the nature and extent of the self-neglect and look at some common causes and functions. These may be helpful in giving some ideas to explore during the assessment and formulation phases.

## Assessing self-neglect

While self-neglect must always be taken seriously it is also important to establish the true extent of the problem. Some individuals learn that shows of apparent self-neglect are effective at eliciting responses from those who support them. They may make dramatic statements and a big performance of not doing something, for example, not eating. It is important to confirm that the individual is really not eating rather than just not eating shared meals in public. Often such individuals will eat later when they are unobserved or were so full up from snacks earlier in the day that they were not hungry at the time of the meal they refused. Key signs to look for are unexplained food wrappers, food going missing from the fridge or cupboards overnight, the individual continuing to have their normal energy levels and no signs of weight loss (some individuals even manage to gain weight while behaving in this manner). Similarly, an individual who has completely stopped drinking will not need to urinate with their usual frequency.

It is also important to think about the role of skills in self-neglect. Is the individual really, deliberately neglecting their health or do they not understand or cannot remember what they are meant to do? It can be very helpful to persuade the individual to let a trusted member of staff observe them carrying out procedures, for example, drawing up an insulin injection to check whether they know the correct dose and can read the calibration on the syringe.

## Reasons for self-neglect

Individuals may neglect themselves for a number of reasons. Neglect can occur when the individual is too ill, either physically or mentally to care for themselves. For example, self-neglect may occur if the individual is developing dementia or experiencing depression. It can also occur when individuals do not know how to care for themselves properly or do not understand the risks of the behaviour. This can occur when the individual has experienced a neglectful and chaotic childhood with no opportunity to learn healthy patterns of behaviour. This situation can also arise when an individual has been over-protected by a family member and has not learnt to care for themselves. If the family member dies, the individual may have no idea how to take on the tasks that were previously done for them. Self-neglect may occur in less able individuals in response to a drop in the amount of support they receive from services, for example, following a re-assessment of need.

Where the neglect is around a particular health issue the individual may not have understood medical advice or may not have grasped the long-term implications of their behaviour. Poor impulse control may also play a role; the individual may be unable to resist the temptation to indulge in something unhealthy or to do something more enjoyable than an unpleasant chore.

Self-neglect can also serve a number of functions for the individual. Some possible functions are given in Box 10.13.

It is also important to remember that behaviours may serve more than one function. Sometimes self-neglect may be triggered by one factor but go on to be maintained by others. For example, an individual may neglect themselves as the result of feeling depressed but might become dependent on the extra support and caring interactions this produced. The self-neglect might then continue after the depression had resolved.

### Formulation

The information gathered should be compiled into a formulation (such as the Five Ps or adapted hot cross bun) before progressing to identify interventions. It is important to take the time to understand what lies behind the self-neglect so

Intellectual Disabilities and Personality Disorder: An integrated approach
© Pavilion Publishing and Media Ltd and its licensors 2014.

that interventions can be tailored to the particular causes. If this is not done, the behaviour will not resolve or will return rapidly once extra support is removed.

---

## Box 10.13: Functions of self-neglect

■ **Communication (implicit meaning of behaviour)**
  ▨ I need someone to care for me
  ▨ I am not worth caring for
  ▨ There's no point (feeling hopeless)
  ▨ I can't do it (feeling helpless)
  ▨ It's too difficult/too much (feeling overwhelmed)
  ▨ You can't control me (defiance/rebellion)

■ **Avoidance**
  ▨ It hurts (eg. medical check ups, blood sugar tests)
  ▨ It's too scary
  ▨ If I behave like I don't have X, it will go away (denial)
  ▨ They will tell me off (eg. avoiding appointments)
  ▨ It's hard work
  ▨ I don't like doing it (eg. washing up)
  ▨ It tastes horrible (eg. certain medications)
  ▨ People will leave me alone (eg. if I look filthy)

■ **Escape**
  ▨ I don't want to be part of this life
  ▨ I want to die

■ **Punishing self**
  ▨ I don't deserve to be healthy/live in a nice place
  ▨ I deserve to be in pain

■ **Punishing others**
  ▨ Look what you made me do
  ▨ Look what they made me do

■ **Achieving things**
  ▨ If you do X then I won't eat/drink/clean my room
  ▨ If you don't do X then I won't eat/drink/clean my room

■ **Pleasurable sensations**
  ▨ I love eating chocolate/drinking cola
  ▨ Fills an emotional emptiness

---

## Interventions

As with other challenging behaviours, the intervention approach will be a positive behaviour support plan with proactive and reactive strategies. The general strategies listed earlier in this chapter are likely to be helpful. Proactive strategies might include treating an episode of depression, providing a combination of nurturing and caring for the individual, education and motivation, boundaries and support, exploring emotions and developing alternative strategies to meet needs. Strategies to address these issues are to be found in earlier chapters.

When an individual severely neglects themselves they may need a lot of help and support to carry out basic care. However, it is important to always keep in mind that the aim is for the individual to return to as much independence as they can. Hence even if they are too unwell to actively participate they should be involved in the process. For example, they might still turn the taps on and pull the plug out even if staff need to do all other aspects of giving them a bath. As they recover they can be encouraged to gradually do more for themselves.

For severe self-neglect it can be helpful to break the activity down into tiny steps (task analysis). Staff can then all follow the same sequence in supporting the individual and can agree which step the person will take over next. This is the approach used to teach less able people how to do tasks and it is very effective at promoting consistency. It may also be helpful to gradually fade out the prompts given, for example, guiding the person physically, telling them what to do, gesturing what to do then waiting to see if they respond independently. It can also be helpful to gradually shorten a verbal prompt or reduce the volume from normal voice to a whisper to silence.

Always keep in mind that the individual may find the interaction involved in supporting them reinforcing. Make the activity itself as rewarding as possible. For example, ensure the bathroom is warm, the water hot enough, the soap is a favourite perfume, there is a nice bubble bath and towels are warm and fluffy. However, make the human contact the minimum necessary to get the person through the task. It may be helpful to say something like *'Let's get this done, so we can sit and have a coffee and a nice chat'*. Ensure praise and interaction is given more in response to efforts to do the task than for not doing it.

As the individual recovers it can be helpful to work with them to make a book, posters or other physical reminders of what they have been taught and are trying to achieve. It can be helpful to place strategic reminders eg. on the food cupboard or in the bathroom. It can also help to build in long-term rewards for healthy behaviour. For example, a support worker might visit once a week to help with the cleaning. However, if the flat is already clean enough they can go out for a coffee together instead. In this way healthy behaviour is not inadvertently punished ie. you cleaned the flat yourself – you don't need support any more. (It is important that the people responsible for funding the individual's care understand the importance of continued contact in maintaining the improvement. If this is not achieved then the level of support is likely to be cut on the basis that it is no longer needed and the individual will quickly regress.)

Where the behaviour is assessed to be motivated by the desire to punish others or as 'emotional blackmail' it is important that the team appear calm and neutral in the face of threats. Make it clear that it is up to the individual how they manage their reaction to staff requests and actions and that the responsibility rests with them and not the staff team.

Finally, it is important to have a crisis plan (see Chapter 12 for more details) as severe self-neglect can be life-threatening and individuals may need admission to a general hospital or mental health service.

Boxes 10.14 and 10.15 give a formulation and positive behaviour support plan for a fictitious individual (based on experiences with a number of individuals) showing self- neglect. Looking at the formulation diagram it appears that this individual's self-neglect may be serving a number of functions. Neglecting their gluten-free diet appears to be associated with a belief that they deserve to be punished. Exposing themselves to the risk of financial exploitation from friends appears to be filling the gap left in their life by losing a job they had enjoyed. Other key factors that might have contributed to the development and maintenance of the behaviour have been underlined, as have factors that might be helpful in developing solutions. These factors are addressed in the behaviour support plan. Notice that the section on proactive strategies (primary prevention) is by far the longest section in the plan.

## Figure 10.14: A formulation of self-neglect for an in individual with intellectual disabilities and personality disorder

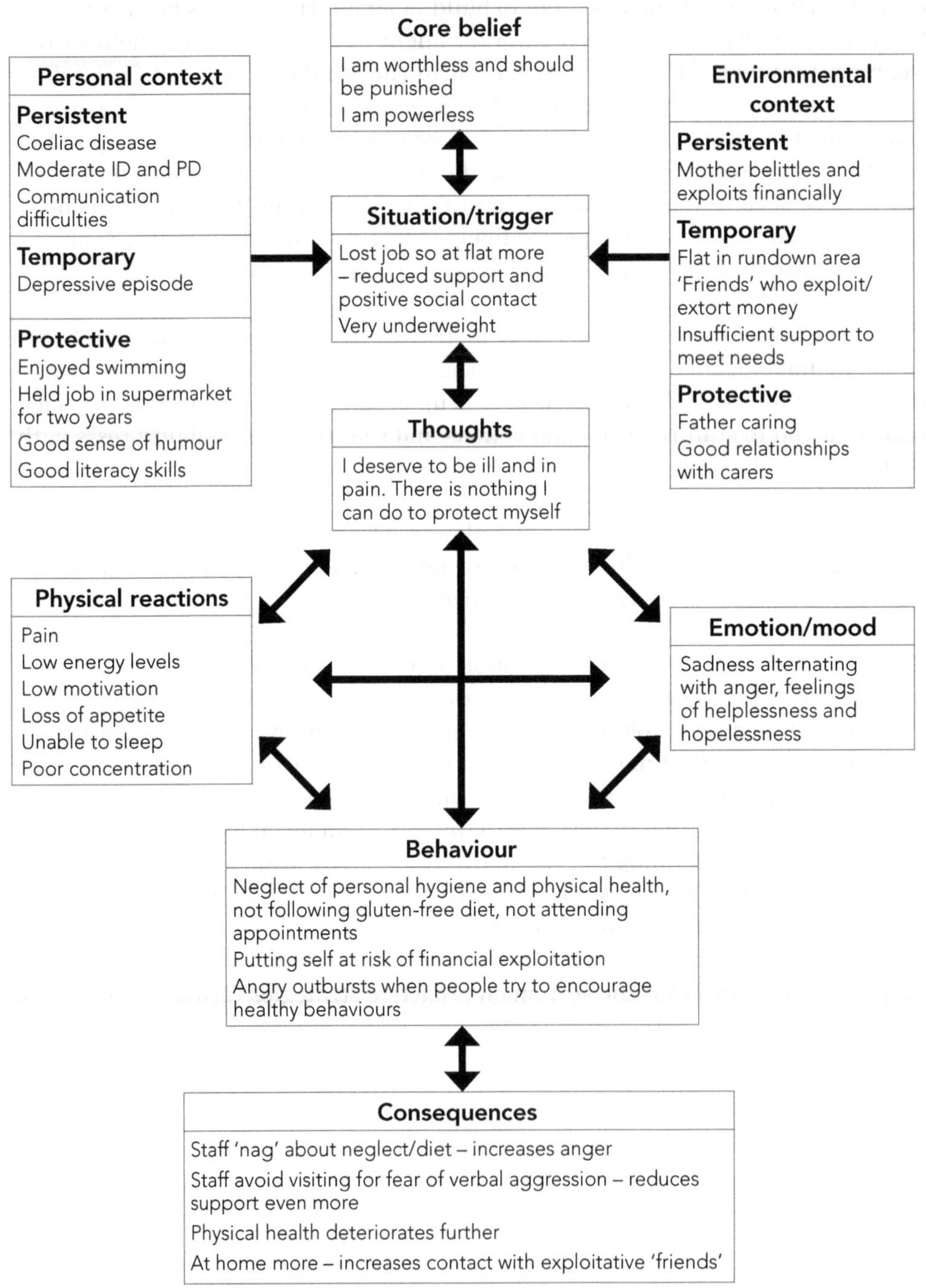

**Core belief**
I am worthless and should be punished
I am powerless

**Personal context**

**Persistent**
Coeliac disease
Moderate ID and PD
Communication difficulties

**Temporary**
Depressive episode

**Protective**
Enjoyed swimming
Held job in supermarket for two years
Good sense of humour
Good literacy skills

**Situation/trigger**
Lost job so at flat more – reduced support and positive social contact
Very underweight

**Environmental context**

**Persistent**
Mother belittles and exploits financially

**Temporary**
Flat in rundown area
'Friends' who exploit/extort money
Insufficient support to meet needs

**Protective**
Father caring
Good relationships with carers

**Thoughts**
I deserve to be ill and in pain. There is nothing I can do to protect myself

**Physical reactions**
Pain
Low energy levels
Low motivation
Loss of appetite
Unable to sleep
Poor concentration

**Emotion/mood**
Sadness alternating with anger, feelings of helplessness and hopelessness

**Behaviour**
Neglect of personal hygiene and physical health, not following gluten-free diet, not attending appointments
Putting self at risk of financial exploitation
Angry outbursts when people try to encourage healthy behaviours

**Consequences**
Staff 'nag' about neglect/diet – increases anger
Staff avoid visiting for fear of verbal aggression – reduces support even more
Physical health deteriorates further
At home more – increases contact with exploitative 'friends'

## Box 10.15: An example of a positive behavioural support plan for self-neglect based on the formulation given in 10.14

### Rationale

### Why I need you to do this

I have been neglecting my health and personal hygiene, care of my flat and exposing myself to risk because I have been feeling very depressed and do not think that I deserve to be well. I have given up hope that I will ever get my life back on track. I need staff to be understanding and patient while helping me get my life back on track.

### Behaviours

- Not following gluten-free diet
- Not attending medical appointments
- Not cleaning the flat
- Shouting at people who try to help

### Proactive strategies

- Move to supported living set-up with staff on site 24/7 in new area
- Get new mobile phone number so that can select which 'friends' will be able to get in touch
- Introduce supported activities including swimming and helping at charity shop – with aim to work towards a new job
- Support to attend appointments with the psychiatrist and to take antidepressants
- Support to attend appointments with clinical psychologist for CBT
- Support from dietitian to explain gluten-free diet and create easy to follow, visual healthy eating plan that takes into account personal preferences
- Negotiate clear contract of support to reduce points of conflict with care staff
- Make time to chat and joke, always start conversations on a fun topic not just what should be doing/haven't done (avoid appearing to 'nag')
- Recognise and praise even very small successes to build self-esteem and increase motivation
- Validate emotions but use distraction techniques to move away from negative thoughts
- Weigh weekly and praise compliance with diet/weight gain/stability
- Support to regularly visit father
- Support to have contact with mother in controlled way eg. by text message/ email rather than phone calls or face-to-face

Continued...

---

**Reactive strategies**

■ Do not 'nag' if individual doesn't do something – use active listening skills to find out why they didn't do it

■ If individual shouts, staff should calmly leave the area but return later

■ If the flat becomes too dirty, book a professional cleaner to come when individual is out. Make sure individual know when the cleaners are coming

■ Monitor health impact of failing to stick to diet

■ Use safeguarding procedure if mother or a 'friends' tries to exploit individual

**Crisis plan**

■ Contact psychiatrist

■ If necessary, be admitted to Y (local specialist assessment and treatment unit) if weight drops below X kg/depression becomes too severe. May require use of Mental Health Act.

---

# Verbal aggression

Verbal aggression is very common and is shown by most individuals with intellectual disabilities and personality disorder. It includes shouting, swearing, unkind personal comments and threats. In its most severe forms it may also include abuse about personal characteristics such as race or sexual orientation. Verbal aggression should be taken as seriously as physical aggression. It has a corrosive effect on staff supporting the individual, destroys the individual's personal relationships and social networks, reduces their social opportunities and may put the individual at risk of prosecution.

Some individuals are indiscriminate in who they shout at; they will yell at anyone who is around when they lose their temper. This may be related to intense emotional reactions combined with poor impulse control. Other individuals may have learnt that there are consequences for shouting at some people or in certain situations (eg. being thrown out of a pub, the police being called). These individuals may be good at identifying whom they can 'get away with' shouting at eg. abusing health or social care professionals but not police or people in the pub. For others it is a part of a wider pattern of bullying behaviour (see Chapter 4). Verbal aggression may also be linked to certain physical states, for example, being tired or under the influence of alcohol. For some it may be related to mental health problems, particularly irritability associated with depression or mania.

Individuals who are verbally aggressive may be hypersensitive to criticisms because of low self-esteem. They may also perceive insults or threats where none were intended as a result of faulty thinking patterns (see Chapter 7). Situations may also be escalated where individuals have an 'eye for an eye' mentality and feel entitled to attack those they consider have wronged them in some way.

Where an individual resorts to comments about race or sexual orientation, this may reflect unresolved personal issues. However, such comments can also be the result of unquestioning acceptance of prejudice or have been reinforced by the intense reaction they often cause.

## Motivations

Some possible functions of verbal aggression are given in Box 10.16.

---

### Box 10.16: Possible functions of verbal aggression

- Social interaction: Being seen as tough/getting 'respect'
- Communication (implicit meaning of behaviour)
  - I need to feel powerful
  - I must be strong or others will hurt me
  - I need to feel in control
  - You can't control me (defiance/rebellion)
  - I can't bear being criticised
- Avoidance: If I shout at you, I won't have to do what you are asking
- Escape: If I shout I won't have to do this anymore
- Punishing others/paying them back/taking down a peg
  - That will teach them not to do that to me again
  - S/he started it
  - S/he's not so smug now
- Achieving things
  - Getting other people to do things
  - Getting people to give things that are wanted
- Pleasurable sensations
  - Enjoyment of 'adrenaline rush'
  - Enjoyment of other people's reactions/distress
- Emotional release
  - Venting anger, frustration, jealousy
  - Achieving revenge, discharging tension built up by holding grudges

---

It is also important that services question their own reaction to verbal aggression. In some settings, shouting can be an effective way of achieving things that cannot be done by talking politely. Other services make allowances because of the individual's intellectual disabilities and personality disorder and protect them from the natural negative consequences that would usually follow such behaviour.

## Assessment

Again, assessment should follow the process suggested earlier in this chapter. The ABC approach is often particularly helpful when looking at verbal aggression as it can highlight triggers, early warning signs and the consequences of the behaviour. It is also helpful to try to explore the individual's emotional reaction to and thinking about the situation that triggered the abuse (see Chapter 7). In particular it is important to explore whether the verbal abuse was targeted at a specific individual in response to perceived wrongs or whether the victim was a 'lightening rod' for emotion that had nothing to do with that person.

## Formulation

The information gathered should be compiled into a formulation before progressing to identify interventions. It is important to take the time to understand what lies behind the verbal aggression so that interventions can be tailored to the particular causes. If this is not done it is likely that the behaviour will not resolve or may even escalate.

## Interventions

As with other challenging behaviours, the intervention approach will be a positive behaviour support plan with proactive and reactive strategies. The primary and secondary preventative strategies listed earlier in this chapter are likely to be helpful. Other proactive strategies might include, building self-esteem, learning about emotions and how to express them appropriately and building social skills. Reactive strategies might include using conflict resolution techniques or the 'no blame' approach to bullying (see Chapter 4).

Anger management training is often suggested to address verbal (and physical) aggression. This can be effective where the individual is struggling to control their emotional reactions but lacks the necessary understanding and skills. However, where verbal aggression is achieving positive outcomes for the individual, anger management is unlikely to reduce the problem. In these situations it is important to both change the outcome of the behaviour and work with the individual to build their understanding of the impact of their behaviour on others and its longer term consequences for themselves. Social Stories™ (Chapter 4) can be helpful with this.

## Tertiary strategies

When responding to verbal aggression, it is important both to consider how to respond to the individual being abusive and how to support the target of the abuse. Techniques given in Chapter 4 for managing interpersonal conflict may be helpful for calmly resolving incidents. Once the incident is resolved thought should be given to how best to support the target. If the target is another individual with intellectual disabilities it will be important to follow the local safeguarding procedure and to ensure that appropriate action is taken to protect the victim. Everyone who has been verbally abused should be given post-incident support. For staff, access to confidential counselling is important. Those who have been the targets of verbal aggression may be reluctant to seek help but may benefit greatly if encouraged to attend such services by supportive managers. It is important that the targets of the abuse are supported to contact the police and take action against the perpetrator if they wish.

Figure 10.17 and Box 10.18 give a formulation and positive behaviour support plan for a fictitious individual showing verbal aggression. Looking at the formulation diagram it appears that this individual's verbal aggression serves a number of functions for the individual; it accesses interaction with staff, escapes and avoids demands and gives them the satisfaction of having revenge on others who have upset them in some way. It appears that the recent change in living arrangements has made the individual feel insecure and this has triggered core beliefs about control, entitlement and revenge. It seems likely that their concrete thinking has made it difficult for them to adjust to the new setting and more likely to misinterpret situations as putting them down or favouring others. The difficulties with their teeth, arising as a consequence of their fear of dentists, cause the individual frequent pain. This is likely to make them more irritable and quicker to anger.

The positive behaviour support plan has a number of strands. The proactive strategies aim to build more positive relationships, clarify boundaries, reduce resistance to demands, increase engagement in meaningful activities and to address their toothache and dental phobia. Reactive strategies aim to resolve incidents as quickly and calmly as possible and to resolve interpersonal conflict. If these are not successful the plan suggests referral for specialist assessment. This might include checking that the individual has not developed a mental health problem as a result of the stress of the move and considering the use of 'as required' medication (this might be helpful in calming difficult situations and also might help get the individual to the dentist). As with the previous example, proactive strategies make up the majority of the plan.

## Box 10.17: A formulation of verbal aggression in an individual with intellectual disabilities and personality disorder

**Core belief**

I can't tolerate restrictions. My needs are more important. People who wrong me must be punished

**Personal context**

**Persistent**

History of neglect and abuse

Mild ID – concrete thinking

PD

**Temporary**

Chronic toothache – refusal of dental care

Fear of dentists

**Protective**

Good verbal communication skills

Enjoys one to one interaction with staff

Enjoys walking

**Situation/trigger**

Having to wait

Requests to do dull tasks/clean teeth

Being alone with person who has upset them

**Environmental context**

**Persistent**

Supported living with five other individuals – was last to move in to an established group

**Temporary**

Recently moved, does not know staff or individuals well

**Protective**

New service has good community links and offers a range of interesting activities

**Thoughts**

Staff can't control me, I'm the boss

I'm always the last to get help

That will teach them for doing …. to me

**Physical reactions**

Pain

Red in the face, jerky movements

Racing heartbeat, short rapid breathing

**Emotion/mood**

Angry, unsettled and insecure

**Behaviour**

Shouting at staff, demanding that things be done immediately

Shouting insults at staff including words such as 'bitch', 'whore' and using racial abuse

Quietly making comments to other individuals such as 'your mother hates you', 'your father's dead' and 'you're a fat slob'

**Consequences**

Staff become flustered, try to calm individual down, offer tea and withdraw demands

Other individuals become angry/upset – individual appears to enjoy watching this

## Box 10.18: An example of a positive behavioural support plan for verbal aggression based on the formulation given in 10.17

### Rationale

### Why I need you to do this

I am feeling insecure and unsettled since my move. It feels to me that I am always getting left out and that others are treated better than me. I find this really difficult and I get very angry. This is made worse by the toothache I have most of the time. I need you to help me sort out my teeth and start to feel more secure so that I change my behaviour.

### Behaviours

- Shouting at staff, demanding that things be done immediately
- Shouting insults at staff including words such as 'bitch', 'whore' and using racial abuse
- Making comments to other individuals such as 'your mother hates you'
- Not cleaning their teeth
- Refusing to attend the dentist

Proactive strategies

- Build better relationships with staff members
  - Daily walk with a member of staff – make sure all staff take part. Use walk to chat (active listening) and get to know each other
  - Key worker to create new person-centred plan to explore all the new and interesting options open in this placement
  - 30 minutes at end of day (7.30pm) to review day. Problem solve options for dealing with any issues identified with individuals/staff
- Build better relationships with other individuals
  - Going out with member of staff and one other individual
  - Chatting with a member of staff and one other individual
  - Support to attend residents' group and contribute views to discussion
- Address toothache
  - Manage toothache – use of paracetamol
  - Support to take part in tooth care education
  - Urgent referral to CTPLD for treatment of dental phobia, support to attend appointments and carry out homework with aim of getting individual to see dentist for treatment of tooth decay
- Negotiate clear contract for rules of living in the house and consequences for breaking them – making clear this applies to all individuals

Continued...

- Use non-confrontational requests eg. *'do you want to …now or this afternoon?' 'Would you like some help to…?' 'Is this a good time to get…done?*
- Name and praise appropriate behaviour however minor
- Keep waiting to a minimum
- Teach strategies for managing waiting, distraction techniques and self-soothing
- Teach consequences of abuse eg. loss of placement, involvement of police

**Reactive strategies**
- Validate emotions and use de-escalation techniques to calm situation
- Use conflict resolution approach to address conflict with other individuals

**Crisis plan**
- Refer for specialist assessment (psychiatrist/psychologist)

# Physical aggression

Physical aggression is also common in individuals with intellectual disabilities and personality disorder. It can be very frightening for staff to support an individual who shows physical aggression. Physical aggression can put staff, other individuals, family members and the public at risk. Less obvious perhaps are the negative consequences that physical aggression has for the individual. It can lead to the breakdown of relationships and placements, to exclusion from health and social services and potentially to criminal proceedings.

Physical aggression is often associated with verbal aggression. Often there is an escalating sequence in which the individual begins by shouting and insulting others but then becomes physically aggressive. More rarely individuals will bottle up their feelings until these explode in physical aggression.

The motivations for physical aggression and the factors that influence it are essentially the same as those for verbal aggression. As are the assessment and formulation processes. Consequently, positive behavioural support plans for physical aggression will have very similar primary and secondary preventative strategies to plans developed for verbal aggression. The main difference is likely to be the need for tertiary prevention; aggression may require the use of restrictive physical interventions. There is greater likelihood that physical aggression will lead to a crisis and hence there will need to be a more detailed crisis plan.

Figure 10.19 and Box 10.20 give a formulation and positive behaviour support plan for a fictitious individual showing physical aggression. Looking at the formulation diagram (10.19) it appears that this individual's physical aggression acts as a vent for pent up negative emotions. The recent relationship breakdown has taken away practical and emotional support and appears to have activated core beliefs about being useless and unlovable. The individual's already poor impulse control has been undermined by getting drunk. The reaction of people to the aggressive behaviour has the result of making the individual feel ashamed and accentuates their feelings of being useless and out of control.

The positive behaviour support plan focuses on trying to reduce stress through added support, building positive mood and reducing temptation to drink through enjoyable activities and to make drinking less likely to lead to violence by choosing a much quieter pub. Reactive strategies have been chosen to try to break the vicious cycle of reactions increasing the underlying feelings of being useless and unlovable. Instead they focus on building hope and the motivation for change.

The crisis plan recognises that the individual may be at risk of experiencing depression, and that the support introduced to the individual's current living arrangements may be insufficient to address their needs. Hence the plan identifies the potential need for admission to a specialist unit or a move to a more supported residential setting. Despite the seriousness of the behaviour the proactive strategies still make up the majority of the positive behaviour support plan.

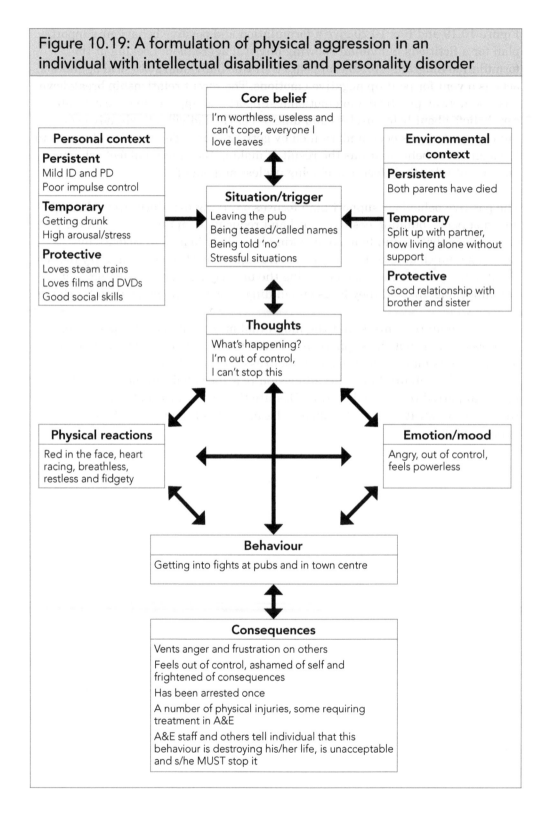

**Figure 10.19: A formulation of physical aggression in an individual with intellectual disabilities and personality disorder**

**Core belief**
I'm worthless, useless and can't cope, everyone I love leaves

**Personal context**

**Persistent**
Mild ID and PD
Poor impulse control

**Temporary**
Getting drunk
High arousal/stress

**Protective**
Loves steam trains
Loves films and DVDs
Good social skills

**Environmental context**

**Persistent**
Both parents have died

**Temporary**
Split up with partner, now living alone without support

**Protective**
Good relationship with brother and sister

**Situation/trigger**
Leaving the pub
Being teased/called names
Being told 'no'
Stressful situations

**Thoughts**
What's happening?
I'm out of control,
I can't stop this

**Physical reactions**
Red in the face, heart racing, breathless, restless and fidgety

**Emotion/mood**
Angry, out of control, feels powerless

**Behaviour**
Getting into fights at pubs and in town centre

**Consequences**
Vents anger and frustration on others

Feels out of control, ashamed of self and frightened of consequences

Has been arrested once

A number of physical injuries, some requiring treatment in A&E

A&E staff and others tell individual that this behaviour is destroying his/her life, is unacceptable and s/he MUST stop it

## Box 10.20: An example of a positive behavioural support plan for physical aggression based on the formulation given in 10.19

### Rationale

### Why I need you to do this

I am very worried and upset by my drinking and aggression but I don't seem to be able to control myself or change my behaviour alone. The worse I feel about it the more I seem to lose control. I need you to help me find new ways of managing my emotions and rebuilding my life.

### Behaviours

■ Getting into fights at pubs and in town centre

### Proactive strategies

■ Provide a package of support to help manage day-to-day tasks eg. shopping, managing money, household chores that were previously done by partner

■ Do tasks with, not for, individual, using task analysis to teach new skills, praise effort not achievement (to build self-confidence and sense of being able to cope)

■ Support to engage in local activities including joining local steam railway restoration group

■ Enlist brother and sister to take to cinema regularly and on high risk evenings

■ One-to-one time to talk about emotions and to learn to manage emotions, relaxation and distraction techniques, encourage to practice daily

■ Support to attend AA meetings/referral for help with low self-esteem

■ Use DVDs of favourite films to improve mood/distract from unhelpful thoughts

■ Encouragement to change pub from busy/rough town centre to quiet local pub

### Reactive strategies

■ Low key response to incidents. Rather than focusing on what happened, give support and encourage focus on what will do to change behaviour. Use active listening and motivational interviewing techniques. Build hope.

■ Avoid using word 'no', use phrases such as *'I'm sorry I can't do that now'*

■ If appears to be becoming agitated with support staff, reduce demands, ask if individual wants staff to leave, give space to calm down.

### Crisis plan

■ If continues to deteriorate may need referral to psychiatrist to check if developing depression and for possible use of medication

■ May need admission to mental health unit (contact numbers)

■ May need to move to more supportive setting

Hopefully, the three examples given in this section show how systematic assessment, formulation and positive behavioural support can be used to address the wide range of challenging behaviours shown by individuals with intellectual disabilities and personality disorder.

# Key learning points

- Behaviour is described as challenging when it threatens the quality of life and/or the physical safety of the individual or others and is likely to lead to responses that are restrictive, aversive or result in exclusion.

- Behaviours have meaning or function (purpose) and do not occur in isolation. Challenging behaviours arise as ways of meeting needs such as initiating social contact or escape from something unbearable.

- Positive behavioural support looks at the interaction between the person and their underlying human needs, their environment and the people around them. It highlights the relationship between challenging behaviours and the setting in which they occur.

- Positive behavioural support is very different from the medical model where specific behaviours are seen as 'symptoms' and assessment looks for the clusters of symptoms that are characteristic of particular physical or mental health problems.

- When this approach is applied with an awareness of both intellectual disabilities and personality disorder it can offer helpful way of addressing problems that might otherwise appear untreatable.

- The use of a structured formulation such as the adapted 'hot-cross bun' can make sense of the large amount of complicated information that is often generated by a thorough assessment.

- Positive behavioural support plans include both proactive and reactive strategies. They aim to prevent the behaviour wherever possible by improving the individual's quality of life and to minimise the impact of the behaviour when it cannot be avoided.

- The positive behaviour support approach highlights the need for 'capable services' which have the skills to develop and implement such plans.

Intellectual Disabilities and Personality Disorder: An integrated approach
© Pavilion Publishing and Media Ltd and its licensors 2014.

# References

McGill P, Clare I & Murphy G (1996) Understanding and responding to challenging behaviour: From theory to practice. *Tizard Learning Disability Review* **1** 9–17.

Royal College of Psychiatrists, British Psychological Society and Royal College of Speech and Language Therapists (2006) *Challenging Behaviour: A unified approach*. London: Royal College of Psychiatrists.

# Further reading

Alexander R & Cooray S (2003) Diagnosis of personality disorders in learning disability. *British Journal of Psychiatry* **44** 28–31.

BILD (2006) *Code of Practice for the Use and Reduction of Restrictive Physical Interventions*. Birmingham: British Institute of Learning Disabilities.

BILD (2002) *Easy Guide to Physical Interventions: for People with Learning Disabilities, their Carers and Supporters*. Birmingham: British Institute of Learning Disabilities.

Department of Health (2007) *Services for People with Learning Disabilities and Challenging Behaviour or Mental Health Needs – revised edition*. Department of Health: London.

Department of Health (2008) *Refocusing the Care Programme Approach: Policy and positive practice guidance*. Department of Health: London.

Donnellan A, LaVigna G, Negri-Schoultz N & Fassbender L (1988) *Progress Without Punishment: Effective approaches for learners with behavior problems*. New York: Teachers College Press

Institute of Applied Behavior Analysis (1993) *Reinforcement Inventory for Children and Adults*. IABA, Los Angeles

Weerasekera P (1993) Formulation: a multi-perspective model. *Canadian Journal of Psychiatry* **38** (5) 351–359.

# Chapter 11: Suicidal behaviour, self-harm and self-injury

This chapter looks at suicide, self-harm and self-injury. It explores what these behaviours are and what motivates them. The chapter looks at how these behaviours are understood in different ways depending on the population being considered and how this can lead to confusion. It looks at these behaviours in individuals with intellectual disabilities and personality disorder and explores how these behaviours may be assessed and managed.

## Key topics

- Suicide

- Self-harm

- Self-harm and suicidal behaviour in individuals with personality disorder

- Self-injurious behaviour, self-harm, suicidal behaviour in individuals with intellectual disabilities

- Self-harm and suicidal behaviour in individuals with intellectual disabilities and personality disorder

- Supporting individuals who show self-harm and suicidal behaviour to access specialist assessment and intervention

- Supporting individuals who show self-harm and suicidal behaviour

## Suicide

Suicide is the formal term for killing oneself. It can be understood as something that a person may do when painful circumstances exceed their resources for coping with that pain. While some people who kill themselves want to die, most do not; they just want the pain they are suffering to end and can see no other way out. Rather than wanting to die, they do not want to live the life they feel trapped in. Often they have become locked in a spiral of negative thoughts and feelings that prevent them from considering other options or communicating their feelings to others in more appropriate ways.

It is estimated that across England and Wales there are about 140,000 attempted suicides every year and about 5,000 people succeed in ending their lives (DH, 2002). The most frequent methods of suicide in the UK are hanging and self-poisoning with psychotropic (medication prescribed for mental health problems) or analgesic (pain killing) drugs. Other methods include: car exhaust fumes (carbon monoxide poisoning), jumping (from buildings, bridges or in front of trains), poisoning with other substances (bleach, pesticides), suffocation (eg. tying a plastic bag around the head), bleeding (cutting wrists, throat or other arteries) and drowning. Choice of method seems to be influenced by a number of factors including gender, culture and availability. For example, death by shooting is more common in countries where there is a more relaxed attitude towards owning guns.

## Risk factors

A number of groups are known to be at greater risk of committing suicide. These include men (especially young men) and those who live alone, are unemployed, have problems with alcohol or drug misuse, or have mental health problems. Those in unskilled work are also at greater risk.

On an individual basis there are a number of life events that can increase the risk of attempting suicide (see Box 11.1). These same events also increase the risk of self-harm.

---

### Box 11.1: Life events that increase the risk of attempting suicide (or self-harm)

■ A recent loss eg. bereavement or the break up of a close relationship

■ The anniversary of a loss or negative life event

■ Anticipated downturn in personal circumstances (eg. worrying about being made redundant)

■ Actual downturn in personal circumstances (eg. actually being made redundant)

■ Painful illness

■ Disabling illness

■ Experiencing an episode of depression

---

# Signs someone may be thinking about suicide

There are sometimes signs that indicate that a person is thinking about killing themselves and these are explored in Box 11.2.

---

### Box 11.2: Signs a person may be thinking about suicide

**Talking about death:** A person may talk about dying, disappearing or going away. They might talk about funerals, suicide methods or other types of self-harm.

**Hopelessness:** A person might say things that suggest they believe that things will never get better; that nothing will ever change, or they might talk about things in the future being irrelevant.

**Change in mood:** A person might not seem themselves.

**Depressed mood:** A person might be distracted, sad, distant or lacking in concentration.

**Calm and peaceful:** Sometimes when people have made the decision to end their life, they feel that a solution has been found and they no longer appear depressed.

**Putting things in order:** If somebody starts putting their affairs in order (like arranging wills, pet or childcare), or giving away their prized possessions, they may be preparing to kill themselves.

---

However, the most effective way to find out if someone is thinking about killing themselves is by sensitively asking them. Many people, including health care professionals, are reluctant to do this. There is a myth that talking about suicide or asking someone if they feel suicidal will encourage suicide attempts. This is not the case; thoughtfully talking about suicide does not create or increase risk, it reduces it. Openly discussing someone's thoughts of suicide can be a relief for them and can be key to preventing the immediate danger of suicide.

For people with depression the time of greatest risk of suicide can be as they appear to begin to recover. Their increased ability to function may give them the capability to put their thoughts into action.

# Self-harm

Self-harm is the term used when a person hurts or damages themselves. This may be done in a number of ways, including taking an overdose of prescribed or over-the-counter medication, cutting or burning themselves, banging or throwing their head or body against something hard, sticking objects into the body or swallowing objects. People self-harm for a number of reasons, including to gain relief from acute distress and feelings (such as emptiness or anger), to access care and support, to give them a feeling of being in control, or to reconnect with feelings after a period of dissociation.

About one in 10 of the general population will self-harm at some time but certain groups are more at risk of self-harm. These include young women, prisoners, asylum seekers, armed forces veterans, gay, lesbian and bisexual people (related to the stress of discrimination) and those who have experienced physical, emotional or sexual abuse during childhood. Self-harm is also associated with mental health problems and misuse of drugs or alcohol. On an individual basis there are a number of life events that may trigger self-harm; these are very similar to those that can trigger suicide attempts (see Box 11.1).

# Distinguishing suicide attempts from self-harm

From the previous descriptions it is clear that there is considerable overlap in the behaviours that characterise self-harm and suicide attempts. There are a number of difficulties in trying to distinguish these behaviours. Superficially, the major difference between suicidal behaviour and self-harm is motivation; suicidal behaviour is intended to end life while self-harm is not. However, motivation cannot be assumed on the basis of the outcome of the behaviour. It is possible that a person may intend to self-harm but that this might accidentally lead to their death. Another person may intend to kill themselves but may unintentionally survive, making the behaviour look like self-harm.

It is also possible that one person may engage in a range of harmful behaviours that may have different motivations at different times. For example, on one occasion they may wish to end their life but on another occasion they may be trying to reconnect with their feelings. Finally, there is a link between having engaged in self-harm and going on to die by suicide. Following an act of self-harm the rate of suicide increases to more than 50 times the rate of suicide in the general population.

Some elaborate definitions have been developed to try to distinguish these behaviours. In other situations, a pragmatic approach has been taken. For example, the national guidance (NICE, 2004) on responding to self-harm adopted the definition that self-harm is: *self-poisoning or self-injury, irrespective of the apparent purpose of the act*.

In clinical situations the important issue is not what the behaviour should be called, but understanding the implications for treatment. When intervening with people who self-harm or attempt suicide it is essential to understand the motivation for the behaviour as this will ensure that the most helpful treatment

Intellectual Disabilities and Personality Disorder: An integrated approach
© Pavilion Publishing and Media Ltd and its licensors 2014.

is provided. Labelling a behaviour as 'self-harm' or 'suicidal' without exploring its motivation is likely to lead to staff teams making potentially unhelpful assumptions about what help should be given. Hence when working with people who engage in self-harm or suicidal attempts it is important to keep an open mind and have a questioning approach to the motivation each time the behaviour occurs. Box 11.3 shows a range of motivations that might underlie acts that are damaging to the person and may put their life at risk. It is particularly important not to make the assumption that as one act did not appear to be intended to end the person's life that a future act will not be intended to do so.

---

## Box 11.3: Motivations for self-harm (including suicidal behaviour)

### Regulate intense emotions and physical tension

- Calm down when anxious, angry, overwhelmed, or tearful
- Release emotional pain and tension
- Take the edge off emotional pain to allow the person to function normally
- Replace emotional pain with something physical that is easier to deal with
- Prevent themselves from taking anger out on other people or hurting them
- Keep happiness under control (where happiness feels alien or there is fear of a come-down)

### Reconnect with life and feelings

- Create a feeling of being alive or being real
- Feel something instead of being numb
- Get in touch with emotions

### Escape

- To trigger dissociation in order to escape from problems for a while
- Feel safe by going through a familiar ritual
- Reduce anxiety and tension that builds up if individual does not self-harm regularly
- Help to get to sleep
- From an unbearable situation that they can see as hopeless
- Physical pain or (increasing) disability
- Emotional pain eg. overwhelming grief, despair and hopelessness
- To end their life

### Avoid

- To avoid a future situation that is perceived as unbearable eg. threat of redundancy, threat of exposure of wrong doing, failure or loss of face

Continued...

---

**Distract themselves** from other problems such as:

■ Difficult life circumstances

■ Nightmares

■ Flashbacks

■ Hearing voices

■ Intrusive thoughts and memories

■ Overwhelming emotions

**Punishment**

■ To punish self – when experiencing feelings of inadequacy, self-hatred, guilt or shame

■ To punish others when feeling angry or impotent

**Control**

■ Feel in control of something in their life, when everything else seems out of control

■ Slow things down when the world seems to be spinning too fast, or when their thoughts are racing out of control

■ Help themselves focus

**Be cared for (nurtured)**

■ Take care of themselves (eg. dressing own wounds afterwards)

■ Be taken care of by others (eg. when having wounds treated)

■ Be admitted to hospital and cared for as if physically ill (rather than mentally ill)

**Communicate**

■ Express feelings that cannot be put into words – communicating this to self and others eg. fear of abandonment or rejection, fear of taking increased responsibility

■ Express how much they hate their body

■ Prove to themselves and others that something is wrong

■ Make others notice them and their problems

# Self-harm and suicidal behaviour in individuals with personality disorder

Individuals with personality disorder are at high risk of engaging in self-harm. Threatening to, or engaging in, self-harm is one of the diagnostic criteria for borderline personality disorder. About half of the people presenting at A&E departments with self-harm meet the diagnostic criteria for personality disorder. Around 60% of individuals with personality disorder make a suicide attempt at

Intellectual Disabilities and Personality Disorder: An integrated approach

some point in their life and about 10% kill themselves. As discussed in Chapter 9, individuals with personality disorder are vulnerable to experiencing episodes of depression. Being depressed increases the number and seriousness of suicide attempts made by individuals with personality disorder. Individuals are also at greater risk of making suicide attempts if they also have difficulties with substance misuse, have difficulties with impulsivity or have a history of abuse.

Where an individual has a diagnosis of personality disorder their self-harm is more likely to be perceived negatively by professionals than that of individuals with other conditions such as depression. The behaviour of individuals with personality disorder is often perceived as being 'manipulative' or 'deliberate' and this can lead to negative responses from those who treat them. For example, they might be left to wait in A&E departments and less care may be taken to minimise pain when their injuries are treated. Individuals with personality disorder report feeling that this view is unfair and illogical. They suggest that it is more helpful and accurate to view self-harm as a means of responding to emotional pain and not as a deliberate attempt to control others. There are now national guidelines on how self-harm should be treated that address these issues.

## Motivations and reasons

All the possible motivations for self-harm/suicidal behaviour given in the earlier section of this chapter may apply to individuals with personality disorder. For these individuals self-harm is often triggered by perceived threats of separation, rejection or an expectation that they take increased responsibility. Endings and transitions are also likely to trigger the need to self-harm. As a result of their experiences in infancy and childhood and consequent maladaptive attachment styles (see Chapter 4) these experiences are likely to make them feel abandoned or rejected. For many individuals with personality disorder, feeling abandoned or rejected leads to the re-emergence of overwhelming grief, panic and anxiety related to their experiences of loss and neglect in infancy. These feelings belong to a time before the individual could speak or had developed the ability to reason. Hence the experience will make little sense to the individual and they will find it very difficult to explain to others why they attempted suicide or harmed themselves.

In addition to being a maladaptive technique to escape a negative emotional state, self-harm may be an attempt to get others to understand the intensity of the individual's distress and get much-needed help and attention. This is often perceived as being 'manipulative' or as 'emotional blackmail'. However, the individual will have learnt that only really worrying behaviour will result in professionals continuing to engage with them. Self-harm can also reaffirm the ability to feel after a period of dissociation or reduce the feeling of being evil by punishing themselves.

For individuals with personality disorder who are experiencing a period of depression, a negative event can trigger a spiral into despair. The individual focuses on negative thoughts, broods on these and becomes increasingly hopeless until they feel there is no point in living.

# Self-harm, self-injury and suicidal behaviour in individuals with intellectual disabilities

It is common for confusion to arise when discussing self-harm in individuals with intellectual disabilities. This is because individuals with intellectual disabilities may show what is called 'self-injurious behaviour' (SIB). This is different from what services for individuals with mental health problems term 'self-harm' or 'self-injury' but, confusingly, is also often referred to as 'self-injury'. There are some similarities in the types of behaviour shown, but otherwise SIB and self-harm are very different. Box 11.4 compares them across a number of areas.

In contrast to the SIB shown by individuals with severe or profound intellectual disabilities, individuals with moderate or mild intellectual disabilities may show self-harm and suicidal behaviour in their more widely understood sense. Very little research has been carried out with this group. However, what research there is suggests that for individuals with milder intellectual disabilities their self-harm arises from similar causes and serves similar functions to those found in more able individuals who self-harm. For example, experiences of sexual, physical or emotional abuse and loss are closely linked to self-harm in individuals with mild intellectual disabilities. Self-harm is linked to feeling restricted with no escape, frustration at others being in control and feeling powerless. It also serves as an outlet for anger and to avoid hurting others. For this group, it is therefore important to consider the relationship of self-harm to the individual's attachment style, early experiences, thoughts, feelings, additional mental health conditions and the way they are being supported. It is also likely that the most effective treatment approaches will be adaptations of those used with more able individuals who self-harm rather than the approaches used for SIB in much less able individuals.

## Box 11.4: Comparison of self-injurious behaviour and self-harm

| Self-injurious behaviour (SIB) | Self-harm |
|---|---|
| Negatively correlated with intellectual ability ie. occurs more often in less able individuals (severe/profound intellectual disabilities) | Seen in individuals from moderate intellectual disabilities to those with superior intellectual ability |
| Associated with genetic syndromes eg. Lesch-Nyhan, Fragile X, Cornelia de Lange, Prada-Willi, Rett, Smith-Magenis | No link to genetic syndromes. Associated with mental health problems and personality disorder. |
| Not linked to impulsivity | May be linked to impulsivity |
| May be linked to an underlying biochemical process | No links biochemical links identified |
| Associated with sensory difficulties eg. blindness | Not linked to sensory problems |
| Associated with communication difficulties | No link to communication difficulties – seen in individuals with excellent communication skills (although may struggle to talk about emotions) |
| No clear association with abuse and loss | Associated with history of abuse and loss |
| May serve simple functions for individual | Complex functions linked to emotions and mental state |
| Not associated with intent to end own life | May be motivated by wish to end own life |
| Common behaviours include: poking or gouging ears, eyes, nose rectum or sexual organs, banging the head, head punching, biting or chewing self (usually arms or fingers) and picking at skin or wounds | Common behaviours include: scratching or cutting self with objects, burning self, overdosing with medication. More rarely may include; banging or throwing head or body against something hard, sticking objects into the body or swallowing objects |
| Associated with increased risk of residential care | Compatible with successful life in community |
| Difficult to treat | Effective treatments available |

There is little research looking at suicide in individuals with intellectual disabilities and the topic is often overlooked. For example, a recent book on mental health issues in individuals with intellectual disabilities does not mention suicide at all. This lack of information may be partly due to beliefs about individuals with intellectual disabilities.

There is some suggestion that staff supporting individuals with intellectual disabilities underestimate the risk of suicide or minimise the seriousness of suicidal behaviour. One study found that for a group of individuals with intellectual disabilities experiencing suicidal thoughts, nearly a third were supported by carers who were unaware of these feelings (Lunsky, 2004). Box 11.5 gives some of the common misunderstandings often held by staff when thinking about suicide and individuals with intellectual disabilities.

---

### Box 11.5: Common misunderstandings about suicide and individuals with intellectual disabilities

- We don't need to worry about her/him, people with intellectual disabilities don't kill themselves.
- S/he has intellectual disabilities – how can s/he kill her/himself?
- S/he's not clever enough to be able to kill her/himself.
- S/he has been saying s/he's going to kill he/himself for years, and s/he's still here!
- S/he's just doing it for attention…
- S/he only took five paracetamol, if s/he was really serious…

From Leeds (undated) *Suicide and Suicidal Behaviour in Learning Disabilities*.
Publication no longer available.

---

Some of these may relate to the archetype of someone with intellectual disabilities being a 'happy innocent', others to assumptions about their level of ability and others to a denial of the intensity of the emotions felt by individuals with intellectual disabilities.

However, the limited information that is available suggests that individuals with intellectual disabilities may attempt suicide and some will kill themselves. The reported rates of suicide are low and may be less than one third of that in the general population. The reasons for individuals with intellectual disabilities killing themselves appear to be same as for the general population. For example, the risk of suicide is associated with mental health problems (especially severe problems or those that have been overlooked), a history of abuse, a history of suicide in the family and low levels of social support. Individuals with intellectual disabilities may also be more likely to attempt suicide if they experience epilepsy.

# Self-harm and suicidal behaviour in individuals with intellectual disabilities and personality disorder

Individuals with intellectual disabilities and personality disorder do not show the SIB associated with severe or profound intellectual disabilities and hence SIB is not explored in the following sections. The self-harm shown by this population follows the same pattern as the self-harm shown by more able individuals with personality disorder. This is an important distinction because of the implications for treatment and also the associated risk of suicide.

Most individuals with intellectual disabilities and personality disorder are supported by specialist intellectual disabilities trained staff (with no additional training in mental health problems). These staff are likely to be familiar with the concept of SIB but may know little or nothing about self-harm. As a result, there is a significant risk that an individual's 'self-harm' will be misunderstood as 'SIB'. Where this occurs there is a risk of staff overlooking many potential causes and motivations for the behaviour and of them being unaware of potentially helpful treatment options. There may also be less awareness of the risk of the individual taking their own life and, consequently, risk assessment and management may be incomplete.

If the behaviours of individuals with intellectual disabilities and personality disorder lead to treatment in A&E departments their behaviour may be correctly identified as self-harm. However, if their personality disorder is also recognised individuals are at risk of being labelled 'manipulative' or showing 'deliberate self-harm' and this may lead to the same negative responses that are received by more able individuals with personality disorder (such as being kept waiting and being denied pain minimising treatment).

Hence individuals with intellectual disabilities and personality disorder are at risk of both being misunderstood by those who regularly support them and being discriminated against by those who support them in emergency situations.

# Supporting individuals who show self-harm and suicidal behaviour to access specialist assessment and intervention

Assessments and interventions for individuals showing self-harm are complex and it is likely that most individuals will need specialist assessment. This section will give an outline of this process and an example of how self-harm might be formulated using the positive behaviour support approach. Issues relating to the day-to-day support of individuals with self-harm are explored in the next section.

In a similar way to the process described in earlier chapters for mental health problems and challenging behaviour, taking a systematic approach can help to achieve a clear understanding of the individual's self-harm and ensure that they have access to the support that they need. These steps include:

- seeking help – supporting the individual to access specialist assessment

- assessing and managing risk

- a holistic assessment and formulation of the individual's self-harm

- integrating recommendations from the specialist assessment into the individual's care plan, CPA or positive behaviour support plan.

## Seeking help

Assessing and intervening with self-harm is complex and the individual will need to be referred to specialist services. The NICE guidelines on self-harm recommend that the most appropriate service for self-harm be determined on the basis of the severity of the individual's intellectual disabilities. They recommend that individuals with mild intellectual disabilities should have access to the same services as more able individuals who self-harm (usually adult mental health services). However, individuals with more severe intellectual disabilities should be supported by specialist intellectual disabilities services.

These decisions clearly need to be made on an individual basis by the GP or professionals who know the individual. For some individuals it may be appropriate for them to be jointly supported by mental health and intellectual disabilities services. Where this is the case NICE guidelines state that the Care Programme Approach (CPA) should be used (see Chapter 9).

Most individuals with intellectual disabilities and personality disorder will understand that their self-harm is damaging and hence they are likely to be willing for a referral to be made. This is important because the more the individual is involved in, understands and supports the plans to prevent and manage their self-harm, the more effective the intervention will be. However, a number of individuals will not accept the need for change and may wish to continue to use self-harm as a way of addressing their difficulties. As discussed in earlier chapters it is therefore important that staff have a sound understanding of issues relating to capacity and consent.

## Capacity and consent

Decisions about whether to respect an individual's choice to continue to self-harm or to use the legal framework to intervene against their wishes will depend on the risks associated with the behaviour and on the individual's capacity. Where the individual has capacity, and the behaviour is not life-threatening, the Mental Capacity Act (2005) gives them the right to make the (unwise) decision to continue with self-harm. Where they lack capacity, intervention may be made following the best interests process. However, if the individual is a danger to themselves the Mental Health Act (1983, amended 1995 and 2007) may be used to keep them safe and provide treatment. It is important to remember that assessing capacity is not a 'one-off' process; capacity can fluctuate and should be reassessed if there is any reason to believe that it might have changed, such as as a result of a deterioration in the individual's mental health.

# Risk management

Assessment of risk around self-harm and suicide should always be done by a multidisciplinary team. A detailed description of risk assessment and management is beyond the scope of this book. However, there are some issues specific to self-harm and suicidal attempts that are important to consider. Risk assessment is likely to focus on two areas; how likely the behaviour is to occur again and how can it be prevented or the harm minimised.

## Likelihood

There is no information available on the likelihood of repeating self-harm specifically for individuals with intellectual disabilities and personality disorder. However, for the general population a number of features are used to predict repetition of self-harm or future completed suicide. These fall into three categories: characteristics of the person, the person's circumstances and characteristics of the act of self-harm. The characteristics of people at risk and the circumstances that might trigger self-harm have been noted in earlier sections. Characteristics of the act of self-harm that are relevant include: its medical seriousness, use of violent methods, evidence of planning or precautions taken to prevent rescue, intent and the choice of method. These issues are also likely to be relevant for individuals with intellectual disabilities and personality disorder. For these individuals it is also important to consider the impact of their intellectual disabilities and personality disorder on the risk of self-harm. For example, intellectual impairment might limit the individual's understanding of the seriousness of the behaviour and might make it more difficult for them to access help. The impulsivity and difficulty managing emotions arising from their personality disorder might increase the risk of repeating the behaviour. Box 11.6 gives some suggestions for assessing the risk of an individual repeating self-harm.

---

### Box 11.6: Assessing the risk of repetition of self-harm or suicide attempts

Consider:

- Methods and patterns of current and past self-harm
- Current and past suicidal intent
- Depressive symptoms and their relationship to self-harm
- The extent to which the person is experiencing 'hopelessness'
- Any other mental health problems and their relationship to self-harm
- Use/misuse of drugs and alcohol
- The personal context eg. specific emotional states, relationships, anniversaries
- The social context eg. support, activities, living arrangements, debt, engagement with services, employment status
- Coping strategies that the individual has used to:
  - limit or avert self-harm
  - contain the impact of personal, social or other triggers
- Significant relationships that may either be supportive or represent a threat (such as possible domestic violence or sexual or physical abuse) and may lead to changes in the level of risk
- Access to means of self-harm eg. medication – own and other people's
- Impact of the individual's intellectual disability
- Impact of the individual's personality disorder

Adapted from NICE (2011)

---

It is important to remember that, however thoroughly undertaken, risk assessment is inexact. It is not accurate enough to make the assumption that someone who appears at low risk of repeating the behaviour is in fact safe.

The results of the risk assessment should be used to identify areas of need that can be addressed. These actions should be fully integrated into the individual's support plans (eg. person-centred plan, positive behavioural support plan and/or CPA).

Risk management needs to address both immediate and longer term risks. It should address the specific factors identified in the assessment as being associated with increased risk and include a crisis plan. It is also important that it considers short-term risk management strategies in the context of long-term therapeutic aims. For example, placing the individual in a safe room with nothing that can be used to self-harm may keep them safe in the short term. However, at some point they will need to leave the room. If the plan has not identified how to help the person keep safe in the real world they will be at risk as soon as they leave that room.

## Holistic assessment and formulation of self-harm

Each specialist service will have its own approach to the assessment and formulation of self-harm. Self-harm is often assessed from a mental health perspective (see Chapter 9). However, when working with individuals with intellectual disabilities and personality disorder, self-harm needs to be considered in the context of the individual's personality disorder, physical health, mental health, intellectual disabilities and their social context. Hence it can be more helpful to widen assessment and use the positive behavioural support perspective (see Chapter 10). This approach ensures that, rather than being seen only as a symptom of mental health problems, self-harm is assessed in relation to possible functions it may serve for the individual. The impact of the systems around the individual will also be considered. The approach's emphasis on improving quality of life and primary prevention also fits well as a response to behaviours that are often desperate measures of individuals who can no longer bear the life they have been living.

Figure 11.7 and Box 11.8 give an example formulation and positive behaviour support plan for a fictitious individual with intellectual disabilities and personality disorder who self-harms. In this example, the self-harm was associated with an episode of depression. The loss of a valued support worker and unplanned reduction in support appear to have made the individual emotionally vulnerable, with the negative contact with family being the trigger for this to develop into a reactive depression. There was a lack of understanding in the system that supported the individual of how emotionally frail and socially isolated they really were. This would have been an easy mistake to make as they had been doing well; holding down a job and managing well at home.

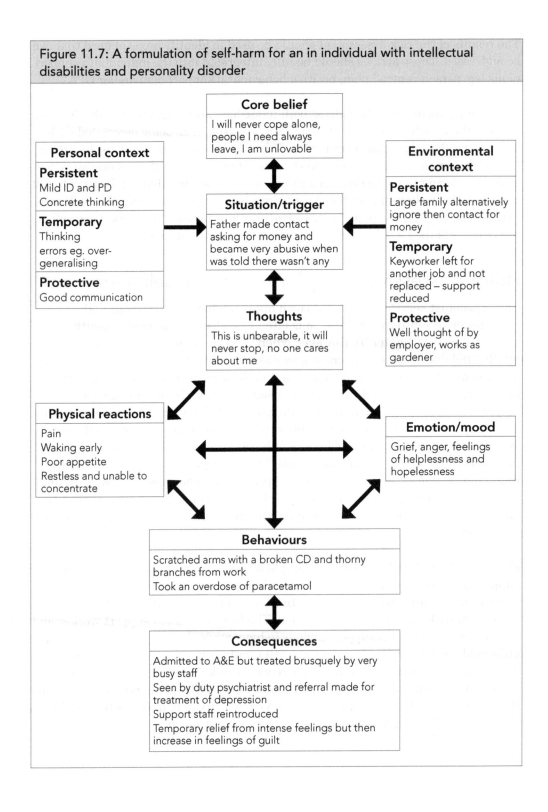

Figure 11.7: A formulation of self-harm for an in individual with intellectual disabilities and personality disorder

**Core belief**

I will never cope alone, people I need always leave, I am unlovable

**Personal context**

**Persistent**
Mild ID and PD
Concrete thinking

**Temporary**
Thinking errors eg. over-generalising

**Protective**
Good communication

**Situation/trigger**

Father made contact asking for money and became very abusive when was told there wasn't any

**Environmental context**

**Persistent**
Large family alternatively ignore then contact for money

**Temporary**
Keyworker left for another job and not replaced – support reduced

**Protective**
Well thought of by employer, works as gardener

**Thoughts**

This is unbearable, it will never stop, no one cares about me

**Physical reactions**

Pain
Waking early
Poor appetite
Restless and unable to concentrate

**Emotion/mood**

Grief, anger, feelings of helplessness and hopelessness

**Behaviours**

Scratched arms with a broken CD and thorny branches from work
Took an overdose of paracetamol

**Consequences**

Admitted to A&E but treated brusquely by very busy staff
Seen by duty psychiatrist and referral made for treatment of depression
Support staff reintroduced
Temporary relief from intense feelings but then increase in feelings of guilt

The self-harm clearly served the function of managing unbearable emotions and trying to escape from what felt like a hopeless situation. However, the episode also had the effect of mobilising a lot of support; help at home was re-introduced with more hours than previously and appointments with a psychiatrist and psychologist were also offered. There is clearly the potential for the individual to learn that the only certain way to get the support they need is through self-harm. Hence the positive behaviour support plan for the individual addresses their current need for extra support, looks to build skills in emotional management, increase their social network and provide safe ways of dealing with crises. However, it also looks at managing reductions of support in planned ways and of having a flexible system so that support can be reintroduced if there are warning signs of a further episode of depression.

---

## Box 11.8: An example of a positive behavioural support plan for self-harm based on the formulation given in 11.7

### Rationale

### Why I need you to do this

I recently took an overdose of paracetamol and scratched myself because life had become unbearable. The doctors think I have been depressed. I need you to support me and help me stay safe while I get over the depression and also to help me learn ways of managing my strong feelings about my family.

### Behaviours

- Scratching self with sharp objects
- Self-poisoning with over-the-counter medication

### Proactive strategies

- Training for support staff on self-harm and how to encourage open communication
- Support levels increased
- **Staffing levels not to be reduced without careful planning**, staged reduction and contingency plan
- **Support to attend appointments with psychiatrist**
- **Support to safely take antidepressants** – initially given by support staff with aim to start using a medication safe
- Lock put on one drawer in the kitchen to keep very sharp objects safe when not in use
- **Support to attend appointments with clinical psychologist for CBT**
- Plan carefully how the ending of this therapy will be managed

Continued...

---

- **Daily 'talk time' with support worker to monitor thoughts and feelings** and promote use of positive ways of managing emotions. Support to talk to boss to work out strategies for managing thorny plant waste
- Teach alternatives to self-harm – wearing elasticated bracelet to 'ping' if need to self-harm when at work
- **Teach self-soothing including use of different tempos of music to calm or distract**
- **Support to build wider social network including attending local music groups**
- **Change phone number so family cannot contact**

### Reactive strategies

- Create 'crisis' box (see Chapter 12)
- Card with contact numbers for people to talk to
- System for quickly adding in support if shows signs of developing depression in the future
- Go to A&E if need treatment for injuries/self-poisoning

### Crisis plan

- Contact psychiatrist
- If necessary, be admitted to Y (local specialist ID and MH assessment and treatment unit) if depression becomes too severe. May require use of Mental Health Act.

## Recommendations of specialist assessment

The treatments and interventions recommended as a result of any specialist assessments need to be integrated into the individual's day-to-day care. The example given earlier shows how ideas from the formulation might be shaped into a positive behaviour support plan. These ideas could also be incorporated into the individual's support plans (such as PCP, CPA or HAP). The important issue is that the recommendations are acted upon and become part of the individual's daily care rather than ending up buried in the individual's file. This is a surprisingly frequent occurrence. Sadly, many individuals with intellectual disabilities and personality disorder have very fragmented care and move around a lot. It is not unusual for individuals to have several thorough assessments of their self-harm on file but for the team currently supporting them to be unaware of these recommendations.

On other occasions, the recommendations may not be acted on because they do not make sense to the staff team or they conflict with their approach to care.

This can arise when the specialist assessment does not fully assess the context in which the individual lives and does not identify gaps in the knowledge, skills or attitudes of the staff team supporting the individual.

The following section explores how to ensure that staff teams are able to implement recommendations and support individuals on a day-to-day basis.

# Supporting individuals who show self-harm and suicidal behaviour

While an individual is participating in specialist assessment, staff will still have to support them on a day-to-day basis and they will also need to help implement the recommendations. Supporting individuals with intellectual disabilities and personality disorder who show self-harm and suicidal behaviour can be frightening and stressful for staff teams. Some individuals may be very distressed and worried by their own behaviour. Others may seem blasé and unconcerned about what seems to staff very worrying and potentially life-threatening behaviour. Staff are likely to be very anxious about the individual but may not know how to address such a sensitive area. The following section explores a number of areas that may be helpful including:

- building positive attitudes to supporting an individual who self-harms
- support style
- talking about self-harm and suicide
- improving an individual's understanding of self-harm
- reducing the need to self-harm
- alternatives to self-harm.

## Building positive attitudes

It is easy for staff to feel deskilled when confronted with self-harm and suicide attempts as they are so frightening and are outside many people's personal experience. There are also many myths around self-harm and suicide that can have a detrimental impact on how individuals are supported (see Box 11.9). These factors can combine to create a negative attitude towards individuals who self-harm.

---

## Box 11.9: Common myths about self-harm and suicidal behaviour

- Talking to someone about suicide increases the risk.
  FACT: Getting it out in the open is the first step to helping.

- If someone talks about suicide, they won't do it.
  FACT: They are expressing a possible intent and reaching out for help.

- As someone starts to get over depression they are less likely to kill themselves.
  FACT: This is the most high-risk time.

- If someone is serious about suicide there is nothing anyone can do.
  FACT: Support and help can change intentions.

- Self-harm is just attention-seeking, ignore it and they will stop.
  FACT: Self-harm is often secretive and is driven by many different motivations, it is likely to get worse if ignored.

- Self-harm is done deliberately and someone can stop self-harming if they choose.
  FACT: The person is coping as best they can, they need help and support to find new ways of coping.

- Individuals who self-harm have a high pain threshold or don't feel pain.
  FACT: Individuals will experience pain in the same way as people who do not self-harm.

- Individuals with intellectual disabilities have a high pain threshold.
  FACT: Most individuals with intellectual disabilities have the same pain threshold as the general population.

---

There are a number of steps that can be taken to promote more positive attitudes towards individuals who self-harm (see Box 11.10).

Training is an important element. Staff need to understand self-harm, why individuals might behave in this way and how they can be helped. Staff also need the opportunity to learn more about the individual as a person and how they have come to self-harm. However, it is not enough to understand these behaviours. Staff also need support in managing their emotional reactions to self-harm and suicidal behaviour. It can be soul-destroying to work with someone who repeatedly tries to harm themselves despite all efforts to help them find other ways of behaving. Good supervision and post-incident support are essential if staff are to remain well themselves and maintain a positive attitude towards the individual they support. This is explored more fully in Chapter 12.

> ### Box 11.10: Building a positive attitude to supporting individuals who self-harm
>
> ■ **Acknowledge own emotional reactions to the behaviour:** Staff may feel shocked, confused or even disgusted by self-harming behaviours. They may feel hopeless, powerless and helpless. They may be angry or frightened. These are natural human responses but staff may feel guilty about these feelings and hence be unwilling to acknowledge them.
>
> ■ **Safely express and address these negative feelings:** Through peer support and supervision.
>
> ■ **Develop compassionate distance** (see Chapter 12)
>
> ■ **Learn about self-harm:** The best way to overcome any discomfort or distaste about self-harm is by learning about it. Understanding why the individual self-harms can help staff see the world through their eyes.
>
> ■ **Learn about the individual and their needs:** The more staff understand about what has happened to the individual and are able to see things from their point of view, the more person-centred and constructive the approach will be.
>
> ■ **Learn about helpful strategies:** It is hard for staff to be hopeful if they don't know how self-harm can be changed.

## Support style

The way individuals with intellectual disabilities and personality disorder who self-harm are supported is crucial to minimising the risk of harm and maximising their quality of life. It is important that any support for self-harm or suicidal behaviour is given using the authoritative support style discussed in Chapter 5. This approach combines the two dimensions of interest and sensitivity to the individual's needs with clear, enforced boundaries and high expectations.

Using this approach, staff respond to acts of self-harm calmly and kindly and with a minimum fuss. Treatment is arranged promptly and given with appropriate pain relief. The individual is not criticised and their behaviour is not judged. Staff do not respond with threats (*'If you self-harm again we will have to…'*), punishment (*'Now you've self-harmed we won't be able to…'*) or ultimatums (*'You've got to make a choice, give up self-harm or…'*). The focus is on preventing or minimising self-harm through actively addressing the individual's needs and building a positive view of their future.

Maintaining an authoritative support style can, however, be very difficult when trying to manage individuals who self-harm. The anxiety created by suicide attempts and self-harm and the determination to stop this behaviour can lead staff to become overcontrolling. This can occur when there is an over-emphasis on physically preventing behaviour, at all costs. Physically preventing self-harm or suicidal behaviour depends on a range of restrictive practices (see Box 11.11).

---

### Box 11.11: Restrictive strategies used to physically prevent self-harm

- Increasing levels of observation eg. within eyesight/within arm's length
- Increasing staffing ratio eg. one-to-one or even two-to-one
- Rooms adapted to prevent self-harm eg. anti-ligature, padding walls
- Controlling movements eg. locked doors
- Limiting access to items eg. locked drawers, removing items from rooms
- Rapid tranquilisation/use of sedating medications

---

While it may sometimes be necessary to use some restrictive practices to keep an individual safe, it is essential that the approach used is the least restrictive option and that it is combined with facilitative strategies (ie. approaches designed to help the individual cope in a more positive way). Some examples of more positive approaches are given in Box 11.12.

---

### Box 11.12: Facilitative strategies for reducing the need to self-harm/making it safer

- Adjusting style of interaction to calm/distract/engage individual
- Channelling physical energy eg. running, swimming, kicking a ball, punching a pillow
- Releasing/expressing emotions eg. popping bubble wrap, writing things down and screwing the paper up
- Managing thoughts/focus of attention eg. supporting to engage in distracting activities/grounding activities/mindfulness
- Developing hope eg. small positive events to look forward to, working together to overcome seemingly impossible problems, breaking them into do-able chunks
- Providing safe alternatives to self-harm
- Teaching 'safer' self-harm
- Creating a crisis box

---

Where staff do not have a full understanding of self-harm they may also become judgemental about the individual and lose hope. When this happens staff are unable to be sensitive to the individual's needs and they may behave more like prison guards than carers.

Over-control and a judgmental attitude often occur together and the combination leads to an authoritarian support style. Once this approach is adopted, care is no longer person-centred. The individual is likely to feel that they are being blamed for their behaviour and to perceive staff as punishing and controlling them rather than helping them.

Authoritarian support can often exacerbate the behaviour it is intended to prevent. This is because of the impact it has on the way the individual feels. It:

- increases feelings of hopelessness, helplessness and inadequacy

- feeds the individual's belief that they are bad and need to punish themselves

- increases the individual's need to experience control in any way possible

- reduces opportunities for positive, distracting and learning experiences.

The authoritarian approach also fails to consider the underlying needs that may be driving the behaviour. For example, if an individual self-harms to block out terrible memories, being isolated in a barren room with no possessions is likely to increase the impact of the memories and hence the need to self-harm. Without access to objects to cut themselves with, the individual might need to throw themselves against the wall and floor to block out the thoughts. Physical restraint might control this behaviour but would again leave the individual tormented by their memories. The behaviour would start again the moment they were released, hence the individual might be restrained for dangerously long periods of time. This would put their life at risk and infringe their human rights. For this individual a safer approach might be to engage them in an enjoyable activity, such as watching a favourite DVD with a member of staff, possibly with the support of some 'as required' medication. This would keep them safe but also work to distract them from the intrusive memories.

## Talking about self-harm and suicide

In order to provide positive support to individuals with intellectual disabilities and personality disorder who self-harm it is important that there is open and honest communication between individuals and staff. There are barriers to this on both sides. Individuals will often be reluctant to talk about self-harm or suicide for fear of other people's reactions and the actions that might be taken. Staff are often reluctant to talk about self-harm or suicide for fear of making things worse or from anxiety about how to approach the topic. Staff may also have concerns about confidentiality and whether they can share with other staff the information the individual might disclose.

The approaches discussed in earlier chapters should help individuals build confidence and trust in the staff supporting them. Once this is achieved it is then necessary for staff to have the skills to help individuals share their thoughts. When thinking about skills in this sensitive area it is important to think about both content and process (see Chapter 2). How things are done is equally, if not more, important than what is done. Working in a way that is characterised by warmth, empathy, genuineness and unconditional regard, together with a non-judgmental approach, will make it much more likely that staff will be successful in efforts to engage individuals in difficult conversations. Staff will also need the skills to get the conversation started and then help the individual open up and express their thoughts and emotions. Some ideas for getting the conversation started are given in Box 11.13.

---

### Box 11.13: Talking about self-harm and suicide attempts

Getting started…

**Time and place:** Think about where and when to have the conversation before you start. Choose a time when the individual appears calm and relatively relaxed and you know you will not be interrupted or have to rush off.

**Approach:** Take a gentle approach, be understanding, tactful and non-judgmental. Use 'open ended' questions (see below). Possible opening comments and questions might be:

*'I've been a bit worried about you'*
*'How are things going? I'd like to help'*
*'How about a cup of coffee and a talk about things?'*

**Gentle prompting:** Encourage the individual to express whatever they are feeling, even if it's something uncomfortable. If the individual hasn't mentioned the self-harm, bring up the subject in a kind, non-confrontational way:

*'I've seen scratches on your arms. I want to understand what you're going through.'*

**Dealing with rebuffs:** If the individual does not want to talk, do not push. Just express calm concern for them and let them know that you're available whenever they do want to talk or need support.

**Respond to approaches:** When an individual is ready to talk they may approach staff but may not express the real reason they want to talk. Make space to discuss minor concerns the individual brings and then ask questions such as 'Is there anything else that's bothering you?'

---

Once the individual is willing to talk it is important that staff have the skills to help the individual express their concerns as fully as possible. An approach that is particularly helpful when trying to talk about difficult topics is that of 'active listening'. This is the approach used by organisations, such as the Samaritans, that work with people who feel suicidal. Active listening is a way of listening that helps people talk through their problems. It uses verbal and non-verbal techniques to help the other person open up and put their thoughts into words. These techniques are explained more fully in Box 11.14.

---

### Box 11.14: Active listening

Active listening is an approach that helps the individual to open up and share thoughts and feelings. Rather than passively leaving the individual to talk, it uses sensitive questions to help the individual express themselves more fully and clarify their thoughts. It does not make assumptions about what the individual is experiencing (eg. *'I know just how you feel'*), does not give glib solutions (eg. *'there's nothing to worry about'*) and is not judgemental (eg. *'how could you!'*).

Useful techniques to achieve this include:

**Body language:** Sit in a relaxed but not totally laid back position. Turn towards the person. Look at them (but don't stare). Use gestures and facial expression.

**Pace and silences:** Let the individual set the pace of the conversation. Don't rush them. Allow some silences, don't jump straight in; it can take time to find the words to express difficult thoughts and feelings. Most people find silence difficult and want to fill it. Resist this temptation. Use the techniques below to gently keep the conversation flowing.

**Open questions:** Questions that cannot be answered 'yes' or 'no'. This opens the conversation up and encourages the person to give more information. For example: *'How are you feeling?'* (answer 'angry') vs *'Are you feeling sad?'* (answer 'no'), *'What are you worried about?* vs *'Are you feeling worried?'*

**Small questions:** Big questions such as *'How can I help?'* or *'What's wrong?* can be overwhelming, the person may not know where to start to answer them.

It is more helpful to ask smaller questions such as *'I can hear you're upset, how long have you been feeling like this'*, *'what led to you feeling like this?'*

**Summarising:** This pulls together what the person has been saying *'So you want your independence but you get lonely in your flat'*. This shows that you have been listening and have understood what has been said.

Continued...

---

**Reflecting:** Repeating back a word or phrase can encourage people to go on. If someone says, *'So it's been really difficult recently,'* but then stops talking, you can keep the conversation going by repeating *'It's been difficult'*. This helps them keep track of what they were saying.

**Clarifying:** Individuals often avoid talking fully about the most difficult things and will just give a hint of what they are thinking. If the individual mentions something important, but does not elaborate, it can be helpful to use questions such as *'Tell me more about…'*, Sometimes just a *'Yes'*, *'Go on'*, or *'I see'* can help.

**Reacting:** It is important to have an emotional balance. An individual may not want to talk if they think what they are saying is upsetting the listener. However if the listener seems completely unmoved this may stop the person because they think they are boring the listener or the listener does not care. Phrases such as *'That must have been difficult'*, or *'You've had an awful time'* show that the listener is aware of but not overcome by the feelings.

It is important that staff think not just about getting the individual to open up but also about what the individual might say once they start talking. Staff need to be prepared, emotionally, to cope with whatever they might hear, however distressing. This requires a balance between emotional connection and emotional distance. By taking up a position of 'compassionate distance' (see Chapter 12) staff will be able to respond with warmth and concern but not be overwhelmed by the distressing nature of the conversation.

Staff also need to think about how to explain the limits of confidentiality to the individual. Staff must share information that suggests the individual may be at risk with others involved in the individual's care. The individual needs to be told what information will be shared and with who, otherwise they may feel betrayed and may be reluctant to share thoughts with staff in the future. This can be discussed openly and the individual can be given choices. For example, staff might say, *'Your doctor needs to know about this. Do you want us to tell her together or would you rather I speak to her? Or would you like to write it down for her?'* This approach gives some choice and control to the individual while ensuring the doctor gets to know the important information.

Once the individual is able to talk about how they are feeling it is much easier to work with them to understand and potentially change their behaviour.

# Improving an individual's understanding of self-harm

It is important that the individual is helped to understand as much as possible about self-harm, to know that they are not alone in showing such behaviours and that there are many things that they can do if they want to change their behaviour. This work should be carried out by specialist professionals, or with consultation and supervision.

It can be helpful to talk about what self-harm is and why someone might want to self-harm (the information given earlier in this chapter should be helpful with this work). These discussions can be recorded in a format that is helpful for the individual. For example, staff can work with the individual to decide on words, pictures, drawings, or paintings that summarise what the individual does and why they do it. Conversations should also be optimistic about the possibility of replacing self-harm and consider some of the options open to the individual.

As this work progresses staff can explore what the individual sees as the benefits and negative aspects of their self-harm. Box 11.15 gives some negative aspects of self-harm that may be useful to explore with individuals.

---

**Box 11.15: Negative aspects of self-harm**

- It brings short-term relief but the feelings soon return.

- It is followed by unpleasant feelings of shame and guilt.

- It can add to the problems it is trying to manage eg. other people taking more control over the individual's life.

- It keeps the person from learning more effective ways of managing their emotions and meeting their needs.

- Failing to learn effective ways of meeting these needs puts the individual at risk of developing other problems including depression and drug or alcohol misuse.

- Self-harm can become 'addictive' and can be very hard to give up.

- There is a risk of hurting themselves more than intended eg. cuts may be deeper or may get infected.

---

These discussions can then explore whether the individual wants to change this behaviour. Where the individual is unsure, the techniques for motivating people described in Chapter 6 may be helpful.

However, many individuals find it hard to give up self-harming behaviour and may choose to continue to manage their emotions in this way. While this is a very difficult thing for staff to accept, individuals with capacity who choose to continue to self-harm, should be given education about ways of minimising the risks of this behaviour.

# Reducing the need to self-harm

When looking at how to reduce the need for an individual to self-harm it is important to look at the whole of their life to see how this can be improved. Generally the happier, healthier, more occupied and more hopeful an individual is, the less they will need to self-harm. Some ideas for doing this are given next, but the suggestions given in Chapter 10 for proactive and reactive strategies to challenging behaviours may also be helpful.

## Healthy lifestyle

Many individuals with intellectual disabilities and personality disorder who self-harm have unhealthy lifestyles. This is easily overlooked as the focus will be on the act of self-harm. However, individuals who self-harm should be encouraged to look at issues such as daily routine, healthy eating, sleep patterns, exercise, activities and relaxation. Leading a healthy lifestyle builds resilience and can give the individual the energy to address their self-harm (see Chapters 3 and 8).

If the individual has difficulty sleeping the reasons for this should be explored carefully; often this will be linked to nightmares, flashbacks or intrusive thoughts. These will need to be addressed if the individual is to sleep better.

## Activities

Activities can be used in a number of ways to help an individual reduce their self-harm. A selection of activities that the individual enjoys should be built into their daily timetable. It is important to include a range of different types of activities including physical activities, those requiring active engagement and passive activities, as each type of activity has different benefits.

Physical activities such as walking, jogging, dancing or swimming can be used to reduce the build-up of, or dispel, physical tension and may also help soothe the individual through their rhythmic, repetitive nature.

Activities such as computer games, wordsearch and handicrafts need active focus and can be totally absorbing. These can be highly effective at distracting the individual. More passive but enjoyable activities such as watching DVDs or listening to music may also provide distraction at times when the individual is too distressed to engage more actively.

Advanced planning of small treats and enjoyable activities can give the individual something to look forward to. These should be short term eg. that afternoon, tomorrow, and longer term eg. next week, next month. This can help to build a more positive outlook and foster hope for their future. These should be recorded in a way that helps the individual remember they are coming eg. in a diary, on a timetable, pictures on a wall or a photo in their wallet.

Enjoyable activities also build positive memories. Hence activities should be recorded eg. by photos or notes in a journal. These might be added to a memory book (see Box 2.10) for the individual to look back on when things get tough.

## Managing intense emotions

Intense emotions are likely to play a role in most episodes of self-harm either directly or indirectly. Hence understanding and managing emotions plays an important role in reducing the need to self-harm. The approaches suggested in Chapter 3 will be very helpful with this. It may also be helpful to explore with the individual ways of coping at the point where they may be about to self-harm. They need to be able to believe that the feeling will pass and that they can cope until it does. It can be helpful to have something to look at or hold that acts as a reminder of something they are working towards eg. a photograph on a keyring. Focusing on this can increase motivation to resist and distract from the urge to self-harm. Some individuals might find it helpful to have a 'crisis' or 'happy' box containing items to help them get through difficult moments (see Box 11.16).

---

### Box 11.16: Crisis or happy box

A crisis or happy box contains items that will help the individual get through the crisis. This might include:

- a copy of their crisis plan (see Chapter 11)

- essential oils, bubble bath, hand cream (check that these are not toxic if used to self-poison)

- favourite books, CDs and DVDs (check risk that these might be broken and used to self-harm)

- relaxation guides/CDs

- photographs

- letters from friends

- cuddly toys

- art supplies (non-toxic and no sharp items such as scissors)

Continued...

---

- alternatives to self-harm (see later in this section)
- one dose of 'as required' medication prescribed for use in a crisis (but don't include large quantities as they might be tempted to take an overdose)
- sweets as a treat or as an alternative to swallowing pills.

Adapted from *See Me Scotland*

The individual should also have contact numbers of people they can ring. These can be added to the phonebook on a mobile or set up as speed-dials on landlines. It can be helpful to incorporate this information into a card, ie. the example in Box 11.17, that can be kept in a wallet or pocket at all times.

### Box 11.17: Example card – what to do if you want to self-harm

If you want to self-harm, **T.A.L.K** –

**T**ell someone what you are thinking and feeling.

**A**sk for help.

**L**isten to advice.

**K**now who to call in a crisis.

Ring 08457 90 90 90 (Samaritans)

## Managing endings and supporting transitions

It is helpful to understand that endings of treatment, services or relationships, anniversaries of significant losses or traumas, and transitions from one service to another are likely to provoke strong feelings and increase the risk of self-harm. Wherever possible, plan in advance of these events with the individual and identify what will help them cope with the event. Plans should be recorded in a format that the individual can access and shared with everyone who supports them. It may be helpful to explore their thinking about these events and identify any unhelpful thinking patterns that surround them (see Chapter 7).

For anniversaries of negative events it is tempting for staff to try to tell the individual to *'Forget it'* or say *'You should be over that by now'*. However, the individual will not be able to do this. Hence it is better to build a constructive ritual around the event.

For a bereavement this ritual might include visiting the grave (or other memorial) and taking flowers, writing a letter to leave there about how much the person is missed but also all the positive things the individual has achieved that year and what they are planning to do in the next one.

For a negative event eg. physical or sexual assault or an accident, it may be helpful to write and illustrate an account of the event and the individual's survival. An example is given in Box 11.18.

---

### Box 11.18: Survival story

On (date) this (event) happened to me.

The memory of (event) makes me feel (list feelings).

I will never forget what happened to me but I have survived.

These are the things I have achieved:

■ ....................................................................................................................
■ ....................................................................................................................
■ ....................................................................................................................

I am going to get on with my life.

These are my plans:

■ ....................................................................................................................
■ ....................................................................................................................
■ ....................................................................................................................

My life may never be the same but I can have a good life and there is much to look forward to.

---

Transitions from one service to another can be particularly traumatic. For example, if an individual has needed admission to hospital to manage their self-harm, they may find it very frightening to return home, however much they may want to do this. In such situations it may be helpful to have a 'transition plan'. For example, the individual might have a period of increasing home leave (an afternoon visit, overnight stay, weekend, a fortnight on leave) before being discharged from hospital. During the transition, individuals may find it difficult to express their fears or worrying thoughts in case these result in them not being discharged. It can be helpful for staff to 'normalise' such reactions with comments such as *'You're bound to be worried about coming home, that's only natural'*. This makes it easier for the individual to raise any concerns they have.

## Medication

Medication can be helpful in a number of ways when trying to support an individual who self-harms. First, it may be an important part of treating the depression that underlies many instances of self-harm. It can sometimes help with anger and anxiety. It may also help some individuals manage impulsivity and hence reduce unplanned acts of self-harm. 'As required' medication may help some individuals at times of crisis. It may provide a means of rapidly calming them at the point where they have gone beyond being able to implement any of the techniques they have been trying to use to replace the self-harm.

However, medication alone is unlikely to be helpful in the long term. It can even act to perpetuate the behaviour by removing responsibility from the individual and creating a psychological dependence on the medication. The use of medication also carries significant risks where the individual manages their own medication. Large supplies of medication may be used to self-poison. Even if small quantities are given at any one time the individual may hoard these for use at a time when they need to self-harm.

# Alternatives to self-harm

Exploring alternatives to self-harm should be carried out by specialist professionals, or by staff with consultation and supervision. Self-harm often performs important functions for individuals with intellectual disabilities and personality disorder. This can make it very difficult for them to stop the behaviour once a situation has gone beyond a certain point. Sometimes it can help if they can find a safer behaviour that will perform the same function and meet their underlying needs. It is very important that alternatives suggested perform the function that is most important for the individual. For example, punching a pillow may be helpful if the individual needs to release physical tension and anger. However, if the individual needs to feel cared for, hitting a pillow is unlikely to help. Instead it may be helpful to have a pampering session such as a warm bath with scented oil followed by massaging in body lotion.

A selection of alternatives, grouped by the function they could serve, are given in Box 11.19.

## Box 11.19: Alternatives to self-harm

**To communicate, express pain or intense feelings**

- Paint, draw, or scribble on a big piece of paper with red ink or paint
- Write feelings in a journal, story or poem
- Write down negative feelings and then rip the paper up
- Play music that expresses the emotion

**To regulate emotions – calming down**

- Take a bath or hot shower
- Stroke or cuddle with a dog or cat
- Wrap up in a warm blanket
- Massage own neck, hands, and feet, rub in scented body lotion (there are videos showing ways of doing this)
- Listen to calming music
- Drink a mug of hot chocolate
- Smell something nice like lavender oil
- Go for a walk in the park or a garden

**To release tension or vent anger**

- Exercise vigorously – run, dance, skip, do press-ups or sit-ups
- Play something that involves hitting/kicking/throwing a ball – squash, swing-ball
- Punch a cushion or mattress or scream into a pillow, use pillow to hit a wall
- Squeeze a stress ball, Play-Dough or clay
- Rip something up (sheets of paper, a magazine, phone book)
- Make some noise (play an instrument, bang on pots and pans, shout loudly)
- Flatten aluminium cans for recycling

**To reconnect with life and feelings**

- Call a friend
- Take a cold shower or bath
- Hold an ice cube in the crook of an arm or leg, squeeze it hard in a hand or press it firmly on the place that would otherwise be burned
- Chew something with a very strong taste eg. chilli pepper, root ginger, peppermint, a lemon or grapefruit peel
- Rub liniment under the nose, or on area that would be burned or cut
- Put a elasticated bracelet on wrists, arms, or legs and snap it

**To escape**

- Go through the ritual but don't actually do the injury
- Use mindfulness techniques

Continued...

**To feel cared for**

- Put on bandages/dressings without the injury
- Have a manicure, pedicure or other pampering beauty treatment
- Look at photos of good friends and read notes they have made about how much they care
- Make a favourite meal/food

**To focus**

- Do a puzzle of some kind – wordsearch, Rubik's cube
- Go through a newspaper crossing out all the 'o's

**To see blood or make marks**

- Draw on self with a red felt-tip pen – pressing very hard
- Trickle red food colouring on the places that would have been cut

**To replace self-poisoning**

- Swallow sweets such as Smarties or Tic Tacs
- Drink something bitter such as tonic water or pure lemon juice

This list is not exhaustive and, with support, individuals may be able to create their own personal alternatives. It is also important to recognise that these alternatives are unlikely to give the same intensity of experience as real acts of self-harm. However, they are all devoid of the negative effects of self-harm and combined with efforts to reduce the need for self-harm in the first place may greatly reduce the frequency or intensity of harm.

It is important to plan in advance what alternatives might be helpful as some may require particular items to be available eg. bracelets, felt-tip pens, food colouring. It can be helpful to add these items to the individual's crisis box. It is also important to think about whether there is a risk of the alternative being used to self-harm. For example, aroma therapy oils are great for providing intense smells and helping an individual reconnect with their senses or to evoke pleasant memories. However, some may be harmful if they are drunk. Where this might be a risk it is better to add the oil to a few tissues and keep it in an airtight pot.

By supporting individuals to access specialist help and using a combination of the approaches suggested above it is possible to support individuals who self-harm safely and positively.

# Key learning points

■ Suicide attempts and self-harm are overlapping behaviours that can often only be distinguished on the basis of the motivation of the individual.

■ Both types of behaviour are complex and potentially life-threatening; many individuals who 'only' self-harm will go on to kill themselves.

■ When looking at these behaviours in individuals with intellectual disabilities the picture is further confused by the occurrence of self-injurious behaviour (SIB) in this population. SIB is a superficially similar pattern of behaviour shown mostly by individuals with severe or profound intellectual disabilities.

■ The term 'SIB' should not be used to describe the behaviour of individuals with intellectual disabilities and personality disorder who self-harm as SIB has different underlying causes, serves less complex functions and has fewer treatment options than self-harm. Using the term 'SIB' can also lead to the risk of suicide being underestimated or overlooked.

■ There are widespread misunderstandings about suicide attempts and self-harm. The resulting unhelpful attitudes can lead to needs being overlooked or to individuals being judged, over-controlled or punished.

■ It is important to recognise the seriousness of self-harm and to support individuals with intellectual disabilities and personality disorder to access specialist assessment and treatment.

■ Assessment of risk around self-harm and suicide should always be done by a multidisciplinary team. Risk assessment is likely to focus on two areas; how likely the behaviour is to occur again and how can it be prevented or the harm minimised.

■ Using the positive behaviour support approach and 'adapted hot-cross bun', formulation can be helpful in untangling the complex causes and functions of these behaviours.

■ Working within the authoritative support model staff can develop the skills to help individuals talk about their self-harm or suicidal thoughts, to minimise the need for individuals to self-harm and to support them to manage their distress as safely as possible.

# References

Department of Health (2002) *National Suicide Prevention Strategy for England*. London: DH.

Lunsky Y (2004) Suicidality in a clinical and community sample of adults with mental retardation. *Research in Developmental Disabilities* **25** (3) 231–244.

NICE (2004) *Self-harm: Short term management. NICE clinical guideline* 16. Available at: www.nice. org.uk/guidance/CG16 (accessed April 2014).

NICE (2011) *Self-harm: Longer-term management: NICE guideline 133*. Available at: www.nice.org.uk/ guidance/CG133 (accessed April 2014).

# Further reading

Alexander R & Cooray S (2003) Diagnosis of personality disorders in learning disability. *British Journal of Psychiatry* **44** 28–31.

Berman A (1992) Treating suicidal behavior in the mentally retarded: the case of Kim. *Suicide and Life-threatening Behavior* **22** 504–506.

British Institute of Learning Disabilities (2008) *Factsheet – self injurious behaviour* [online]. Available at: www.bild.org.uk/EasysiteWeb/getresource.axd?AssetID=2525&type=full (accessed April 2014).

Department of Health (2002) *National Suicide Prevention Strategy for England*. London: DH.

Department of Health (2002) *Mental Health Policy Implementation Guide: Adult acute in-patient care provision*. London: DH.

DesNoyers-Hurley A (2002) Potentially lethal suicide attempts in persons with developmental disabilities: review and three new case studies. *Mental Health Aspects of Developmental Disabilities* **5** (3) 90–95.

Duperouzel H & Fish R (2008) Why couldn't I stop her? Self-injury: the views of staff and clients in a medium secure unit. *British Journal of Learning Disabilities* **36** 59–66.

Finlay W & Lyons E (2001) Methodological issues in interviewing and using self-report questionnaires with people with mental retardation. *Psychological Assessment* **13** 319–335.

Fish R (2000) Working with people who harm themselves in a forensic learning disability service – experiences of direct care staff. *Journal of Learning Disabilities* **4** (3) 193–207.

Harker-Longton W & Fish R (2002) Cutting doesn't make you die: one woman's views on the treatment of her self-injurious behaviour. *Journal of Intellectual Disabilities* **6** 137–151.

Hillary J & Dodd P (2007) Self-injurious behaviour. In N Bouras & G Holt (Eds) *Psychiatric and Behavioural Disorders in Intellectual and Developmental Disabilities*, pp 225–237. Cambridge: Cambridge University Press.

James M & Warner S (2005) Coping with their lives – women, learning disabilities, self-harm and the secure unit: a Q-methodological study. *British Journal of Learning Disabilities* **33** 120–127.

Merrick J, Merrick E, Lunsky Y & Kandel I (2006) A review of suicidality in persons with intellectual disability. *Israeli Journal of Psychiatry & Related Sciences* **43** (4) 158–264

Patja K (2004) Suicide cases in a population-based cohort of persons with intellectual disability in a 35-year follow-up. *Mental Health Aspects of Developmental Disabilities* **7** (4) 117–123.

Phillips J (2001) Risky Business. *Learning Disability Practice* **4** (3) 18–24.

Royal College of Psychiatrists (2014) *Self-harm* [online]. Available at: www.rcpsych.ac.uk/mentalhealthinfoforall/problems/depression/self-harm.aspx (accessed April 2014).

Sellars C (2011) *Risk Assessment in People with Intellectual Disabilities* (2nd edition). Chichester: BPS Blackwell.

# Useful websites

Help Guide: www.helpguide.org/mental/self_injury.htm

The Samaritans: http://www.samaritans.org.uk/

See Me Scotland: http://ww.seemescotland.org/findoutmore/aboutmentalhealthproblemsandstigma/suicide

Sirius Project: www.siriusproject.org/alternatives.htm

# Chapter 12: Crisis management

This chapter looks at what a crisis is, how crises are experienced by individuals with intellectual disabilities and personality disorder, and the challenges these present for the staff supporting them. The chapter explores how to support individuals through each stage of the crisis cycle and how to reduce the likelihood and seriousness of future crises.

## Key topics

- Crises

- Impact of crises on people

- Crises and individuals with personality disorder

- Crises and individuals with intellectual disabilities

- Crises and individuals with intellectual disabilities and personality disorder

- Supporting individuals with intellectual disabilities and personality disorder through crises

- Formulation

- Developing/improving strategies to manage crises

- Helping the individual to cope better

- Supporting staff through the crisis cycle

- Successful crisis management

## Crises

A crisis is an unstable period, especially one of troubling or dangerous events. When applied to people, crises may take the form of a sudden change, usually for the worse, in their social functioning, physical or mental health. Crises may be triggered by a wide variety of events that lead to the person being overwhelmed by internal or external stressors. These may include major life events such as being made homeless, losing a job, a breakdown in a relationship or a bereavement. Crises may also be triggered by financial difficulties (such as court proceeding for debt) or problems with the police (for example, being arrested for drunken behaviour or petty crimes).

Crises relating to physical health may occur when a new health problem develops or there is a sudden deterioration in a chronic health problem such as asthma or diabetes. When a person is unable able to cope with their symptoms, comply with treatment or manage the impact on the rest of their life, the situation may spiral out of control.

In a similar way, crises relating to mental health may occur with the onset of mental health problems or a relapse in problems that were previously well managed.

While some crises are unavoidable, it is also important to recognise that people may also, unintentionally, contribute to crises occurring. An unhealthy lifestyle, poor money management or irresponsible behaviour may all increase the risk of crises happening.

Crises will happen at times in everyone's lives. How people are able to respond to these crises depends on a number of individual and social factors. Some people are more psychologically resilient; they can bounce back from negative events, solve problems and adjust well to things they cannot change. Others find this much more difficult. People also cope better with crises when they have a strong social support network and access to good physical and mental health services.

# The impact of crises on people

Being in crisis is accompanied by a number of changes in how people think, feel and behave. The body also responds differently, creating a number of different sensations. These changes are associated with a primitive reaction to perceived threat that prepares the body to defend itself through a number of changes including the release of stress hormones such as adrenaline. This pattern of responding to threats is sometimes called the fight or flight response.

## Impact on thinking

As a result of evolution, there are some different ways a fully developed and undamaged brain can operate (see Box 12.1).

Depending on their stress level and skills at managing their thoughts, people can switch between logical, intuitive and emotional ways of thinking. The change may be a conscious choice, for example, engaging in mindfulness exercises to promote the intuitive mind. More often the change is simply a reaction to the situation the person is in; the more stressed or distressed a person becomes the more likely it is that the emotional mind will take over. Hence most people will be in their 'emotional mind' during a crisis. Consequently, they cease to think logically. Their behaviour becomes driven by instinct and emotion and feels out of conscious control. They are unlikely to hear, let alone respond to reason. They will, however, be very sensitive to the emotional climate around them. For example, they will become more fearful if those around them are anxious.

This state of mind was important for survival; logical thinking takes too long in a dangerous situation. However, it causes difficulties in modern life where stressful situations are rarely life-threatening and often require problem-solving skills (logical/reasonable mind).

## Impact on feelings

When in crisis, people are most likely to feel either fear or anger. Depending on the situation and how others respond to them, people may also switch suddenly between these two emotions. Such emotional switches may result in changes of behaviour, from running away to attacking.

## Impact on behaviour

When in crisis a person's senses become heightened as they vigilantly look and listen for signs of danger. They will be unable to relax and are likely to have difficulty sleeping. They will have difficulty concentrating, may be jumpy and startle easily. There will be a build-up of physical tension and energy in readiness for action. A perceived threat will trigger one of three instinctive reactions, acting out (fighting), running away (fleeing) or shutting down (freezing).

When in this state, people may be much stronger physically than when they are relaxed because of the way adrenaline causes blood to be pumped into muscles and they will tire less quickly because of the build-up of energy. People may also continue to fight or run away despite physical injuries or to carry out acts that would normally be avoided because of pain. This is because high levels of adrenaline can reduce perceived pain.

If pent up energy is not released it can make it very difficult to calm down and makes people vulnerable to 'flaring up' again at the smallest provocation.

## Box 12.1: Ways the brain can operate

| Logical/ rational mind | **Logical and rational**<br>■ Uses front of the brain (frontal lobes) to process information<br>■ Uses cause and effect reasoning to guide the choices and behaviour:<br>　■ Plans, looks at the long-term<br>　■ Thinks objectively, looks at the facts<br>　■ Focuses attention<br>　■ Problem solves<br>　■ Tests things out (scientific)<br>　■ Attempts new approaches<br>■ Cool, measured and controlled<br>■ Acting, doing, achieving, striving<br>■ Judging<br><br>**'This is what I should do'**<br><br>(Can be cold, detached from feelings, not seeing bigger picture) |
|---|---|
| Wise/ intuitive mind | **Intuitive**<br>■ Frontal lobes and base of brain work together<br>■ Takes both logic and emotion into account when making decisions:<br>　■ Attempts to integrate the logical and emotional mind<br>　■ Tries to find compromises between the logical and emotional perspectives<br>　■ Looks at the bigger picture<br>■ Accepting<br>■ Being, flowing, calming, soothing<br>■ Knowing what is right<br><br>**'This is what is right for me'**<br><br>(Warm, involved, engaged, balanced. Mind state sought by some eastern religions through meditation and also promoted by some treatment approaches such as DBT)<br><br>Continued... |

| Emotional mind | **Instinctive**<br>■ Uses primitive structures in the base of the brain<br>■ Uses energy level, feelings and psychological needs to guide choices and behaviour:<br>  ■ Facts are distorted to fit emotional reality<br>  ■ Thinking is illogical, based on attitudes, prejudices and preconceptions<br>  ■ Actions are immediate and uncontrolled<br>  ■ Responses are automatic, based on habit/instinct<br>  ■ Considers only the immediate impact – not the long-term consequences<br>■ Instinctive, impulsive, beyond control<br>■ Unthinking<br>■ Feeling<br>**'This is what I want to/need to/must do'**<br>(Hot, impulsive and over-involved) |
| --- | --- |

## Impact on physical sensations

The hormones released when a person is stressed create a range of bodily sensations. These are the result of changes to blood circulation, heart rate and breathing that prepare the body for violent activity. People may feel sick (or actually vomit) and need to urgently empty their bowels and bladder. This is because the body takes blood away from the digestive system to support action and also wants to get rid of any unnecessary weight. They may experience a pounding, racing heartbeat, may sweat more and breathe more rapidly. If the person does not understand the cause of these changes they may fear that they are having a heart attack or other physical illness.

## After the crisis

Eventually, if the stress continues, the person may become completely mentally, emotionally and physically exhausted. Once the threat has resolved the person's thoughts, emotions and physical sensations gradually return to their usual state. The person may become aware of pain from injuries they were not aware of sustaining. They may struggle to remember or make sense of what happened during the crisis. This is because their behaviour during the crisis became instinctive rather than reason based and hence makes little sense when looked at logically.

# The crisis cycle

The changes described earlier can be understood as a cycle. As a person moves through the crisis, they go through different stages. Each is characterised by different combinations of state of mind, physical reactions, emotion and behaviour. These stages are summarised in Table 12.2.

| Table 12.2: The crisis cycle: mind states, arousal, emotions and behaviour | | | | |
|---|---|---|---|---|
| **Stage of crisis** | **Mind state** | **Arousal level** | **Emotion** | **Behaviour** |
| Pre-crisis | Rational | Typical for person | Typical | Typical |
| Crisis | Emotional | High | Fear/panic or rage | Flight/fight/ freeze |
| After crisis | Emotional/ rational | Raised arousal/ total exhaustion<br><br>Returning to typical | Shame, embarrassment, guilt, feeling unworthy<br><br>Returning to typical | Restless, jumpy /immobility<br><br>Returning to typical |
| Trigger events | Rational/ emotional | Increasing | Emotional outbursts | Coping responses<br><br>Twitchy/ difficulty sleeping |
| Next crisis | Emotional | High | Fear/panic or rage | Flight/fight/ freeze |

It may be noted that the intuitive or wise mind state does not appear in this box. This is because being in the intuitive mind state switches off the flight or fight response. Hence people who are skilled at promoting this mind state do not go into crisis. Some of the interventions mentioned later in this chapter work by promoting the intuitive mind state and the physical and emotional calm associated with it.

# Crises and individuals with personality disorder

Individuals with personality disorder, particularly those with borderline personality disorder, are vulnerable to experiencing crises for a number of reasons. Their lifestyles may be chaotic, thereby creating situations where important actions are forgotten or warning signs are overlooked. Impulsive behaviour may place them in risky situations. When problems do occur, individuals with personality disorder may have difficulty controlling their emotional reactions. This can lead to failure to think rationally about what action is needed to resolve the problems and to situations spiralling out of control. Individuals with personality disorder often have difficulty trusting people. This means that they often lack the social support that other people rely on in a crisis.

Finally, staff members' prejudice, outdated understanding of personality disorder and lack of skills mean that individuals are often not well served by A&E departments and the mental health services that are meant to be there for them in crisis. Difficulties accessing support, and the negative attitudes of staff once help is accessed, can both exacerbate the crisis.

# Crises and individuals with intellectual disabilities

For most individuals with intellectual disabilities, crises are rare events. Where crises do occur they are usually associated with the onset or worsening of additional problems such as mental or physical health problems or challenging behaviours. Crises may also occur as a result of placement breakdown or life events such as illness or death of an elderly carer. Having intellectual disabilities can make individuals more vulnerable to experiencing crises in response to certain life events as they have fewer resources and may have difficulty responding to unexpected events. They may also be vulnerable to misunderstanding or overlooking important changes. For example, they might not understand the implications of changes to the way rent is being collected. This can lead to problems such as debt or eviction. Individuals with intellectual disabilities are also likely to struggle with problem solving and may not know how to access specialist help. Coping with bereavements such as the death of a parent is difficult for anyone. However, for an individual with intellectual disabilities who has lived at home all their lives, this loss may be compounded with needing to leave home because they have also lost their unpaid carer.

## Support services

Most support services for individuals with intellectual disabilities are designed to provide routine, rather than crisis, care. Most services operate on the basis of a referral system and are open 9–5pm Monday to Friday. Few operate outside these hours and out of hours support may comprise an answer phone message with phone numbers and perhaps an on-call specialist psychiatrist. Hence when an individual with intellectual disabilities does experience a crisis it can be difficult to access help quickly. Where the crisis is related to physical health, general hospital staff may struggle to understand and meet the individual's needs (see Chapter 8). This can lead to health problems deteriorating dramatically or even death.

# Crises and individuals with intellectual disabilities and personality disorder

Individuals with intellectual disabilities and personality disorder experience a 'double whammy' when it comes to crises. They have the increased vulnerability to crises that is associated with personality disorder including chaotic lifestyles, impulsivity, thinking errors, intense and poorly controlled emotions, lack of social resources and difficulty trusting others. They will also have the issues arising from having an intellectual disabilities including difficulties with problem solving and recognising the seriousness of certain events, reduced capacity to cope and greater dependence on carers.

Individuals with intellectual disabilities and personality disorder seem particularly vulnerable to cycles in which a seemingly minor event triggers a series of other events until the situation spirals out of control. This applies across their physical health, mental health and everyday lives. Appointments are missed, prescriptions not picked up, treatments are not followed accurately or important actions are not taken. In this way the individual can ricochet from one crisis to the next. This can be both exhausting and frustrating for those trying to support the individual. When difficulties continue for a long time or behaviour escalates beyond a containable level, living arrangements or placements may break down.

Crises can also be triggered by the way services are provided. Social care and support is given to people who are unable to cope. Once the individual appears to be coping better, support is often reduced. If support is reduced below a critical threshold the individual may then be very vulnerable to going into crisis if anything changes or goes wrong for them. Most health services for mental health and intellectual disabilities offer short courses of input that end when the person recovers. They also usually have waiting lists. Sometimes the only way for an individual to have ongoing regular support is by having a crisis every time the input ends.

# Impact of crises on the individual

During a crisis individuals with intellectual disabilities and personality disorder will react in the ways described earlier in this chapter. Some common responses are summarised in Box 12.3.

---

### Box 12.3: How individuals with intellectual disabilities and personality disorder may think, feel and behave during a crisis

- Reacting instinctively
- Thinking will be emotionally driven and will consider only the immediate situation
- Feeling overwhelmed, hopeless, helpless and exhausted
- Feeling terrified
- Feeling intense physical and/or emotional pain
- Experiencing high levels of physical arousal and tension
- Becoming highly agitated
- Behaving erratically
- Attempting self-harm or suicide
- Experiencing psychotic symptoms eg. hearing voices, seeing things
- Shutting down to the extent of not eating or drinking
- Using drugs or alcohol to cope
- Exposing self to risk of abuse by seeking support from inappropriate people
- Damaging property
- Showing verbal and physical aggression towards people perceived as a threat including staff trying to care for them

---

Once the crisis is over individuals with intellectual disabilities and personality disorder often feel ashamed or embarrassed about their behaviour during the crisis and are likely to wish that the situation would not happen again. While this might be expected to motivate them to want to change their response, this is not usually the case. More often the shame and embarrassment mean that they do not want to think about what happened, talk about it or learn new coping strategies. It is too scary to think it might ever happen again and is more comfortable to deny this and get on with more enjoyable things.

# Supporting individuals with intellectual disabilities and personality disorder through crises

In order to successfully support individuals through a crisis it is necessary to tailor the support given to the stage of the crisis. Figure 12.4 shows the type of interventions that are needed at each stage of the crisis.

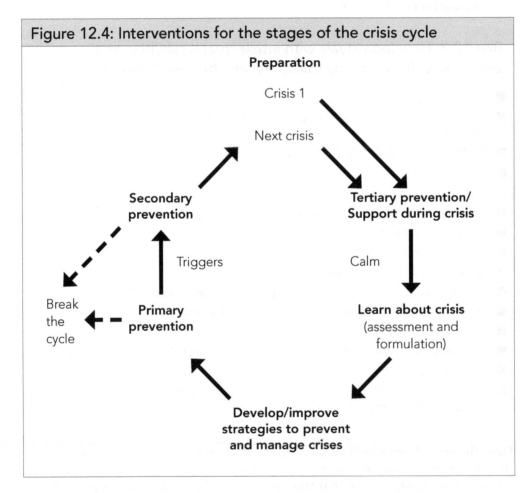

**Figure 12.4: Interventions for the stages of the crisis cycle**

By tailoring support to the individual's way of thinking, arousal level and emotional reactions at each point of the crisis cycle, it is possible to minimise the effect of a crisis, resolve it more quickly and reduce the risk of future crises occurring.

This section explores:

■ preparation

■ supporting the individual during a crisis

■ learning about the crisis once it has resolved

■ assessing an individual's readiness to contribute to avoiding future crises

■ teaching coping skills to the individual.

# Preparation

It is by definition difficult to prepare in detail for crises and individuals with intellectual disabilities and personality disorder are unlikely to be willing to spend time thinking about bad things that might happen. However, at the minimum every individual should work with staff to create a hospital/care passport to maximise the chances of their needs being met if they need admission to hospital or a crisis house. More able individuals may be able to work with staff to create advanced directives that say how they would wish to be supported in the event of a future crisis.

# Supporting the individual during a crisis

As an individual goes into crisis there are a number of important actions that need to be taken to promote the physical safety of the individual and that of other people. However, it is equally important to provide emotional containment and to interact with the individual in a way that both helps them to calm down and lays the foundations for future work. Consequently, it is important to think not just about what needs to be done but also about the way it is done. All actions need to be taken calmly, quietly and thoughtfully. The more anxious and stressed the staff team appears, the more distressed the individual will become. This in effect means ensuring that support continues to be delivered within the framework of an authoritative support style (described in Chapter 5) despite the stresses of a crisis situation.

This section explores:

■ promoting physical safety

■ emotional containment

■ taking a long-term view.

# Promoting safety

When responding to a crisis it is important to ensure that **everyone is safe**. This means considering the safety of the individual, those who live with or support them, and the general public. The work of resolving the crisis cannot happen until this has been achieved.

Safety may be achieved in a number of ways depending on the severity of the crisis, the individual's preferences and their insight into the dangers. It might be sufficient to increase staffing support at home or to see a psychiatrist to arrange a review of medication. The individual might wish to be admitted to hospital or to stay in a crisis house for a brief respite.

To maintain safety it may also be necessary to use restrictive physical interventions. These should be the least restrictive methods that will keep the individual and others safe and should be carried out by trained staff (see Chapters 3 and 10). However, it should be noted that in an extreme situation, everyone is allowed by law to use reasonable and proportional force to escape a situation if they believe they are in danger.

Achieving safety becomes more difficult if the individual does not perceive the risk or is unwilling to co-operate with actions intended to make them and others safe. However, there are a number of options depending on the individual's mental state and capacity to make decisions. If the individual is experiencing mental health problems it may be appropriate to use the Mental Health Act to take them to and detain them in a place of safety. Where the individual is assessed to lack capacity, the best interests process laid out by the Mental Capacity Act should be used and, if necessary, Deprivation of Liberty Safeguards applied (this provides a framework for an individual without capacity to be moved even if they are unwilling, if it is in their best interests). Where the individual has capacity and the behaviour does not fall under the auspices of the Mental Health Act, actions may still be possible on the basis of duty of care (a common law responsibility on everyone to prevent harm). In extreme situations the police may need to be called.

## Going into hospital

Sometimes individuals will need to be admitted to hospital as a result of the crisis. This might be a general hospital, an acute mental health ward or a specialist unit for individuals with intellectual disabilities. While everyone may be in a state of panic it is important to take the time to think about how to manage this process so that it is as positive as possible for the individual. Box 12.5 gives suggestions about how this can be done.

Intellectual Disabilities and Personality Disorder: An integrated approach
© Pavilion Publishing and Media Ltd and its licensors 2014.

---

### Box 12.5: Going into hospital

- **Explain what is happening:** Use short sentences and a calm, positive tone. Give honest information. (It is dishonest to describe it as a short break or a holiday. This will destroy trust in the person giving the information and create problems for hospital staff.)
- **Take the time to collect essentials:** Individuals will be more comfortable and will settle more quickly if they have all the items they need:
  - several changes of day clothes and underwear
  - slippers/light shoes for indoors
  - night clothes
  - toiletries (eg. shower gel/soap, shampoo, deodorant, favourite scent, tooth brush and toothpaste)
  - hair brush/comb
  - bath and hand towel
  - small amount of money in a purse or wallet
  - soft toy or photo etc that would provide comfort
  - coat/jumper if the weather is cold so they can go out
  - current medication
  - hospital/care passport (see Chapter 9).

**Be cautious taking valuable items they may be stolen/damaged** and this will only increase the person's distress.

---

## Creating a sense of safety for the individual

Wherever the crisis is managed, it is important that, as well as safely containing the individual, attention is paid to making the individual feel safe in themselves. This is because the more frightened the individual is, the more they will respond instinctively and the harder it will be to manage their behaviour. Ways of creating a sense of safety in the physical and social environment are given in Chapter 3. Being honest with the individual is essential. If staff use 'white lies' in an effort to shield the individual from the reality of what is happening, this is likely to increase the individual's anxiety in the longer term as they will no longer be able to trust what is being said to them.

# Providing emotional containment

The aim of interacting with individuals in crisis is to provide emotional containment and hence allow them to calm down as quickly as possible. There are a number of strategies and techniques that can help achieve this. There are also a number of responses that need to be avoided because they will intensify or prolong the crisis. These are summarised in Box 12.6.

---

### Box 12.6: Interacting with individuals in crisis

Do

- Maintain respect at all times
- Keep interactions short and matter-of-fact
- Use short sentences and keep choices to the minimum
- Convey a sense of calm and normality
- Use simple questions and observations of body language to establish if the individual will calm down more quickly with staff staying close or giving more space
- Use de-escalation techniques (see Chapter 3)
- Support individual to use **well learnt** calming techniques
- Validate the individual's emotions (see Chapter 3)
- Agree on and stick to a single plan of support (follow the crisis plan if there is one)
- Treat wounds gently with minimum fuss
- Respond promptly but calmly to extreme behaviours
- Maintain hope and have an eye on the future – how will the current response look/seem when the crisis is over?
- Be ready to **listen** the moment the individual feels calm enough to talk about what has happened to them – use active listening (see Chapter 11)

Do not

- Try to get the individual to explain their behaviour/use probing questions – they will not be able to and this will escalate the situation
- Try to teach the individual new skills – they are too distressed to learn
- Ask them to make complex choices – they will not be able to see the wider picture
- Keep trying new approaches to try to end the crisis – it needs to run it course
- Tell the individual off, use punishment or overly restrictive practices – these will escalate the situation and damage future relationships with the individual
- Respond to extreme or unhealthy behaviours in ways that are likely to reward them and increase their frequency in the future eg. great expressions of concern, angry condemnations or harsh criticisms

---

Some of these approaches are self-evident. However, some are worth exploring in more detail.

## Respect and validation

All interactions with individuals in crisis need to be respectful. This sounds obvious but in a crisis it is easy to lose sight of the vulnerable individual staff will have to work with once the crisis is over. Instead, the individual may be experienced as selfish and demanding or as a frightening, life-threatening monster. Consequently, the little social graces, body language and voice tone that are so important in maintaining respect may be forgotten (see Chapter 2).

It is also important that staff validate the individual's emotional reaction (see Chapter 3). This can be difficult when staff may view the individual as 'over-reacting'. However, 'invalidating' responses are likely to escalate the situation. Some examples of invalidating responses that are likely to escalate difficult situations are given in Chapter 3.

## Simplify communication

At the peak of the crisis the individual will not be able to absorb or process much information. Interactions should be matter-of-fact and aimed at conveying a sense of calm and normality. Sentences should be short and grammatically simple to avoid overloading the individual with information. Choices should be kept to a minimum as too many options will only feed the individual's sense of chaos.

## Space or company?

Some individuals are calmed by having someone present but others calm better if they are given more space. A simple question to ask might therefore be *'Would you like me to stay with you?'* However, staff should be relaxed about whether or not they get an answer as the individual may not be able to put this into words. Instead they should observe the individual's body language; do they relax or tense up if staff move slowly towards them, or retreat out of the door?

## Calming techniques

If staff know that the individual has previously learnt techniques to help them calm in a crisis, it may be worth seeing if they can be encouraged to use those techniques. However, the peak of a crisis is not the time to try to teach someone new skills or to practice skills they have only just begun to learn. This may feel counter intuitive – surely everything should be tried to help the individual? However, learning new skills is stressful, difficult and can make people feel like a failure. These feelings will only add to the crisis. David Pitonyak (2009) has a powerful image to help understand this: *'Remember: You don't teach swimming lessons to a drowning man.'*

## Consistent support

It is important to agree on and stick to a single plan of support. When consulting with a staff team about a crisis it is common to hear the phrase *'We tried everything we could think of and nothing worked'*. In fact, if the team had stuck with any one of the things they thought of, the crisis would have resolved more quickly. This is because once a crisis is underway it needs to run its course; it is a reaction to events that have already happened and cannot be changed. Often there isn't *anything* that *anyone* can do to help the individual feel better during a crisis. However, there are a lot of things that can be done that will make the individual feel worse. Frantically trying different things creates an anxious atmosphere that feeds the individual's sense of fear. Constantly changing how staff react makes building confidence and trust much more difficult. Creating calm and consistency are the most effective ways of ending a crisis as quickly as possible.

## Taking a long-term view

While managing a crisis it is important to have one eye on the future. Staff should consider if their response will make such behaviour more or less likely in the future. It is possible for caring staff to reinforce unhelpful crisis behaviours by the way they react to them. For example, if wounds or injuries trigger great outpourings of concern and distress that do not occur in response to more moderate behaviours, the individual may be drawn to repeating self-harm to elicit this response. Instead wounds should be treated gently but with minimum fuss and no expressions of great concern. In contrast, efforts to talk about emotions and engage with staff should be greeted warmly and with full attention.

However, it is important not to take this too far and try to punish unhelpful behaviours, for example, by delaying treatment, neglecting pain relief or telling the individual off. Such responses will be perceived as rejecting and hurting the whole individual and will undermine the formation of a good working relationship once the crisis is over. They are highly unlikely to have any impact on reducing the likelihood of such behaviors in the future.

## Learning about the crisis once it has resolved

Once the individual has calmed down it is important to take the opportunity to learn about the crisis and hence how future crises might be prevented or managed more successfully. The learning process has two main strands:

- exploring the crisis with the individual
- staff reflecting on and learning from the crisis.

# Exploring the crisis with the individual

Timing is critical when trying to find out what the individual understands about the crisis. Asking them probing questions during the crisis will not provide helpful information and is likely to escalate the situation. As the crisis begins to resolve the individual may want to talk about their experiences. It is important that they are able to do this whenever they feel ready to. What they say needs to be taken seriously and should receive a warm, caring and compassionate response from understanding staff. The active listening techniques described in Chapter 11 can be helpful at this point. It is important that the individual is allowed to lead conversations and is not pressurised to go further than feels comfortable.

Once the individual is calm and settled staff may begin to try to explore specific questions they would like answered. However, staff should not be worried if the individual is still not ready to talk. Quietly spending time with them, for example, going for a walk, kicking a ball around, sitting over a cup of tea or doing a puzzle together can help build trust. This is much more likely to encourage an individual to open up than repeated questions.

Once the individual begins to open up, they should be involved as much as possible in understanding what has happened to them and thinking about what can be done in the future. Some individuals may be reluctant to think about the crisis and their role in causing or exacerbating the situation. Consequently, if staff do not talk to them sensitively the individual may refuse to take part in this process. It is important to remember that the aim is to get the individual's perspective, not to correct them or show that they misunderstood events. If the conversations show that misunderstandings played an important role in the crisis, this should be added to the other information gathered and ways of addressing it can be explored later.

It is also important not to minimise or trivialise the reasons the individual may give for the crisis. It is very easy to make statements such as *'Surely all that fuss wasn't just about your mum forgetting to send a birthday card'*. If a reason given does seem trivial, it can be helpful to validate it but also use it as a base for further questions. For the example given, staff might respond: *'So you were really upset about your mum forgetting the card, has she done that before? Can you tell me what happened?'* Such questioning may expose other issues in their relationship with their mother, inflated expectations around events such as birthdays, or social isolation (eg. mum was usually the only person who remembered).

At this point it is also not helpful to start offering solutions or telling the individual how they must do things differently in the future. Possible solutions should only be shared with the individual once information gathered from all sources has been combined and carefully thought over. It is, however, appropriate to explore with the individual how they see their role in the crisis and whether they have any ideas about how things might be different. This is helpful for two reasons. Clearly the individual may have helpful insights into how future crises may be avoided and it is important that these are shared and integrated into the plans for the future. However, often the ideas the individual expresses will show that they are not ready to accept that they played a role in events and that they may not see any need to change their behaviour. Their responses can be used to understand where the individual currently is on the 'change cycle'. This in turn can be used to make decisions on the most effective way to involve them in work to prevent future crises.

## The change cycle

The concept of the change cycle was developed by Prochaska, Norcross & DiClemente (1994) as part of their Transtheoretical Model (TTM) of change. This approach challenges the assumption that people must want to change behaviours that others see as problematic. Rather, there is a progression from failure to see any problem at all, to proactively making changes. The stages of the cycle, responses characteristic of each stage and what the individual might need, are given in Box 12.7.

| Box 12.7: The TTM change cycle | | | |
|---|---|---|---|
| | **Stage** | **Individual response** | **Needs** |
| Hasn't entered the change cycle | Pre-contemplation (Not ready) | Appears unaware behaviour is causing problems and not intending to take action<br><br>Under-estimates negative impact on selves and others | Learn more about healthy behaviours<br><br>Think about benefits of changing behaviour<br><br>Think about the negative impact of behaviour on self and others (motivational interviewing – Chapter 6) |

Continued...

Intellectual Disabilities and Personality Disorder: An integrated approach
© Pavilion Publishing and Media Ltd and its licensors 2014.

| | | | |
|---|---|---|---|
| **In the change cycle** | **Contemplation (Getting ready)** | Begins to recognise behaviour is causing problems<br><br>Starts looking at pros and cons of change<br><br>BUT pros seem to balance cons, hence limited motivation to change | Learn more of the benefits of change<br><br>Talk to peers who have changed<br><br>Motivational interviewing may be helpful |
| | **Preparation (Ready)** | Is thinking about changing and may begin taking small steps toward change eg. they may say that they want to change | Talk about their plans, support from friends, peers and professionals, use strategies to help them make and maintain change (see below) |
| | **Action (Doing)** | Has made some changes to their problem behaviour or shows some new healthy behaviours | To learn how to strengthen their commitment to change and to fight urges to slip back, continue to use change strategies |
| | **Maintenance (Keep doing)** | Has been able to continue with the changes and is trying not to slip back into old ways of coping | To be aware of situations that may tempt them to slip back into doing the unhealthy behaviour – particularly stressful situations<br><br>Spend time with people who behave in healthy ways<br><br>Reminded to engage in healthy activities to cope with stress |
| | **Relapse (Slipping back)** | The individual slips back to an earlier stage in the cycle | To normalise relapses, be non-judgemental and supportive<br><br>Adjust approach to reflect the needs of the stage the individual has returned to |
| **Exits the change cycle** | **Resolution (Automatic)** | Healthy ways of coping and behaving have become automatic and there is little risk of a return to old behaviours | Opportunities to share their positive achievement with peers |

Each stage of the change cycle requires a different approach from those supporting the individual to enhance the chances of them engaging in work to address the problems (in this case to prevent future crises). However, staff frequently make the mistake of assuming that the individual with intellectual disabilities and personality disorder shares the staff team's readiness to take action and hence will offer support that is appropriate for the 'Preparation' or 'Action' stages. If the individual is at an earlier point on the cycle, this will not fit with their needs. This mismatch makes it more likely that the individual will feel misunderstood or that they are being controlled by staff. They are then more likely to refuse to work with staff to prevent future crises.

## Staff reflecting on and learning from the crisis

One way of reflecting on and learning from the crisis is for the staff team to meet and discuss:

■ how best to help the individual calm down during a crisis

■ how the crisis arose in the first place.

### How best to help the individual calm down

It can be helpful to make two lists; what helped the individual to calm down and what made them more distressed. Often staff have few ideas about what helped the individual to calm down but will be much more confident about what made things worse. This is just as useful, as often doing the opposite is likely to help the person calm down. This process will identify strategies for tertiary prevention, that is approaches that will reduce the severity, intensity and duration of the crisis. Some areas to explore are given in Box 12.8.

This work can then be drawn together to provide tertiary strategies to help the individual calm down as quickly as possible in any future crises. A summary of the most helpful approaches can be added to the individual's crisis plan.

Intellectual Disabilities and Personality Disorder: An integrated approach
© Pavilion Publishing and Media Ltd and its licensors 2014.

## Box 12.8: Examples of things that may calm an individual or distress them more

**Things that might help an individual to calm down <u>or</u> distress them more**

| | |
|---|---|
| ■ Being alone | ■ Someone being with them |
| ■ Being in control | ■ Staff taking control |
| ■ Making simple choices | ■ Choices being made for them (on the basis of known preferences) |
| ■ Being supported to do as they choose | ■ Being told what to do |
| ■ Having a warm bath/shower | ■ Relaxing standards of personal hygiene until they feel better |
| ■ Having a warm drink | ■ Having a cool drink |
| ■ Having something to eat | ■ Not pushing them to eat until they feel well enough |
| ■ Staff being silent | ■ Staff talking to them |
| ■ Staff using a firm tone of voice | ■ Staff using a gentle tone of voice |
| ■ Watching TV/DVD | ■ Avoiding TV |
| ■ Listening to loud music | ■ Listening to relaxing music |
| ■ Running and jumping | ■ Sitting still, curling up under a blanket |
| ■ Seeing friends/relations | ■ Having a break from friends/relations |
| ■ Having 'as required' medication | ■ Not using 'as required' medication |

### Understanding how the crisis arose

With hindsight, it is often possible for staff to identify factors that contributed to the crisis and signs that things were not going well. Each individual will have a unique pattern to their crises. Box 12.9 gives some common triggers, vulnerabilities and warning signs.

## Box 12.9: Some common triggers, vulnerabilities and warning signs

### Triggers

- Life events eg. loss, deaths, redundancy, relationship breakup, house move, homelessness, in trouble with the police, being attacked or abused
- Practical changes eg. level of support, changes to finances
- Staffing changes eg. familiar staff leaving, high staff turn-over
- Changes to support style eg. relaxing boundaries, inconsistent responses
- Physical health eg. onset of new problem or deterioration in existing problem
- Mental health eg. onset of new problem or deterioration in existing problem
- Pain (physical and emotional)
- Medication: changes, not taking correctly, not taking at all, adding in unhelpful medications

### Vulnerabilities

- Low self-esteem and lack of self-worth
- Lack of practical skills and knowledge
- Unhelpful thinking patterns
- Lack of skills to manage intense emotions
- Small social network
- Few sources of enjoyment and fulfillment in their life
- Drug or alcohol misuse
- Poor engagement with support services
- Insufficient support or the wrong type of support
- Support staff lacking skills/knowledge/attitudes to support when in difficulties

### Warning signs

- Increase/decrease in phone calls/contacts with services
- Less contact, more missed appointments
- Erratic attendance at job/day centre
- Talking more about problems and concerns
- Talking less
- Decline in personal hygiene
- Increase in use of alcohol or drugs
- Increase in self-harm
- Change in general demeanour eg. more angry, sadder, more irritable
- Change in personal appearance (hair, dress, weight loss/gain)
- Change in pattern of behaviour (sleeping more/less, eating more/less, going out more/less)

## Timeline

Where there is a lot of confusion about why a crisis occurred it can be very helpful to draw up a 'timeline'. This puts all the events that occurred in the correct sequence. This is important because it helps clarify if certain behaviours were triggers for an event or the consequences of the event. For example, it may be known that the individual had a letter about eviction that was followed through, was drunk, self-harmed and was admitted to A&E. Box 12.10 gives two possible timelines for these events.

| Box 12.10: Example timelines showing the impact of the sequences of events | | |
|---|---|---|
| | **Timeline 1** | **Timeline 2** |
| ↓ | Letter about eviction | Cautioned for drunken behaviour |
| | Cautioned for drunken behaviour | Self-harm |
| | Evicted | Admitted to A&E |
| | Self-harm | Letter about eviction |
| | Admitted to A&E | Evicted |

In Timeline 1, there appears to be a connection between behaviour and the process of being evicted. Drunken behaviour follows the letter, while self-harm follows the eviction. In Timeline 2, the eviction does not appear to have been directly related to the behaviours of drunkenness and self-harm. In this case, eviction might be an indirect consequence, for example, the individual may be spending all their money on alcohol rather than paying the rent.

# Formulation

Once information about the crisis has been gathered from the individual and the staff team the formulation process discussed in Chapter 10 can be very helpful in making sense of all the information. The adapted 'hot-cross bun' may be useful in summarising the information gathered. The formulation process should also consider the point the individual is at on the change cycle. This will help to ensure that the interventions proposed and crisis plan developed match with the stage the individual is at and, where appropriate, include interventions to help them move on to the next stage of the change cycle.

# Developing/improving strategies to manage crises

Once as much as possible is understood about the crisis it is time to start working on plans to prevent or minimise the impact of future crises. The process of reflecting on the crisis will have identified how to help the individual calm as quickly as possible (tertiary prevention). Discussions with the individual may also have identified how they might like things to be managed in the future. For individuals who, when well, have the insight and capacity to know what is helpful for them in a crisis but who lose capacity during the crisis, these ideas may be turned into 'advanced directives'. These are instructions about how they would like to be treated if another crisis occurs in the future. This information can then be pulled together to form a crisis plan. Examples of crisis plans can be seen in Box 12.11 and also Boxes 10.15,18, 20 and 11.8.

---

**Box 12.11: Example crisis plan**

If I do not have the right kind of support on the anniversary of my father's death I will be unable to manage my conflicting emotions and this can spiral into an episode of severe depression. I may feel suicidal, may self-harm and stop eating. I may also have hallucinations, hearing my father and seeing him in my bedroom. If the hallucinations become very severe I may begin to destroy the furniture in my room and will attack staff and other individuals with the broken pieces. My positive behaviour support plan gives strategies for preventing this and for supporting me in the early stages of a depressive episode. However if I still go into a deep depression, follow this crisis plan.

- Contact Dr X consultant psychiatrist and arrange an urgent assessment.
- Increase staffing levels so that I am within eyesight during all waking hours.
- Support me to pack away all the objects in my room I might use to self-harm (scissors, CD cases, electric cords).
- If you see me trying to self-harm, intervene if it is safe to do so. Ask me calmly to put down anything sharp I may be using. Do not shout or use a forceful tone of voice. This reminds me of my father and will make me more likely to cut myself. If necessary, techniques X or Y can be used by staff to guide me to a safe place.
- If I have self-harmed, calmly assess the injuries and either give first aid or take me to A&E. Do not tell me off or make a fuss about the injuries. Comments such as *'You must have been feeling really upset to do this'* may help me relax and talk to you about why I needed to self-harm.
- Support me to engage in low key activities such as colouring, wordsearch and chatting about my favourite celebrities to distract me from my distress.

Continued...

---

■ Do not pressure me to eat big meals. Offer me the choice of a small snack from my list of favourites or fortified milkshake eg. *'Would you like a banana or a chocolate milkshake?'* Do not push me if I say no, just offer again later.

■ Validate my feelings (often a mixture of distress, guilt and fear) but remain calm. Remind me that it is natural to be sad that my father died but to be relieved as it means he can no longer hurt me. Remind me that I have got over my distress before and that I will do so again.

■ Offer to look at my survival story with me.

■ If I am having hallucinations, stay with me. Say that you know what I am seeing and hearing feels real to me but that I am safe now. Use short sentences and a calm but firm tone of voice.

■ If my weight drops below X kg seek an urgent review with the dietician – it may be necessary to admit me to hospital.

■ If I am admitted to hospital make sure you pack all the items on my hospital list and bring my hospital/care passport.

Worst case scenarios

■ If I go missing, call the police immediately and give them the pre-made description and contact sheet.

■ If I stop drinking take me to A&E as dehydration can quickly become life-threatening.

■ If I begin to destroy my room, clear the area and call the police. I will need admission to a place of safety.

The focus at this point then shifts to how to reduce the risk of crises and how to respond to the early warning signs through primary and secondary prevention. It is important that the individual is involved in this process in a way that reflects their point on the change cycle. For example, fully involving someone who is at the 'Action' stage but simply taking into account the preferences and wishes of someone at the 'Pre-contemplation' stage.

## Primary prevention

As discussed in Chapter 10, primary prevention focuses on ensuring that the individual's needs are met and that they have the correct support. This includes considering physical and mental health, social support networks, activities, hobbies and employment, accommodation and their support package. Ideas for identifying and addressing these needs can be found in the earlier chapters of this book and proactive strategies are summarised Box 10.10.

For individuals who have reached the Preparation/Action stages of the change cycle, primary prevention may include offering a referral for therapy that addresses some of the issues that make them vulnerable to repeated crises.

## Secondary prevention

Strategies for secondary prevention may be seen as falling into two main groups:

- ensuring that support services are accessed or provided in a timely fashion
- helping the individual cope better with the trigger situation.

## Accessing support services

Often crises escalate because the right support is not received at the right time. The most important factor in ensuring an individual has access to the right support is establishing whether the individual will actively seek help if they understand how to do this or if they are unlikely to do this.

For individuals who lack the insight or motivation to seek help, it is important that teams have proactive ways of keeping in touch and monitoring the situation. Missed appointments should be actively followed up. It may be helpful to meet individuals at regular intervals for a coffee and chat or a pleasant walk. This will make contact a more enjoyable experience and reduce the feeling that staff are trying to catch them out. It also offers staff the opportunity to watch for early warning signs that they would not otherwise be aware of. For such individuals, the suggestions in Chapter 13 may help staff to promote more active engagement with services.

Individuals who are motivated to seek help need to know how to contact services. It is important to make sure that individuals have clear information on who to contact and when. It can be helpful to spend time with the individual, adding numbers to their mobile phone or creating email contacts. Reminders of who to contact can be made into small prompt cards to go in a wallet or purse. An example card is given in Box 12.12. If the individual has a crisis box (see Box 11.16) a copy of the card could also added to the box.

Developments in technology may also be helpful; increasingly apps are being developed for use with smart phones that allow individuals to alert staff about their mental state, emotional or physical well-being.

## Preventing admissions

If an individual has needed admission to hospital in a previous crisis, thought should be given to how this might be avoided in future and what measures would need to be in place to allow them to remain at home. Agreement might need to be sought for flexible funding to allow increases in staffing levels or links built with local crisis services so that there are no issues about eligibility (many crisis services exclude individuals with intellectual disabilities).

---

**Box 12.12: Example crisis card**

**Crisis support**

**If you are feeling unwell or distressed**

Let us know what is going on

- ■ Text Joe on _____ (key worker/care co-ordinator – NB the text goes to a team number that will be addressed even if Joe is on holiday)

If you need to talk
- ■ Ring or text X (a friend or family member)

If you feel suicidal
- ■ Ring the **Samaritans (0845 90 90 90)**

If you feel unwell
- ■ Ring **111** for advice

---

# Helping the individual to cope better

For individuals who accept that their behaviour or lack of coping skills contributed to the crisis it may be helpful to spend some time developing new skills. There are four steps to this process:

1. Identifying helpful skills

2. Learning to use the skills

3. Identifying when to use them

4. Practicing them regularly so they are not forgotten by the time of the next crisis.

## Identifying helpful skills

This is best done working with the individual; they are much more likely to use skills that they feel comfortable with and understand than ones that seem alien to their nature or do not make sense to them. The earlier chapters of this book contain a range of skills that would be helpful in preventing crises (see Box 12.13).

| Box 12.13: Helpful skills | |
|---|---|
| **Skill** | **Chapter/Box** |
| Relaxation | Box 3.12 |
| Self-soothing | Box 3.13 |
| Distraction | Box 7.14 |
| Mindfulness | Box 7.15 |
| Pain management | Chapter 8 |
| Grounding techniques | Box 9.12 |
| Alternatives to self-harm | Box 11.19 |

## Learning the skill

Once helpful skills have been identified, thought needs to be given to how they will be taught. When thinking about this it is important to remember that the individual will often have been using their unhealthy ways of coping for many years. These patterns of responding will have become automatic and consequently will be very hard to change. **New skills need to be practised over and over again for weeks or even months if they are to stand a chance of competing with these well-established patterns of behaviour**. In addition to regular practice it is important for individuals to think about how they are progressing, to have feedback from others about their performance and to be encouraged to continue with the learning process.

When working with an individual to teach coping skills it can be helpful to compare the process with learning to play a musical instrument or a skilled game such as football (choose an example that resonates with the individual's experiences and interests). No one would expect someone to become a concert pianist or premier league footballer on the basis of being shown a piano or football and being told to hit the keys or kick the ball in the goal. Rather it takes daily practice, help from skilled coaches and years of persistence to become expert at a skill.

It is important also to remember that, by definition, individuals with intellectual disabilities and personality disorder, find it harder to learn new skills than other people and that they may have problems remembering what is said to them. Sessions may need to be shorter in length, more frequent and take place over a longer period of time than would be needed for more able individuals with personality disorder. It can also be helpful to build the new coping skills into a book using words and pictures that the individual can understand so that they can consult this to remind them what they need to do.

## Identifying when to use skills

Once the individual has mastered the skill they then need to learn *when* to use it. This is perhaps the most difficult step because individuals are often unaware of the subtle changes that indicate they are becoming upset and once they are really upset it is usually too late to use their new coping strategies.

It can be helpful to have a list of the early signs identified by staff and to go through these with the individual. Do they recognise them? Are there other things that they feel or think that staff have not noticed? If the individual does not have a good understanding of thoughts, feelings, physical reactions and behaviour it may be necessary to work with them to improve this (see Chapter 3).

Once the individual understands what they are looking for staff can then prompt them to carry out frequent spotchecks on their own feelings to identify when they should use the coping skill. Staff can then gradually reduce the role they play in reminding the individual to use the skill until the individual can do this independently. Box 12.14 gives this process in more detail.

---

### Box 12.14: Helping individuals develop skills to prevent/manage crises

- Working with the individual, select self-soothing, relaxing, distracting or grounding techniques that they would find helpful. Try to choose a mixture of active and passive activities and include some that can be done alone. Look for activities that have a clear beginning, middle and end.
- Make a visual menu of these activities that the individual can understand and that looks attractive to them.
- Make a record form that the individual can tick to show which techniques they have practiced.
- Encourage the individual to go to the list and choose an activity to carry out. Aim to do this 5–10 times every day.
- Do this for at least three weeks.
- Make a list of things that show that the individual is beginning to get stressed Help the individual to recognise these early signs eg.' You look tense, how about doing something on your calming menu?'
- Support the individual each step of the way to complete the activity.
- Congratulate the individual on making a better choice about how to deal with their stress.
- Keep giving the individual lots of opportunities to practice their new skills.

---

However, some individuals may continue to be dependent on others to remind them when to use their coping skills. If this is the case it is very important that this is recognised and that the individual is not blamed for failing to use the skill independently. Rather their support package needs to be adjusted to build in external monitoring of their emotional state and to include sufficient support so that there are staff available to remind them to use their coping skills.

# Supporting staff through the crisis cycle

Supporting individuals with intellectual disabilities and personality disorder through crises can make huge demands on services, teams and individual staff members. Frequently, staff teams will be ill-prepared to deal with these demands. Staff in intellectual disabilities services may have little knowledge of personality disorder or of supporting individuals in crisis. Staff in mental health and crisis services will have training in these areas but they often lack the skills and confidence to apply these skills to individuals with intellectual disabilities.

Whatever service they are based in, staff often find individuals with intellectual disabilities and personality disorder require much more time than staff have available and cause a great deal of anxiety. Individuals with intellectual disabilities and personality disorder also often create conflict in teams that support them. This adds to the challenge of supporting them in crises. These difficulties are explored more in Chapter 14.

## The impact on those supporting the individual through a crisis

Crises have a significant impact on the people around the individual. Staff can feel overwhelmed by the needs of the individual. This may result in panic with unco-ordinated and inconsistent responses. As the crisis progresses staff may lose hope that the individual will recover. Where the individual shows verbal and physical aggression, staff may fear for their own safety or that of other individuals living in the service. Where the individual is self-harming or expressing suicidal thoughts, the staff may fear for the individual's safety. Staff may find it difficult to switch off at the end of the working day and may lose sleep worrying about the individual. They may dread coming to work and may suffer from stress-related health problems.

Those supporting the individual may make heroic efforts to rescue them. However, as exhaustion sets in this may switch to anger and frustration at the individual's failure to get well, stay well or do the work needed to prevent future crises. Where the individual is living with family or a partner this exhaustion may lead to them being thrown out of the home and becoming homeless with all the risks that this entails.

Where the individual lives in supported living or residential care, exhausted staff teams may decide that they do not have the skills to support an individual and may act to find them another placement or transfer them to the care of a more skilled team. Where this cannot be achieved, the exhausted team has to continue to provide care. Such services often suffer from high levels of sickness and staff turnover. Staff who stay may stop connecting emotionally with the individuals they support in an effort to protect themselves. These staff are at risk of becoming uncaring and uninterested in the people they support and may begin to blame the individual. In this situation there is a risk that more aversive and restrictive strategies may be used and that the service, or certain staff within the service, will abuse the individual.

To ensure that staff are able to successfully support individuals with intellectual disabilities and personality disorder through the crises it is important to ensure that they have the right knowledge, skills and attitudes to cope with each stage of the crisis cycle. They will also need practical and emotional support. This section will look at how to support staff at each stage of the crisis cycle.

## Preparing for crises

Crises feel totally unpredictable both in terms of when they will happen and also the form they will take. However, with thought, it is possible to be prepared practically and emotionally for most eventualities and to develop the confidence to support individuals through crises whenever they occur and whatever form they take. This is the approach taken by emergency services; they never know what they will encounter but train so that they have the skills to deal with whatever they might find and can remain calm and confident in the face of new problems.

Preparation may include:

- learning about local services
- learning about the legal context
- selecting and developing staff.

## Understanding local services

One of the most consuming aspects of crises is trying to find out, often outside office hours, what help is available. To avoid this it is important to have an easily accessible resource that gives clear information about what services are available, what they do and how to access them. Box 12.15 suggests some of the information that might be helpful.

---

### Box 12.15: Information that may be helpful in a crisis

- Contact numbers for out of hours support for that service eg. duty managers
- GP out of hours numbers
- Numbers for crisis phone lines
- When to use 111
- Contact details for local crisis support services
- Minor injury units – opening hours – location and postcode/map of how to get there
- Local accident and emergency units – location and postcode/map of how to get there
- Location of local Section 136 beds (used by the police in emergencies for individuals with mental health problems)
- Location of PICU (psychiatric intensive care unit)
- Number for local social services duty team
- The admission criteria and process for local mental health inpatient services including units for individuals with intellectual disabilities

---

Often much of this information has already been pulled together by other services. Networking and internet searching can often save a lot of work. It can be helpful to have flowcharts for common types of problems, for example, physical illnesses or injuries, mental health issues, self-injury or self-poisoning and accommodation/housing issues. These give 'at a glance' information on what action to take depending on the severity and timing of the crisis. These need to be reviewed regularly as services often change locations or phone numbers.

## Understanding the legal context

Sometimes in crises individuals may not understand or accept the need for help or treatment. The law deals effectively with many of these situations through the Mental Health Act, The Mental Capacity Act and the common law duty of care. However, crises often continue for much longer than necessary because those involved do not understand the legal framework and are trying to understand what actions can lawfully be taken at the same time as making urgent decisions about how to support the individual.

Staff who are prepared with a good understanding of the relevant legislation and common law are able to take the necessary action quickly and confidently. It is beyond the scope of this book to explore the legal framework for making decisions about care. However, there are many clear and helpful resources that have been developed by government and others to help staff understand these issues. Details of some of these are given in the Further reading section.

## Developing, preparing and supporting staff teams

Individuals in crisis need calm, confident support. It is important to recognise that being able to cope with crises is based on personal characteristics: if everyone could cope with crisis situations the selection process for fire and rescue staff would not be so intensive. While they should not be the only characteristics considered, it may be helpful to include the ability to cope with crises as part of the person specification when recruiting. Box 12.16 gives some of the characteristics that have been identified in staff who cope well when people with intellectual disabilities and challenging behaviour are in crisis. These are also likely to be applicable where those challenges arise from having a personality disorder.

---

### Box 12.16: Characteristics of staff who cope well with crises

- Not easily overwhelmed
- Prepared for the worst
- Know what to do when things get tough
- Able to remain calm even when the situation appears impossible
- Able to convey verbally and non-verbally that they are OK and will do what is needed to make sure no one gets hurt
- Have been through tough times before
- Almost always have a sense of humour, but would consider jokes at the individual's expense a serious character flaw
- Project a sense of hope to the individual about the future

Adapted from Pitonyak D (2009)

---

However, calmness and confidence also come from having the right knowledge, skills and back up. They can be built and maintained through preparation and practice. Box 12.17 gives some suggestions for how staff teams might be developed and supported to ensure they are able to cope when crises occur.

---

### Box 12.17: Preparing staff for potential crises

- Knowledge: the crisis cycle and approaches needed at each stage, legal context
- Skills: de-escalation, restrictive physical interventions (Chapters 3, 10), supporting individuals in crisis (see earlier in this chapter)
- Support:
  - Systems for rapidly accessing additional support/staff when needed at short notice to ensure that regular staff are able to take breaks and holidays despite the crisis
  - Supervision: regular, supportive with permission to explore uncomfortable issues
  - Post-incident support system: needs to be in place *before* incidents occur
  - Access to confidential counselling service
  - Network of professional connections and links with support services
- Self-care: Encouragement to develop work-life balance including activities that restore, heal and meet spiritual needs

---

## Support staff during the crisis/tertiary prevention

A well-prepared staff team is in a good position to successfully support an individual during a crisis. However, it is easy for staff to be overwhelmed by events and to find it difficult to put what they have learnt into practice. It is important to continue to support staff to promote a calm, confident and caring atmosphere or at least the appearance of calm despite the prevailing panic. A number of approaches can help staff remain positive during a crisis. These include promoting:

- compassionate distance
- reframing
- taking the long-term view
- taking care to prevent exhaustion.

### Compassionate distance

Maintaining a calm, confident and caring atmosphere is very helpful in resolving crises as quickly as possible. Individuals in crisis need staff to be warm, caring and compassionate but they also need staff to remain cool, calm and collected in the face of the crisis. If staff panic, are afraid or become confused and overly emotional in their response they will be unable to think clearly or provide the emotional (and sometimes physical) containment that is needed by individuals in crisis. However, if staff are too cool, controlled and detached this can make individuals feel uncared for, vulnerable and alone. Such feelings are likely to escalate the crisis. This balance between emotional connection and emotional distance has been described as maintaining a *'compassionate distance'*, *'let people affect you, but don't join them in the drowning'* (Pitonyak, 2009) or *'staying warm and keeping your cool'* (Bell, 2005).

It is also important not to respond in a dramatic, 'over-the-top' manner. Intense, forceful responses that rush to take over the situation and 'control' the individual are unhelpful as they are likely to increase panic and may lead individuals to fight back to regain some control for themselves.

## Reframing and externalising the problem

Sometimes it can be hard to feel compassion for an individual as their behaviour seems unreasonable and their problems seem self-inflicted. Reframing is a useful mental 'trick' that can help staff to see situations in a more helpful way, in this instance one that allows staff behave with compassion. If staff know an individual they can be helped to think of how the individual is when they are well and how they will be distressed by the way they have behaved when they calm down. If they also know about events that have happened to the individual, staff can try to understand how things might feel for the individual. If staff do not know the individual it can help to imagine how the member of staff would themselves want to be treated if they were the person in distress or what they would want done if that individual was a close friend or relative. It can also help to attribute the difficult behaviour to an illness or situation rather than the person. For example, *'That is their depression talking, I won't let it trick me into being disrespectful'.* This is called 'externalising the problem'. It allows anger, frustration and hurt to be directed at 'the problem' rather than the person with the problem.

## Long-term view

Staff need to be able to take a long-term view and not to despair when the individual appears to be getting worse or not responding to their efforts to help. It is important to remember that an individual's response may be the result of lifelong difficulties including multiple traumas, mental and physical health problems. Such problems can take years to overcome or may never be fully resolved. So staff need to be able to maintain faith in their ability to manage the situation and hope for resolution in the long term.

## Preventing exhaustion

Staying calm, confident and caring is much easier if staff are not exhausted. They need breaks both within a working day and over the longer time period. No one should be asked to support an individual in crisis for longer than two hours at a time; systems need to be in place for staff to swap roles and have short breaks within a shift. Staff should also still be able to take their usual number of rest days to enable them to 'recharge their batteries'. As a rule of thumb, no one should work more than five days without a rest day. If they do so, their emotional health and ability to cope are likely to be compromised.

During the crisis, staff should have regular opportunities to talk about what is going on, to express their feelings and to agree consistent plans of action. Part of the emotional reaction around a crisis makes this difficult to achieve; people are likely to respond *'how can we take time out now, we've got a crisis to deal with?'* However, if this is not done it is easy for splits to emerge in staff teams resulting in conflict and inconsistent responses (also see Chapter 14). Those supporting staff also need the opportunity to find out what staff need to feel safe in the situation.

## Learning from the crisis

Once the crisis has resolved it is tempting for staff to go back to 'business as usual' (mirroring the reaction of individuals who find it too painful to think there might be another crisis). However, this is the best time to try to understand what has happened and work out how to do things better in the future. It is important to explore:

- what actually happened in the crisis
- what staff feared might happen
- how to build the confidence to cope in future crises.

This can be done in parallel with the process described earlier in this chapter for finding out how to better support the individual through the crisis process.

### What happened in the crisis

It can be helpful for staff to meet as a team and share their thoughts, feelings and experiences about each step of the crisis cycle. It is important that this is done in a non-judgemental way. If staff feel this is about finding out what they did wrong, they are unlikely to share, what may be vital information for fear of being reprimanded. It is important to use this time to explore the impact on the staff team and to think about what might help them cope better in the future.

### Fears of what might have happened

Often it is the fears of what might happen, rather than the reality of an individual's behaviour, that cause a staff team to panic or lose confidence during a crisis. These might be fears about serious injury or death, of letting down the individual or colleagues, of doing something they know to be wrong (like shouting back or hitting the individual) or losing their job. If these fears are not explored, they are unlikely to resolve naturally and will often mean that staff continue to be unable to support the individual successfully in future crises. Some questions that may be helpful in exploring this are given in Box 12.18.

---

**Box 12.18: Questions to identify what support staff need at the height of a crisis**

■ What is the worst case scenario? What did you fear would happen in the darkest moments?

- To the individual
- To other people
- To yourself (individual staff member)
- To your colleagues
- To the public

How could this be managed safely?

■ What would you need if the individual had a terrible day and nothing you could do would make them calm down?

■ What would you need to feel safe?

■ What would you need so that you can go home at the end of a day without a knot in your stomach?

■ What would you need to cope with X, Y & Z (feared outcomes)?

Adapted from Pitonyak (2009)

---

Paradoxically, thinking about the worst case scenario can help reduce the severity of any future crisis; staff who know what to do if things get really bad are more relaxed, calm and confident. These qualities help individuals feel contained and hence help them calm more quickly.

## Prevention of and preparation for future crises

A crisis is not the time for staff to be learning new skills. Hence it is important that any training needs identified in the review of the crisis are met promptly and that those skills are regularly refreshed. These skills need to be 'over-learnt', that is they need to be practised until the point that they are used automatically and the staff member does not even need to think about how to respond. In this way the staff team will become confident of their ability to manage any future crisis. Again, paradoxically, the more confident the staff team are that they can manage a crisis, the less likely it is to happen.

## Complacency

If a crisis has been successfully managed and an individual has been stable for a long period of time, it is easy for staff teams to 'forget' about the crisis and the lessons learnt. Staff changes may mean that there is no one left who experienced the crisis. It is therefore important to have an approach that reviews the crisis plan as part of the individual's annual review, checks that it is still accurate (for example, key personnel, services or phone numbers may have changed) and incorporates it into the most recent care plan (whether that is a PCP, HAP or a CPA). In this way it will remain available should a crisis occur. Sending the plan to archives on the basis that the individual is 'better' and 'that would never happen again' is, sadly, usually wishful thinking.

# Successful crisis management

Successfully managing crises has significant benefits for the individual and those who support them. It can build stronger, more trusting relationships, lead to a more helpful and individualised support plan and build the resilience and confidence to tackle difficult situations in the future. However, it is not always easy to tell if an approach is being successful.

If the approach taken to crisis management is totally effective, this is very obvious: there will be no more crises. In reality, some crises are likely to occur despite good preparation and implementation of primary and secondary preventative strategies. It may also take time for an approach to become fully effective. This can leave staff unclear as to whether the approach is working or not. However, there are a number of indicators that will show whether crises are becoming less frequent or less severe.

Where there is effective crisis management, individuals are likely to have fewer placement breakdowns, less frequent and shorter admissions to hospital, be on more effective medication regimens (and generally less medication overall), experience fewer and less intrusive episodes of restrictive physical interventions and have less contact with emergency services. By monitoring these variables a much clearer picture will emerge as to whether the plan is being effective.

If crises continue despite the plan it is important not to blame the individual and to remember that a crisis is an indication of unmet need. When an individual has repeated crises it is a message that the services being provided are not effectively meeting the individual's needs. It may even be that the service is reinforcing the behaviours it is trying to reduce. It is then important to repeat the processes outlined above to identify key issues that may have been overlooked in previous crises.

Intellectual Disabilities and Personality Disorder: An integrated approach
© Pavilion Publishing and Media Ltd and its licensors 2014.

# Key learning points

■ People may experience crises in the form of a sudden change, usually for the worse, in their social functioning, physical or mental health.

■ Crises may be triggered by events that lead to the person being overwhelmed by internal or external stressors.

■ Crises often seem to come out of the blue and can overwhelm both the individual and those who support them. However, it is possible to respond to crises proactively in a manner that can build stronger, more trusting relationships, lead to a more helpful and individualised support plan and build the resilience and confidence to tackle difficult situations in the future.

■ Staff teams need to understand the crisis cycle and the actions that are most helpful at each stage. They need to understand how to keep the individual and themselves safe during the crisis.

■ Maintaining a calm, confident and caring atmosphere is very helpful in resolving crises as quickly as possible. Individuals in crisis need staff to be warm, caring and compassionate but they also need staff to remain cool, calm and collected in the face of the crisis. This is often termed 'compassionate distance'.

■ Once the crisis is over staff need to work together with the individual to build a clear understanding of the recent crisis. This information is then used to develop primary, secondary and tertiary preventative strategies.

■ Primary and secondary strategies can be integrated into the care plan, while tertiary strategies are used to create a crisis plan.

■ Care must be taken to ensure that the crisis plan continues to be updated and that staff have the skills, confidence and resources to follow it.

# References

Bell L (2005) *Managing Intense Emotions and Overcoming Self-destructive Habits: A self-help manual.* Hove: Routledge. (Chapter 7: Investigating and modifying thinking habits and beliefs.)

Pitonyak D (2009) *Upside Down and Inside Out: Supporting a person in crisis / supporting the people who care.* Available at: www.dimagine.com/Upside.pdf (accessed April 2014).

Prochaska JO, Norcross JC & DiClemente CC (1994) *Changing for Good.* New York: Avon Books.

# Further reading

Barksby J & Harper L (2011) *Duty of Care for Learning Disability Workers*. Exeter: BILD & Learning Matters.

Department for Constitutional Affairs (2007) *Mental Capacity Act 2005 Code of Practice*. London: TSO. Available at: www.legislation.gov.uk/ukpga/2005/9/contents (accessed April 2014).

Department of Health (2008) *Code of Practice: Mental Health Act* 1983. London: TSO.

Cambridge University Hospitals (2014) *Hospital passports* [online]. Available at: http://www.cuh.org.uk/resources/pdf/patient_information_leaflets/easy_read/passport_CUH.pdf (accessed April 2014).

Ministry of Justice (2008) *Mental Capacity Act 2005: Deprivation of liberty safeguards*. Code of Practice to supplement the main Mental Capacity Act 2005 Code of Practice. Norwich: TSO.

Mind (2011) *Listening to Experience: An independent enquiry into acute and crisis mental health care*. Available at: http://www.mind.org.uk/media/211306/Listening_to_experience_web.pdf (accessed April 2014).

Pitonyak D (2009) *Upside Down and Inside Out: Supporting a person in crisis / supporting the people who care*. Available at: www.dimagine.com/Upside.pdf (accessed April 2014).

Pitonyak D (2008) *Jumping Into the Chaos of Things*. Version 28. Available at: www.dimagine.com/Jumping.pdf (accessed April 2014).

Sellars C (2011) *Risk Assessment in People with Intellectual Disabilities* (2nd edition). BPS Blackwell, Chichester.

Sane (2014) *Crisis*. Available at: http://www.sane.org.uk/what_we_do/support/crisis/ (accessed April 2014).

Unison (2011) *Duty of Care Handbook: For members working in health and social care*. UNISON: London. Available at: https://www.unison.org.uk/upload/sharepoint/Best%20Practice%20and%20 Procedures/Duty%20of%20Care%20handbook%20-%202011.pdf (accessed April 2014).

Wilson S (2001) A four stage model for management of borderline personality disorder in people with mental retardation. *Mental Health Aspects of Developmental Disabilities* **4** 68–76.

# Chapter 13: Difficulties engaging with services

This chapter explores the concept of engagement with services, why it is difficult for individuals with intellectual disabilities and personality disorder to engage with services and how these difficulties may be overcome. Its main focus is on what support services can do to make their services more accessible and responsive to the needs of these individuals.

## Key topics

- Engagement
- Engagement with individuals with personality disorder
- Engagement and individuals with intellectual disabilities
- Engagement with individuals with intellectual disabilities and personality disorder
- Enhancing engagement
- Service design

## Engagement

Engagement is the process of connecting to and working with professionals and services to resolve problems. There are a number of steps to the process (see Box 13.1). These steps are related to the change cycle explored in Chapter 11.

---

### Box 13.1: The steps to engagement with services

- Identifying the need to seek help
- Making the decision to seek help
- Putting that decision into action
- Forming a working relationship with staff
- Committing to completing a course of treatment
- Putting possible solutions into action

---

A multiplicity of factors can impact on this process. Some of these factors are given in Box 13.2.

---

## Box 13.2: Factors impacting on engagement with services

### Individual characteristics

- Ability to recognise problems
- Comfort with acknowledging there is a problem
- Belief that the problem can be changed (hope)
- Belief that they are deserving of help
- Having the vocabulary (practical and emotional) to express problems
- Recognising that others might be able to help with the problem
- Comfort with accepting help from others
- Attitude towards professional helpers/services
- Degree of trust, shyness or embarrassment
- Extent and quality of previous contact with services
- Ability to organise self eg. to get to appointments, to put plans into action

### Staff characteristics and behaviour

- Personal qualities eg. personality, warmth, empathy, positive regard
- Skills eg. building rapport, listening skills, creative solutions
- Attitudes eg. being hopeful, accepting and non-judgemental
- Continuity ie. being able to see the same person over a long period of time
- Managing interactions (ability to contain emotions and make person feel safe)
- Collaborative approach – working with people, not imposing on them
- Managing endings (so person feels able to return if necessary)

### Service characteristics

- Visibility – do people know the service is there?
- Outreach – degree to which it takes services to people
- Accessibility eg. location, transport links, opening times
- Flexibility eg. different options for keeping in contact
- Confidentiality
- Links with community
- Skills mix – having the right staff
- Gate-keeping (who is referred/which referrals are accepted)
- Allocation of resources (money, facilities, priority given to service)

### Social factors

- Attitudes – towards the problem and those who seek help
- Stigma – the negative perception of individuals with particular characteristics
- Taboos – things that cannot be talked about
- Consequences of engaging with services eg. impact on work opportunities

---

Intellectual Disabilities and Personality Disorder: An integrated approach
© Pavilion Publishing and Media Ltd and its licensors 2014.

Engagement is important as, without it, people struggle with problems on their own or, if they seek help, treatment may not be completed. This increases the risk of crises and of negative outcomes.

# Engagement and individuals with personality disorder

It is widely recognised that individuals with personality disorder often have difficulties engaging with services. Individuals may not seek treatment. If they do seek help they may not attend consistently, may leave before treatment has finished or may only partially comply with treatment. When seeking to improve engagement it is important to understand the characteristics of individuals with personality disorder, staff teams, services and wider society that contribute to these difficulties.

## Individual factors

Individuals with personality disorder have a number of characteristics that can make it difficult for them to engage with services. Individuals may have low self-esteem and feel that they do not deserve or would not benefit from help. They may become angry or frustrated with staff and be unable to inhibit expressing this. Individuals may be suspicious of others and lack the trust or social skills to build working relationships with staff. They may have patterns of thinking that lead them to misinterpret staff intentions. For some, a sense of entitlement may lead them to make impossible demands on staff trying to help them. Others may not perceive that they have a problem or not understand that there is anything that can be done to address the difficulties they experience. The factors underlying these characteristics have been explored in earlier chapters (see Box 13.3).

| Box 13.3: Individual factors that make engagement difficult | |
| --- | --- |
| ■ Low self-esteem | Chapter 2 |
| ■ Difficulties managing emotions | Chapter 3 |
| ■ Difficulties with relationships | Chapter 4 & 5 |
| ■ Unhelpful thinking patterns | Chapter 7 |
| ■ Not recognising problems/need for change | Chapter 12 |

# Experiences of services

In addition, many individuals with personality disorder have had negative experiences when they have tried to seek help. These negative experiences make them more reluctant to seek help in the future and make it harder for them to establish trusting, working relationships with staff.

# Staff characteristics and behaviour

The attitude, knowledge and skills of staff who come into contact with individuals with personality disorder have also been found to contribute to the difficulties individuals have engaging with services.

### Negative attitudes

Many staff have negative attitudes towards people with personality disorder. They may hold the outdated belief that personality disorder is untreatable. They may have negative views of individuals with personality disorder using terms such as 'time-wasters', 'difficult', 'manipulative', or 'attention seekers'. Where staff hold such negative views, individuals are likely to feel that they are blamed for their problems. Individuals with personality disorder may feel that staff are prejudiced against them, are belittling or patronising them. Consequently, individuals may feel rejected, that they are a nuisance or that there is no point attending appointments as there is nothing that can be done to help them.

### Lack of skills or confidence

Some staff are more positive towards individuals with personality disorder but feel a lack of knowledge and skills to help them. They may try to direct individuals with personality disorder to other services. While this may be well intentioned, the individual with personality disorder is still likely to feel rejected and will be less likely to seek help in the future.

If unskilled staff try to help individuals with personality disorder they may be overwhelmed by the intensity of the individual's distress and the amount of time that the individual needs. This can lead to the individual with personality disorder feeling unsafe and uncontained. It can also lead to the member of staff experiencing burnout and withdrawing from working with the individual.

### Endings

Sometimes staff are able to work well with individuals and progress is made. However, endings are very hard for individuals with personality disorder. Hence things can deteriorate if ending the work is not handled carefully. The individual is likely to feel abandoned, that staff only care for them when they are ill and do not value them when they are well. Remembering the pain the individual felt on ending may discourage them from engaging with treatment in the future.

# Services

Many services do not see helping individuals with personality disorder as their responsibility. GPs generally do not feel they have the skills to help individuals with personality disorder and will usually refer them on to other services. Most existing mental health services were set up at a time when personality disorder was seen as untreatable and consequently they may not see themselves as the right service to treat individuals with personality disorder. They may refer on to specialist services that again may not see this as their job and these services may refer them back to their GP. If individuals go to A&E after self-harming they may encounter staff who consider that the individual with personality disorder is abusing a service that is for people who are 'really ill'.

Individuals who become caught up in this cycle of rejection can become increasingly disillusioned with services and may be reluctant to approach them except when totally desperate. These issues have been recognised and there is now a national personality disorder strategy that seeks to address these issues. However, change takes time and old attitudes and lack of skills remain an issue.

## Model of care

Most health services are designed to offer short courses of treatment that stop as soon as the individual recovers (the 'acute' model of care). This model of care does not work well for individuals with personality disorder who tend to need long term, low level contact to help them remain stable and prevent crises (the 'chronic' model of care). Hence, even when staff have the skills to manage endings well, the service model may push them into ending contact in a way that is unhelpful to the individual.

The need for on-going contact is being increasingly recognised in treatment approaches designed for individuals with borderline personality disorder such as DBT. These are designed to be carried out over longer time periods, often 18–24 months. However, these services are expensive to run (although they may be highly cost-effective in the longer term) and are still not widely available.

Other practical aspects of services may make them unattractive or inaccessible to individuals with personality disorder, for example, opening times or the need for a formal referral. These practical aspects were explored in Chapter 12.

## Stigma

The diagnosis of personality disorder carries many negative associations in society (see Chapter 1). Individuals may avoid services for fear of being labelled. They may also be embarrassed or ashamed to use mental health services. These feelings can make individuals more reluctant to seek help and more likely to drop out of treatment.

# Engagement and individuals with intellectual disabilities

Individuals with intellectual disabilities generally engage well once they come into contact with professionals and support workers. Many individuals with intellectual disabilities are socially isolated and consequently may enjoy contact with paid carers and professionals. However, there is a risk that individuals will misunderstand the professionals' roles and view them as friends or potential partners (see Chapter 5). Such confusions over roles can complicate the process of engagement with services.

Many less able individuals with intellectual disabilities will have lifelong contact with services. For these individuals the main issues tend to be referrals made on their behalf, without the individual being involved in or made aware of the referral. This can raise issues of consent and capacity.

For the most able individuals, living relatively independent lives, their intellectual disabilities are likely to make it more difficult for them to understand their own needs, to seek help and to organise themselves to see treatment through. Some of these individuals may feel stigmatised by being viewed as having intellectual disabilities and may avoid services with the term in their title. They may prefer to use mainstream services.

Services for individuals with intellectual disabilities have traditionally been organised on a 'chronic' health care model, providing long-term support and contact, for example, through an annual review process. However, with cost constraints many services are moving to a more 'acute' model of care; working to referrals for specific pieces of work with cases then being closed.

# Engagement and individuals with personality disorder and intellectual disabilities

Engagement with individuals with intellectual disabilities and personality disorder is likely to be influenced by the issues associated with both personality disorder and having intellectual disabilities. Individual factors associated with personality disorder (such as place on the change cycle and cognitive distortions) are likely to influence their ability to engage with services. Their intellectual disabilities will to make it harder for them to understand issues and organise themselves. Some individuals may feel doubly stigmatised by the labels 'personality disorder' and 'intellectual disabilities' and may want to avoid both mental health and intellectual disabilities services.

Like their colleagues in mental health, staff in intellectual disabilities services may hold negative attitudes or lack the knowledge and skills to work with these individuals. However, intellectual disabilities services are often more sympathetic to individuals with long-term needs as this is a characteristic of the population they serve.

Many individuals with mild intellectual disabilities and personality disorder will have had experience of being treated in acute mental health wards or of being treated by A&E before being directed to intellectual disabilities services. For some individuals these will have been positive experiences. Sadly, for many these will have been unpleasant, rejecting or even damaging experiences. These experiences may make it harder for them to engage with staff when they are offered support from intellectual disabilities services.

In addition, as explored in Chapter 12, services for individuals with intellectual disabilities are not designed to deal with crises. This mismatch can have a negative impact on the individual's relationship with the service and can hinder engagement.

## Enhancing engagement

The key to enhancing engagement with individuals with intellectual disabilities and personality disorder is to understand that the process **must be led by staff and services**. Individuals with intellectual disabilities and personality disorder are not in a position to change how they respond to services. It is too easy to blame the individual if they have not sought help or have not responded to the help offered. Rather it is for services to develop a greater understanding of personality disorder, the needs of individuals and what helps and hinders their engagement with services. Individuals may be able to give helpful and insightful opinions about the support they need and have (or haven't) received if approached thoughtfully and sensitively. However, individuals are unlikely to volunteer this information and they need services to listen to them if their insights are to be used constructively.

It is important to understand that even when staff and services get things right, individuals may not engage fully with the service. It may take several contacts for the individual to build up trust and be in the right place mentally to work with a service. Some may be so fearful that they only engage when compelled to, for example, being detained under the Mental Health Act. The secret is to do the right things and keep doing the right things in the knowledge that they are most likely to engage the individual in the long term.

# Staff development

In order to engage individuals with intellectual disabilities and personality disorder staff need knowledge, positive attitudes, skills and emotional resilience.

## Knowledge

Staff will need to understand personality disorders, what causes them and how they appear in individuals with intellectual disabilities. They also need a good understanding of the approaches that are helpful for these individuals. It is also important to have a good understanding of human motivation and the change process as this can be critical in establishing how to work with an individual at any one time. All of these are explored in earlier chapters of this book.

## Positive attitude

Sound, up-to-date knowledge provides the basis for developing positive attitudes. First, this dispels the old-fashioned belief that personality disorder cannot be treated. This creates the opportunity to develop hope, optimism and high expectations for change. Second, it challenges the negative perceptions of behaviours shown by individuals with personality disorder by identifying the underlying causes and functions served by challenging behaviours. With this understanding negative labels such as 'attention seeking' and 'manipulative' can be replaced with less blaming, more constructive terms such as 'attachment seeking', 'survival strategies' and 'emotional distress'.

## Skills

Many skills needed generally to work with individuals with intellectual disabilities and personality disorder are explored fully in the earlier chapters of this book (for example, active listening, emotional validation, authoritative support style). Perhaps the most important skill for enhancing engagement that has not been explored so far is timing.

To maintain engagement it is important to match the skills used not just to what the individual might need overall but to what matters to them at that particular time. In addition to thinking about where the individual is on the change cycle (see Chapter 12), it can be helpful to think about what stage treatment is at (see Box 13.4).

---

### Box 13.4: Stages in treatment

- Keeping safe/managing crises
- Establishing a working relationship, and dealing with immediate problems (such as panic attacks or depression)
- Working together to create a long-term support plan (positive behaviour support plan and crisis plan)
- Learning skills to control feelings and impulses
- Exploring, processing and potentially resolving longstanding psychological issues

---

The approach to the individual and the skills needed are different at each step in the treatment process. For example, when in crisis the individual needs to be emotionally and physically contained and it is unhelpful to explore their understanding of issues or try to teach new skills (see Chapter 12). In contrast, once an individual is ready to learn new skills a much more active style of interaction is needed.

Using the skills appropriate to the point individuals are at will enhance engagement. If the issues related to one stage are successfully resolved the individual may be more open and willing to engage in the work necessary for the next stage.

## Creating engagement

The first interactions with an individual will set the tone for their work with that service and can strongly influence the quality of their engagement. First, interactions may be planned and structured, for example, a referral for anxiety or moving into a new home. At other times they may be the result of a crisis, for example, an urgent referral or emergency admission. In a crisis situation engagement will be promoted by following the approach presented in Chapter 12.

Regardless of whether the first contact is routine or crisis, it needs to be warm, accepting and the individual should feel that they have been listened to. These early interactions also need to begin building trust. The acronym SET has been used to summarise the qualities needed in these interactions (see Box 13.5).

---

## Box 13.5: Effective communication

Effective communication should include three elements:

1. **S**upport: commitment to and wish to help the individual

2. **E**mpathy: letting the individual know that you are aware of what they are experiencing

3. **T**ruth: accurate and honest information eg. what will happen, what is understood about the situation, given without judgement or anger

Kreisman J & Straus H (1991)

---

## Telling the truth

The hardest element of SET to maintain is often 'Truth'. Staff may be reluctant to tell the truth for a number of reasons. They may fear the individual will become angry and might even physically assault them if the news is not what the individual wants to hear. This reason for withholding information is particularly reinforcing for individual staff members as it usually postpones the emotional reaction until the time that someone else tells the individual. However doing this will damage that staff member's relationship with the individual. The individual may well be angry with that staff member when they find out the truth and will be much less likely to trust them in the future, even disbelieving them when they are telling the truth.

Sometimes staff may withhold information out of misjudged kindness; they do not want the individual to be upset. They feel that the individual will not understand the facts, particularly if things are complex. Sometimes the truth is uncomfortable, for example, staff may not want to admit that they have no control over certain events.

Staff may also be concerned about the impact of the individual's intellectual disabilities on their ability to understand complex issues, particularly those involving the future, long timescales or with a number of possible outcomes. They may also be concerned about overwhelming the individual with too much information or a multitude of possibilities.

Dishonesty also makes it much harder for staff teams to give a consistent message. There is usually one truth, however there are as many untrue answers as there are team members. Inconsistent messages can often cause more confusion and distress than the painful truth staff were trying to avoid.

## Expectations

In early interactions staff should also make clear what is expected of the individual in the future. They should explain that the individual will be expected to actively work with the staff team to achieve agreed goals and to eventually do more for themselves. It may be helpful to present this in the form of a contract or a more general plan with stages in it (using a format that the individual can understand). If the individual will be expected to leave the service or the intervention is intended to come to an end, this should be gently mentioned in the earliest stages so that the individual does not make up their own plan and then feel let down when it does not reflect reality.

# Sustaining engagement

Once things have got off to a good start it is important to pay attention to sustaining engagement. Individuals with intellectual disabilities and personality disorder are at risk of giving up on services. Often the problems only become apparent once the individual has been working with a service for a while; the individual does not attend appointments consistently, does not make the progress expected, fails to co-operate with efforts to help them or experiences repeated crises. This may be related to two different factors:

- where the individual is on the change cycle
- the impact the individual has in triggering unhelpful reactions in staff members.

## Change cycle and motivation

A breakdown in engagement after a promising start can be understood by looking at where the individual is on the change cycle (see Chapter 12). If the individual is at the pre-contemplation or contemplation stages, they may have initially engaged with services because of their level of distress or need for help with practical problems. However, once the distress had subsided or the problem is resolved, they did not understand the need to work on the underlying issues that had created the problem. In this situation staff need to use motivational interviewing and the change enhancing strategies given in Chapter 6 to increase the individual's motivation to engage with staff.

Lack of engagement can be less visible in residential settings. An individual may be willing to continue to live in a setting, but closer examination shows that they spend little time engaged in constructive activities, let others do things for them that they are able to do themselves and avoid anything actively therapeutic. Such individuals may have slipped into a safe, passive and dependent role. This can be difficult to challenge as efforts encourage independence and activity will be experienced as rejection and abandonment. The motivational techniques described in Chapter 6 can be helpful in addressing this. Other individuals may show their lack of engagement with residential settings by demanding to move home after the initial 'honeymoon' period is over. This is often related to underlying core beliefs the individual holds about 'perfect care' and 'black and white' thinking such that small, inevitable disappointments are seen as proof that the placement is no good. Rather than simply finding a series of new placements for the individual, it may be helpful to explore their thinking with them using the approaches in Chapter 7.

## Triggering unhelpful staff emotions and behaviour

Warmth, empathy and active listening are often sufficient to make a positive initial contact with individuals with personality disorder. However, sustaining engagement is often much harder than creating the initial connection. Staff teams need to build the skills to manage their own emotional reactions to repeated rebuffs and rejection. They need the emotional resilience to bounce back again and again. They also need to understand the way that individuals with intellectual disabilities and personality disorder can trigger difficult emotions and unhelpful behaviours in those supporting them.

Individuals with intellectual disabilities and personality disorder unconsciously trigger the emotions that they themselves are feeling in those who support them. For example, if the individual fears rejection, they are likely to make staff feel rejected, if the individual feels hopeless, they are likely to make staff feel ineffectual. This will be true for all staff members but will have a particular impact on staff who have a vulnerability to that feeling. (The mechanisms that underlie this process are explored more fully in Chapter 14.).

Individuals may also behave in ways that can trigger unhelpful behaviours in staff. For example, a member of staff who needs to rescue people may be vulnerable to becoming over-involved in trying to keep an individual safe. A staff member who needs to feel in control may be drawn to over-restrictive practices in an effort to contain an individual who appears out of control. Staff may be drawn into behaving in ways that replicate the interactions the individual has had with parents or other carers in the past. These patterns of behaviour are explored more in Chapter 14.

If staff do not have good self-awareness and do not think about how they are feeling in relation to what the individual is going through, the situation can escalate. It can lead to significant distress, potentially damaging their working relationship with the individual and, in extreme situations, to blaming the individual and engaging in inappropriate, potentially abusive management approaches. Box 13.6 gives some questions that help explore areas where individual staff may be vulnerable emotionally.

---

## Box 13.6: Soul-searching questions

Knowing the honest answer to these questions will help staff understand the things that might 'get to' them when working with individuals with intellectual disability and personality disorder.

- Do you need the individual to like you?
- Do you see the individual as a child?
- Do you need the individual to be dependent?
- Do you need the individual to be grateful?
- Do you need the individual to get better?
- Do you need to fix things?
- Do you need to feel competent?
- Do you need to feel wise and have the answers?
- Do you need to feel in control?
- Do you blame victims?
- Do you need to rescue individuals?
- Do you need to protect individuals and keep them safe?
- Do you need other people to be happy all the time?

Be totally honest, pretending your answer to a question is 'no' when really it is 'yes' will not help address the issue.

Adapted from Bell (2005)

---

Warning signs that an individual is triggering unhelpful responses can include intense personal feelings, urges to act in unprofessional ways or frustration and tension in relationships with other members of staff. For other examples see Box 13.7.

Worrying staff behaviours might include staying late to get things done for an individual, neglecting other work, doing things that are not really the staff member's role because of anxiety that others will not do it well enough, or not being able to sleep for worry about the individual.

Staff members need to monitor their own reactions and those of their colleagues. There needs to be informal and formal opportunities to do this, including individual, peer and team supervision. Ways of doing these are discussed in Chapter 14. By engaging in these approaches staff will be able to create and maintain the compassionate distance that is essential for maintaining engagement.

> ## Box 13.7: Staff responses that may damage engagement
>
> - Replicating the negative behaviours of other care figures in the individual's life
> - Acting out intense emotions inappropriately:
>   - Anger
>   - Rejection
>   - Despair
>   - Anxiety, fear and panic
> - Feeling the need to punish the individual or let them 'know what it feels like'
> - Feeling the need to control the individual and 'show them who's boss'
> - Having inappropriate expectations then getting critical or impatient when the individual doesn't meet them
> - Making promises that cannot be kept
> - Being confrontational eg. 'Why don't you....?'
> - Being over persuasive eg. 'You really should......'
> - Blaming the individual eg. 'That is really bad for you.......'
>
> Adapted from Bell (2005)

# Managing endings

If an individual has successfully engaged with a service and this has been sustained it is easy to forget about the importance of ending work thoughtfully. While some individuals will do so well that they never need services again, most will have multiple episodes of care. Endings need to be managed sensitively so that the individual feels that they can return if they need to, without feeling they have failed or let people down. Equally, attention needs to be given to the feelings triggered by the ending. However well the individual may appear, a bad ending can leave them feeling rejected and abandoned. Such feelings will make it hard for them to return if they become unwell in the future or may trigger a relapse.

Leaving an inpatient unit, after a period of treatment, can be particularly difficult for individuals with intellectual disabilities and personality disorder and needs to be managed sensitively. Ideally there should be a carefully planned transition period with the opportunity to build relationships with new staff or build links with the community. Individuals may have spent a lot of time telling staff how much they hate being in hospital and how much they want to leave. It can then be very difficult for them to admit how scared they are about forming new relationships and leaving behind the security of staff who have (hopefully) supported them with compassion during a very difficult time. It can be very helpful for individuals if staff raise these issues in a matter of fact and considerate way. Gentle humour is often helpful at these times. Staff might make comments such as *'I know you are fed up with all of us but it is always difficult to make a new start. Everyone feels a bit frightened when they have to make new relationships'*. This would help create an environment in which the individual feels comfortable to acknowledge their fears.

## Service design

Evidence increasingly shows that to be effective, treatment and support for individuals with personality disorder needs to be proactive, person-centred, intensive, collaborative and, frequently, long term. This is also likely to apply where the individual also has intellectual disabilities. Where service design does not take this into account it can be very hard to sustain engagement. Services need to take a critical look at their contribution to the 'cycle of rejection' rather than blaming individuals for not responding well to what is offered.

When trying to improve a service it can be most helpful to consult 'experts by experience'. These are individuals who have experienced problems and services themselves and are able to give opinions and advice based on that experience. Their insights are invaluable and may be crucial in identifying small but highly significant changes that can be made to improve services and enhance engagement.

## Key learning points

- Engagement is the process of connecting to and working with professionals and services to resolve problems.

- Engagement is influenced by a wide range of factors including characteristics of the individual, the staff and the service.

- Engagement is important because, without it, people struggle with problems on their own or, if they seek help, treatment may not be completed. This increases the risk of crises and of negative outcomes.

- Some individuals with intellectual disabilities and personality disorder may feel doubly stigmatised and may want to avoid both mental health and intellectual disabilities services.

- It is easy to pay too much attention to factors within the individual and to blame them for any problems with engagement.

- It is important to pay attention to the knowledge, skills and attitude of staff team and the design of services.

- A well-skilled staff team with positive attitudes and a good understanding of the needs of individuals with intellectual disabilities and personality disorder will maximise the chances of individuals engaging with and benefiting from services.

# References

Bell L (2005) *Managing Intense Emotions and Overcoming Self-destructive Habits: A self-help manual*. Hove: Routledge.

Kreisman J & Straus H (1991) *I Hate You, Don't Leave Me: Understanding the borderline personality*. New York: Avon books.

# Further reading

NIMHE (2003) *Personality Disorder: No longer a diagnosis of exclusion: policy implementation guidance for the development of services for people with personality disorder*. Leeds: NIMHE. Available at: http://www.candi.nhs.uk/_uploads/documents/miscellaneous/pd-no-longer-a-diagnosis-of-exclusion. pdf (accessed April 2014).

NIMHE (2003) *Breaking the Cycle of Rejection: The personality disorder capabilities framework:* Leeds: NIMHE. Available at: http://www.spn.org.uk/fileadmin/spn/user/*.pdf/Papers/personalitydisorders.pdf (accessed April 2014).

# Chapter 14: Tensions, disagreements and unhelpful responses within and between teams

This chapter explores the way that individuals with intellectual disabilities and personality disorder create strong emotional reactions in those who support them and how this can lead to tensions and disagreements within the teams that support them. It explores a number of psychological concepts that are helpful in making sense of these processes including: 'projection', 'transference', 'countertransference', 'splitting' and 'reciprocal roles'. It looks at how these processes can be managed to avoid teams becoming paralysed and how to enable teams to act together to constructively support individuals. It also examines the long-term consequences of failing to address these issues, such as high staff turnover and burnout.

## Key topics

- Processes influencing interactions between people
- Unhelpful responses triggered by individuals with personality disorder
- Unhelpful responses triggered by individuals with intellectual disabilities
- Unhelpful responses triggered by individuals with intellectual disabilities and personality disorder
- Promoting and maintaining motivated, energised and effective team work
- Team work
- Case discussion
- Supervision
- Recognising burnout
- Preventing burnout

# Processes influencing interactions between people

Interactions and conversations between people appear deceptively simple; one person has something they wish to communicate, they share it with the other person. That person hears and understands what is communicated and makes a response. The process continues in this way with each person understanding the other. However, from some of the issues discussed in earlier chapters it will be clear that the process is by no means so simple in real life. Interactions can be distorted by a wide range of factors, some of which are given in Box 14.1.

---

**Box 14.1: Factors influencing interactions between people**

■ Ability to understand own thoughts, feelings and motivations (mentalising) (Chapters 1, 2 and 3)

■ Ability to express thoughts, feelings and concepts eg. in words, signs, writings

■ Ability to interpret the content of communications

■ Ability to interpret others' thoughts, feelings and motivations (mentalising) (Chapters 1, 2 and 3)

■ Impact of core beliefs, stereotypes and prejudices and cognitive distortions on how situations/communications are understood (Chapter 7)

■ Impact of the emotional state of the person on their thinking (emotional mind/ logical mind/intuitive mind) (Chapters 3 and 7)

■ Impact of past experience

■ Projection (ascribing own, unacceptable feelings to other people)

■ Transference (applying attitudes and feelings from a past situation to a current interaction)

■ Countertransference (past attitudes and feelings are triggered by a current interaction)

■ Splitting (introduced in Chapter 7 but explored more fully in this section)

■ The influence of reciprocal roles (patterns of interaction where one person takes a particular role, pushing the other to take the opposite, partner role eg. attacker – defender)

---

In addition to the factors explored in earlier chapters, the processes of projection, transference, countertransference and reciprocal roles are helpful in understanding how interactions between people can become distorted. These concepts highlight how, in any interaction, people's responses can be shaped not just by the present situation but also by their own past experiences and the past experiences of the person they are interacting with. These concepts are explored more fully in the following sections.

# Projection

Projection is a process by which people unconsciously try to avoid, or defend themselves from, their own unpleasant feelings. For example, someone might be uncomfortable about personal characteristics or behaviours such as their body image, sexual behaviour or uncontrolled anger. Rather than accept and cope with these difficult feelings they 'project' them onto those close to them. The person may show this by being overly critical of the rejected characteristics in others (for example, telling a plump friend that they are fat and should go on a diet). They may also misinterpret well-meant comments as showing that others feel about them in the way they find unacceptable. Projection may be encountered in many different interactions including between family members, within personal relationships, between staff and the individuals they work with and between staff members. Box 14.2 gives an example of how projection might occur within a personal relationship.

---

### Box 14.2: An example of projection

After five years of marriage a woman finds herself becoming bored with her husband and is attracted to a work colleague. She has always believed that marriage is for life and only 'sluts' have affairs. Rather than deal with these feelings she 'projects' these thoughts on to her husband. She accuses him of being bored with her and sees signs of attraction every time he looks at another woman. If he is late home from work, she accuses him angrily of no longer loving her and asks if he is seeing someone else. The husband is initially distraught; he loves his wife and has never thought of anyone else. However, as the groundless attacks continue he begins to wonder if he married the right person. He begins to think about an ex-girlfriend who was kind and supportive and wonders if she is still single…

---

Projection does protect the person from their difficult feelings but at the expense of distorting their relationships with others and preventing open communication. Those around the person feel hurt, confused, misunderstood and unfairly criticised. This can develop into anger and frustration with the person as they continue to misunderstand well-intentioned interactions. Projection can also be a self-fulfilling process. People who initially felt positively towards the person may begin to really feel the negative feelings that are projected onto them.

# Transference

The concept of transference was developed by Freud to explain why some of his patients responded to him in ways that seemed far too intense for the time that they had known each other and did not seem to fit with Freud's behaviour, as a therapist. Freud came to believe that he was triggering the same intense emotions in his patients that they had felt towards their parents or other significant people in their lives. These feelings might be love, hate, fear or anger. He came to think that patients unconsciously 'transferred' feelings and attitudes from a person or situation in the past on to a person or situation in the present. Hence he named the process 'transference'.

---

## Box 14.3: Identifying transference

■ **Is there a mismatch between your comments and the person's reactions?**
  ■ Does it feel as if the person does not hear or see you?
  ■ Does it feel like they are responding to/seeing someone else?
  ■ Is it hard to make sense of their reactions to you?
  ■ Does it feel as if they are seeing or hearing something beyond/different from the message you intended?

■ **Does their reaction seem out of proportion?**
  ■ Saying *'you are the best ever …'* having only just met you
  ■ Bursting into tears at the thought of you having a day off
  ■ Exploding with anger and saying you don't care when you are a few minutes late because of traffic

■ **Do you find yourself wondering:**
  ■ *'What on earth have I done to make them feel like that about me?'*
  ■ *'What ever did I say to make them think that?'*
  ■ *Why is everything I say and do wrong?'*

■ **Does the individual trigger unusual responses in you?** (subtle transference is often only spotted when it triggers countertransference, see next section)

If the answer to any of these questions is 'yes', transference may be occurring.

---

While the process of transference was identified in the context of therapy, it has become understood that this process often occurs in interactions in everyday situations. The extent to which people 'transfer' feelings and expectations from the past on to people they meet in the present varies greatly. Healthy people with good past relationships may not do this to any noticeable degree. However people with difficult past experiences who have been emotionally damaged may project these negative feelings and expectations on to many relationships where they are not appropriate. In effect, such people are not reacting to others they met as unique human beings; rather they are responding to a template from their past, triggered by some characteristic of the person they are interacting with. This can lead to repeated patterns of unhelpful behaviours, such as rejecting help or becoming angry with others. Box 14.3 gives some questions that may help to identify when transference is occurring.

# Countertransference

Freud also came to recognise that aspects of the patient might trigger strong emotions or thoughts in the therapist by connecting with the therapist's past experiences or relationships. Freud called this process 'countertransference'. Where countertransference is not recognised the therapist can find themselves responding in very inappropriate ways, for example, falling in love with a patient and trying to seduce them or being so hostile to them that they are not able to help them.

Although Freud identified countertransference in the context of therapy, it is now recognised that countertransference can occur in other types of interactions between staff and the individuals they support. Box 14.4 gives one way of identifying staff reactions that might be countertransference.

---

### Box 14.4: Identifying counter-transference

■ **Is this reaction characteristic for you? Do you feel like this much of the time?** This response is about you, not the individual you support.

■ **Is the response triggered by something unrelated to the individual you support?** Eg. being hungry, tired, arguing with your partner, problems with the job. This response is about you and your lifestyle, not the individual.

■ **Is the response related to the individual in a direct way?** Eg. are you upset because they are screaming abuse and have broken the new TV? This is an obvious and natural response to the individual's behaviour.

■ **Is this reaction uncharacteristic for you?** Ie. you rarely feel like this and **Is this reaction related to one individual?** This is likely to be countertransference. It is worth exploring this reaction as it may avoid you reacting inappropriately and may help to understand the individual better.

Adapted from Reidbord (2010)

---

# Splitting

Splitting (also termed 'black and white' thinking or 'all-or nothing' thinking) is one of the unhelpful thinking styles explained in Chapter 7. When someone thinks by splitting, things are seen as good or bad, right or wrong, a total success or utter failure. They will see themselves as either 'good' or 'bad' and other people as intimate friends or arch-enemies, victims or oppressors. This thinking style allows no shades of grey or middle way and no recognition that nothing is ever perfect. Splitting makes it very difficult for a person to hold balanced, integrated, stable views of themselves or others.

Splitting is thought to characterise the thinking of very young children (18–36 months). At this age children find it hard to cope with ambiguity. When someone meets the child's needs they are all-good or perfect. When someone frustrates those needs, or is not there when needed, they are all-bad. The process of splitting protects the child from the painful anxiety experienced when trying to make sense of contradictory feelings such as how can you love someone yet also hate them at the same time? As the child develops they learn to cope with this anxiety. This allows them to see that all people have good and bad in them. They learn that when someone they love lets them down they are not a villain; they are just human.

However, some children may not take this next step in the development of their thinking, perhaps because of the way they are treated. For these children this way of viewing other people persists into adulthood. Other people are idolised or demonised. The moment an idolised figure makes a mistake the person may change their view of them to being bad. For those who think in this all or nothing way, other people are split into two completely different groups; the good and the bad. Specific people may swap groups if their behaviour is perceived to no longer fit the group they were in. However, there is no middle ground of flawed but well intentioned and loveable.

## Impact on relationships

Once another has been 'categorised' by the person as an angel or a demon, then the person behaves towards them on that basis. This behaviour is then likely to provoke behaviours in the other person that reinforce that view. For example, a 'good' person may be greeted with smiles and jokes and will respond positively. However a 'bad' person may be greeted with *'Oh, no not you again, that's ruined my day.'* It would be natural for the second person to respond in a less positive way. However, this is likely to be seen as more evidence of dislike and the other person will continue to be seen as 'bad'.

Intellectual Disabilities and Personality Disorder: An integrated approach
© Pavilion Publishing and Media Ltd and its licensors 2014.

At any one time all the people known to the person will occupy one of these categories. Often family members will have set roles, for example, one parent is good while the other is bad. These will be maintained despite evidence that contradicts this view. The person will often be very sensitive to perceived criticism of the 'good' family member, as if the criticism is believed, they will then have two 'bad' parents.

If, however, someone 'good' does something that upsets the person enough this may result in a switch to perceiving them as 'bad' with associated change in behaviour towards them. This is likely to be accompanied by an intense emotional reaction with the person sometimes shouting, being verbally or even physically aggressive.

Sometimes a pattern can emerge of all new people being seen as 'good' only to later be rejected when they are found to be only human. People showing this pattern often spend all their time seeking out new relationships in search of the perfect person who will never let them down.

## Reciprocal roles

A role is the function or part played by a person in a situation. In many social situations roles are related to each other. For example, the role of doctor relates to that of patient, while the role of teacher relates to that of pupil. These roles have a function, for example, the doctor is there to treat the patient. However, they also have a part or pattern of behaviour associated with that function. In the example of doctor-patient, the doctor is expected to try to find out what is wrong with the patient and suggest how it might be treated. The patient is expected to be unwell in some way and to co-operate with the doctor in finding out what is wrong and treating it. In this way the interaction follows a characteristic pattern.

Some reciprocal roles are linked clearly to functions, others are associated with relationships, for example parent-child, and some are associated with particular ways of interacting such as leader-follower. Some other examples of healthy reciprocal roles are given in Box 14.5.

In many such interactions there will be social pressure to follow the expected pattern of interaction. Mostly the roles taken are helpful or harmless and the pressure is subtle so most people are unaware of this process and slip unconsciously into the expected role.

| Box 14.5: Healthy reciprocal roles |
| --- |
| ■ Carer – cared for |
| ■ Comforter – comforted |
| ■ Teacher – learner |
| ■ Supporter – supported |
| ■ Nurturing – nurtured |
| ■ Healer – healed |
| ■ Protector – protected |
| ■ Empowering – empowered |
| ■ Complimentary – complimented |
| ■ Valuing – valued |

## Developing reciprocal roles

The development of reciprocal roles begins in childhood interactions with parents and continues through later social experiences. The child learns both their own role in the interaction (such as being cared for) and also the parent's role (in this case carer). Children will often act out or practice reciprocal roles in their play. For example, they will comfort, teach or reprimand their toys, often using the same words that their parents have used to the child. Consequently, most people have extensive repertoires of roles.

Within any particular culture many of the experiences that lead to the development of roles will be shared. Consequently, many people will share similar templates for reciprocal roles. This means in many situations if a person adopts one of a pair of reciprocal roles the other person will instinctively adopt the other role. However, very different experiences can lead to a different repertoire of roles. This can become very clear if a person moves to a different country and suddenly has no idea what is expected of them in social interactions.

## Unhelpful and harmful reciprocal roles

Within a particular culture the range of roles a person develops may be restricted by negative life experiences such as loss, deprivation or abuse. As well as limiting the opportunities to develop helpful roles, such experiences make people vulnerable to absorbing roles that are unhelpful or even harmful outside of the survival situation in which the role was learnt. These roles are often characterised by extreme and inflexible behaviours, with no 'middle ground' or adaptability. Box 14.6 gives examples of some of the unhealthy reciprocal roles that may be learnt in difficult circumstances.

---

## Box 14.6: Some harmful or unhelpful reciprocal roles

- Controller, dominator – controlled, submitter
- Controller – rebel
- Abuser/bully – victim
- Neglecting – abandoned
- Criticising and conditionally loving – criticised and conditionally loved
- Contemptuous – contemptible
- Attacker – attacked
- Punisher – punished

---

People who have absorbed these harmful reciprocal roles are likely to act these out through other interactions in their lives. For example, a person who had learnt the roles 'contemptuous – contemptible', might respond to comments intended to be constructive criticism as a personal attack. They might reply either in a highly aggressive attacking way or be totally devastated by the comments. Such, seemingly inappropriate, responses may then draw the other person into becoming more critical, with responses such as *'Why the overreaction? It's totally out of order to speak to me like that!'*

## Pressure to respond in particular ways

The processes of projection, transference, countertransference and reciprocal roles all have the effect of complicating interactions. The person is not responding to the communications of the other person in the current context: they are responding to a misperception of the situation that is distorted by their own emotions and past relationships. This process puts unintended, intense pressure on the other person to respond in the same, negative way as people from the past. The comments or behaviours that create this behaviour might be likened to emotional 'hooks' that 'reel' the other person in. For example, it is very hard to avoid being pleased and responding positively to someone who says *'You're the best, no one understands me like you do'*. In contrast it is hard not to become angry if, after great efforts to sort something out, the response is *'Why have you done this, I didn't ask you to, you're just like all the others, trying to control me'*. Such interactions may trigger responses such as feelings of unfairness, anger, hostility, rejection, smothering or paralysis in the other person. Other examples of hooking comments are given later in this chapter. If the other person does not understand what is happening, it becomes very difficult to make or sustain a positive relationship. If the other person resists this pressure and does not behave in the expected way, or directly challenges the role adopted, this can cause the person to flip into the opposite role or a different role altogether.

# Unhelpful responses triggered by individuals with personality disorder

Individuals with personality disorder (particularly borderline personality disorder) frequently rely on projection and splitting as ways to protect themselves from painful emotions and ambiguity. Their difficult past experiences mean that they may 'transfer' past negative relationships onto others, often triggering countertransference reactions in those who support them. Many individuals with personality disorder think about themselves and other people in the extreme terms characteristic of splitting. They have not learnt to be able to integrate good and bad aspects and consequently are unable to see themselves and others as flawed but loveable human beings. They also often have a narrow range of unhealthy reciprocal roles. This means that they may switch between extreme behaviours such as being totally controlling or totally passive. These switches can happen in response to the behaviour of others but also in response to thoughts, memories or mood changes. The impact of all these processes is to make their behaviour appear unpredictable and unreasonable to the person interacting with them. Everything a staff member says or does seems to be misunderstood and does not have the effect the member of staff intended or hoped for.

These ways of interacting can trigger a range of unhelpful reactions in individual staff members, within and between staff teams (such as blaming or wanting to punish the individual). These responses can lead staff to act in uncharacteristic and sometimes unprofessional ways such as being rude to individuals or overstepping professional boundaries (see Chapter 5).

Sometimes the reaction of one staff member will be reflected throughout the whole team. The team may work heroically to rescue the individual or will unite in rejecting them as not being suitable to work with. More commonly, the individual will trigger different reactions in each staff member they come into contact with. Staff members will then see the individual in very different ways, leading to tensions and conflict about how best to support the individual. These conflicts can be very severe; staff members who usually work well together can find themselves arguing furiously or questioning each other's competence.

Individuals with personality disorder often come into contact with a number of different services. These tensions and conflicts can then arise between the different teams. The individual can end up being given conflicting and inconsistent advice in an atmosphere of chaos, fear or anger.

# Unhelpful responses triggered by individuals with intellectual disabilities

Individuals with intellectual disabilities can also trigger unhelpful responses in the staff who support them. These reactions have their origins in a number of unhelpful stereotypes about intellectual disabilities rather than necessarily the patterns of interaction between the individual and staff members. However, there may be some interaction between behaviour and stereotypes, such that certain behaviours by the individual may be more likely to trigger some stereotypes than others. For example, an individual showing extreme challenging behaviour may be seen as a menace or less than human, while a survivor of abuse might be seen as an object of pity. Some of the most commonly held stereotypes are given in Box 14.7.

---

### Box 14.7: Common stereotypes of individuals with intellectual disabilities

- Eternal child/innocent – sweet and gentle
- Object of pity/victims – weak/tragic
- Object of charity/a burden on society
- Non-sexual being
- Source of profound wisdom (eg. Forest Gump)
- Object of ridicule/clown/court jester – butt of jokes
- Outcast – not part of society, should be hidden
- Less than fully human – not part of the human race, different
- Object of fear, horror or menace to society

---

These stereotypes can have a profound influence on the way individuals with intellectual disabilities are treated and the reactions staff may have to such individuals. These responses may vary depending on whether the individual conforms to or challenges the stereotype. For example, if an individual is seen as an eternal child they may be protected and comforted. However if that individual tries to assert their independence, staff may respond by being controlling and punishing. Where the individual is viewed as less than fully human staff may try to exclude and avoid that individual. They may react with fear or anger if the individual tries to be included. The negative impact of such views on the health care received by individuals with intellectual disabilities is discussed in Chapter 8.

Intelligence is a quality that is highly valued in Western society. Staff who hold this value may find it difficult to recognise the extent of an individual's intellectual disabilities at the same time as valuing that individual. This can lead to an unhelpful response of denying the extent of the individual's intellectual disabilities. This, in turn, can lead to the individual not receiving the help that they need and, consequently, struggling. However, if staff recognise that the individual needs more help, they must also see the extent of their intellectual disabilities. To avoid this some staff will then see the individual as 'lazy', 'stubborn' or 'difficult' and as not worthy of help.

While all staff may hold unhelpful stereotypes, there is evidence to suggest that these are more commonly held by untrained staff and staff who do not regularly work with individuals with intellectual disabilities. These differences can create tensions within and between teams. For example, a specialist intellectual disabilities team may advocate that a crisis team should support individuals with intellectual disabilities when they are in crisis. However the crisis team may say that individuals with intellectual disabilities should be excluded from their service as the team lacks the skills to support them.

## Unhelpful responses triggered by individuals with intellectual disabilities and personality disorder

Individuals with intellectual disabilities and personality disorder will trigger strong emotions in staff teams in the same manner as more able individuals with personality disorder. They are likely to use projection and splitting to protect themselves from painful emotions and ambiguity. They are likely to have learnt a narrow range of unhelpful reciprocal roles.

However, this pattern will be complicated by the stereotypes that staff hold about individuals with intellectual disabilities. This adds another layer of complexity when trying to understand the tensions and conflicts that arise in the teams that support them. Staff will be responding to the behaviour of the individual that arises from their personality disorder, as seen through the 'filter' of the stereotypes they hold about intellectual disabilities.

A common reaction is for staff members to 'split' around whether or not they see the 'intellectual disabilities' or the 'personality disorder'. Rather than seeing that both are part of the individual and need to be addressed together, staff may argue about which service is the most appropriate to support the individual and will focus only on the needs arising from one or other of the conditions.

If the effects of projection, transference, countertransference, splitting, reciprocal roles and stereotypes are not understood then staff can become confused; the individual's reactions will not make sense. Individuals may be seen in negative ways and may be given labels such as 'demanding', 'manipulative', 'attention seeking' or 'over-dependent'. This process will also trigger intense reactions in staff. Some examples of these reactions are given in Box 14.8.

---

### Box 14.8: Potential staff responses if interpersonal processes are not understood

- Righteous indignation – rescuing the individual from inadequate/incompetent/ uncaring situation
- Anxiety and panic – frantic efforts to save individual or paralysed and overwhelmed
- Blaming the individual – *'They never do anything I suggest to help'*
- Being angry with individual – *'Why on earth did you do that?'*
- Rejecting individual – *'I don't want to work with them'*
- Punishing the individual – *'You've missed two appointments, I can't offer you another one for six weeks'*
- Trying to control the individual
- Feeling de-skilled – *'I don't have the skills to work with them'*
- Exhaustion – *'I can't do any more'*
- Hopeless – *'It will never change'*
- Helpless – *'There is nothing I can do'*

---

There is a risk of staff being drawn into a reciprocal role and acting out parts that are unhelpful for the individual or even unprofessional. Box 14.9 gives some examples of unprofessional behaviours that sadly occur far too frequently when staff are supporting individuals with intellectual disabilities and personality disorder.

## Box 14.9: Unprofessional responses that may be triggered in staff by individuals with intellectual disabilities and personality disorder

- Being rude to the individual, colleagues or other services
- Taking on roles or responsibilities that are not part of the job
- Taking on actions that are beyond their experience or training
- Refusing to do things that are part of their responsibilities
- Not doing things they are trained to do because of loss of confidence
- Working excessive hours
- Neglecting other individuals or important parts of their workload
- Rejecting advice and support from colleagues because it does not fit with their experience of the individual
- Failing to take important actions such as contacting child protection/police
- Seeking advice and supervision from multiple sources but not following any
- Failing to keep accurate records
- Not giving pain relief while treating injuries
- Blaming, criticising the individual and giving invalidating responses
- Over-use of restrictive interventions
- Over/under prescription of medication

Within a team, some staff may be drawn into becoming critical, controlling, rejecting or neglectful. This can lead to repeating past patterns of rejection and even abuse. Other staff might become overprotective and overinvolved, making promises of special care that they are unable to deliver. This can undermine independence and repeat patterns of overdependence and over-involvement. Staff may feel rejected, powerless and incompetent. Staff may become demoralised, lose empathy with the individual and may become emotionally and physically exhausted creating the state called 'burnout' (see Box 14.10).

---

## Box 14.10: Burnout

Burnout is a state of long-term exhaustion, diminished interest and loss of sense of achievement. It was identified in the 1970s by Maslach. Some of the signs of burnout are given below.

**Emotional signs**

- Feeling overwhelmed
- Feeling ineffective, sense of failure and self-doubt
- Feeling helpless, trapped, defeated
- Feeling empty
- Lacking motivation, everything is too much effort
- Being 'beyond caring'
- Feeling unhappy and dissatisfied
- Feeling mentally drained
- Mental health problems eg. depression

**Thoughts**

- Negative outlook – nothing will change, nothing will make a difference
- Cynical attitudes – people deserve the problems they have, blaming the victim

**Physical signs**

- Feeling physically drained
- Tired all the time
- Headaches/back ache
- Change to appetite
- Problems sleeping
- Increased vulnerability to physical illness
- Stress-related illnesses

**Behavioural signs**

- Reduced job performance, coming in late, going home early
- Putting things off, not getting things done
- Detachment, not engaging with others
- Taking frustrations out on others, shouting, criticising, undermining
- Use of food, alcohol, drugs to cope

---

In this situation staff teams are likely to experience conflict between team members. Each team member will hold a different view of the individual and how they should be helped. Team members may begin to pull in different directions, criticise each other and cease to work in a co-ordinated way. Where more than one team is involved in the individual's care, conflicts are likely to develop between the different teams.

In addition to the stress this places on individual staff members, this conflict can lead to fragmented, uncoordinated and inconsistent support for the individual. This can lead to individuals or their families being justifiably dissatisfied with the care they have received. This can lead to criticism, anger and complaints. Where care is fragmented and uncoordinated, risks may go unnoticed or not be effectively managed. This can place individuals or staff members at risk and, in extreme situations, may lead to harm.

The intensity of emotional reactions and unrealistic expectations that are associated with some individuals' search for the perfect carer can also leave staff vulnerable to unfounded allegations. Despite delivering appropriate services they may be accused of neglect or be unfairly criticised.

## Promoting and maintaining motivated, energised and effective team work

There are a number of measures that can protect teams from the potential negative effects of supporting individuals with intellectual disabilities and personality disorder and others that can be taken to address problems at an early stage. Some of these measures can be taken by individual staff members, others need a co-ordinated team approach and good management systems. The aim of all these measures is for all staff to stay motivated, energised and effective.

The 'deskilling' effect of individuals with intellectual disabilities and personality disorder is so powerful that staff often think that special measures or the input of an expert 'guru' or 'tsar' is needed. However, all the actions proposed below are the standard approaches for building good teams and resolving conflicts. Perhaps the most difficult step in maintaining a positive approach is to believe that individuals with intellectual disabilities and personality disorder can be managed effectively by a confident and united team that works professionally, within clear boundaries. Once this belief is established, the rest is straightforward.

# Training and understanding

To work effectively and manage emotional reactions, staff need a good level of understanding of:

■ personality disorder in individuals with intellectual disabilities, the problems presented and how these can be addressed

■ the processes by which individuals can cause intense emotional reactions in those who support them

■ their own attitudes, motivations and areas of emotional vulnerability.

The better staff members understand these areas, the easier it is for them to spot the signs of projection, transference, countertransference and unhelpful reciprocal roles. Self-reflection will help them recognise their own reactions and also notice situations where the views of team members are becoming polarised with the risk of splits developing.

It is important that all members of a team who work with individuals with intellectual disabilities and personality disorder have appropriate training. This includes administration staff who may be dealing with 'urgent' phone calls and apparent 'crises'. If some staff have a good understanding and others are untrained this can act to increase rather than decrease tensions and splits.

# Individual staff

At the level of individual staff members there are two areas that need to be addressed:

■ creating a work context that will help them remain positive

■ developing the skills to spot the behaviours that individuals show that can draw staff members into behaving in unhelpful ways and how to respond if this is taking place.

## Work context

Box 14.11 summarises the factors that need to be present in the work situation to prevent staff becoming overstretched physically and emotionally. A sense of humour and permission to laugh (provided the joke is not at the expense of the individual) when things get tough are also very helpful in relieving stress and tension.

---

### Box 14.11: Preventing burnout

Ensuring that the following are in place will help staff stay motivated, energised and effective.

■ Training
■ Peer support
■ Reflection: space to think about self and work
■ Supervision: individual, peer and team
■ Clear job role: maintaining boundaries, using contracts
■ Balanced workload
■ Teamwork
■ Support network
■ Work-life balance
■ Relaxation and stress busting
■ Rest – sleep, short breaks and holidays

---

These are the same factors that were identified in Chapter 12 in helping staff cope with crisis situations.

## Supervision

The importance of good supervision is often underestimated and it can be one of the first things to slip when situations become pressurised. When working with individuals with intellectual disabilities and personality disorder, supervision is essential to maintain perspective and a positive attitude. Box 14.12 gives some pointers for making supervision effective.

---

### Box 14.12: Effective supervision

■ Create an environment where it is safe to discuss (negative) emotional reactions to individuals and other members of staff

■ Protect time – ensure that case discussion is not squeezed out by management issues

■ Use supervision to work through the countertransference checklist and to explore any issues that this raises

■ Look for signs of taking up unhealthy reciprocal roles and for the beginnings of unprofessional behaviour (eg. shift in priorities, taking calls when not at work)

■ Review professional boundaries – how are they being challenged? Have they been breached?

■ Problem solve: look for ways of resolving underlying issues eg. arranging case discussion, arranging personal counselling to resolve own issues, agreeing contracts and boundaries for future work

---

## Spotting emotional 'hooks'

Once there is a supportive work context it is important to ensure that staff have the skills and insight to identify when they are being drawn or 'hooked' into particular roles or positions in relation to the individual with personality disorder and potential sources of conflict with other team members. Box 14.13 gives some common roles individuals may take, indicative comments and some ways staff may react.

## Box 14.13: Common roles individuals may take, indicative comments and some ways staff may react

| Role and common 'hooking' comments | Common staff reactions |
|---|---|
| **Seeking perfect care giver** | |
| 'You're the only one who can help me' | Feel special |
| 'You're the only one who understands' | Feel superior to colleagues |
| 'You're the only person I can talk to' | Strive to provide perfect care |
| 'No one else listens/cares/knows me' | Give out private phone no., see when should be on leave |
| | Criticise/blame colleagues/other services |
| **Neglected/abandoned/victim** | |
| 'No one ever helps me' | Striving to help, long sessions |
| 'People always let me down' | Giving more than fair share |
| 'No one ever listens to me' | Giving priority |
| 'No one bothers about me' | Neglect other work |
| 'I just get forgotten about' | Give up/neglect |
| 'It's not fair, I'm always last' | Exhaustion – nothing is good |
| 'Everyone is against me' | enough |
| 'Everyone hates me' | |
| **Passive** | |
| 'What's the point?' | Strive to motive |
| 'Nothing will make any difference?' | Take control |
| 'Why ask me?' | Ignore the person |
| 'You don't take any notice of what I say?' | Feel useless |
| 'Do whatever you think' | Despair, give up |
| 'What do I know about anything?' | |
| 'Nothing anyone can do will make this better' | |
| **Aggressive/attacking/blaming** | |
| 'It's all your/their fault' | Defensive/blaming |
| | Feel abused/used |
| **Rejecting** | |
| 'What do you know about anything?' | Become upset |
| 'You don't understand' | Avoid |
| 'P*** off, you make me sick' | Refer on/pull out of the work |
| 'I've GOT to do this alone' | Dislike |
| 'I don't want to live here' | |

Continued...

**Controlling/rebelling**

| | |
|---|---|
| *'You can't make me ... '* | Feel helpless |
| *'If you don't, I'll ... '* | Feel powerless, panic, placating |
| *'Why haven't you finished my ... yet?'* | Feel inadequate/manipulated |
| *'I need more medication'* | Over-medicate |
| *'(Name) said I must ...'* | Anger at colleagues |
| | Become forceful |

**Contemptible/useless**

| | |
|---|---|
| *'I don't deserve to ... '* | Act as if this is true |
| *'It's my fault'* | Give up |
| *'Nothing I do ever goes right'* | Treat with contempt |

There are a number of things that individual staff members can do to help them stay motivated, energised and effective, despite pressure to behave less positively. Some ideas are given in Box 14.14.

It is also helpful to carry out the self-reflection exercises in Chapter 13, to help identify individual vulnerabilities. It is really helpful for staff to know their own weak spots and to be prepared to cope with their reactions if the individual hits upon them. Staff may also find it helpful to consider their own expectations of their relationships with individuals. It is unrealistic to expect individuals with intellectual disabilities and personality disorder to nurture staff, provide unconditional positive regard, fulfil a need to feel successful, or be grateful for the help provided. These needs have to be met from elsewhere.

However, it is very difficult to maintain a positive approach all alone. It is important that teams work together to address these issues.

## Box 14.14: Things that can help staff stay motivated, energised and effective

**Stay calm:** Anger only escalates situations. Intense reactions eg. distress at self-harm, only act to reinforce unhealthy behaviours.

**Pause and think:** 'Knee jerk' reactions are always unhelpful and often make things much worse. Use the countertransference checklist and list of reciprocal roles to find out where the emotional reaction is coming from.

**Look for patterns:** Does the individual have recognisable, recurring states each characterised by mood, behaviour, sense of self and others? Do they draw staff into particular ways of behaving?

**Don't take things personally:** You may be the 'lightening rod'. The comments/reaction/behaviour may relate to other things in the individual's past or current situation/relationships.

**Don't jump to conclusions:** What you are told someone said or did may not be accurate. Look for the evidence to support it.

**Clear expectations:** What is practically possible? What is good enough? What would you do for any other individual? Question the individual's judgement of your (and other people's) efforts. Are they expecting perfection?

**Clear boundaries:** Set realistic limits and stick to them. Remember professional standards and behaviour, don't break them however 'special' or 'urgent' the situation.

**Write it down:** Keep good, timely, notes, write down agreements and write guidelines, contracts etc. These avoid confusion at the time and allow things to be checked, help reduce conflict and can highlight even very small positive changes.

**Keep a sense of proportion:** Remember that no one is perfect (even if someone is telling you so!). Are things really as black as they are painted?

**Reality checking:** One individual saying something about you does not make it true. There are two sides to every story. Other people may have a different view on what happened. Wires may have got crossed – someone may not have said or done what you have been told they did.

**Step back and look at the wider picture:** Everything looks huge and terrifying when looked at through a microscope.

**Acceptance:** There are things you can't do, things you can't change, people you don't like, people who don't like you. That is reality, not the end of the world.

**Commitment:** Continue to care and do what is right whatever is thrown at you.

Intellectual Disabilities and Personality Disorder: An integrated approach
© Pavilion Publishing and Media Ltd and its licensors 2014.

# Team work

A team may be defined as a group of people with complementary skills who are committed to a common purpose and hold themselves mutually accountable for its achievement. Successful teams are characterised by a team spirit comprising trust, mutual respect, helpfulness and co-operation. More characteristics of effective teams are given in Box 14.15.

---

## Box 14.15: Characteristics of effective teams

**Effective teams**

Have:
- A team identity
- Shared vision and team objectives
- Good communications

They:
- Participate and collaborate
- Negotiate and resolve issues
- Reflect and self-assess

Effective teamwork results from:
- Membership, size and resources (including time-frame) that match the task
- Good leadership and attention to team-building
- The development of team goals and a shared vision
- A sense of common ownership of the task at hand and joint responsibility for its achievement
- Co-ordinated effort and planned sharing of tasks evenly across the team
- The open exchanges of information within the team
- Time for and commitment to reflection and self assessment
- Honesty and frankness among team members
- Openness in identifying and resolving conflict
- Acceptance of risk so that it is neither neglected nor over-responded to

Adapted from Department for Trade and Industry (2004)

---

These characteristics apply equally, whether the team is building a house, creating an advert for shampoo or supporting individuals with intellectual disabilities and personality disorder. However, individuals with intellectual disabilities and personality disorder are much more likely to 'destruction test' a team and highlight all its previously unnoticed weaknesses. Supporting individuals with intellectual disabilities and personality disorder makes particular demands on team leaders. Hence this aspect is worth exploring in more detail.

## Leadership

Effective leaders need to reflect on team performance. They need to be able to draw on a number of different leadership styles in order to respond to complex, often rapidly changing, situations. Difficulties may develop if the leader lacks particular skills, is unable to rapidly assess what approach is required for a particular situation or is unable to adapt their leadership style. Box 14.16 suggests some leadership competencies that may be particularly helpful for the range of challenges presented by individuals with intellectual disabilities and personality disorder.

---

### Box 14.16: Leadership capabilities appropriate for addressing frequently encountered issues

| Situation | Competence |
| --- | --- |
| Individual in crisis | Effective decision making and direction, ability to take charge |
| Novel, complex and unexpected problems | Resourcefulness, flexibility, persistence and problem solving |
| Pressure on team/individual members to take on excessive/inappropriate roles/activities | Maintaining boundaries and professional standards, line management skills |
| Addressing splits within the team, need for consensus and consistent working | Maintaining group effectiveness, resolving conflict and building relationships |
| Fear/anger/despair arising from interactions with individual/risk | Validating and containing emotions |
| Intense, prolonged involvement with apparently intractable problems | Motivating, engaging and involving |

---

If good leadership and the characteristics of effective team working are present, the team will be in a much stronger position to provide effective decision making and risk management. Such teams will be able to quickly address the tensions that arise when supporting individuals with intellectual disabilities and personality disorder and to avoid splits developing. They are less likely to become polarised and this reduces the risk of staff blaming each other for management or treatment difficulties.

## Case discussions

Well-functioning teams will also be able to take pro-active measures to prevent splits occurring, such as organising case discussions about individuals who appear to be presenting challenges to the team. There are a number of formats for doing this and teams will find the way that is most helpful for them. The important factors are that the team has time to share their knowledge of the individual, that there is a safe space for each team member to share their concerns and ask any questions they may have. An example of how this might be done is given in Box 14.17.

---

### Box 14.17: Example format for case discussion

- Identify a suitable facilitator (team member or external to the team)
- Establish group rules eg. confidentiality, taking turns, listening respectfully to others even if you disagree, everyone to contribute
- Share information about the individual (history, characteristics of their intellectual disabilities and personality disorder, areas of need, strengths, social situation
- Identify current issues eg.:
  - feeling stuck
  - the type and amount of support needed
  - keeping the individual safe
  - identifying the most effective approach
  - the extent of and boundaries to team involvement.
- Explore how this is making the team feel and where these feelings are coming from (projection, transference, counter transference, reciprocal roles)
- Problem solve
- Agree an action plan

---

## Team building

If a team is not functioning well and conflicts occur, it may be necessary to take the time to work on the foundations for effective teamwork. There is not space to explore approaches to team building and improvement here but there are many helpful resources and programmes that teams can use to help them in this process. Some of these are given in the Further reading section.

However, some teams are basically healthy but lack the skills to resolve the conflicts so easily generated by individuals with personality disorder. This is often the case for teams that do not work frequently with such individuals. Hence it may be helpful to explore some ideas about conflict resolution.

# Conflict resolution

Chapter 4 explored how a 'problem solving' approach could be used to resolve interpersonal conflicts between individuals with intellectual disabilities and personality disorder. While this approach can also be helpful in resolving minor conflicts within professional teams, it can be helpful to have a deeper understanding of issues to deal with more serious conflict.

In thinking about conflict resolution within teams it is again helpful to think of the process at both the individual and team levels. If individual staff members are aware of their personal responses to conflict situations they can reflect on whether this is a helpful style and if not how they might deal with conflict more positively. It is also important for teams to have a process by which conflicts can be explored and resolved.

## Individual approaches to conflict

One widely used model for understanding how individuals respond to conflict is the Thomas-Kilmann model. This suggests that there are two dimensions to an individual's response: the extent to which the individual seeks to satisfy their own concerns (assertiveness) and the extent to which the individual seeks to satisfy the other person's concerns (co-operativeness). These two dimensions can be combined to give five different modes of responding to a conflict situation. These modes are given in Figure 14.18.

Everyone is capable of using each of the five modes and each mode may be more or less appropriate and helpful in any given conflict situation. However, people tend to rely more heavily on some modes than others. It can be very helpful for each team member to know their own 'default' conflict mode and to think about situations where they might need to consciously try a different approach.

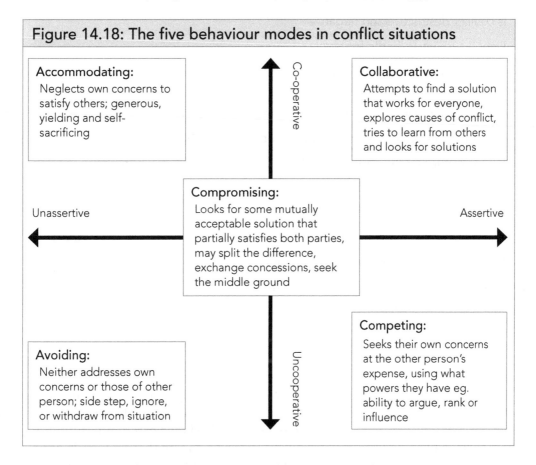

## Figure 14.18: The five behaviour modes in conflict situations

**Accommodating:**
Neglects own concerns to satisfy others; generous, yielding and self-sacrificing

**Collaborative:**
Attempts to find a solution that works for everyone, explores causes of conflict, tries to learn from others and looks for solutions

Co-operative

Unassertive

Assertive

**Compromising:**
Looks for some mutually acceptable solution that partially satisfies both parties, may split the difference, exchange concessions, seek the middle ground

**Competing:**
Seeks their own concerns at the other person's expense, using what powers they have eg. ability to argue, rank or influence

Uncooperative

**Avoiding:**
Neither addresses own concerns or those of other person; side step, ignore, or withdraw from situation

## Team approach to conflict

It can also be helpful to take some time out to think about the team's approach to conflict. Box 14.19 gives some questions that may be helpful.

---

### Box 14.19: Exploring how a team approaches conflict

**How is conflict expressed in the team?**

Is conflict destructive and negative?

Does it turn into a battle for power?

Are there competing factions and patterns of alliances? (often within and between different professions)

Are particular team members scape-goated?

Can everyone have a say or are some people excluded?

Is conflict suppressed and avoided? eg. difficult decisions are not made

Is debate open and productive?

What are the differences in the team?

What are the similarities in the team?

How are differences managed in the team?

How is competition managed in the team?

Are individuals' feelings about competition and conflict explored and acknowledged?

Adapted from RCN (2005)

---

Understanding how the team manages conflict generally will help make decisions about the best way to tackle a specific issue. For example, teams that have clear factions and divisions may need a strong and highly skilled external facilitator to help them explore an issue constructively. However, a team that frequently and constructively debates difficult issues may only need the time and space for a team discussion to enable them to find a solution for themselves.

Box 14.20 gives some practical suggestions for how to organise the process of conflict resolution.

It can also be helpful to think about other occasions when the team has successfully resolved conflict. What was done then? Could that approach be used for the current issue? It is tempting to think that there should be a 'special' approach to resolving conflict about an individual with intellectual disabilities and personality disorder. However, this is not the case. Other than including a few specific exercises to explore what staff think and feel about the individual, what is needed is a robust, tried and tested approach to resolving team conflict.

## Box 14.20: Practical steps to healthy conflict resolution

- Acknowledge that conflict is acceptable, even valuable, when it is dynamic, robust and controlled
- Create a blame-free culture by getting the team to focus on joint team solutions, not who is responsible for the problem
- Build trust so that team members can say what really happened and what they really feel rather than what they think is expected
- Get the entire team together so that they can identify the sources of conflict, to allow frustrations to be aired and identify possible solutions
- Identify someone to facilitate the discussion (this might be a team member not working with the individual discussed or someone trusted from outside the team)
- Establish clear rules eg. listening to others, taking turns, respect
- Ensure all team members have the opportunity to contribute fully both their frustrations and concerns and ideas for solutions
- Use constructive questioning to:
  - explore issues relating to the perception of the individual with intellectual disabilities and personality disorder
  - identify the causes of conflict, for example, different perceptions of need
  - identify areas of agreement eg. may have same aim but be approaching it using a different approach
  - separate out assumptions from facts
  - explore reasoning behind views and decisions
  - look at roles and responsibilities
  - help identify potential solutions
- Put things down on paper eg. using flipcharts, Post-it notes
- Consider drawing a 'time line' of events leading to the current situation
- When looking at solutions, assess every different competing option and produce the best overall solution – taking shared responsibility for its implementation
- When conflicts are resolved, celebrate the success of the resolution.

Not essential, but good tea/coffee and a homemade cake or special chocolate biscuits can really help the energy levels!

Adapted from DTI (2004)

Where splits have emerged in a team it can be helpful to get each team member to talk about the individual, how they feel and think about them, and how these thoughts and feelings arose (eg. things the individual has said/done, things the staff member knows about their past experiences). These feelings and thoughts can then be pulled together to explore if that individual takes different roles, what roles they take with whom and when. This can really help understand the wider picture and give everyone a richer understanding of the individual. Some other ideas for exercises that might be helpful are given in Box 14.21.

---

### Box 14.21: Exploring the impact of an individual with intellectual disabilities and personality disorder on a team

**Hunt the emotion:** Stick up pages of flipchart around the room each with an emotion written on it (eg. anger, fear, happiness, sadness, hopelessness). Split the page in half – individual's initials/staff. Each member of staff says how the individual makes them feel. Team then share ideas about how the individual might be feeling. Team take the time to explore where these feelings are coming from and what processes are operating (eg. projection/splitting), how is this being acted out between team members?

**Hunt the role:** Stick up pages of flipchart with common reciprocal roles on each. Think of difficult times with the individual. What role might they have been taking? What role was that pushing staff to take? Do they take certain roles with particular members of staff? Why might that be? What impact is that having on team relationships?

**Compare and contrast:** Each team member takes time to think about how they react to the individual and what they have done for them/want to happen for them. They then compare this with what they feel about/do for other people on they work with. What is different? Why is it different? Team share their experiences and look for patterns, how might these be leading to conflict in the team?

---

Using these approaches will help reduce and resolve conflict. However, it is important to remember that some level of disagreement in teams is both unavoidable and perfectly healthy. If a team starts seeking to eliminate all conflict it has probably failed to recognise that it is seeking to be the 'perfect team' that can give 'perfect care' to the individuals it supports.

# Key learning points

- Interactions between people are complex and can be distorted by a number of factors. In any interaction, people's responses can be shaped not just by the present situation but also by their own past experiences and the past experiences of the person they are interacting with.

- A number of psychological concepts are helpful in making sense of these distortions. Helpful concepts include; 'projection', 'transference', 'countertransference', 'splitting' and 'reciprocal roles'.

- Individuals with intellectual disabilities and personality disorder often interact in ways that trigger strong reactions in those supporting them.

- These emotional reactions can create tensions and disagreements within and between staff teams. Splits may develop within and between teams. If these reactions are not understood and actively managed, staff teams can become paralysed and unable to act together to constructively support the individual.

- If the difficulties persist, staff can become exhausted, frustrated and de-motivated. There may be problems with staff turnover (going to other jobs) or burnout (physical and mental exhaustion).

- Teams need to develop understanding of key psychological processes. This will give them the ability to reflect on and resolve conflicts.

- If this is done, teams will be able to manage these difficulties in a way that enriches their understanding of the individual and allows them to work together constructively to meet the individual's needs.

# References

Department for Trade and Industry (2004) *Effective Teamwork: A best practice guide for the construction industry.* London: DTI.

RCN (2005) *Developing and Sustaining Effective Teams: Getting started – an introduction and overview.* London: RCN.

Reidbord S (2010) Counter-transference, an overview: What is counter-transference. Available at: http://www.psychologytoday.com/blog/sacramento-street-psychiatry/201003/countertransference-overview (accessed April 2014).

# Further reading

Bennett D, Pollock P & Ryle A (2005) The states description procedure: The use of guided self-reflection in the case formulation of patients with borderline personality disorder. *Clinical Psychology and Psychotherapy* **12** 50–57.

Berne E (2010) *The Games People Play*. London: Penguin.

Bland A & Rossen E (2005) Clinical supervision with nurses working with patients with borderline personality disorder. *Issues in Mental Health Nursing* **26** 507–517.

Cocks E (2001) Normalisation and social role valorization. Guidance for human service development. *Hong Kong Journal of Psychiatry* **11** (1) 12–16.

Denman C (2001) *Cognitive-analytic Therapy: Advances in Psychiatric Treatment*. Available at: http://apt.rcpsych.org/content/7/4/243.full (accessed April 2014).

Department for Trade and Industry (2004) *Effective Teamwork: A best practice guide for the construction industry*. London: DTI.

Flynn A & Taggart L (2011) Personality disorders and substance misuse. (Contains helpful exploration of splitting.) In N Bouras, S Hardy S & G Holt (eds) *Mental Health in Intellectual Disabilities: A reader* (4th edition). Brighton: Pavilion.

Golynkina K & Ryle A (1999) The identification and characteristics of the partially dissociated states of patients with borderline personality disorder. *British Journal of Medical Psychology* **72** 429–445.

Helpguide.org (2012) *Preventing Burnout: Signs, symptoms, causes and coping strategies*. Available at: http://www.helpguide.org/mental/burnout_signs_symptoms.htm (accessed April 2014).

Helpguide.org (2013) *Conflict resolution skills* [online]. Available at: http://www.helpguide.org/mental/eq8_conflict_resolution.htm (accessed April 2014).

Huber D (2010) *Leadership and Nursing Care Management* (4th edition). Maryland Heights Missouri: Saunders Elsevier.

Huges P & Kerr I (2000) Transference and counter-transference in communication between doctor and patient. *Advances in Psychiatric Treatment* **6** 57–64. Available at: http://apt.rcpsych.org/content/6/1/57.full (accessed April 2014).

Main T (1989) *The Ailment and Other Psychoanalytic Essays*. London: Free Association Books. (The original description of splitting arising from caring for individuals with personality disorders.)

NHS Institute for Innovation and Improvement & Royal College of Nursing (2005) *Developing and Sustaining Effective Teams: Getting started – an introduction and overview*. London: Royal College of Nursing.

NHS (20140) *Productive series resources* [online]/. Available at: www.institute.nhs.uk/quality_and_value/productivity_series/the_productive_series.html (accessed April 2014).

Scott V (2010) *Conflict Resolution at Work for Dummies*. New York: Wiley & Sons.

Weeks D (1994) *The Eight Essential Steps to Conflict Resolution*. New York: TarcherPutman.

# Chapter 15: Difficulties with relatives, family and partners

This chapter explores what families are, how they influence development and some of the challenges that families face. It looks at common issues that may arise in families where an adult member has intellectual disabilities and personality disorder and how these issues may be addressed.

## Key topics

- Families

- Families, relationships and individuals with personality disorder

- Families, relationships and individuals with intellectual disabilities

- Families, relationships and individuals with intellectual disabilities and personality disorder

- Frequently encountered difficulties

- Good practice

## Families

A family may be defined as a group of people linked by blood or co-residence. Families may take many forms. In recent Western tradition, the family has been seen as comprising two parents (usually married) and their children. This form is often called the nuclear family. The wider family network comprising parents, children and other members of the family (such as grandparents, aunts, uncles, cousins, in-laws) is called the extended family. Extended families living together as one household are common in many cultures. In current Western society families also come in many other forms, including single parent families, blended families (where single parents form new households) and single sex couples (with and without children).

# Healthy families

Whatever form it takes, a healthy family has a number of characteristics. Healthy families generally have healthy interpersonal relationships. Family members spend time together; working together to achieve family goals (such as getting the chores done), having fun and celebrating (for example, birthdays, festivals, milestones and achievements). Healthy families have good communications and can talk about emotions, fears and wishes. There is trust that they will meet each other's needs and help each other in times of crisis.

Healthy families protect children and keep them safe, making them feel secure and loved. They teach children to understand and manage their own emotions, to think about their own behaviour and to understand the thoughts and feelings of others. Families build a child's image of themselves and the world, providing the basis for self-esteem and core beliefs about the world. Families foster skills and build independence, giving children a range of responses to the situations that will arise and helping them build a social network outside the family. Families also teach children moral, social or religious values, providing them with a context to evaluate their conduct and make choices about how to act.

# The family lifecycle

Families may be seen as having a lifecycle with different stages. The exact sequence may vary depending on the type of family (for example, nuclear, single parent or blended). Figure 15.1 shows how people might move though the family lifecycle.

At each stage the family needs to successfully achieve certain tasks. People need to adapt to their changing circumstances, first as independent adults, then part of a relationship and then a parent. Parents need to create a safe and healthy environment in which their children can develop. They need to adapt their parenting style to meet the needs of babies, toddlers, young children and adolescents. Parents need to successfully launch their children into the world and then to adapt to life without children at home.

Families also need to adapt and respond to life events such as moves, separations, disabilities, illnesses and deaths. They will need to respond to external factors such as economic changes (for example, unemployment) and widespread events (such as flooding or wars).

Most families successfully negotiate these changes. However, problems can arise when families become stuck at a particular stage and cannot adapt or move on.

For example, a family may successfully parent small children but be unable to give them the increasing freedom they need as adolescents. Where this happens there will be conflict and tension within the family and some members may behave inappropriately.

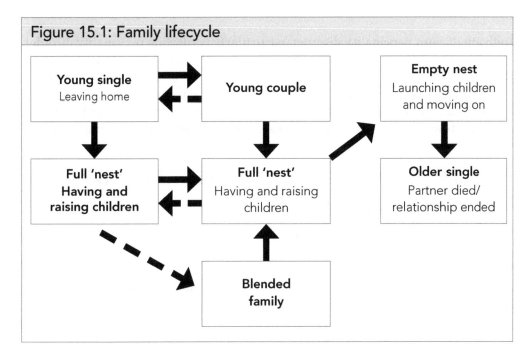

Figure 15.1: Family lifecycle

# Families, relationships and individuals with personality disorder

Individuals with personality disorder rarely come from healthy families and often have complex family backgrounds. Their parents may have mental health problems or issues with drug or alcohol use. There may be a history of abuse or neglect. There are likely to be issues with attachment resulting from difficult early relationships with parents. The patterns of over- or under-involvement and invalidation in childhood that contributed to the development of personality disorder often persist into a parent's relationship with their adult child.

These difficulties are likely to mean that relationships between an individual and their family will be inconsistent and strained. These strained and inconsistent interactions can be a source of great distress to the individual who may continue to seek affection and validation from family members who are unable or unwilling to change their views of the individual. Sometimes, therapists support individuals to cut off contact with their family as this can allow them time to address their own needs and build the resilience to cope with how their family treat them. This is generally straightforward as individuals with personality disorder usually function independently of their parents and have already left or are easily able to leave home.

Individuals with personality disorder, particularly borderline personality disorder, often take the difficulties they experienced in their family of origin forward into their own relationships. Their relationships are volatile and intense. They may be characterised by desperate attempts to prevent the partner from leaving, alternating with feeling overwhelmed and smothered. Individuals may behave abusively towards their partner or tolerate abuse rather than face being alone.

# Families, relationships and individuals with intellectual disabilities

There are two important factors that influence family relationships for individuals with intellectual disabilities:

- the impact of having a child with intellectual disabilities on the family of origin
- social attitudes towards individuals with intellectual disabilities forming their own families and having children.

## Impact of having a child with intellectual disabilities

Having a child with intellectual disabilities can have a wide reaching impact on the family, including:

- altering the family lifecycle
- emotional reactions to having a child with disabilities
- disrupting bonding and attachment.

The impact of these factors is carried forward into adulthood, shaping the pattern of interaction between the adult child with intellectual disabilities and their family. Hence it is important to have an understanding of these influences.

### Family lifecycle
Having a child with intellectual disabilities can impact on the way families move through the lifecycle stages. For example, parents may spend much longer in the

phase of care typical for young children. Young adults with intellectual disabilities may live at home for longer and may not move on to create their own family. This can create challenges for the family, for example, balancing the need to protect a vulnerable young adult against the young person's need to develop more independence. Parents may struggle to recognise their children as adults and may continue to exert influences over many areas of their lives in a way that would not occur for individuals without intellectual disabilities.

## Emotional impact

Having a child with intellectual disabilities has been likened to a bereavement; the parents need to grieve for the 'perfect' child they had expected and to come to accept, and to love the disabled child. This grieving process may be seen as having stages (see Box 15.2).

---

### Box 15.2: The stages of grief

**Denial:** Parents cannot see that their child has disabilities. They will not want to listen or think about the difficulties. This denial means that parents are unable to advocate for the child or to seek the best support. Instead they may endlessly seek a diagnosis that will disprove or cure the disability. They may reject the use of any aids or adaptations that mark the child out as different from others eg. refusing to attend groups, not learning sign language.

**Anger:** Parents are angry at what has happened. This anger may be directed at partners, family, friends, services, fate/God, or the child.

**'If only' (bargaining):** This stage is characterised by 'if only.' Parents may attribute the disability to a fall, an event, illness or medical treatment and think that they failed to prevent the disability. This leads to feelings of self-blame and guilt.

**Depression:** Parents can become overwhelmed and struggle to carry on. They cannot see the point in trying to do anything.

**Acceptance:** Parents accept the loss of the 'perfect' child. They are able to see the child with disabilities as they really are and start to have hopes and dreams for that real child.

---

The family need to address and resolve these feelings or they may become stuck in that phase of the grieving process and the negative feelings will persist. However, the bereavement process is not a one-off event following the diagnosis of the disabilities. The process often recurs as the child grows up. At significant milestones the family may need to grieve again for the things the child cannot do. For example, stages of schooling, when siblings go to university, get married or have children.

Families may struggle more with the grieving process when there are additional problems in the family such as physical or mental health problems or having more than one child with disabilities. Where unresolved bereavement issues persist, families may have difficulties recognising their adult child's needs. Where there is unresolved anger and blame they may also find relating to health professionals difficult.

### Attachment and bonding

When a child with intellectual disabilities has a difficult early start or is difficult to parent, the attachment and bonding processes may be disrupted. This can make it harder for parents to become attached to and build love for their child. These difficulties can continue into adulthood and may lead to unhelpful patterns of contact or to total abandonment.

## Attitudes to individuals with intellectual disabilities forming their own families

In the recent past there were strong negative views on individuals with intellectual disabilities forming personal relationships, marrying and having children. While attitudes have become much more positive, it is still very difficult for individuals with intellectual disabilities to form families. They are at much greater risk of having their children taken into care at birth. Hence while many individuals with intellectual disabilities aspire to create their own families, this is often not a straightforward undertaking.

## Families, relationships and individuals with intellectual disabilities and personality disorder

It should be kept in mind that an individual with intellectual disabilities and a strong genetic vulnerability may develop personality disorder despite having a caring and generally well-functioning family. The combination of genetics, intellectual disabilities and the traumas associated with growing up with intellectual disabilities may result in personality disorder despite overall good parenting. Such families may have successfully raised their other children to be healthy and happy adults. These families may be a great source of support to their adult child.

However, many individuals with intellectual disabilities and personality disorder come from damaged families where relationships are complex and unhealthy. Like the families of more able individuals with personality disorder, these families may have difficulties arising through mental health problems or difficulties with drug or alcohol misuse. For families that are already challenged by other difficulties, having a child with intellectual disabilities can be overwhelming. Often families do not successfully resolve the bereavement process associated with having a child with disabilities; they may deny the disabilities, continue to seek a cure or be overwhelmed by anger, guilt or hopelessness. Consequently, individuals with intellectual disabilities and personality disorder often experience a 'double whammy' of difficulties with their families.

For most individuals with intellectual disabilities and personality disorder, difficult relationships with their family continue to have a negative impact on their lives as adults. The individual may still crave the love, attention and approval of their family, despite many years of experiencing that this is unlikely to be provided. Sometimes staff blame families for these difficulties and exclude them from therapy, when in fact their involvement might lead to positive changes. However, where this has been attempted without success, it is much harder for an individual with intellectual disabilities and personality disorder to distance themselves from their family, than it is for more able individuals. Their intellectual disabilities may make it difficult to leave home without the help of other people. Sadly, sometimes families will seek for an individual to continue living with them in order that their benefit payments can increase the family income, while giving the individual the message that they are a drain on the household. Even when the individual leaves home, families often have a much more powerful role than they do in the lives of more able children. For example, families are consulted as part of the best interests process for decisions where the individual is assessed as lacking capacity.

Where the parents have mental health issues or also have a personality disorder, this can have a destabilising impact on the individual. If the individual lives with their family there may be frequent crises and highly inconsistent care. If the individual has left the family home, they may receive frantic phone calls at all hours of the day and night about family crises or to tell the individual how cruel they were to abandon their family. Often contact is erratic; visits are cancelled, phone calls are missed.

These unresolved issues often impact strongly on the families' relationship with the services that support the adult child; services may be blamed for excluding the family, failing to 'cure' the child or failing to provide 'perfect care'.

## Personal relationships

These difficulties experienced with their family of origin are often perpetuated in the personal relationships formed by individuals with intellectual disabilities and personality disorder. Often, they appear to be magnetically attracted to people who abuse them or are a 'bad influence' and draw them into unhelpful behaviours. Partners may have similar difficulties to the individual and may undermine attempts to help the individual change their lifestyle or coping mechanisms. Even if they leave an abusive relationship, they may simply form another that follows the same pattern.

# Frequently encountered difficulties

It is important to keep an open mind about the families and partners of individuals with intellectual disabilities and personality disorder. They may be caring and supportive and may be able to work constructively with services to help the individual. Where this is the case, they are important allies. Sadly this is often not the case. Frequently staff comment that supporting the individual is the easy part; coping with their family is much more difficult.

The difficulties often encountered may be seen as falling into two main groups:

- Difficulties arising from the individual's relationships with family and friends
- Issues relating to family involvement with services provided to the individual.

Some of the most frequently encountered difficulties are discussed in the following sections.

## Difficulties arising from the individual's relationships with family and friends

The first group of difficulties impact directly on the individual, through the effect they have on the individual's care, by impacting on the opportunities the individual has to develop or through the distress and intense emotions they cause the individual.

### Chaotic contact

Family, partners or friends may show a chaotic pattern of interaction with the individual. For those living at home or with partners this may take the form of alternate smothering and rejection. For those who have left home, there may be multiple phone calls which leave the individual in tears followed by periods when calls stop altogether and attempts to contact the family are ignored. Visits may be arranged but cancelled or the family just does not arrive. Individuals may find themselves smothered with loving gestures one moment only to be ignored or shouted at the next time they have contact. This chaos can be very distressing for the individual and also disrupts efforts to provide consistent support.

Intellectual Disabilities and Personality Disorder: An integrated approach
© Pavilion Publishing and Media Ltd and its licensors 2014.

## Over-involvement

Some families are heavily over-involved or over-protective of the individual. They may want to be involved in all appointments, conversations and decisions, blocking all opportunities for the individual to develop their independence or make their own decisions. These families are unable to distinguish their own thoughts and wishes from those of the individual and are often intolerant of differences. Often the individual will develop challenging behaviours or mental health problems as a reaction to this smothering. However, the family will not see their role in triggering these difficulties. Rather they will seek medical treatment for the difficult behaviours, often looking to medication as the answer.

Staff may feel helpless when the individual appears unable to see that their family are not helping them. If the individual tries to be more independent, staff may find themselves being abused for keeping the family in the dark. Over-involved families may make complaints and in extreme situations they may threaten or take legal action over being 'excluded'. Such situations are particularly difficult for less able individuals who may lack capacity to make many decisions. The best interests process expects the involvement of family members. In these situations decision making can become a highly stressful process.

Where the individual lives at home, heavily over-involved families may obstruct the individual's access to services that the family view as unhelpful.

## Medication

Where families are dysfunctional there is a risk that medication may be misused. Families who are stuck in 'seeking a cure' may look for alternative or additional diagnoses, such as ADHD, that can be treated with medication. This can lead to an individual being on excessive amounts of medication. In chaotic households, medication may be given erratically. For example, it might be stopped as soon as the individual appeared better only for the leftover tablets to be given as soon as they appear unwell, without discussion with the individual's doctor. Sometimes controlling families will disagree with the medical diagnosis and will not give medication as prescribed. Individuals living at home may continue to deteriorate, to the perplexity of doctors who do not realise that the medication is not being given. Where an individual no longer lives at home but returns for visits, medication may be stopped during the visit. Again, if this is not recognised it can lead to dose increases or a potentially effective medication being dismissed as ineffective.

## Emotional abuse

Sometimes families or partners have patterns of interactions with individuals that professionals may consider emotionally abusive. This might comprise belittling and undermining the individual, repeatedly letting them down, for example, not visiting or calling when agreed, applying pressure for them to behave in unhelpful ways or having unrealistic expectations. This can cause a lot of emotional distress for the individual and can undermine work to help build self-esteem and more positive patterns of behaviour.

## Financial abuse and exploitation

Sadly, some families, partners or 'friends' may exploit the individual. Often this is in small ways such as expecting extravagant presents while giving nothing in return. Sometimes it can be much more serious, for example, involving them in criminal activities. Some signs of financial abuse are given in Box 15.3.

---

### Box 15.3: Possible indicators of financial abuse

- Unexplained withdrawals from the bank
- Unusual activity in the bank accounts
- Unpaid bills
- Unexplained shortage of money
- Reluctance on the part of the person with responsibility for the funds to provide basic food and clothes etc.
- Reluctance on part of person with responsibility for the funds to share basic information eg. bank details, bank statements, bank balance
- Frequent purchase of expensive items that disappear, with unconvincing explanations eg. they were broken, lost or stolen
- Reluctance to let the individual move out of the family home

---

Individuals can be vulnerable to abuse because of their need to feel loved and wanted. They may become angry with professionals who try to intervene as their fear of losing their family and 'friends' is much greater than their personal distress at being exploited.

## Physical and sexual abuse

Sadly, many individuals with intellectual disabilities and personality disorder have experienced abuse as children. Often this pattern continues into adulthood, with individuals being abused by partners. Sometimes individuals will recognise that they have been or are being abused. These experiences are often all the individual has known hence they may not understand that the behaviours are abusive. Others may understand but may tolerate abuse out of fear of losing the relationship.

# Family involvement with services

The families and partners of individuals with intellectual disabilities and personality disorder will have their own history of contact with services. Many of the issues discussed in Chapter 13 as interfering with engagement will apply to them and may make it difficult for them to work constructively with services. Each family is unique, but there are a number of issues that frequently occur when working with the families of individuals with intellectual disabilities and personality disorder. Some of the most frequently encountered issues are discussed below.

## Crises

Families may repeatedly make contact with services in crisis situations, calling late in the day and needing urgent help. However, this is often linked to an inability to engage with professionals and take the actions necessary to prevent future crises from occurring.

## 'No one helps us'

Families of individuals with intellectual disabilities and personality disorder sometimes tell professionals that they have never received the help they need. This can make staff angry on the family's behalf and cause tension with the services that appear to have neglected them. Often, on investigation it is found that multiple professionals and agencies have tried to engage with the family. However, the support offered has not been taken up and the service was then withdrawn. This pattern can be repeated each time there is a crisis in the family.

## 'Nothing works'

Families may repeatedly ask for help, but report that everything suggested fails. As time goes on professionals are met with *'we tried that before and it didn't work'* until they run out of suggestions and are exhausted and baffled. If the individual leaves the home setting for a period of inpatient care, it is often found that the 'ineffective' treatments work well on the ward, only to become 'ineffective' once the individual returns home. Such families may be too chaotic to implement treatments effectively, may misunderstand what is involved or be too exhausted and overwhelmed by feelings of hopelessness to persist long enough for treatments to work.

## Insistence

Families may find it difficult to accept the limits of support available and may be very insistent that they are given all the support they feel that they need. This may take the form of repeated, increasingly angry, phone calls, demanding and confronting interactions with professionals or seeking backup by complaining or using the media. They may behave in a way that is sometimes graphically described as 'bulldozing'. This behaviour may be understood as seeking for 'perfect care'. Underlying it may be the unrealistic belief that if the services were good enough then the individual would be 'cured' and there would be no further problems.

## Chaotic contact

Families may have chaotic contact with professionals. They may repeatedly miss appointments, be out when professionals call, turn up when they are not expected or call in a panic wanting help that minute. Important paperwork goes astray and letters are not received or are not answered. When they do make contact with services the information they give and the needs they express constantly change and are often contradictory.

## High expressed emotion

Family members will often become highly emotional at times of stress. They may shout, be abusive or burst into tears. When things are going well they may be ecstatic, overwhelming staff with thanks, presents and compliments. This can be exhausting and confusing for staff.

## Splitting

Family members may confide in one professional that another has let them down, been rude, unhelpful or inconsiderate. They may idolise some professionals while 'rubbishing' others. This can create tensions within and between teams.

## Making frequent complaints

Families may make complaints about the support and services they have or have not been given, individual professionals or care staff or other aspects of their support. While these will sometimes be justified, more often they are found to be groundless. Sometimes, in the general chaos, the family will have forgotten the help that was offered but refused or given successfully at the time but now no longer effective. At other times the complaints may seem more vengeful, perhaps directed at staff who have correctly refused to overstep professional boundaries.

# Good practice

Many of the problems faced by individuals with intellectual disabilities and personality disorder in relating to their family are difficult, if not impossible, to change. Families are usually not 'patients' of the service and trying to 'fix' them is therefore not within the service remit. Often the difficulties have to be understood and managed rather than changed. Many of the ideas discussed in Chapter 13 (barriers to engagement) and Chapter 14 (tensions and conflict) will be helpful in trying to understand issues with families. It can be very helpful to apply the concepts of projection, transference, splitting and reciprocal roles when thinking about interactions with the family members of individuals with intellectual disabilities and personality disorder. Conflict resolution skills may also come in handy.

The following ideas may also be helpful in developing a caring, responsive but robust approach to issues with families, partners and friends:

- developing self-awareness of family issues
- building empathy with families
- understanding the legal context
- keeping good records
- monitoring medication
- using contracts, maintaining boundaries and promoting clear communication
- managing care planning and meetings
- helping the individual manage their finances
- recognising and responding to signs of abuse
- supporting the individual to manage contact with their family
- reviewing the individual's level of support and engagement
- working on relationships through counselling or therapy
- working with the whole family.

## Self-awareness

Everyone is influenced by their own experiences of families; both while growing up and by their present family situation. When encountering dysfunctional families it is important that staff take time to think about their own attitudes and sensitivities about families. For some ideas on how this might be done see Box 15.4.

If this is not done it is easy to be drawn into taking sides with resulting conflict and splitting within teams. For example, young, single staff may be more sympathetic to the needs of a young adult, still living at home, to achieve independence. In contrast, staff married with young children may connect more easily with parental concerns about vulnerability and the need for protection. In addition to thinking about their own issues with families, it is also important for staff to be aware of their own particular emotional 'hooks' that will draw them in. The ideas given in Chapter 13 are as useful for staff in interacting with dysfunctional families as they are for interacting with individuals.

---

## Box 15.4: Questions to help develop self-awareness of family issues

- What form is your current family? (eg. single adult, single parent, empty nest)
- What is your family style? (eg. supportive, highly involved, laid-back, pushy)
- Are there any types of family you are uncomfortable with?
- What stage of the family lifecycle are you currently at?
- What earlier stages have you found difficult?
- Is there a future stage you are dreading?
- Do you find yourself taking the 'side' of particular members of an individual's family? If so, which, and how does this relate to your own experiences?
- Is there a family member you have strong negative feelings towards? If so, which, and how does this relate to your own experiences?

---

# Empathy with the family

Some families behave so badly that it is hard for staff not to feel angry or even to demonise them. It is also easy to slip into seeing the family environment as 'toxic' and to blame family members for causing the individual's difficulties. While there may be much truth in these feelings, they are not conducive to effective working.

It is important to find ways of connecting with the family and withholding judgement. It can be helpful to maintain curiosity about each family's story and to consider what has led to them behaving in such an unhelpful way. They may have had many traumatic experiences, survived abuse themselves or be struggling with mental health problems. Family members may have repeatedly experienced being rejected by or let down by services. Thinking about these experiences can make it easier to manage the emotions triggered by the behaviour of family members and to be tolerant of the difficulties that cannot be changed.

## Perspective taking

It can be helpful to try to work out the perspective of family members and the emotions the individual's behaviour or contact with services may have triggered. It can be helpful to look at the bereavement process related to having a child with intellectual disabilities and to consider if the family have become stuck at a particular stage. For example, they might refuse to listen to the results of an assessment if they are still in denial about their child's difficulties or might react with anger because advice is perceived as criticism of their own care. If any of these are identified it may suggest openings for building more positive relationships.

## Legal context

It is important that staff have a clear understanding of the legal rights of both the individual and their family and friends. Families may often think that their rights and responsibilities remain unchanged as their child becomes an adult. This is not the case. Staff need to be aware that legal changes that apply at given ages occur irrespective of the presence of intellectual disabilities. Once an individual reaches 18 they legally become an adult and parents' rights are much reduced compared to those held in regard to younger offspring.

It is important to understand the Mental Capacity Act (2005). Where an individual has capacity to make a particular decision, staff need to work with that decision however unwise it may seem to them or however strongly their family objects to it. Where the individual lacks capacity, the best interests procedures need to be followed. Of course this makes the situation appear more straightforward than it is. In reality an individual's capacity may fluctuate. It is also possible for splits to develop within teams or between staff and the individual's family where there are differing views about whether the individual has capacity. The approaches given in Chapter 14 will be helpful in preventing or managing such splitting.

It is also important to understand the legal context around confidentiality and data protection. Families do not have an automatic right to information about the individual. Where the individual has capacity, it is important to agree with them whether or not they want to share information and who they want to share it with. Their decision needs to be recorded, reviewed regularly and complied with.

Some helpful guides about these legal issues are available and examples are given in the Further reading section.

## Good record keeping

It is important to make accurate and timely notes of interactions with families. This may seem obvious; however chaotic families will often ring repeatedly or call late in the day. This makes it more likely that a conversation will not be recorded in detail or will be missed altogether. It is also easy for events to get out of sequence. Good records are very helpful in supervision or other times when staff are trying to make sense of what is going on. They will help show patterns of contact or responding. Exploring these may suggest better ways of supporting the family.

If there is a complaint at a later stage, accurate records play a key role in establishing whether or not the complaint can be upheld. Knowing that the records will show that they behaved in a professional manner can give staff the confidence to stick to agreed therapeutic actions despite fears that families may challenge this because of their own emotional issues.

## Monitoring medication

It is important that someone takes the role of actively monitoring all the medication prescribed to an individual with intellectual disabilities and personality disorder. This includes that from GPs, physical health specialists, psychiatrists and emergency or crisis services. Thought needs to be given to how that medication is dispensed, for example, the use of medication safes, bubble packs and other systems that simplify administration. Clear accessible information needs to be given about what the medication is for, how to take it and the risks of not taking it properly. Motivational interviewing techniques (see Chapter 6) can be used to encourage families to support medication seen as essential or to think about the need for other medications that may not be necessary.

Careful record keeping can often show up 'blips' in behaviour that might be linked to not taking medication. Staff are often afraid to raise such concerns with families. However, avoiding the issue just perpetuates the problem. These should be investigated sensitively. Using the SET formula for communications (see Box 13.5 and the next section) may be helpful.

For example, *'Our records show changes in X's behaviour every time they come back from leave. I want to try to help X settle back more smoothly. I know you have a lot of concerns about his medication and the long-term side effects. It would really help me to know how giving the medication works when X is at home. Are you finding any problems?'*

GPs and physical health doctors may find it helpful to have information about the individual's diagnosis and some awareness of the need to seek medication as a 'cure' for problems that really need a change in behaviour. This may help them resist the 'pester' power of families convinced that medication is the only answer to their adult child's difficulties.

# Clear contracts, boundaries and communication

Families may have unrealistic ideas about what services should offer the individual. It can be helpful to spell out for them what is offered, what can and what cannot be done. For example, a family may not have thought about when a service is open and may assume that it offers 24/7 support. Giving them this information and also details of where they can get support outside these hours may resolve some issues.

## SET

The acronym SET (see Box 13.5) is also helpful in creating effective communication with families. Each interaction should convey Support and the wish to help, Empathy for their experience and Truth, in the form of accurate and honest information.

## Assertiveness

When interacting with family members who are aggressive 'bulldozers' or are highly critical of services and are rude to staff, it can be helpful to draw on assertiveness techniques. Assertiveness is a way of behaving and communicating which is honest, direct, clear, persistent and respectful. Some helpful assertiveness techniques are given in the Box 15.5 and suggestions are given in the further reading section for more detailed information on assertiveness at work.

## Boundaries

It is important that staff remember that it is not acceptable for family and partners to be rude to staff. Most organisations have policies for responding to verbal and physical aggression to staff; policies are there to be used. It is important to let people know when their behaviour has overstepped the mark and to ask them to calm down or to leave and return when they are able to speak calmly about the issue. This should be done quietly and firmly using the assertiveness techniques given above. For example, repeating. *'Mrs X, I want to help you but I need you to calm down and tell me what is bothering you. If you keep shouting I will have to ask you to leave / end this telephone call'*. If this does not work staff need to follow through. *'I'm really sorry Mrs X, I'm going to end the call now / I'm going to call security. I will be happy to talk to you when you are calmer.'*

Staff often worry about how that person will respond next time they meet. However, often the person will appear to have totally forgotten the incident and will behave as if nothing occurred.

Teams need to be united in taking these assertive approaches; otherwise the non-assertive team member may find themselves repeatedly being subject to the abuse that other team members have resisted.

## Box 15.5: Being assertive

- Keep what you want to say clear and to the point. Avoid long explanations.
- Look at the other person, use open gestures, keep voice low, warm and calm.
- Be polite but firm.
- Cultivate 'two-track listening'
  - Be aware of your own and the other person's feelings
  - Try to distinguish whose feelings are whose
  - Empathise with the other person and validate their feelings
  - But avoid taking on other person's feelings – keep an eye out for 'hooks' and avoid being hooked in (see Chapter 13 for examples of 'hooks')
- Consider using the 'scratched record' technique:
  - State the key message eg. *'the earliest appointment is…..'*
  - Keep repeating the key message, whatever the other person says to deflect, challenge or ignore it eg. *I'm sorry… but the earliest appointment is…'*

**Responding assertively to criticism – 'defusing'**

- Resist the natural urge to counter-attack or to passively accept unfair criticism.
- Do not take hurtful comments to heart (see them as the person's emotional response to a situation that is overwhelming them, a habit they have got into or a survival skill for getting their needs met in a difficult world).
- Use active listening to identify how the person is feeling and any substance to their insult.
- Calmly agree and accept the appropriate part of the criticism. eg *'It looks like we forgot to put that appointment in the diary…'* If the criticism is very general ask the person to clarify. eg. *'I'm sorry you think the service is rubbish, can you tell me more about what is bothering you?'*
- See any criticism as a chance to learn what could be done better eg. *'What can we do to make sure that doesn't happen again?'*

# Care planning and meetings

When families behave in particularly difficult ways, it can be tempting for staff to try to exclude them as much as possible. This is generally counter-productive; the more excluded a family feel, the less they will trust teams and the harder they will try to be involved. Where an individual has chosen to have their family involved in their care it can be helpful to meet regularly and to share clear, specific plans with the family.

As many family members behave inappropriately in meetings, it is important to give thought to how this will be managed. It may be necessary to have a staff-only 'pre-meeting' to iron out differences within the team to ensure that the family are not able to accentuate these conflicts (see Chapter 14 for more ideas to avoid splits in teams). It is always helpful to have an agenda shared at the beginning of the meeting. It can also help to agree specific rules such as taking turns to talk, no shouting or abuse. These rules must then be implemented. For example, the chairperson may need to make comments such as *'Mr X, please can you let Dr Y finish what she is saying'* (making sure that they then give Mr X the opportunity to talk next) or *'It's getting a bit heated in here, I'm going to stop the meeting for five minutes to give everyone the chance to calm down'*.

## Managing finances

If family members, partners or 'friends' appear to be exploiting an individual financially, the problem must be reported through the safeguarding adults process. It will be important to assess an individual's capacity to manage their money. There are assessment tools available to help with this process.

Where the individual has capacity, they have the right to use their money unwisely. However, staff can still try to help them budget more wisely and encourage them to think about the implications of their choices. As many unwise actions are made on impulse and are regretted later it can be helpful to put practical barriers in the way of accessing money. For example, the individual may agree to transfer money being saved for a holiday into a separate account and to leave the card or passbook for that account with a trusted person or safe place. This will mean that when tempted by family or friends to give away their money, they cannot immediately access that money. By the time they have arranged to access the book, they may have also had time to think about what it means for them to give that money to someone else. So called, 'jam jar' bank accounts may be helpful for some individuals.

Where the individual lacks capacity to manage their finances, staff need to follow the processes to arrange for someone else to do this for them, for example by having an appointee. If it is the appointee who is misusing the money, this needs to be investigated through the safeguarding process.

## Recognising and responding to abuse

It is important that staff are aware of, and are vigilant for, signs that an individual may be being abused. Box 15.6 gives some ideas about possible indicators of physical, emotional or sexual abuse.

---

## Box 15.6: Possible indicators of abuse

- Multiple bruising – unexplained, in unusual places, bruises of different ages eg. fresh and old
- Fractures
- Burns
- Fear – avoiding people, not wanting to go out
- Depression
- Unexplained weight loss
- Uncharacteristic hitting out at others
- Symptoms of PTSD – flashbacks, dissociation

**Possible indicators of emotional abuse**

- Fear
- Depression
- Confusion
- Loss of sleep
- Unexpected or unexplained change in behaviour

**Possible indicators of sexual abuse**

- Loss of sleep
- Unexpected or unexplained change in behaviour
- Bruising
- Soreness around the genitals
- Torn, stained or bloody underwear
- A preoccupation with anything sexual
- Sexually transmitted diseases, urinary tract infections
- Pregnancy
- Symptoms of PTSD – flashbacks, dissociation

---

It is important to recognise that these are only 'possible' indicators. These signs may be due to any number of different causes. For example, multiple bruises may indicate health problems or depression may arise because of a bereavement. It is just as dangerous to assume these signs prove abuse as it is to ignore them. It is surprisingly easy to miss signs of abuse in individuals with personality disorder because of the variability of their behaviour and the complexity of their social networks. So, signs of abuse might be dismissed because, for example, *'he loves her so much, he would never hurt her'*, *'it's most likely self-harm'* or *'it's part of their personality disorder'*. The important point is that such indicators should never be ignored and that an open mind should be kept about all possible causes.

Unexplained physical injuries and bruises should always be reported through the safeguarding process.

### Responding to disclosures of abuse

All disclosures or allegations of abuse should be taken seriously and reported through local safeguarding processes. The decision of how seriously an allegation should be taken rests with those involved in the safeguarding process and not the member of staff who was told the allegation.

### Confidentiality

Sometimes individuals will want to tell something to only one member of staff, asking in advance that it be kept secret. It is important that staff make clear that there are some things that they cannot keep private; staff must share information if the individual is at risk, is a risk to others or if they share information about past abuse. Some staff find this difficult; they fear it will deter individuals from telling them things. However if they agree to keep something secret and it turns out to be something that should be reported, that member of staff is in an impossible position. If they report, the individual will feel they have broken their promise; if they do not, they breach their duty of care to keep the individual and others safe.

Sometimes individuals will repeatedly tell different people about abuse from the past as if this is a new disclosure. This should still be reported, in case it gives more information.

## Managing an individual's contact with their family

Many individuals who no longer live in the family home appear to find contact with their family distressing. It is important to talk this through with the individual. Do not try to talk about this at a time when they are distressed about family contact. Choose a time when they are calm and settled as they will be more able to focus on the issues. Ask them in a neutral way what they think about their contact with their family and the effect it has on them. Acknowledge both aspects of the contact; that the individual loves their family but that speaking to them is upsetting. Explore what they would like to have happen and how likely the family are to be able to do this.

It may be helpful to plan phone calls for a time when there is someone around to support the individual, to make visits shorter but more frequent, to meet in neutral places or for a more structured and time-limited activity such as a meal out.

Together you may be able to agree on strategies to make contact less distressing. This plan should be put in writing. The individual may need support to share this with their family. Sometimes an individual may choose to cease contact with their family for a while. They should be supported to do this but staff need to regularly check if they still feel this way and record these discussions. If this is not done then staff may be vulnerable to accusations of depriving the individual of their liberty to see family members.

It is highly likely that, having achieved what seems to be a clear plan about managing contact, the individual will change their mind and may get angry with staff who remind them of the agreement. Again do not try to resolve this at the time. Wait until the individual is calm and then suggest that if the plan isn't working and can you write a new one together. When calm, they may think the plan is still right and this gives an opportunity to talk about what when wrong.

## Level of support and engagement

Where an individual has difficulties with peer relationships it is often as a result of having insufficient support and a lack of constructive activities. A fresh start in a setting with more support and a plan of appropriate activities can often create a healthier pattern of interaction. The individual may then have the opportunity to form more healthy relationships. Sadly, because of the additional costs often involved, this can be difficult to achieve. Professionals can feel helpless as they watch the individual being abused and exploited by more able peers. In such situations staff need to use the safeguarding adults procedure and also seek the support of the police in protecting the individual.

## Personal relationships

Individuals may be helped to explore the impact of their personal relationships in individual therapy or counselling. This may help them recognise unhealthy patterns in relationships and to explore other ways of behaving. Support staff may also have opportunities to explore these issues with the individual. Where the individual is in a long-term relationship it may be helpful to have relationship counselling from an organisation such as Relate. It may also be helpful for the partner to attend a support group. The approaches discussed in Chapter 4 may also be helpful.

## Family work

Caution needs to be exercised when sharing with families information about the individual's diagnosis of personality disorder. Being told, in isolation, that childhood adversity is linked with personality disorder can add to the family's distress and sense of guilt and hopelessness. It is important that information is balanced and shows families how they may help the individual.

If they are available, it may be helpful for families to attend support groups or special programmes designed for those close to individuals with personality disorder such as the STEPPS programme for individuals with borderline personality disorder (**S**ystems **T**raining for **E**motional **P**redictability and **P**roblem-**S**olving).

Where the individual and family consent, it may be helpful to work with the whole family. There is some evidence that such work can be beneficial. This work may allow families to explore lifecycle issues, think about each other's perspectives, see some problems from a different angle, see the good as well as the bad, and improve their communications. However, it is also important to be aware that some unhealthy patterns of interaction are so entrenched that they are almost impossible to change. In this situation offering family work may create opportunities for emotional abuse to continue. To be effective this work needs to be done by skilled individuals. Access to professional supervision from a family therapist is also essential. Referrals of family work may be made through the individual's GP, psychologist, psychiatrist or community team.

The ideas given in this section may be helpful in developing a caring, responsive but robust approach to issues with families, partners and friends. However, many difficulties are intractable and staff teams need the confidence and resilience to maintain a positive approach in the face of such long-term difficulties. The techniques described in Chapter 14 will be very helpful in accepting the difficulties but remaining motivated, energised and effective.

# Key learning points

- Families take many forms. When healthy they move through a number of stages. They are able to work together, support and care for each other.

- It should be kept in mind that an individual with intellectual disabilities and a strong genetic vulnerability may develop personality disorder despite having a caring and generally well-functioning family. These families are an important resource.

- Many, but not all, individuals with intellectual disabilities and personality disorder come from damaged families where relationships are complex and unhealthy. Like the families of more able individuals with personality disorder, these families may have difficulties arising through mental health problems or difficulties with drug or alcohol misuse. There may be entrenched patterns of over or under involvement. Some families may be abusive.

- The families, partners and friends of individuals with intellectual disabilities and personality disorder often have difficult relationships both with the individual and the services that support the individual.

■ To address these difficulties staff need to have a good understanding of how families work and the impact having a child with intellectual disabilities may have on families.

■ Staff need to think about their own experiences and attitudes, to help them avoid being drawn into conflicts. This knowledge and self-awareness will allow them to use a range of techniques to contain and manage the interactions of families, partners and friends with the individual and the service.

■ Staff need a good understanding the law relating to confidentiality. This will help ensure that they act lawfully in sharing information with families.

■ It is important that staff are aware of, and are vigilant for, signs that an individual may be being abused. Staff need a good understanding of safeguarding issues and, where appropriate, must be confident to seek protection for the individual.

■ Services need to have clear, well-enforced boundaries, keep good records and have the ability to respond assertively to inappropriate expectations.

# Further reading

Back K & Back K (2005) *Assertiveness at Work: A practical guide to handling awkward situations*. Maidenhead: McGraw-Hill.

Hardie E & Brooks L (2012) *Brief Guide to the Mental Capacity Act 2005: Implications for people with learning disabilities*. Birmingham: BILD.

Suto I, Clare I & Holland A (2012) *Financial Decision-making: Guidance for supporting financial decision-making by people with learning disabilities*. Birmingham: BILD.

Information Commissioner's Office (2014) *Guide to Data Protection: Definitions, principles and practical examples* [online]. Available at: www.ico.gov.uk/for_organisations/data_protection/the_guide.aspx (accessed April 2014).

General Medical Council (2014) *Confidentiality Guidance: Sharing information with a patient's partner, carers, relatives or friends* [online]. Available at: www.gmc-uk.org/guidance/ethical_guidance/confidentiality_64_66_sharing_information.asp (accessed April 2014).

GMC (2014) *Confidentiality Guidance: Disclosures about patients who lack capacity to consent* [online]. Available at: www.gmc-uk.org/guidance/ethical_guidance/confidentiality_57_63_patients_who_lack_capacity.asp (accessed April 2014).

Health Concordia (2014) *Guide to Healthy Relationships* [online]. Available at: http://www-health.concordia.ca/pdf/healthinfo/healthyrelationships.pdf (accessed January 2014).

# Glossary

Where possible, everyday language has been used throughout this book. Where words have been used in a technical sense their definitions are given below.

**Advanced directives:** Information about how a person wants to be treated should they develop certain physical or mental health problems.

**Behavioural contract:** An agreement between an individual and their carers about what behaviours are expected on both sides and what consequences will apply. This is one means of setting boundaries and providing containment.

**Boundaries:** Consistent limits that show when behaviours are no longer acceptable and when consequences will apply. For example, *'If you are racially abusive, I will end the interview'*.

**Cognitive behaviour therapy (CBT):** A talking therapy that aims to help people manage problems and change their behaviour by understanding the relationship between thoughts, feelings and behaviour.

**Comfort object:** An item such as a soft toy, doll, quilt or weighted blanket that can be cuddled or wrapped tightly round someone to provide comfort when they are distressed or unhappy to be alone. This may also be called a 'transitional object'.

**Compassionate distance:** The balance between connecting with another person's feelings and keeping a distance to avoid being sucked in and overwhelmed by what they are going through.

**Containment:** Holding behaviour within agreed limits or boundaries. This creates a sense of safety and value.

**Counter-transference:** Feelings that an individual generates in the staff supporting them.

**Dialectical behaviour therapy (DBT):** A talking therapy developed to help individuals with borderline personality disorder. It evolved from CBT but is wider ranging and addresses issues such as how to tolerate distress and manage intense emotions.

**Dissociative state:** An automatic response to a situation that is too much to cope with mentally. The person partially or completely switches off from the situation. Afterwards they may have no memory of the event or may have experienced it as if it happened to someone else, like watching a film.

**Downward comparison:** Increasing self-esteem by making comparisons with a group that will be inferior on a particular characteristic, putting down peers or denying membership of a devalued group.

**Emotional containment:** Being able to remain calmly supportive in the face of extreme emotion expressed by other people. Helping them hold the emotions within limits.

**Empathy:** Using imagination to understand and enter into another person's feelings and experiences.

**Executive functions:** The abilities that allow people to self-motivate, plan, organise, problem solve, inhibit impulses and to monitor their behaviour.

**Expert by experience:** People who have experienced difficulties and services themselves who are able to give an opinion or advice based on these experiences.

**Genuineness:** Being yourself when interacting with someone. Not pretending or putting on a show.

**High expressed emotion:** Where strong emotions such as fear, anger and jealousy are given free rein. This may create a sense of high drama and a feeling of being overwhelmed.

**Internalising:** Absorbing the comments and views others have and taking them as our own. This is often unconscious, so we are unaware of where the view has come from.

**Limit:** A clear point beyond which behaviour is not acceptable.

**Low expressed emotion:** Where strong emotions are contained and resolved with minimum fuss.

**Mentalising:** A way of making sense of your own and other people's actions by thinking about what is going on in your own and the other person's mind.

**Natural consequences:** The natural outcomes of behaviour. For example, speeding may result in a fixed penalty notice, screaming abuse on the street may lead to the police being called.

**Primary prevention:** A way of stopping an unwanted behaviour or feeling before it has even started. For example, having a busy social schedule may stop someone becoming lonely.

**Rumination:** Over-thinking or obsessing about a negative event, setback, loss or an abstract issue. Going over and over possible causes or consequences. It comprises reflection (a positive reaction to think over what happened) and brooding (dwelling on the negative aspects of the event).

**Secondary gains:** Unintended benefits of a situation. For example, attention may be a secondary gain of an injury that requires treatment.

**Secondary prevention**: A way of stopping an unwanted behaviour or feeling by responding to early warning signs. For example, having a list of people to phone if someone begins to feel lonely.

**Self-regulation:** Ways for a person to manage their impulses, behaviour and emotions.

**Self-soothing:** Ways for a person to calm themselves and manage strong emotions. These may be positive; for example, meditation or potentially harmful; for example, use of drugs or alcohol.

**Social comparison:** Judging self-worth by comparing self to others on a range of roles and characteristics.

**Stigma:** Mark of social disgraced or unacceptability.

**Tertiary prevention:** Ways of reducing the harm or damage once a situation has occurred.

**Validation (emotional):** Showing someone that you believe what they are feeling is real (however different it is from how you would feel) and that how they are feeling is important to you.

**Warmth:** A calm and friendly feeling of caring about others.

*9781909810358*

#0001 - 310818 - C0 - 246/186/25 - PB - 9781909810358